D1596774

SOUND states

SOUND

Innovative

STATES

Poetics

Edited by

and

Adalaide Morris

Acoustical

The University of North Carolina Press

Technologies

Chapel Hill and London

© 1997
The University of North Carolina Press
All rights reserved
Manufactured in the United States of America

The paper in this book meets the guidelines for
permanence and durability of the Committee on
Production Guidelines for Book Longevity of the
Council on Library Resources.

Library of Congress
Cataloging-in-Publication Data
Sound states: innovative poetics and acoustical
technologies / edited by Adalaide Morris.
p. cm.
Includes bibliographical references and index.
ISBN 0–8078–2364–3 (cloth: alk. paper).—
ISBN 0–8078–4670–8 (pbk.: alk. paper)
1. Sound in art. 2. Arts, Modern—20th century.
3. Postmodernism. I. Morris, Adalaide Kirby,
1942– .
NX650.S68S69 1997
700'.9'04—DC21   97–9884
                            CIP

01 00 99 98 97   5 4 3 2 1

Quotations from H.D.
copyright © 1997 by Perdita
Schaffner; copyright © 1961
Norman Holmes Pearson.
Used by permission of New
Directions Publishing Corporation.
Quotations from Edward Kamau
Brathwaite's "Wings of a Dove,"
published in *The Arrivants*, are used
by permission of Oxford University
Press.
Quotations from John Cage's
"What You Say . . . ," first published
in *Formations* (Spring–Summer 1987),
courtesy of the John Cage Trust.
James A. Connor's "RADIO free
JOYCE" is reprinted by permission
of *James Joyce Quarterly*.
Michael Davidson's "Technologies
of Presence" appears, in slightly
different form, as a chapter in his
*Ghostlier Demarcations: Modern Poetry
and the Material Word* (Berkeley:
University of California Press, 1997);
used by permission of the publisher.
Nathaniel Mackey's "Cante Moro"
is reprinted by permission of Anne
Waldman and Andrew Schelling,
eds., *Disembodied Poetics: Annals of the
Jack Kerouac School*, and the University
of New Mexico Press.

Sign of sound
sibilant wind

> Susan Howe, *Articulation*
> *of Sound Forms in Time*

Look into thine own ear & read

> Zukofsky on advice from
> Pound, letter to Lorine Niedecker,
> 9 March 1938

[A poetics is] a question
of technology as well as
inspiration

> Jerome Rothenberg,
> "Pre-Face (1967)"

And lo: there are poets, poets
from this book, on MTV! It's the
nineties! Poems are being
written with television cameras,
composed in recording studios,
downloaded via computer
networks . . . .

> Bob Holman, *Aloud: Voices from*
> *the Nuyorican Poets Cafe*

We see the poem, read it, hear
it, feel it—is it, in the midst of
these various experiences, the
same? Does it change? Where
is the poem?

> Fred Moten, "Tragedy, Elegy,
> Improvisation"

CONTENTS

ILLUSTRATIONS

CD TRACKS

1. James A. Connor, radio collage (2:44)

2. H.D., Helen is of course that Helen (2:43)

3. H.D., In the sanctuary (3:01)

4. H.D., Much has happened (0:58)

5. John Cage, "What You Say . . ." (4:13)

6. Bengt af Klintberg, "Calls," 1968 (1:08)

7. F. T. Marinetti, "Bombardamento di Adrianopoli," 1912 (3:04)

8. Hugo Ball, "Gadji Beri Bimba," 1915 (1:44)

9. Christian Morgenstern, "Das grosse Lalula," 1905 (0:52)

10. Paul Scheerbart, "Kikakokú! Ekoralaps!," 1897 (0:48)

11. Raoul Hausmann, "b b b b et F m s b w," 1918 (1:11)

12. Isadore Isou, "Rituel somptueux pour la Selection des Espèces," 1965 (2:11)

13. Aleksei Kruchenykh: "Dyr bul shchyl," 1912; "Kr dei macelli," 1920; "Zanzera, velano," 1922 (2:48)

14. François Dufrêne, "Cri-rhythme" (2:49)

15. Henri Chopin, "Le Ventre de Bertini," 1967 (1:51)

16. Lee "Scratch" Perry, "Well Dread" (0:35)

17. King Tubby, "A Rougher Version" (1:02)

18. Anthony McNeill, "Ode to Brother Joe" (2:01)

19. Edward Kamau Brathwaite, "Wings of a Dove" (3:32)

20. Mutabaruka, "The People's Court" (2:24)

21. Pastora Pavón, "Ay Pilato" (2:32)

22. Miles Davis, "Saeta" (3:45)

23. Miles Davis and John Coltrane, "All Blues" (5:44)

24. Mississippi Fred McDowell, "Everybody's Down on Me" (3:13)

25. Mississippi Fred McDowell, "Jesus Is on the Mainline" (1:55)

26. Rahsaan Roland Kirk, "The Business Ain't Nothin' but the Blues" (2:25)

27. [Iranian singer], "Love Song" (2:45)

28. Sonny Rollins, "East Broadway Rundown" (3:07)

29. Cecil Taylor, "Chinampas" (5:07)

ACKNOWLEDGMENTS

The experience of putting together this collection of essays has been exhilaratingly plural. I thank Jim Connor, in on it from the start, and Michael Davidson and Marjorie Perloff, encouragers all along the way. I am grateful to Garrett Stewart's writing, which taught me to hear how reading voices, and to Fred Moten's improvisations, which helped me to understand how sounds think. Bill Dolde, Jocelyn Emerson, Rick Lattanzio, Kate Lewis, Sarah MacDonald, Richard Quinn, Julie Schmid, Lara Trubowitz, and the other students in my sound states seminars at the University of Iowa heard, amplified, and enriched the ideas that generated this collection.

For material support, I am grateful to Laura Dubek, Traci Kyle, Lori Muntz, Jessica Renaud, and, especially, Angela Brown. Tom Schipper, audio engineer and director of the University of Iowa's Audio Department, was a crucial partner from the project's inception to the final fade on its last track. His skills, energy, patience, and generosity were integral to the development of the book.

The University of North Carolina Press has been bold in its willingness to support both the inked and the aired components of our arguments. It is our hope that the book's sound states will not just amplify the archives available to students of innovative writings but also encourage additional acoustical ventures. Peter Quartermain's acute reading of the manuscript made a difference in its development. Stephanie Wenzel, our copyeditor, and Pamela Upton, the project editor, have been unceasingly helpful. Finally, I thank our editors at the Press, two keen listeners: Barbara Hanrahan, who gave the idea its first hearing; and Sian Hunter White, who heard it through to the end.

SOUND states

**Tawny owl (*Strix aluco*) addicted to BBC Radio. Postcard, 1935,
Eric Hosking/Acme Cards, London.**

INTRODUCTION

Sound States

"Writing has been bottled up in books since the start," the poet Robert Carleton Brown proclaimed at the end of the 1920s: "It is time to pull out the stopper" (*Readies* 28). His hypothetical un-corker—"Bob Brown's Machine"—aimed to give "the up-to-date reader . . . an eye-ful" (*Readies* 1). First the movies, then the talkies, now "the readies": "Without any whirr or splutter," Brown announced, "writing will be readable at the speed of the day—1929—not 1450" (*1450–1950* facing title page). As Jerome McGann describes it, Bob Brown's machine would "provide the reader with the power to read in all directions and at any speed, to change type size and type-face at will, to leap forward or backward in the text: to browse, to speedread, to connect any and all parts of the text in any and all ways" (*Black Riders* 88). However implausible such a device must have seemed in 1929, by 1992 its equivalent sat on hundreds of thousands of library, school, and office desks. The technologized words that burst from Brown's imagination—"print-in-action-at-last-moveable-type-at-full gallop" (*1450–1950*)—take their place in a lineage that runs from Gutenberg's Bible forward to the digitized hypertexts now playing on hard drives everywhere.

The notion of a stopped-up culture of the book has been elaborated in different directions by scholars such as Eric A. Havelock, Walter J. Ong, and Marshall McLuhan, on one hand, and Richard Lanham and George P. Landow on the other. The point these scholars make is foundational to the essays in this collection, all of which assume that we read, write, think and feel, position ourselves within, and move through the world in the web of power, technologies, and signifying marks that Friedrich A. Kittler calls a "discourse network." Ready or not, contemporary readers and writers exist in a technologized culture that has since the 1920s set the material conditions for the generation, transmission, and reception of the signals we call "literature."

The stuck stopper the essays in this collection work to loosen is not visual but aural. Our aim is to give the reader an earful. Like Brown, most twentieth-century thinkers draw their models for reading, writing, and the formation of subjectivity from mirrors, lenses, cameras, screens, and other paraphernalia of the gaze. For them, as for Brown, the processing, storage, and transmission of data is an ocular event, in which readers catch a glimpse, scan, attain an overview, or gain perspective through the eye. It takes only a slight displacement, however, to notice moments when we lend an ear, keep our ears open, even become all ears. If we begin our analysis, as Havelock and Ong did, before the onset of writing; listen, as Jack Goody and Kamau Brathwaite have, to master storytellers; tune in to children, stand-up comics, talk show hosts, politicians, teachers, and preachers; or attend, as the essayists in this collection do, to the boom of radio, loud-speakers, microphones, and tape recorders, it is impossible to ignore the data that also and incessantly pours into consciousness through the ear.

Animal cries, waterfalls, thunderclaps, horses' hooves, church bells, steam engines, the shriek and grunt of industrial machines, factory sirens, the ring of phones, the buzz and blare of loudspeakers, radio background noise, jamming, feedback, static, undertones, in-your-ear headphones, sound tracks, voice-overs, the hum, whirr, and sosumi-twang of computers —past or future, live or on tape, we are always suspended in a surround of sound. It's not just Eskimos who live in an "ear world" (Frizzell and Mandeville 45); it's not just talk poets who think with an "ear mind" (Antin). Even the most book-bound European is, in Joyce's acoustical slide, also an "earopean" (*Finnegans Wake* 310.21, qtd. in McLuhan 302).

To judge from contemporary critical vocabularies, most readers have a tin ear for sound in texts. With the exception of New Critics trained in prosody, even our best close readers have not also been close listeners. Attention to the play of textualized sound is so rare, in fact, that exceptions— Debra Fried's elegant capture of the phenomenon she terms "the call of the phoneme" (88), for example, or Garrett Stewart's kinetic apprehensions of the "underestimated dimension of textuality" he calls the "phonotext" (28) —seem lush, thick, and startling. The sound states Fried and Stewart hear go beyond euphony, cacophony, assonance, and alliteration to the fundamentals of textual understanding. The questions they open cannot be answered with our old vocabularies, vocabularies in which it seems plausible to refer to "oral literature," "silent reading," or even, to borrow John Cage's blunt example, "silence."

As Havelock and Ong began to argue in the 1960s, the term "oral literature" is oxymoronic. Narratives of a primary oral culture—a culture untouched by writing—are so qualitatively different from those of a culture with a knowledge of writing that they cannot be subsumed under the same rubric. The term "oral literature" is, in fact, not just mistaken but obtuse. "Our concept of oral performance has long been derived from our concept of literature," Ong explains, "despite the fact that in actuality it is literature which grows out of oral performance. A parallel . . . would be to refer to a horse never as a horse but always as a four-legged automobile without wheels" (*Presence* 21).

While it is a mistake to collapse orality and literacy into one category, however, it is no less a mistake to divide them by consigning orality to a preliterate past. As the first sense organ to develop in utero, the ear opens our initial access to the world. Even the most print-dependent thinkers begin as oralists and continue throughout life to orient themselves by ear as much as by sight. Since the 1920s, furthermore, our ears have been roused and supplemented by acoustical technologies such as telephones, microphones, loudspeakers, phonographs, radios, walkie-talkies, tape recorders, compact discs, and now cellular phones, digital voice mail, and talking computers. As Ong suggests, these and other electronic technologies have generated a new or "secondary" orality. At once like and unlike primary orality, secondary orality combines the participatory mystique, preoccupation with the present, and formulaic bent of primary orality with the penchant for analysis, inward turn, and insistence on closure characteristic of literacy (*Orality* 136). Within print cultures, Jack Goody insists, the registers of orality and literacy remain so intricately entangled that no neat division between the two can hold. "Strictly speaking, therefore," Goody concludes, we should think not of the oral and the literate but, rather, of "the oral and the oral plus the written, printed, etc." (xii).

The term "silent reading" designates one of many ways to access Goody's "written, printed, etc.," but it too relies on an unthought dichotomy: the apparently obvious opposition, in this case, between the "voiced" and "unvoiced" processing of texts, between "reading aloud" and "reading to oneself." Because phonetic alphabets by definition always engage the ear of the reader, each lexical act involves a crisscross—even a double- or triple-cross—between a text's graphics and its phonemics. Every "graphotext," in Stewart's terminology, has as its companion and counterpart a "phonotext" or articulatory stream of soundings. "In alphabetic language," Stewart writes, "the 'glyphs' are not of course pictograms but rather the indication (rather than transcription) of acoustic (though not vocal) signifiers" (28).

Acoustic signifiers can be spoken aloud or merely evoked, summoned under suspension in the pronunciations of "silent reading." In Stewart's dazzling phenomenology of reading, the friction between "graphotext" and "phonotext" generates "the ceaseless interrelationship and relativity, the mutually implicated biplay, the virtual *dramaturgy*, of aural sequencing" (101). The operative distinction in this case is not the difference between sound and no sound but, more precisely, the difference between scriptive characters processed by the eye and phonemic characters evoked for the inner or the outer ear. Whether or not it is voiced, "reading" always, to cite Stewart's title, "voices." It depends, that is, on a rich, supple, uncontainable aurality, an acoustics we are only beginning to learn how to access (2).

In a flash that changed the course of his career, finally, John Cage undid a third, even more fundamental opposition: the division, in this case, between "sound" and "silence." After an experience in Harvard's anechoic chamber, Cage composed his music and wrote his poems in the conviction that there is no such thing as silence, only a failure to pay attention to sound. Like the term "white noise," "silence" for Cage describes that which we hear but do not apprehend: unintended sounds, unattended sounds, sounds that exceed or elude our abilities to detect or measure them. To illustrate this point, Cage referred again and again to Harvard's laboratory chamber in which instead of stillness he heard a constant high-pitched ring and a low pulse: the singing tones of his nervous system, the throbbing of his blood (Revill 162). To borrow Barthes's terminology, in this case the operative distinction is not between "silence" and "sound" but between "hearing" and "listening." The first is an ongoing, often subthreshold, physiological phenomenon; the second, a psychological act (245). "Music . . . is continuous," said Cage, echoing Thoreau; "only listening is intermittent" (preface 3).

Writing about/listening to the literary phonotext has been sporadic and uneven. Critics with a keen ear tend to turn not to literature but to classical or operatic music, blues, jazz, rock, rap, hip hop, and the advancing technologies of youth music and youth culture (see, for example, Rose and Ross). Although they do not exactly plug their ears, most contemporary media critics tend to look rather than listen. For every two dozen good books on photography, cinema, television, or video, there are at most one or two good essays on radio, phonography, or tape art. Until the marketing of inexpensive tape recorders in the 1950s, sounds routinely slipped away as they emerged, but even after the widespread availability of recording technologies, sound events remain difficult to archive and all but impossible to transcribe on the page.[1] For these and other reasons suggested in the essays that follow, the interplay between textuality and twentieth-century acoustical technologies remains largely undocumented and undertheorized. "The deafening silence surrounding sound was made to be broken," Douglas Kahn and Gregory Whitehead proclaim in the preface to *Wireless Imagination: Sound, Radio, and the Avant-Garde*, their groundbreaking anthology of work by artists, historians, and theorists of sound: "Let the clamor begin!" (xi).[2]

Some of the most sophisticated writing about sound in contemporary media occurs with reference to theories of gender, the gaze, and subject formation in cinema.[3] Notions of silence, noise, groove, transmission, and interference continue to circulate through various domains of contemporary theory, but as Kahn and Whitehead point out, these and other acoustical terms "are most typically employed like migrant workers, obliged to cultivate somebody else's juicy literary analogies before being trucked off to the next field" (ix). A few highly suggestive psychoanalytic hypotheses have the potential to tend their own field—Julia Kristeva's famous elaboration of the semiotic register, for example, or Micheline Veaux's much less familiar suggestion of a vocal equivalent for the mirror stage[4]—but it is telling that for the most part theories of aurality are deployed to mark the point at which lucidity disintegrates. When the ear is evoked primarily to signal moments of destabilization, slippage, or even psychosis, it becomes the one sense through which nothing much can make sense.

Literary analysts of sound generally turn either to poetry, conventionally the most sound-saturated of genres, or to the dense and intricate prose of writers such as James Joyce, Samuel Beckett, and William Burroughs. Critics of lyric poetry in particular, however, are quick to override the slide of the phonotext with the stability of the graphotext. They are eager, that is, to motivate puns, explain away echolalia, submit rhythms to regularizing prosodic analysis, or soft-pedal textual acoustics into a sort of emotional background music. New Critical close readings and conventional thematic analyses alike tend to position earnestness and stability at the heart of "serious" literature.[5] To constitute a literary text as a static, truth-telling object, abstruse, hieratic, and linear, however, not only mutes the roar Joyce called "soundsense" but also strands the text in a private, timeless, hermetic isolation, a seclusion that is not only out of earshot of but antithetical to the acoustical technologies that ground the inquiry of this collection of essays.

Recent trends in literary criticism and theory continue to hold sound not so much in our ears as—to borrow Stewart's pun—"in arrears" (7). Historicist criticism, for example, situates texts as nodes in a ceaseless circulation of power, points of relay important not so much for their linguistic intricacies as for their ability to transmit extralinguistic codes and messages. Deconstructive criticism, on the other hand, situates texts as inscriptions that exceed the codes of spoken language. The catchwords of this philosophical position—"phonocentrism," for example, or "presence"—emphasize its rejection of the paired assumptions that writing represents speech and that speech exists in a direct and natural relationship with meaning. In opposition to unending discussions of lyric poetry conducted in terms of hearing the poet's "voice," finding one's own "voice," and/or "voicing" one's vision, critics persuaded by Derrida's attack on the Logos have preferred to avoid all things phonemic. "Though inner audition need not in any sense subscribe to a myth of an originary Voice before the letter, still," Stewart writes, "the resistance to a supposedly 'undemystified' orality has created a veritable deaf spot in the tenets of even the most sophisticated reception theories" (3). "Phonocentrism" has, in fact, slid so far toward the aversion Stewart labels "phonophobia" that most contemporary academic criticism of lyric poetry avoids sound states altogether.[6] Even though the term "lyric" situates the most prevalent poetry as a sonorous event, it remains, as Kahn and Whitehead have observed in another context, "almost unheard of to think about sound" (ix).[7]

In auditing the intersection between modern and contemporary textuality, contemporary literary theory, and acoustical technologies, the essays in this collection run counter to a critical tendency that pits graphotext against phonotext as if the town were not big enough for both. "Literary Language is Optical, speaking language Vocal," Bob Brown declared in throwing his weight on the side of optics. His hypothetical machine would turn "the gap between them . . . [into] a gulf" (*Readies* 39). Modern and postmodern literary language *is* optical, to be sure. As both Jerome McGann and Cary Nelson have recently demonstrated, modernism took shape in the emphatic graphics of countless small press publications, fine printed books, and broadsides containing work by authors such as William Morris, Yeats, Pound, Stein, Williams, Langston Hughes, Paul Dunbar, Malcolm Cowley, and the poets of the political left.[8] Recognizing that texts appeal to the ear as well as to the eye, however, engineers of the contemporary equivalents of Bob Brown's machine—the speediest Macs and the IBM Power-Readies—have installed stereo sound systems; CD audio players; scrapbooks of quacks, falling droplets, beeps, and wild eeps; and a microphone that attaches to the side of the screen for easier sound input.

Although they can be discussed separately, the optical and the acoustic are not easily split from each other. Because of print's appearance on the page, it is tempting to think of poems as silent, solid, even stolid, entities: "I thought once that poems were like words inscribed in rock or caught in amber," Louise Glück admits. "I thought in these terms so long, so fervently, with such investment in images of preservation and fixity, that the inaccuracies of the metaphor as description of my own experience did not occur to me until very recently" (128). What is left out of these images is, of course, the slip and slide of the phonotext, which Glück identifies as contact, presence, or voice. In an essay that argues from different assumptions in a different vocabulary, Charles Bernstein reaches a similar conclusion: "In*hear*ing in a poetics of vision or reflection (as if to counter a visualist frame of reference in these terms) is," he writes, "a poetics of sound. Words [must be] returned to a sonorousness that does not require the validation of fixed images, of sight and insight, nor deny its common roots with visibility" ("Words" 160). Our aim in these pages is to release the genie of sound bottled up in books, dial up the volume on printed volumes, and suggest some ways to look at, listen to, and talk about literary texts in a digitalized and hypertextual age.

Complex, plural, and supple methods of interpretation—methods that register more than one sense—become ever more urgent as information continues its migration from print to computerized multimedia. Like a poetics, editorial theory is a matter not just of aesthetic convictions and interpretive know-how but also of available information-processing technologies. The ideal of a definitive or authoritative edition—an edition designed to be as ageless as rock or amber—responds not only to New Critical convictions about texts and their authors but also to the relative stability of printed books. More recent editorial theory, by contrast, responds to poststructuralist assumptions about textuality and the capabilities of contemporary multimedia technologies.[9] When CD-ROM memory, hypertextual software, instant cross-referencing and search capacities, electronic journals, and online access shuttle information between files, libraries, offices, and homes, through modems, nets, and worldwide webs, from screens to printers and back to screens, texts exist as fluid, social products, products that are more easily downloaded, modified, saved, reproduced, and relayed than fixed in any one authoritative or definitive form. Multimedia computer technologies do not generate brides of quiet sequestered in expensive, limited variorum editions but something closer to what the poet Susan Howe calls, in appropriately unstable syntax, the "articulation of sound forms in time."[10] As Donald Reiman suggests, then, it may be time to borrow a term from acoustical mixing and speak not of "editing" but rather of "versioning" the texts we put into circulation (169).[11]

Several projects now in process or in distribution suggest that sound editing practices need no longer downplay the element of sound. As Richard Lanham argues, "The fundamental 'operating system' for the humanities is changing from the book to the digital multimedia computer screen."[12] Variorum editions in the humanities can now easily incorporate not only all known versions of a text, relevant drafts, historical and artistic references, and extensive supporting documentation but also aural performances of poetic scores. The editors of the electronic hypermedia edition of Yeats's *The Tower*, currently in preparation for distribution on CD-ROM, for example, plan to include recordings of all twenty-eight poems in the volume, supplementing extant recordings by Yeats with readings by contemporary Irish poets. *The Norton Anthology of Poetry*, fourth edition, and *The Norton Introduction to Poetry*, sixth edition, now come with a *Norton Poetry Workshop* on CD-ROM, edited by James F. Knapp, containing the sounds of poems. On Voyager's widely distributed CD-ROM *Poetry in Motion*, performances, interviews, and poetic texts by twenty-four contemporary writers are accessible at the click of a mouse. The magical graphics of Robyn and Rand Miller's computer adventure game *Myst* are accompanied by exquisite sounds that players must process in order to solve its puzzles. Hybrid sound-prints such as The Last Poets' "jazzoetry" and "spographics" are published on audio CD, and print-sounds such as those performed at the Nuyorican Cafe are available in anthology form (Algarín and Holman). These contingent, collaborative, enigmatic, plural, technologized states of sound—sound states—are both the topic and the hypothesis of the essays in this anthology.

In ink, on air, miked, muted, magnetized, digitalized, or virtualized, sound has the versatility and insistence of water. Fixed in phonetic writing, thawed by reading, scattered in speech, stored for replay on tape, record, disk, or drive, sounds pass through multiple phases, forms, and structures, all of which claim our ear but few of which gain a hearing. The twelve essays in this collection track various forms of earplay in texts composed or received after telephones, phonographs, radios, loudspeakers, microphones, and tape recorders became facts of everyday domestic and political life.

As the essays by James A. Connor, Adalaide Morris, Toby Miller and Alec McHoul, N. Katherine Hayles, and Michael Davidson emphasize, the acoustical technologies that grew up with modernism also prepared the swerve toward the postmodern. In the 1920s, Joyce, Pound, and H.D. spun the knobs of their brand-new radio receivers to tune in ghostly, foreign, yet strangely familiar murmurings from around the globe. Radio transmissions gave writers, politicians, advertisers, and religious broadcasters alike the opportunity to "voice" their era: to tell a story, spell out the news, or sell soap. This contested public airspace is also a local front available to the activist-commentator Miller and McHoul call the "wired intellectual," a figure who can, like other writers and theorists, make imperfect, incomplete noises in culture, sound interventions that may not control the production and dispersal of culture but can, nonetheless, make claims to influence aspects of its circulation.

In 1925, three years after Eliot "did the police in different voices," a patent was issued for the electrodynamic loudspeaker that boomed the voices of Hitler, Mussolini, Roosevelt, Churchill, and de Gaulle across the 1930s and 1940s. In the 1950s, as Davidson and Hayles explain, inexpensive tape recorders made it possible for the first time for poets to hear their own voices. In addition to promoting a new oral imperative, as Davidson argues, tape technologies also allowed performers such as David Antin, Laurie Anderson, and Steve Benson to become active agents in the demystification of voice. Tape's eerie ability to detach voices from bodies led Samuel Beckett to create *Krapp's Last Tape* and William Burroughs to write *The Ticket That Exploded*, texts that Katherine Hayles positions as crucial to the formation of not just a postmodern but a posthuman subjectivity.

The essays of Part II attend to sounds performed or ritualized on stage, in the streets, at bars or cafes: the grounded sounds of John Cage, Henri Chopin, the deejay-poets of the emerging Caribbean, Bob Kaufman, Amiri Baraka, and Cecil Taylor. These poet-performers deploy language less for its segments of meaning—its lexemes, morphemes, and phonemes—than for a buzz or hum that can be heard in Cage's "musicated language," Nathaniel Mackey's "speaking more than one knew what," or Taylor's "sound in florescence." "I have not yet carried language to the point to which I have taken musical sounds," Cage explained to an interviewer in the early 1970s, but, he added, "I hope to make something other than language from it." As Marjorie Perloff demonstrates, Cage fine-tuned his mesostics to release words from syntactical linearities into multidimensional zones of resonance. In his history of sound poetry, Steve McCaffery traces a similar florescence from the early twentieth-century phonetic performances of Futurist and Dadaist "sonosophers" to Henri Chopin's micro-engineered, speed-changing, electroacoustic "audio-poèmes," the first poetry achievable only through the use of tape-recording technologies.

As soon as inexpensive sound equipment allowed cultural noises to be captured, dubbed, sampled, and versioned with cut-'n-mix technologies, brilliantly innovative electroacoustical artists took their art from the streets into the studio and back again.[13] In her analysis of Caribbean performative sounds, Loretta Collins hears the "riddims" and "rub-a-dub" of Rastafarians, Rude Boys, politicians, and poets as they coalesce in the mix Brathwaite called "nation language" and Collins calls "a dread black consciousness."

Like the "Cante Moro" or "dark sounds" to which Mackey draws our ear, the technical competence—the virtuosity—of this art exists at the other side of skill: "You get there," Mackey explains, "by not being satisfied with skill." "Words don't go there," Fred Moten says in preparing to play with—to attune to—Cecil Taylor's musicked language. The resonance that Mackey and Moten teach us to hear is a wavering, troubled, unbound sound that rides on frequencies outside and beneath the lexical range, a strain that takes language far past its familiar limits.

In this volume's two concluding essays, Garrett Stewart and Jed Rasula reconnect aural and ocular registers, premodern and modern moments, and literary and filmic effects. Both begin with "voice"—the act of giving voice, the poet's voice, voice-print, voice recording, and voice-over—and complicate their hearings with observations about Chris Marker's experimental videos. In "Modernism's Sonic Waiver," Stewart offers the operations of the filmstrip as a parallel to the reeling-by—the "s/tripping"—of words in syntactic focus. Arguing that modernism is continuous with the discontinuities of literary language itself, he begins with aural cuts from *Jane Eyre* and *Dr. Jekyll and Mr. Hyde* and ends with a visual sequence from Marker's *La Jetée*. Arguing that poetry loses touch with its voice-over when it appropriates voice for the purposes of subjectivity, Rasula returns to mythopoetic scenarios of poetic origins. Long, long before acoustical technologies, he notes, poets were wired for sound: if Hesiod acted as the Muses' radio transmitter, Orpheus doubles as the speaker/broadcaster for the cosmos.

As if pressing against the constraints of the page, several recent books that argue (that) sound matters deploy postmodern page layouts, shifting typefaces, and innovative cover designs. Avital Ronell's *The Telephone Book: Technology, Schizophrenia, Electric Speech*, Jacques Derrida's *Cinders*, and Kahn and Whitehead's *Wireless Imagination* all speak for sound through the eye rather than to the ear. Reviews of *Wireless Imagination*, convinced by its content, lament its muteness. "Think of the book as a radio station with some really good shows. Think of yourself as a radio," one reviewer writes, but still he asks, "Where's the CD?" (Clover 30). "It's impossible to read [this book] without aching for some sound," another reviewer suggests, "an audio supplement [to] highlight the fades, cuts, collages, and contortions of the volume's audio pioneers." "At least someone broke the silence," he adds, "even if they did do it without making a sound" (Strauss 62).

As more and more humanities reference materials leave paper and bindings behind, a few recent university press books have broken the sound barrier that constrained the *Wireless Imagination*. In 1990, for example, Harvard University Press published John Cage's Norton Lectures *I–VI* with accompanying audiotapes, and in 1994 the University of North Carolina Press published important studies of blues and of country music with accompanying audio CDs (Titon; Tichi). Since *Sound States* contends that acoustical technologies have changed the subject, the definition of community, and the conduct of politics; enriched the auditor's sensorium; and profoundly altered our cultural imaginary, it seems appropriate to mix audio with optical signals and back our claims with soundtracks of early radio sounds, poetry readings, Dada cabaret performances, jazzoetry, audiopoèmes, and contemporary Caribbean DJ dub poetry. It's time, we say, to lend an ear.

Containing contributions from literary scholars, communication theorists, cultural historians, poets, and public intellectuals, *Sound States* is indebted to the work of several communities of thinkers. Each essay has its own array of influences, but the collection as a whole is especially indebted to Ong, Havelock, and McLuhan, who grew up listening to radio and were the first to theorize the interplay between orality and literacy; to Garrett Stewart, who has elegantly demonstrated that literature need not be oral for its aurality to work on its readers; to Marjorie Perloff, whose book *Radical Artifice* tunes in the interplay between poetry and the electronic media; and to a remarkable group of poet/theorists that includes Michael Davidson, Nathaniel Mackey, Steve McCaffery, and Jed Rasula. This collection was also sparked by Kahn and Whitehead's *Wireless Imagination* and by the radio-texts of Neil Strauss and Toby Miller. May the clamor continue!

NOTES

1. See Davidson and Tedlock.

2. For two other excellent beginnings in this endeavor, see Toby Miller's "Radio-Sound" issue of *Continuum*, containing essays by Australian sound theorists and artists, and Neil Strauss's "Radiotext(e)" issue of *Semiotext(e)*.

3. See, for example, Silverman and Lawrence.

4. See Kaplan 8–9.

5. See Ahl and Culler for spirited analyses of this literary critical default mode in classical and contemporary scholarship.

6. See Perloff's review of Hošek and Parker, *Lyric Poetry*, a collection of twenty-one essays from a symposium at the University of Toronto, published in 1985. "What does it mean to write of lyric poetry," Perloff asks, "as if its sound structure were wholly irrelevant, a mere externality?" ("Can(n)on" 17).

7. See, in a happy example, Bernstein, *Close Listening*.

8. For stunning examples of these graphics, see the illustrations in McGann, *Black Riders*, and Nelson.

9. For sustained discussion of these points, see Bornstein; Schillingsburg; and McGann, "What Is Critical Editing?"

10. *Articulation of Sound Forms in Time* is, of course, the title of Susan Howe's poem published in a beautifully designed edition by Awede.

11. See discussion in Bornstein.

12. See "Implications of Electronic Information," printed in summary form, available by anonymous ftp from cni.org, in the directory cni/documents/tech. schol.human/papers. See also Lanham's *Electronic Word*.

13. For other arguments that listen to the poetic energies in the streets, see Damon and Talarico.

WORKS CITED

Ahl, Frederick. *Metaformations: Soundplay and Wordplay in Ovid and Other Classical Poets*. Ithaca: Cornell University Press, 1985.

Algarín, Miguel, and Bob Holman. *Aloud: Voices from the Nuyorican Poets Cafe*. New York: Holt, 1994.

Antin, David. *tuning*. New York: New Directions, 1984.

Barthes, Roland. "Listening." *The Responsibility of Forms: Critical Essays on Music, Art, and Representation*. Trans. Richard Howard. New York: Hill & Wang, 1985. 245–60.

Bernstein, Charles. "Words and Pictures." *Content's Dream: Essays, 1975–1984*. Los Angeles: Sun & Moon, 1986. 114–61.

———, ed. *Close Listening: Poetry and the Performed Word*. New York: Oxford University Press, forthcoming.

Bornstein, George. "What Is the Text of a Poem by Yeats?" *Palimpsest: Editorial Theory in the Humanities*. Ed. George Bornstein and Ralph G. Williams. Ann Arbor: University of Michigan Press, 1993. 167–94.

Brathwaite, Edward Kamau. *History of the Voice: The Development of Nation Language in Anglophone Caribbean Poetry*. London: New Beacon, 1984.

Brown, Bob. *The Readies*. Bad-Ems: Roving Eye Press, 1930.

———. *1450–1950*. Paris: Black Sun, 1929. New York: Jargon, 1959.

Cage, John. *I–VI*. Cambridge, Mass.: Harvard University Press, 1990.

———. Preface to *"Lecture on the Weather." Empty Words: Writings '73–'78*. Middletown, Conn.: Wesleyan University Press, 1979. 3–5.

Clover, Joshua. "The Avant-Garde Art of Noise." Review of *Wireless Imagination: Sound, Radio, and the Avant-Garde*. Ed. Douglas Kahn and Gregory Whitehead. *San Francisco Review of Books* 18.2 (1993): 30–31.

Culler, Jonathan, ed. *On Puns: The Foundation of Letters*. New York: Blackwell, 1988.

Damon, Maria. *The Dark End of the Street: Margins in American Vanguard Poetry*. Minneapolis: University of Minnesota Press, 1993.

Davidson, Michael. " 'By ear, he sd': Audio-Tapes and Contemporary Criticism." *Credences* n.s. 1.1 [1981]: 105–20.

Derrida, Jacques. *Cinders*. Ed. and trans. Ned Lukacher. Lincoln: University of Nebraska Press, 1991.

Fried, Debra. "Rhyme Puns." *On Puns: The Foundation of Letters*. Ed. Jonathan Culler. New York: Blackwell, 1988. 83–99.

Frizzell, Rev. Dwight, and Jay Mandeville. "Early Radio Bigwigs." *Semiotext(e)* 6.1, no. 16 (1993). Ed. Neil Strauss. 39–46. *Semiotext(e)* no. 16 is also titled "Radiotext(e)."

Glück, Louise. "Death and Absence." *Proofs and Theories: Essays on Poetry.* Hopewell, N.J.: Ecco, 1994. 125–28.

Goody, Jack. *The Interface between the Written and the Oral.* Cambridge: Cambridge University Press, 1987.

Hošek, Chaviva, and Patricia Parker, eds. *Lyric Poetry: Beyond New Criticism.* Ithaca: Cornell University Press, 1985.

Howe, Susan. *Articulation of Sound Forms in Time.* Windsor, Vt.: Awede, 1987.

Kahn, Douglas, and Gregory Whitehead, eds. *Wireless Imagination: Sound, Radio, and the Avant-Garde.* Cambridge, Mass.: MIT Press, 1992.

Kaplan, Alice Yaeger. *Reproductions of Banality: Fascism, Literature, and French Intellectual Life.* Minneapolis: University of Minnesota Press, 1986.

Kittler, Friedrich A. *Discourse Networks 1800/1900.* Trans. Michael Metteer, with Chris Cullens. Stanford: Stanford University Press, 1990.

Kristeva, Julia. *Revolution in Poetic Language.* Trans. Margaret Waller. New York: Columbia University Press, 1984.

Lanham, Richard A. *The Electronic Word: Democracy, Technology, and the Arts.* Chicago: University of Chicago Press, 1993.

———. "The Implications of Electronic Information for the Sociology of Knowledge." Printed in summary form and available through the Internet.

Last Poets. "Jazzoetry." *Chastisment.* Celluloid, 1992.

Lawrence, Amy. *Echo and Narcissus: Women's Voices in Classical Hollywood Cinema.* Berkeley: University of California Press, 1991.

McGann, Jerome. *Black Riders: The Visible Language of Modernism.* Princeton: Princeton University Press, 1993.

———. "What Is Critical Editing?" *Text* 5 (1991): 15–29.

McLuhan, Marshall. *Understanding Media: The Extensions of Man.* New York: McGraw-Hill, 1964.

Miller, Toby, ed. "Radio-Sound." *Continuum* 6.1 (1992).

Nelson, Cary. *Repression and Recovery: Modern American Poetry and the Politics of Cultural Memory, 1910–1945.* Madison: University of Wisconsin Press, 1989.

Ong, Walter J. *Orality and Literacy: The Technologizing of the Word.* London: Methuen, 1982.

———. *The Presence of the Word: Some Prolegomena for Cultural and Religious History.* New Haven: Yale University Press, 1967.

Perloff, Marjorie. "Can(n)on to the Right of Us, Can(n)on to the Left of Us: A Plea for Difference." *Poetic License: Essays on Modernist and Postmodernist Lyric.* Evanston: Northwestern University Press, 1990. 7–29.

———. *Radical Artifice: Writing Poetry in the Age of Media.* Chicago: University of Chicago Press, 1991.

Reiman, Donald H. *Romantic Texts and Contexts.* Columbia: University of Missouri Press, 1987.

Revill, David. *The Roaring Silence: John Cage, a Life.* New York: Arcade, 1992.

Ronell, Avital. *The Telephone Book: Technology, Schizophrenia, Electric Speech.* Lincoln: University of Nebraska Press, 1989.

Rose, Tricia, and Andrew Ross, eds. *Microphone Fiends: Youth Music and Youth Culture*. New York: Routledge, 1994.

Schillingsburg, Peter L. "Text as Matter, Concept, and Action." *Studies in Bibliography*. Vol. 44. Charlottesville: University Press of Virginia, 1991. 31–82.

Silverman, Kaja. *The Acoustic Mirror: The Female Voice in Psychoanalysis and Cinema*. Bloomington: Indiana University Press, 1988.

Stewart, Garrett. *Reading Voices: Literature and the Phonotext*. Berkeley: University of California Press, 1990.

Strauss, Neil. "Talk Radio." Rev. of *Wireless Imagination: Sound, Radio, and the Avant-Garde*. Ed. Douglas Kahn and Gregory Whitehead. *Village Voice* 2 February 1993: 62.

Talarico, Ross. *Spreading the Word: Poetry and the Survival of Community in America*. Durham: Duke University Press, 1995.

Tedlock, Dennis. "Learning to Listen: Oral History as Poetry." *Boundary 2* 3 (1975): 707–26.

———. "The Speaker of Tales Has More Than One String to Play On." *Vox Intexta: Orality and Textuality in the Middle Ages*. Ed. A. N. Doane and Carol Braun Pasternack. Madison: University of Wisconsin Press, 1991. 5–33.

Tichi, Cecelia. *High Lonesome: The American Culture of Country Music*. Chapel Hill: University of North Carolina Press, 1995.

Titon, Jeff Todd. *Early Downhome Blues: A Musical and Cultural Analysis*. 2nd ed. Chapel Hill: University of North Carolina Press, 1994.

Veaux, Micheline. "Réflexions Vocales dans un miroir et voix mythiques." *Bulletin d'Audiophonologie* 16.4 [1983]: 435–47.

PART ONE

Radio and Tape

SOUNDINGS

Transmissions

JAMES A. CONNOR

RADIO FREE JOYCE

Wake Language and the
Experience of Radio

In *The Human Use of Human Beings: Cybernetics and Society*, Norbert Wiener spoke of the uses of improbability in communication: "Messages are themselves a form of pattern and organization. Indeed, it is possible to treat sets of messages as having an entropy like sets of states of the external world. Just as entropy is a measure of disorganization, the information carried by a set of messages is a measure of organization. In fact, it is possible to interpret the information carried by a message as essentially the negative of its entropy, and the negative logarithm of its probability. That is, the more probable the message, the less information it gives" (21). If you think about it, this makes a kind of strange linguistic sense. If you could predict the contents of a message beforehand, why would it need to be sent? How useful could such a message be? But Wiener means something more than this. What he is saying is that up to a point, chaos itself increases information by increasing the possibilities of that information's content, up to the point when the very randomness of the signal makes it less and less able to bear meaning. If you graph this change, as did Claude Shannon in his "Mathematical Theory of Communication," it forms a bell curve, with information rising to a point, then dropping off at an equal rate.

Long before Shannon put this complex insight into the large, economy-size mathematics of information theory, modernist poets, painters, musicians, and novelists were experimenting with concrete examples. Cubists "opened up" three-dimensional objects to give impossible views of ordinary things. Dadaists experimented with pure sound. Novelists such as William Faulkner and James Joyce experimented with shifting points of view, multiple voices, and direct readings of thoughts. This is especially true of Joyce's last, arguably his greatest, and certainly his strangest novel, *Finnegans Wake*, which seems, at first glance, to be nearly pure chaos but is, slyly, not so. Here is a text that stands at the top of Shannon's bell curve, halfway between pure order and pure chaos, constructed, and yet constructed in such a way that it packs a measure of improbability into every line.

How could they have come up with such an idea? Something was in the air with these modernists, something to which they were responding, something that opened their ears, if not also their eyes, to a new way of communicating. This essay suggests that something, at least for *Finnegans Wake*, was radio. In those days radio signals were as far from our kind of digital stability as the Wright brothers' plane was from Apollo 11. Radio air was full of noises, wandering signals, high altitude skips, and super-heterodyne screeches, and anyone who listened to it had to gradually attune themselves to a cacophony of voices all speaking at once. For Joyce the exile, Joyce the aficionado of popular culture, radio air was not something to be ignored.

Voices All at Once: Early Radio

In the early twentieth century, radio had more influence on cultural change than did most other technological developments. For the first time, people living hundreds, sometimes thousands of miles apart had instant contact on a mass scale. This quantum jump in communication radically reduced the cost of influencing large numbers of people. It did not require paper or ink. It did not require a large distribution network. It only required a transmitter, a studio, some entertainment, and an audience, who paid for their own receivers and license fees for the privilege of listening. Capitalism had a new tool powerful enough to colonize the very art forms that produced it. Like Samuel Beckett with the tape recorder or William Butler Yeats with radio, Joyce was attuned to the technologies around him. First in *Ulysses* and then in *Finnegans Wake* he reformulated the language of advertising and the structure of technology and reset them in an older form, the novel. In so doing, he increased the amount of information that could be passed from one place to another with language. In a real sense he reset the linguistic level of entropy.

Irish radio was an early player in the development of radio. Having its roots in the uprising of 1916, when a group of republicans carried a radio set from one building to another in order to evade the British news blackout, the first Irish commercial station came on the air from Dublin on the first of January 1926 (Mink 459). Broadcasting from Little Denmark Street, the transmitter was moved in the early 1930s to a spot two miles east of Athlone.

At first it was not a very powerful station—on the average of 1 kilowatt (Gorham 9)—paltry by today's standards but average in those days, with a range of little more than a hundred miles.[1] "The evening programme began with a Stock Exchange List, News Bulletin, and Market Reports, and closed with a Weather Forecast" (Gorham 45), but there was a station trio, which eventually became an orchestra, and an overload of ballad singers.[2] And of course there were speeches. The opening address was given by Dr. Douglas Hyde, the founder of the Gaelic League, a fact that did not stop the league from condemning the station at least once a year for years to come.

The call sign for Radio Eireann, which Joyce referred to as "Radio Athlone," was 2RN, chosen to echo the final words of "Come back to Erin" (Gorham 23). Although the station relied heavily on relays from the BBC, Seamus Clandillon, the first director, emphasized Irish language programming. Broadcasts were informal affairs, done on the cheap.[3] By 1933, however, the Athlone station began to broadcast at 60 kilowatts (Gorham 86), so that on still nights, without much interference from sunspots, its signal reached Paris, where Joyce picked it up—an immediate connection with home, with its tidbits of news, weather, drama, and poetry. Although the airwaves were not nearly as crowded in the early 1930s as they are today, Radio Athlone had to compete for the most efficient frequencies, but it was the single channel where an Irish expatriate could hear Irish voices, not anglicized, and pick up Irish news. For a man who "each day, and each hour of the day" thought of Ireland, and each day, each hour of the day "lived and relived his memories" (Soupault 116), such a radio link must have been like water in the desert.

The power of radio in the lives of people in the 1930s cannot be overstated. Night after night entire families—if they were affluent—sat mesmerized around a large speaker. Others sat alone beside a crystal set, wearing headphones, their hands clutched over their ears, their faces screwed up with concentration as they picked out their station through all the noise. Noise was always a problem. And worse, transmissions were never steady—they appeared and disappeared like desert highways. These were the days before adjustable frequency stabilizers (my father invented the first one in 1950).[4] Blocks had to be put in or taken out to hold the frequency and keep it steady. Moreover, signals from the other side of the world sometimes bounced off the Heaviside layer and overrode more local signals so that an Abbey Theatre broadcast could be interrupted by a snow report from Minsk or a farm journal from Chicago.[5]

Factors like temperature drift also varied frequency. As a transmitter warmed up, its signal meandered off course, so that a listener would have to constantly tune and retune the receiver. What is more, if someone at the transmitter opened the door to the radio room, the transmitter tubes cooled suddenly and the frequency would stray again, so that everyone would have to try to follow. Then, on top of all this, there were squeals and whistles, howls like banshees keening through the airwaves. If any two radio frequency signals are close to each other, the difference between them becomes an audial signal, an eerie wail on the headphones, like the voice of a poor dead soul bouncing up and down along the Heaviside layer.[6] These voices—moving, shifting, piling on top of one another, settling, whistling, humming, and screeching—must have sounded in all their constant flux like the coils of hell.

In radiospeak, taken together these noises are called static, a term with two basic meanings: (1) generic radio interference, including words and unintelligible sounds—pops, whistles, squeals, and what have you—and (2) that hissing sibilant white noise, close to pure chaos, that is sometimes quiet enough to be ignored, sometimes loud enough to drown out everything else. While frequency shifts fade signals in and out, without the proper filters, the radio frequency hiss would be a nearly constant irritation. Any kind of electrical machinery causes man-made static, or QRN. Power lines and electric motors, generators, and automobiles are common culprits.[7] Natural static, or QRM (why these last letters are reversed, why M and not N for "natural" I don't know), is caused by sunspots and attendant atmospheric discharges, especially the aurora borealis.

CD1

The experience of radio in the 1930s, then, was a wondrous, often mysterious jumble of signal and noise. Benjamin's observation about the work of art in an age of technological reproduction also applies to the utterance, which like the work of art lost its uniqueness, its singular place in time and space (220). The word "spread out" over the landscape. The hearer and the speaker could be halfway across the world from each other. Moreover, the fact that a single utterance could be "reproduced" in so many homes in so many different places, at such great distance, and could be so altered along the way by so many electromagnetic forces meant that the spoken word was set into the world in an entirely new way. This new way is what Walter Ong calls "secondary orality," like and yet decidedly unlike the ancient primary orality of Homer (136).

At the same time that radio was becoming commonplace, Joyce was experimenting with language that reproduced its audial characteristics. Joyce himself admitted that in his *Work in Progress* "there is not even a chronological ordering of the action. It is a simultaneous action, represented by the novel's circular construction" (Hoffmeister 132). Simultaneous action, everything happening at once—what could be a better description of radio before digital dials, noise filters, and stereophonic sound? The language of the *Wake* flows and shifts, is noisy and hard to grasp, much like competing radio signals, so that a reader must listen with the same intensity as a radio hound in 1933. Joyce was, of course, aware of this connection, for as Michael Begnal points out, "Within the text are constant allusions to a wireless or short-wave radio as a central symbol or unifying device, and the basic problem in an understanding of the action is the recognition on the part of the reader of the individual voices of the characters" (Begnal and Eckley 26). A number of dreamers and a number of voices—HCE, ALP, Issy, Shem and Shaun, the Four Old Men—communicate across space like dream radios.

In book II, chapter 3, the Four are speaking, sitting on the posts of the bed. The dreamers are connected by a "high fidelity daildialler, as modern as tomorrow afternoon." Their "supershielded umbrella antennas" are "for distance getting" and are "capable of capturing skybuddies, harbour craft emittences, key clickings, vaticum cleaners, due to woman formed mobile or man made static and bawling the whowle hamshack and wobble" (309.14ff). These dreamers give and receive radio signals. They capture skybuddies, experience skip off the Heaviside layer, hear key clickings of Morse code and man-made static. They hear "bawling the whowle ['howl' and 'whole'] hamshack [ham radio shack] and wobble." Radio is everywhere in their dreams, for it is the medium of their communication.

John Gordon, following Margaret Solomon, points out that the radio is actually the body of the sleeper: "The radio introduced at the start of the chapter is also the sleeper's head and trunk, his cranium ('a howdrocephalous enlargement'), brain ('harmonic condenser enginium'), mouth ('vitaltone speaker'), eyes ('circumcentric megacycles'), heart ('magazine battery'), arteries ('twintriodic singulvalvulous pipelines') front and back ('up his corpular fruent and down his reuctionary buckling')—and the most prominent feature is the ears, the 'umbrella antennas for getting distance'" (194–95). Throughout the *Wake* the bodies of HCE and ALP are at once flesh and land and river, city and waterway—the world is linked to the body, the body to the world in a tradition that goes back to Leonardo da Vinci's *Man in a Circle and Square*, to the Roman *umbilicus mundi*, to the primitive omphalos or "navel of the world" (Edgerton 11)—but for Joyce this old image takes on a new, more technological form. While the dreamers are connected by dream radio, their bodies are themselves bound into the circuit; there are no headsets, no wires that are not already parts of their bodies. Machines and flesh share functions. The dreamer does not merely listen. The dreamer is the signal, the message, and the noise. The dreamer sends and receives.[8]

Much of book II, chapter 3, is mingled with radio transmissions. According to Gordon the downstairs radio plays throughout: "In fact, there are two main broadcasts being recalled here, often overlapping—a result of the reception's wandering from frequency to frequency and the interference which is especially bad at night, when as Shaun's inquisitors later say, anyone with a wireless can 'peck up bostoons' (489.36–490.01). (The radio does in fact get signals from Norway and Czechoslovakia)" (196). The chapter opens with the "tolvtubular high fidelity daildialler" (309.14) mentioned above, a two-way radio in which gossip about HCE passes back and forth (Tindall 189), then returns to the story of the Norwegian Captain, a story about Earwicker that was left off in chapter 2. Weaving in and out of this is a sermon, which begins pleasantly enough, until the volume on this "low frequency amplification" signal is turned up (312.33). Not only is the signal wandering, but dials are being manipulated. With its volume raised, the sermon becomes a tub thumper and a hell raiser—"Sets on [the radio set is on] sayfohrt [say it forth]! Go to it, agitator!" (313.4). In the midst of the sermon are words that sound like background static—a thousand faint signals, indiscernible noises that come through the speakers: "Bothallchoractorschumminaroundgansumuminarumdrumstrumtruminahumptadumpwaultopoofoolooderamaunsturnup!" (314.8–9).

This linguistic monster is at first composed of individual words strung together—"Both all charactors chummin around"—then fades into an onomatopoeic thrumming and drumming of radio interference that gives way to "looderamaunsturnup!"[9] This is not simply white noise, a long stream of sibilance, for it contains recognizable sounds, faint and nearly indiscernible, sounds like those at the edge of the telephone, far in the background, strange, ghostly people, half-heard conversations, drum beats, whistles, recorded messages, rising to the surface to tease and irritate. Then, immediately after the static word, almost as if tired of the noise, after first ordering a drink (317.20–28), the channel is changed several times:

Till they plied him hehaste on the fare. Say wehrn!
—Nohow did he kersse or hoot alike the suit and solder skins, minded first breachesmaker with considerable way on and (first change)
—Humpsea dumpsea, the munchantman, the secondsnipped cutter the curter. (second change)
—A ninth for a ninth. Take my worth from it. And no mistaenk, they thricefold the taler and they knew the whyed for too. The because of his sosuch. (Gordon 199)

This turns into a speech about Daniel O'Connell, who gets mixed up with O'Connor Power, an Irish politician known for his dark prophecies and "premonitory alarms" (Gordon 199). From here we go back to the sermon, then once again to the speech, with a few more references to radio parts—"selenium cell" (323.25). The radio dial is spun once more. "Radiose wodhalooing" (324.18). A few truncated words are picked up as the vernier spins past:

Am.
Dg.[10]

Each half-word is located on a separate line, as if silence lay between them, the voices barely able to get out a syllable or half-syllable before the dial passes them by. Finally the channel changer lights on a weather report:

Welter Focussed.
Wind from the nordth [note compression of German "Nord" with English "north"].
Warmer towards muffinbell, Lull. (324.23ff)

Radio reports come and go throughout the chapter, until at the end of the section there is a radio horse race (341.18ff). In an explicit example of what Joyce does implicitly throughout the book, signals come and go with mindboggling rapidity. The reader can hardly keep up. The book begins not with a capital letter, not with a new sentence, but halfway through a sentence: "A way a lone a last a loved a long the . . . riverrun, past Adam and Eve's, from swerve of shore to bend of bay, brings us by a commodius vicus of recirculation back to Howth Castle and environs" (628.15–16, 1.1–3). We begin in the middle of a message, as if that station, whatever it is, has been on all along and we are now just picking it up. After a prelude of seven pages introducing the main landmarks of the story, we follow the traveler to peer through the bedroom keyhole to the Waterloo section (reminiscent of both the water closet, or water-loo, and the famous battle). We are near and far away, at once in the familiar and the distant, down the hall in the toilet and far away in France (8.10–10.23). Entering the water closet, we are told to "Mind your hats goan in!" Suddenly we are in the Wellington Museum, or the Willingdone Museyroom (8.10–11). Water closet—museum. When leaving, we are told, "Mind your boots goan out. Phew!" (10.20–23). The sudden jumps from image to image are similar to the jumps on the old wireless from channel to channel.[11]

Joyce and the Structures of Radio

In *Understanding Media: The Extensions of Man*, Marshall McLuhan notes that "the personal and social consequences of any medium — that is, of any extension of ourselves — result from the new scale that is introduced into our affairs by each extension of ourselves, or by any new technology" (7). Since the medium of radio extends us and changes us, its structure is as influential as its content. As what McLuhan calls a "hot medium," radio extends one sense only — in this case, hearing — producing an intimacy between speaker and listener that television has not been able to match. Television provides the audience with a visual experience confined to a small screen, thereby undercutting the sense of presence that radio induces. The experience of radio, therefore, is in some ways more powerful: "If we sit and talk in a dark room," McLuhan writes, "words suddenly acquire new meanings and different textures. They become richer, even, than architecture, which Le Corbusier rightly says can best be felt at night. All those gestural qualities that the printed page strips from language come back in the dark, and on the radio" (303).

Cheryl Herr has demonstrated in *Joyce's Anatomy of Culture* that "for Joyce culture is largely constituted by the censoring efforts (that is, the conventionalizing, stereotyping, and hegemonic maneuvers) of institutions" (34). Herr argues that Joyce subverted the constraining forces of culture by foregrounding their ideological basis. Critiquing the social relations of the Irish middle class, he also "called attention to those cultural sites where ideological or semiotic conflict occurs — where one set of institutional values clashes with another or where ideological practice is crumbling under the pressure of lived experience" (17). Joyce did this by mixing codes from opposing ideological systems in his language. His "sin was to mingle the codes reserved for pornographic writing with those governing other forms of literature and behavior. Bloom not only appreciates the eroticism of *Sweets of Sin* but also supports Arthur Griffith's politics, which included a stance on sexual purity" (35–36).

This subversion was not restricted to the level of content; it also took place between content and structure. While radio content, especially advertising, tried to implement unanimity of thought, its structure provided a bandwidth broad enough to permit a multitude of conflicting ideas. National censorship of radio, which was tried in Ireland, was difficult because radio is by nature international. In radio, Joyce found a medium well-structured for his purpose, "not only a mighty awakener of archaic memories, forces, and animosities, but a decentralizing, pluralistic force"

(McLuhan 307) that by its very structure undercut a literate society's tendency toward centralization. Joyce's encyclopedic mix of codes from opposing forms was already in place in the structure of radio. Because "at first," according to McLuhan, "electric media merely followed the established patterns of literate structures" (306), radio in its early days was moving in two directions at once: content often supported those social forces that sought to depress pluralism, while structure tended to subvert those same forces.

Radio Content: Sponsored Programs and Advertising

In 1920 Dr. Frank Conrad, the engineer in charge of Westinghouse Corporation's experiment in radio telephony, began playing phonograph records over the air from his home in Pittsburgh as an escape from talking to the numerous radio amateurs in his neighborhood. Working on the first radio telephone, Conrad quickly tired of chit chat, but then something odd happened. The amateurs began telephoning him off the air and sending him cards and letters, asking him to play music at regular intervals so they could entertain their friends. So at 7:30 P.M. on Wednesdays and Saturdays, Dr. Conrad played music across his transmitter, borrowing the records from a local music store. The merchant, realizing the value of this free publicity, asked him to announce the name of his store from time to time in return. Thus commercial radio broadcasting and radio advertising were born as twins (Archer 199).[12]

Sponsored programs began on Radio Athlone in 1933. By 1934 sponsored programming was bringing in nearly as much money as licensing fees on receivers, which had until that time supplied most of the financial support for transmitters. As commercial broadcasting expanded, the "prospect of big money from advertisers became irresistible" (Gorham 87). Advertising on Irish radio never set a very high standard, however. According to Gorham, "The I.B.C. [Irish Broadcasting Company] had plenty of experience of commercial broadcasting, but it proved very difficult to sell time at the full rate on Radio Athlone. So the advertising programmes and the products they advertised were mostly cheap: record programmes—and not always very new records—advertising patent medicines and cosmetics were typical of the fare. Only the Hospitals Trust, the body that ran the famous Irish Hospitals Sweepstakes, continued to put on programmes of a higher standard" (88). For this reason, among an array of others, commercial broadcasting came under attack as "un-national, unworthy of the national station, and unfit to be transmitted to listeners abroad" (88). In the end, financial considerations lost out to considerations of national image, and advertising was banned from Radio Athlone in 1934, with the sole exception of the Hospitals Trust. Thus radio advertising was in the strange position of being censored, along with much of the rest of popular culture and nearly all of Joyce's own works.

Elsewhere the spread of the medium, and advertising within it, occurred faster than anyone expected. Radio hams were soon overtaken by casual, nontechnical listeners. Within a few short years, radio was a medium of mass communication, a concept with a theory already well in hand. In 1896 the French sociologist Gabriel Tarde published *Les Lois de l'Imitation*, which held that "the general laws governing imitative repetition . . . are to sociology what the laws of habit and heredity are to biology, the laws of gravitation to astronomy and the laws of vibration to physics. Sociology is imitation and imitation is a kind of hypnotism" (79). As Bloom points out in *Ulysses*, "For an advertisement you must have repetition. That's the whole secret" (Joyce, *Ulysses* 323). In post-Darwinian psychology, "A human society . . . must be rather the same as a nest of ants—to understand it, one ignored the individual and looked at the mass, and its primal imitative behaviour" (Smith 23). The notion of mass communication, with its assumption of repetition and imitation, reencoded the old class system in a new form. Those communicating could look at those receiving not as individuals with personal autonomy but as a species with a primal and instinctive group mind. As Matthew Arnold pointed out, mass communication was not to be equated with culture, which "works differently" and "does not try to reach down to the level of the inferior classes" (69).

Radio was still new when advertising had already become a noble profession, promoting the idea of mass communication. Throughout the 1920s "there developed a widespread feeling that in mass society the individual has less and less influence on the flow of events" (Smith 29). During World War I, books and magazines—the vehicles of mass communication—were developed into various means of propaganda. With the advent of radio advertising, commerce, propaganda, and entertainment merged, and a sense of autonomy quickly gave way to groupthink. By the time that 2RN was established on Little Denmark Street, these movements were far along. The very fact that radio advertising was so easily censored in spite of its financial benefits would have confirmed Joyce's initial sense of the inescapability of censorship.

With print, the censors purged offensive words, phrases, and ideas. Their control came through marginalization, by excising dissent with a blue pencil or by refusing publication altogether. Censorship could masquerade as every editor's right to publish what he deemed to be the best. Social values were reinforced through repetition, which in turn reinforced censorship, because fewer and fewer new ideas could be explored. At a print level, repetition was relatively slow: newspapers were published daily; magazines, monthly; books, only once or twice. Radio, on the other hand, could supply a constant barrage of repeated messages. Because it was often cheaper to leave the station running than to turn it off and on, stations could broadcast advertising over and over. This was a new, dynamic form of control. Not only could censors cut out what society found offensive, society could now enforce its values through constant repetition.

To Joyce, who was hyper-aware of censorship in any form and also an avid collector of advertising tidbits, radio offered double enticement. Advertising fascinated him. As Jennifer Wicke has shown, in *Ulysses* advertising is not a sideshow but the main language. "Advertising's presence changes the scene," Wicke writes: "*Ulysses* absorbs it to get beyond it, leaving Joyce the final option of creating his own language or nothing. Voila! *Finnegans Wake*" (124). I would extend Wicke's point to advertising on radio as well as in print. Advertising, after all, developed from narrative:

> Having borrowed its techniques from those of aesthetic representation, most specifically narrative fiction, and having created a system of exchange modeled on that of literary production, advertising by 1920 had established itself as a prerequisite for doing business of any kind. Ads had become a self-referential system, an exotic form of social reading whose meanings far exceeded the original ostensive meaning of early ads: here is announced my product. The configuration of ads told a collective story —a narrative—to its society at a given moment. The sudden profusion of ads and their creation of social narrative in the newly dis-continuous way naturally reshaped the reception of narrativity as a whole. (Wicke 120)

Sponsored programs often slipped advertising into a musical introduction or a bit of radio play dialogue: "Wouldn't you like a nice cup of Ovaltine, Sandy?" says Little Orphan Annie. "Arf!" says Sandy. Joyce used this sly propaganda technique a number of times throughout the *Wake*: "Your fame is spreading like Basilico's ointment since the Fintan Lalors piped you overboarder," he writes (25.9–10). Mixing codes from personal letters, breakfast food, the church, and toilet humor, the narrative has the calm radio voice of a fireside chat:

> Everything's going on the same or so it appeals to all of us, in the old holmsted here. Coughings all over the sanctuary, bad scrant to me aunt

Florenza. The horn for breakfast, one o'gong for lunch and dinner-chime. As popular as when Belly the First was keng and his members met in the Diet of Man. The same shop slop in the window. Jacob's letter-crackers and Dr. Tibble's Vi-Cocoa and the Eswuards' desippated soup beside Mother Seagull's syrup. Meat took a drop when Reilly-Parsons failed. Coal's short but we've plenty of bog in the yard. And barley's up again, begrained to it. The lads is attending school nessans regular, sir, spelling beesknees with hathatansy and turning out tables by mudappli-cation. Allfor the books and never pegging smashers after Tom Bowe Glassarse or Timmy the Tosser. (26.25–27.1)

Note the mellow, Arthur Godfrey tones of "in the old holmsted here." It's just everyone's Uncle Jim spreading the news about the sweet doings back home. And if a few lines about "Jacob's lettercrackers and Dr. Tibble's Vi-Cocoa and the Eswuards' desippated soup beside Mother Seagull's syrup" slip in, well, that's commerce. According to W. Dygert's *Radio as an Advertising Medium*, a handbook for admen from the period, "Commercial announcements, dramatic or straight, should never be just 'dropped' into the program on the hour and half hour like suburban buses. The program should be designed for the commercials. There should be a logical and sensible spot for each announcement. In other words, announcements should as nearly as possible be an integral part of the program, so adroitly led up to, so naturally placed, that the listener has no occasion to resent their introduction" (129).

As radio stations grew in number, it became clear that listeners had one advantage over the sender: they could change the channel. The bubbling instability of the airwaves reprieved the audience; a twist of the dial gave them a power they had not had before. Radio changed the way people communicated, the way they lived, the way they thought, the way they conceived of the world, and the way they occupied space and time. This utterance in a competing field of signals, a battlefield of information, prepared an audience for the near-chaos of ultra-informational language in *Finnegans Wake*. In embracing this new medium of communication, Joyce gave back to print a fluidity as rich and multiform as the storm of electromagnetic signals that constituted the experience of early radio.

NOTES

1. The BBC station 2LO at that time had only 1.5 kilowatts. Radio telegraphy had a significant history in Ireland, since the republican forces took the Irish School of Telegraphy on O'Connell and Lower Abbey Streets during the Easter Rising of 1916. The radio telegraph equipment there was their only link with the

outside world through much of the war. J. J. Walsh, originally the Irish postmaster general, then the minister for posts and telegraphs, said that on its 1-kilowatt power the station could be heard for twenty-five miles on crystal sets, fifty miles for one-valve sets (costing about 10 pounds), and eighty miles for two-valve sets (costing 20 pounds) (Gorham 30). However, the *Irish Times* claimed that the opening show was "probably heard by somebody in every country of Europe, and possibly by many in America" (Gorham 24).

2. A good portion of their programming was a relay from the BBC, which surprisingly enough had very good relations with 2RN, even after the years of rebellion. However, according to Gorham, "On one occasion a London relay was cut short when a sketch called 'Loyalty' was substituted for the one billed, and there was a mention of Queen Victoria. On another, Belfast was similarly cut, when an old drinking song proposed a health to the King" (9).

3. The minister for finance had to grant special permission even for substitute employees during an outbreak of flu. Letters went back and forth between the station and the ministry for days every time someone new came down with a case, and the ministry was asked to deliberate on each new substitute.

4. John A. Connor, personal telephone interview, 28 November 1990. Much of the information about the experience of radio listening in the 1930s is gathered from him.

5. Named after Oliver Heaviside, the British informal genius—scientist and inventor—who discovered it, the Heaviside layer is a shell of charged particles that covers the earth at about the same altitude as our communication satellites fly. Because of the strong charge, radio frequency signals often cannot penetrate and are reflected back—"skip"—to earth in places continents away from their transmitters. During World War II the study of the Heaviside layer led to the development of radar. One odd feature of the Heaviside layer was that its effects were more pronounced at night than during the day. This meant that while conditions were better for Joyce to pick up Radio Athlone at night, there was likely to be more interference at that time.

6. Another cause of such radio noise was lightning flashing south of the transmitter. Since 2RN was so far north, "whistlers and squealers," as they were called, would have been more pronounced.

7. Automobiles were a major problem. Shielding ignition systems so that they would not cause radio frequency interference was vital, not only for the development of commercial radio but also for avionics in World War II.

8. Begnal points out another place in book III of the *Wake* where the body of Shaun (then called Yawn) acts as a radio receiver for the Four Old Men. "His dream monologue was over, of cause, but his drama parapolylogic had yet to be, affact" (476.4).

9. I would like to distinguish between two types of words in the *Wake*. Both are often referred to as "thunder words," but I think that there are thunder words and static words, each with different characteristics. The example of the latter found above can be contrasted with "bababadalgharaghtakamminarronnkonnbronnton-nerronntuonnthunntrovarrhounawnska wntoohoohoordenenthurnuk!" found on page 1. In this case the onomatopoeic jumble has fewer distinguishable words and

more hard consonants, followed by the short *u* and double *o* sounds that are standard imitations of rolling bass sounds like thunder. Static words have more crackle and hiss, with more distinguishable words strewn about, as if the signal were coming and going.

10. An alternative interpretation here is that if you put the two truncated words together, you get AMDG, an acronym for Ad Majorem Dei Gloriam, the Jesuit motto.

11. At the tail end of book I, chapter 2 (i.e., from 43.21–47), we have what appears to be part of a radio show, introducing and describing a ballad:

> The wararrow went round, so it did, (a nation wants a gaze) and the ballad, in the felibrine trancoped metre affectioned by Taiocebo in his Casudas de Poulichinello Artahut [43.21–23]. To the added strains (so peacifold) of his majesty the flute, that onecrooned king of inscrewments, Piggott's purest, ciello alsolito which Mr Delaney (Mr Delacey), horn, anticipating a perfect downpour of plaudits from the rapsods [43.31–34]. . . . It's cumming, it's brumming! The clip, the clop! (All cla) Glass crash [a special effect]. The (klikkaklakkaklaskaklopatzklatschabattacreppycrottygraddaghsemmilhsammihnouith appliuddyappladdypkonpkot!) [44.19–21] . . .
>
> Ardite, arditi!
> Music cue.

Then comes the Ballad of Persse O'Reilly. The thunder word in 44.20–21 is an imitation of a glass breaking, with some of the characteristics of static words encoded in the middle ("creppy" and "crotty" and "laddy").

12. There was in fact some controversy over advertising on the radio. Before this time the wireless was viewed as a means of two-way communication, to be used for emergencies and in time of war. But as commercial radio grew, only two alternatives presented themselves for its support: a tax on radio sets, and the use of advertising on the airwaves. Great Britain chose the first, while the United States chose the second (Archer 285).

WORKS CITED

Archer, Gleason L. *History of Radio to 1926*. New York: American Historical Society, 1938.

Arnold, Matthew. *Culture and Anarchy*. Ed. J. Dover Wilson. Cambridge: Cambridge University Press, 1932.

Begnal, Michael H., and Grace Eckley. *Narrator and Character in "Finnegans Wake."* Lewisburg, Pa.: Bucknell University Press, 1975.

Benjamin, Walter. "The Work of Art in the Age of Mechanical Reproduction." *Illuminations: Essays and Reflections*. Ed. Hannah Arendt. Trans. Harry Zohn. New York: Schocken, 1968. 217–51.

Dygert, Warren G. *Radio as an Advertising Medium*. New York: McGraw-Hill, 1939.

Edgerton, Samuel Y., Jr. "From Mental Matrix to *Mappamundi* to Christian Empire: The Heritage of Ptolemaic Cartography in the Renaissance." *Art and Cartography: Six Historical Essays*. Ed. David Woodward. Chicago: University of Chicago Press, 1987. 10–50.

Gordon, John. *"Finnegans Wake": A Plot Summary*. Syracuse: Syracuse University Press, 1986.

Gorham, Maurice. *Forty Years of Irish Broadcasting*. Dublin: Talbot, 1967.

Herr, Cheryl. *Joyce's Anatomy of Culture*. Urbana: University of Illinois Press, 1986.

Hoffmeister, Adolph. "Portrait of Joyce." Trans. Norma Rudinsky. *Portraits of the Artist in Exile: Recollections of James Joyce by Europeans*. Ed. Willard Potts. Seattle: University of Washington Press, 1979. 127–36.

Joyce, James. *Finnegans Wake*. New York: Penguin, 1967.

——. *Ulysses*. New York: Vintage, 1961.

McLuhan, Marshall. *Understanding Media: The Extensions of Man*. New York: McGraw-Hill, 1964.

Mink, Louis O. *A "Finnegans Wake" Gazetteer*. Bloomington: Indiana University Press, 1978.

Ong, Walter J. *Orality and Literacy: The Technologizing of the Word*. New Accents Series. London: Routledge, 1989.

Shannon, Claude E. "A Mathematical Theory of Communication." *Bell System Technical Journal* 27 (July, October 1948): 379–423, 623–56. Repr. in *Claude Elwood Shannon: Collected Papers*. Ed. N. J. A. Sloane and Aaron D. Wyner. Piscataway, N.J.: IEEE Press, 1993. 5–83.

Smith, Anthony. *The Shadow in the Cave: The Broadcaster, His Audience, and the State*. Urbana: University of Illinois Press, 1973.

Soupault, Philippe. "James Joyce." Trans. Carleton W. Carroll. *Portraits of the Artist in Exile: Recollections of James Joyce by Europeans*. Ed. Willard Potts. Seattle: University of Washington Press, 1979. 108–18.

Tarde, Gabriel. *Les Lois de l'Imitation*. Paris: Etude psychologique, 1895.

Tindall, William York. *A Reader's Guide to "Finnegans Wake."* New York: Farrar, Straus and Giroux, 1969.

Wicke, Jennifer. *Advertising Fictions: Literature, Advertisement, and Social Reading*. New York: Columbia University Press, 1988.

Wiener, Norbert. *The Human Use of Human Beings: Cybernetics and Society*. New York: Da Capo, 1954.

ADALAIDE MORRIS

SOUND TECHNOLOGIES AND

THE MODERNIST EPIC

H. D. on the Air

Those who use the telephone today, the telegraph, the phonograph, the train, bicycle or automobile, the ocean liner, dirigible or airplane, the cinema or a great daily newspaper ... do not dream that these diverse forms of communication, transportation and information exert such a decisive influence upon their psyches.
> F. T. Marinetti, "Destruction of Syntax" 45

As to Cantos 18–19, there ain't no key. Simplest parallel I can give is radio where you tell who is talking by the noise they make.
> Pound, qtd. in Carroll F. Terrell,
> *Companion to the Cantos of Ezra Pound* 75

Ezra Pound's *Cantos*, T. S. Eliot's *The Waste Land*, Hart Crane's *The Bridge*, H.D.'s *Trilogy* and *Helen in Egypt*, and William Carlos Williams's *Paterson* reverberate with subway rumbles, rolls of thunder, snatches of song, knocks, horns, even the "whhsssh, t ttt" of a buzz-saw (Pound, *Cantos*, canto 18/83) and the "zrr-hiss" of a rocket dropping through air (H.D., *Trilogy* 58). "What is that noise?" Eliot's neurasthenic asks, alerting us to the poem's surround of sound. "What is that noise now?" (33). In epics composed, read, recited, and recorded between 1917 and 1960, sounds cut in, rise, then fade away as other sounds intrude, as if we were tapping into a party line on a municipal phone exchange, spinning down a radio dial, or sampling a stack of records. Sound technologies enter the *Cantos*, *The Waste Land*, *The Bridge*, *Trilogy*, and *Helen in Egypt* sometimes as things, sometimes as themes, sometimes as models or types of communication, but in this essay I argue that their most crucial effect was generative. The acoustical technologies that grew up with the generation of poets born in the late nineteenth century set up conditions conducive to a brief but intense resurgence of epic poetry in the first half of the twentieth century.

Whether orally or aurally, in air or in ink, the epic has been, from its beginnings, a noisy affair. First vocalized by bards reciting to an audience, then evoked by poets writing for readers, epics solicit the public ear. Epic composers speak as citizens to other citizens, engaging a tribe, community, nation, or alliance in order to move it through moments of crisis. The term "modernist epic" signals a handful of poems written in response to two world wars, global economic collapse, and the development of nuclear armaments. Although these poems are by no means identical, they have in common an ambition and urgency, a set of ancestors, and an array of allusions, tropes, and gestures that invite us to consider them together. However dependent they are on capaciousness and continuity, these are not simply "long" or "serial poems." Their reach is requisite to the magnitude, eloquence, and structural complexity they need to mobilize a culture's historic, spiritual, and/or mythic heritage and suggest a route toward durable release.[1]

Like their predecessors, modernist epics have an aural opulence that produces, in Garrett Stewart's pun, not just "semantic excess" but "somatic access" (2). Their sounds solicit the body. Epics of primary orality, composed and recited before acoustically sophisticated audiences, directly engaged the body's vibratory field. In the scene set by Eric A. Havelock, Albert B. Lord, and other scholars of the oral epic, as the epic composer-performer intones and strums, auditors hum, clap, and sway, partially hypnotized by the intricately coordinated verbal, vocal, instrumental, and physical rhythms that surround them (see Havelock, *Preface* 152). Stewart's proposition in *Reading Voices* is that so-called silent readers also process sound somatically, for the act of reading sets in motion not just the organs of sight but also the diaphragm, the throat, the mouth, and the tongue—all the organs of vocal production (1). In this sense, then, as poets from Vergil to Walt Whitman insisted all along, literary epicists also "sing." They produce an articulatory stream of sound—a "phonotext"—which takes place within the body of the reader. If in the earliest epics sound traveled from the mouth of the bard to the ear of his auditors, in later epics sound travels from the poet's sensorium through the spaced letters of a phonetic alphabet to the body of a reader. This highly charged phonotext makes the reader's body a sounding board for the language of the poem.

The acoustical technologies developed in the first half of the twentieth century enticed and enhanced the ear of an audience that had come to conceptualize poetry—particularly the elite poetry of written epic—as a silent inner event. For Havelock and Walter J. Ong, the mediated, amplified, insistent sounds of telephones, radios, loudspeakers, and tape recorders created a new orality, a "secondary orality" that "preserves much of the mind-set of primary orality" (Ong 11). Secondary orality is not, however, a reversion to a distant past, for as Havelock emphasizes, technologized sounds, no matter how pervasive and insistent, can never re-create the conditions of preliterate orality. Rather, Havelock continues, new acoustical technologies produce "a forced marriage, or remarriage, between the resources of the written word and of the spoken, a marriage of a sort which . . . reinforce[s] the latent energies of both parties" (*Muse* 33). The epic of secondary orality—the modernist epic—engages the newly energized ear of its audience with a phonotext that is peculiarly jagged, insistent, and insinuating. Mr. Paterson's "thought is listed," Williams informs us, "in the Telephone / Directory" (9). To ring it up is to initiate a decisively aural interchange. "What is that sound high in the air?" Eliot asks toward the close of his poem (43). "Hear me," Pound commands at the opening of his (*Cantos*, canto 4/13). "Do you hear me?" H.D.'s Helen asks. "Listen," she whispers, "it is no matter" (*Helen* 175, 177).

How has the no-matter of sound come to matter so little in our discussions of the modernist epic? Leading critics of these poems for the most part ignore their shifting, speeding, slurring, sliding, and slowing phonotexts in order to pay attention to a more stable set of visual analogs and antecedents. Joseph Frank was the first to argue that the *Cantos* and *The Waste Land* are "based on a space-logic that demands a complete reorientation in the reader's attitude toward language" (13). These epics are, he concludes, poems for the eye rather than the ear. In the thirty years since this reorientation, Marjorie Perloff has placed the poems of Pound and his contemporaries "in the context of the 'documentary' collages, Futurist as well as Cubist, that were its exact contemporaries" (*Dance* 34), Hugh Kenner has situated *The Waste Land* as an imitation of newsreel quick-cutting (*Mechanic* 9) and the *Cantos* as an array of written ideograms (*Pound Era*), and most recently, Jerome McGann has located the "visible language" of modernist poetry as "a direct function and expression of the Renaissance of Printing that began in the late nineteenth century" (xi). As these and other critics have shown, typewriters, linotype machines, photographs, paintings, cinema, and video all provide useful entries into modernist poetic structures and strategies. What happens, however, if we close our eyes and prick our ears instead to the ring of a phone, the crackle of the radio, the creak of a capstan driving a tape?

"Brrrr-rrr . . . Ye-e-e-e-*es*." In H.D.'s fictionalized autobiography *HERmione*, the twenty-three-year-old apprentice poet, author-to-be of two modernist epics, lifts a receiver outside Philadelphia to hear "tin pan noises, little tin pan against my ear and words striking, beating on it." It's the twenty-four-year-old author-to-be of the *Cantos* calling. "I didn't know you were here," she opens. "I'm not here," he retorts (41–42). Tympanums vibrating, puns drumming, these two young poets improvise a logic of sound across distance through the aural overlap of "here," "not here," "hear," and "ear." In the realm of the eye, previous to the development of video broadcasting, it was impossible to be at once "here" and "not here," but in the realm of the ear at the turn of the century, newly available technologies routinely transported voices, as H.D. put it, "far and far . . . out of something, out of nothing, holding something, holding nothing" (41). Like the homophones H.D. and Pound deploy to make this paradox audible, telephones—at least at first—were all about illogical connections.[2] Because, as Marinetti suggested, the tin-pan noises of early twentieth-century communication technologies had a decisive influence on the psyche of the modernists who first used them, this call between poets has a peculiar resonance with their calling as modernist poets, a calling that developed in tandem with two other technologies that mark significant moments in their careers.

By the 1930s, as Pound and H.D. achieved middle age, a series of inventions had made it possible, at least in theory, for a single voice addressing a single audience on a single occasion to be heard by the entire population of the western world (Havelock, *Muse* 31). This fact was not lost on Pound in the 1940s as he shouted again and again into the microphones of the Italian Broadcasting System, "EUROPE CALLING! POUND SPEAKING! EZRA POUND SPEAKING!" "If yew hadn't bin such *mutts*," he yelled into living rooms across the United States, Canada, the Pacific, New Zealand and Australia, "you woulda *heerd* me . . . long before now!" (qtd. in Carpenter 588). Extending the range of transmission and generalizing the audience of address, radio gave poets like Pound and H.D. an opportunity not only to invade the homes of strangers but to imagine a global audience for their work, a possibility H.D. first apprehended during a visit to Manhattan in 1937. "I was called to the telephone," she reports to a friend. " 'Your islands were on the air,' I was informed, 'and read beautifully.' 'Where?' I asked. 'Radio City, just a few minutes ago' " (letter to Pearson, 12 December 1937). The poem on the air, "The Islands," superimposes Corfu, Rhodes, and Crete with a river island in Pennsylvania, where she was born, and ocean islands off Maine, where she had traveled (*Collected Poems* 124). To hear of this poem's broadcast as she arrived "here in this island" from the island of England offered evidence for an intuition that sustained not only many of H.D.'s lyrics but her two epics as well: the sense that all space and time converge in a vast "here" and "now," a cosmic matrix, a kind of global Radio City that is intermittently accessible to listeners through the transmissions of dream, vision, and art.[3]

By the 1950s, as Pound and H.D. entered old age, the development of inexpensive tape technologies made it as easy to preserve sound across time as it had become to transmit it through space. In January 1955, at the urging of Norman Holmes Pearson, the sixty-nine-year-old H.D. leaned into the microphones of a studio in Zurich to record for posterity portions of her epic *Helen in Egypt*. Just as Pound chose to begin his *Cantos* with a rendering of Odysseus' visit to the spirits of the underworld, H.D. opened her taping with a meditation on the theme of disembodied presences, presences that are, like voices on the air, both "here" and "not here." Now, more than three decades after her death, by sliding a cassette into a player it is possible to hear her voice, thin as a reed, retelling the events at Troy: "Do not despair," she says, "the hosts / surging beneath the Walls, / (no more than I) are ghosts" (1).[4]

CD2

To measure a development in poetics by reference to a shift from print to acoustics or, within acoustics, by reference to a development from telephone to radio to tape is no less potent—and potentially much more interesting—than to use the more familiar markers of biography or aesthetics. In face of virtual reality, cyborg consciousness, and the World Wide Web, the status of literature as a transcendent discourse has dissolved along with the status of authorial subjectivity, individual mind, or inner being as the source of meaning or action. Epic commitments do not emerge from thin air. As numerous critics have shown, Pound, Eliot, H.D., and Williams had ample models and motives for their labors. Their educations prepared them to reverence the poems of Homer, Vergil, Dante, and Milton; they lived in a time of sustained political, social, and spiritual crisis; they held poets responsible for cultural continuities; and finally, as colleagues and rivals for over half a century, together they prepared an audience to receive their difficult writings. There was, however, another factor that nourished these poets' epic ambitions. In the years between 1917 and 1960, telephones, radios, and tape recorders restored key conditions of primary orality by linking sound to vivid imaginings, enriching and expanding rituals of listening, gathering a vast potential audience for cultural pronouncements, and making perceptible a cosmos in which voices routinely emerged "out of something, out of nothing, holding something, holding nothing."

One reason the rise, flourishing, and fading of the modernist epic can be calibrated to the rise, dominance, and supersession of acoustical technologies is that texts—like telephones, radios, loudspeakers, and tape recorders

—are a means of processing, storing, and transmitting information. In his recently translated *Discourse Networks, 1800/1900*, Friedrich A. Kittler presents a dense and compelling argument for the constitution of literature in and through technological media. Literature changes, Kittler maintains, according to the material and technical resources at its disposal. In the thirty years on either side of 1900, Edison's two great inventions, film and the gramophone, decisively altered the nature of poetry and literature. In 1912, toward the end of this thirty-year period, Marinetti heralded the "complete renewal of human sensibility" through these optical and acoustical technologies. Although Marinetti was excited by cinema, however, he reserved his greatest enthusiasm for the technology contemporary critics have overlooked or, more accurately, underheard: the "multiple, simultaneous consciousness" of the "wireless imagination," "the art of noise and . . . words in freedom" (45).

Unlike film, television, video, and the emerging media of virtual reality and cyberspace, technologies of the wireless imagination have eluded the attention of many otherwise acute cultural critics.[5] If, as Marjorie Perloff points out, "we have yet to understand the interplay between lyric poetry, generally regarded as the most conservative, the most intransigent of the 'high' arts, and the electronic media," we know even less about the relation between such auditory technologies as telephones, radios, and tape recorders and the imaginations of the poets to whom the epic once again seemed a fresh and compelling endeavor.[6] The epics composed between 1917 and the early 1960s were sustained and ambitious experiments in the art of noise. What aspects of these texts—positive and negative—resonate with the newly reorganized sense ratios of secondary orality? What sorts of solutions to twentieth-century world crises can emerge from the ghostland or dreamland of the wireless imagination?

One of the earliest recorded acoustical machines is an oddly familiar contrivance: a golden bird perched in the boughs of a gold and silver tree (Davies 15). Metalworkers in ninth-century Baghdad were reported to have fashioned this legendary device for Abbasid Khalif Abdallah al-Ma'mun, but it is of course familiar to us as one of the signal images of modernism: the "miracle, bird or golden handiwork" presiding "in glory of changeless metal" over William Butler Yeats's Byzantium (243). The bird's golden tones announce a realm of remote perfection to which listeners are summoned with songs, calls, and gongs. Yeats's poem invokes the ear as the most attenuated of all senses, the least contaminated by "complexities of mire or blood" (243), but in 1930, the year his poem emerged, the ear of the public had been prepared by almost a decade of listening to transmissions that seemed to audiences of the time only slightly less miraculous than golden birds singing in gold and silver trees.

Although many of the devices used to capture, save, send, and/or receive sound were invented in the decades flanking the birth of Yeats, Eliot, Pound, H.D., and Williams, it was not until after World War I that acoustical technologies became a feature of daily life.[7] During the 1920s tens of thousands of radios were produced, distributed, purchased, and installed in places of honor in homes across the Western world. News photos, cartoons, sketches, and advertisements introduced consumers to the proper vocabulary for this technology, a set of customs surrounding its use, and an array of ways to conceptualize its peculiar combinations of art, technology, and power. The paradoxes these popular documents take up are the same paradoxes of disembodied presence that H.D. and Pound processed through the aural overlap of "hear" and "here." Advertisements and cartoons of the 1920s and 1930s again and again worry the enigmatic convergence of "hear," "here," and "not here." In sketch after sketch, musical instruments, dance bands, entire symphony orchestras, snatches of song lyrics, political speeches, and advertising slogans ride the sound waves out of radio speakers into bourgeois living rooms. Dogs perk up their ears, teenagers cut a rug, couples spoon, matrons sew, and old men snooze in their armchairs, each enveloped in the wavy lines that came to represent radio signals.

Cartoons of the period register both excitement and anxiety about radio's intrusive reach. In one, a little girl asks her mother, who bends and stretches to commands from a disembodied voice, "What will he say if you don't do it?" In another, a mother tosses a tea tray into the air, a baby screams, and a boy, a dog, and a cat all rush from the room with bristling hair as a lion's "G-R-R-R" spills out of a radio speaker (Hill 67; see figs. 1 and 2). Habits formed across this decade were elaborate enough to turn the physiological act of hearing into a series of culturally charged rituals of listening. At first, in order to coax broadcast signals through the chatter of thousands of amateur and commercial stations, at least one member of each family had to arrange and rearrange batteries, crystal detectors, vacuum tubes, and antennae (see Connor). As the technology improved, however, increasingly sophisticated receivers set into podium-sized, "Temple Style" cabinets allowed the whole family to sit back while components with names such as "Beam-a-scope" and "Dynapower" made "all barriers of time and space seem to fall away" and "the unseen curtain of distance" lift.[8]

The General Electric advertisement from which this copy comes is captioned "Don't Cry Mother . . . It's *Only* a Program!" An opulent, full-page, illustrated spread on the inside cover of *Life* magazine, it features family

Figure 1. "What will he say if you don't do it?" Cartoon, 1940s.

members gathered in their living room on either side of a GE "golden tone" cabinet-style receiver. "What a wonderful thing this radio is!" the text exclaims. "Its magic conjures people, nations, castles and kings right out of the air! It carries you on thrilling journeys to exciting places — brings colorful people to call who become closer friends than the folks next door. Summons interesting guests . . . brings countless bits of radiant color to weave into the pattern of gray days" (see fig. 3). The illustration is, among other things, a lesson in the art of listening. In it the unknown fits so snugly into the known that no one needs to rush from the room. The family is anchored by Father, who sits to one side reading his paper. Mother, at the opposite side, moved by what she hears, puts down her mending to dab at her eyes with a handkerchief. Leaning over her shoulder, finally, her golden-haired daughter murmurs, "Don't Cry Mother," reminding her of the differences between representation and reality. Although the transmission may be, as the copy says, *only* a program, the radio sits at the center of the scene as if it were another member of the family, a storytelling elder or a neighborhood bard. On its gleaming surface, doubled by a golden mirror suspended behind it, stands a bouquet of white blossoms radiant enough to adorn an altar.

Figure 2. "Listenin'!" Postcard, 1923, reproduced in Jonathan Hill, *The Cat's Whisker: Fifty Years of Wireless Design*, with photographs by Trefor Ball (London: Oresko Books, 1978).

"Don't Cry Mother.. It's <u>Only</u> A Program!"

OF COURSE daughter is wrong. It's not just a program—it's real and the people in it live! Mother's tears and smiles are the natural reaction of one good neighbor to another neighbor's everyday problems.

She shares the heartbreak of a girl who is hundreds of miles away—yes, farther than distance itself, for she lives in the land of make-believe. But it isn't make-believe to this lady because, thanks to the golden tone of her General Electric Radio, every program is close, intimate and personal—an actual visit from the interesting neighbors on the other side of the dial.

What a wonderful thing this radio is! Its magic conjures people, nations, castles and kings right out of the air! It carries you on thrilling journeys to exciting places—brings colorful people to call who become closer

friends than the folks next door. Summons interesting guests whose songs and smiles crowd with pleasure hours that once were empty and lonely for so many of us—brings countless bits of radiant color to weave into the pattern of gray days.

The golden tone of the General Electric Radio affords such realistic reproduction that every word and sound sweeps in with full depth and color. It's almost like another dimension in radio. And, listening to G-E, all barriers of time and space seem to fall away. The unseen curtain of distance is lifted.

Great improvements are constantly being made in G-E Radios. G-E engineers have perfected a new Beam-

a-scope (eliminating aerial and ground wires), a new Dynapower speaker, a new super-powered chassis, a new tone monitor circuit, and other great contributions to finer radio reproduction. These developments mean reception of greater depth and brilliancy of tone—*realism!* All this adds up to greater radio enjoyment—a better seat at the greatest show in the world.

Radio plays such an important part in your daily life that you should enjoy it at its best. You can, for G-E golden-tone radios are priced to fit all purses.

And remember—it ceases to be *"only a program"* when it comes to you via the rich, golden tone of the new General Electric Radio.

GENERAL ⓖⓔ ELECTRIC RADIO

LISTEN   TO   THE   GOLDEN   ♪   TONE   OF   GENERAL   ELECTRIC

Figure 3. Advertisement for General Electric Radio, from *Life*, January/February 1940, inside front cover. Reproduced by permission of James Harman, General Electric.

On dashboards, bedside tables, and kitchen counters or in a sport-model headset, late twentieth-century radio seems little more than a glorified timekeeper, weather monitor, exercise pacer, and commercial bulletin board. Early radio had higher aspirations. In 1936 to Rudolf Arnheim and other influential cultural commentators, radio was no less than "the great miracle of wireless": an extraordinary event, an ethereal intervention, a cause for pride, excitement, wonder, and fear, available day and night through "forty million sets . . . scattered over the world" (14). The hold of radio technology on the public imagination was not just its novelty or rapid improvements but the utopian dreams it suddenly made plausible: "the omnipresence," in Arnheim's list, "of what people are singing or saying anywhere, the over-leaping of frontiers, the conquest of spatial isolation, the importation of culture on the waves of the ether, the same fare for all, sound in silence" (14). And not only this. Gregory Whitehead, in his survey of radio art in the wireless age, enumerates a series of even grander dreams: "communication with alien beings, the establishment of a universal language, instantaneous travel through collapsing space," even "the achievement of a lasting global peace" (254).

Just as in the unrevised version of his first canto Pound declined to "sulk and leave the word to novelists" ("Three Cantos" 118), he and his compan-ions refused to cede dreams of disembodied transmission and overleapt frontiers to radio. With Yeats, Eliot, Joyce, Wyndham Lewis, Gaudier-Brezska, and many other prominent artists of the 1920s and 1930s, Pound and H.D. described their work in terms borrowed from the new technolo-gies of reception and transmission. For Pound, artists were "the antennae of the race"; for H.D., more elaborately, they had "the right sort of brains" to act as "receiving station[s]" and "telegraphic centre[s]" relaying "flashes of electric power" across "the world of dead, murky thought."[9] "[The artist] draws," Pound says, "from the air about him," for "the best of knowledge is in the air."[10] The spirits these poets invoke to superintend their airborne transmissions are not just the messengers of primary orality but also, and more strikingly, the trademarks of Western Union, RCA, Ekco, Gramo-phone, and other corporate agents of secondary orality: Hermes with his winged sandals, Mercury with his lightning bolt, the nymph Echo, and the Gramophone angel etching a message on a wax tablet.[11] When Edison called his invention the "phonograph" and Emile Berliner named his the "gramophone," their coinages made a single compound: "sound-writing," "writing-sound." Had the element of sound not so thoroughly disappeared from our considerations of writing, these terms might more easily remind us of yet another contrivance for the capture and relay of sound: the sound-writing of the phonotext.

Bell's telephone, Edison's "aerophone," Cros's "paleophone," Bell's "photophone," Edison's "kineto-phonograph," the marconiphone, the microphone, the paleophone, the dynamophone, the aetherophon, and the phonoautogram are only a few of the many sound devices invented, patented, improved, and distributed between 1880 and 1960.[12] The phono-text is as ancient as the first phonetic alphabets. Although our assumptions about so-called silent reading and our critical fascination with the image, the gaze, and other aspects of the visible have dulled our ability to apprehend this aspect of writing, the intermixture of phonic and graphic is foundational to lexical meaning-making. Like a record or tape, the phonotext stores and transmits sound. It is, then, in a sense that is only partly metaphoric, an acoustical track or trace activated by the process of reading. The technologies of secondary orality that enrolled the ear as a crucial processor of information prepared a generation of readers to tune in to the aural opulence of texts: it is no accident that R. P. Blackmur, William K. Wimsatt, Cleanth Brooks, and the other New Critics grew up in living rooms that featured for the first time telephones, phonographs, and General Electric's golden-toned, cabinet-sized, podium-style radio receivers.

The majority of contemporary critics who attend to writing's phonic component tend to position it as a sort of soundtrack that backs the main action of the text: a euphony or cacophony that accents meaning made elsewhere or otherwise. The concept of the phonotext foregrounds sound's generative aspect: its capacity to make or unmake meaning. As the work of critics such as Garrett Stewart, Frederick Ahl, and Jonathan Culler so amply demonstrates, this capacity is most perceptible through breached word boundaries and puns that complicate and confuse the process of meaning-making. To give just one example — one that opens into the main case study of this essay — the drift of a single phoneme between adjacent lexical units in H.D.'s *Helen in Egypt* switches the compound "inked-in" to its phonic parallel, "ink-din." An example of the phenomenon Stewart calls the "transegmental drift," this oscillating phoneme "undercuts the spaced succession of words by cutting across them at an angle oblique to inscription, generating in the phonotext an ambiguously inflected contiguity, severing and assimilative at once" (31). As H.D.'s Helen reads the Egyptian temple symbols, the graphic hieroglyph — that which is "inked-in" — manifests itself as "ink-din" (23).[13] This dynamic semantic waver is phonotextuality in action.

The audience for the dense, jagged, and powerful phonotext of the modernist epic was prepared by the incessant flow of fact, intention, and persuasion over the international airwaves between World War I and World War II. Among early radio's most avid listeners were not only the writers who devised the modernist epic but the scholars who first theorized the orality of the ancient epic. Between 1962 and 1963, in three different countries, five different thinkers published volumes that examined the dynamics of orality in the history of culture. The authors of these publications — Claude Lévi-Strauss, Jack Goody and Ian Watt, Ernst Myer, Marshall McLuhan, and Eric Havelock — could not at the time have been aware of one another's research, but all had long been immersed in rituals of technologized listening.[14] Havelock recounts a memory of hearing in October 1939 a speech that could also and simultaneously have been audited in England, Italy, Switzerland, and New Jersey by Eliot, Pound, H.D., and Williams. "I recall standing on Charles Street in Toronto adjacent to Victoria College," Havelock writes,

> listening to an open air radio address. We all, professors and students, as by common consent had trooped out to listen to the loudspeaker set up in the street. It was broadcasting a speech from Hitler, with whom we in Canada were, formally speaking, at war. He was exhorting us to call it quits and leave him in possession of what he had seized. The strident, vehement, staccato sentences clanged out and reverberated and chased each other along, series after series, flooding over us, battering us, half drowning us, and yet kept us rooted there listening to a foreign tongue which we somehow could nevertheless imagine that we understood. The oral spell had been transmitted in the twinkling of an eye, across thousands of miles, had been automatically picked up and amplified and poured over us. I have sometimes wondered whether McLuhan as a young man in Toronto at that time would have heard the same speech, shared the same experience (*Muse* 32).

Radio made a new type of demand on the attention, exercised a new kind of power on the mind. If, as Havelock speculates, the effort to understand the personal and political effects of this demand led these scholars to generate their theories of orality and literacy, these theories also, in their turn, help us comprehend the ambition, buoyancy, and address of the epics that emerged and faded during radio's glory days. As the "ink-din" of H.D.'s *Helen in Egypt* and the "radio . . . noise" of Pound's *Cantos* solicit the reader's ear, what styles of thought, what social and subjective configurations, what apprehensions of the cosmos do they create? A close listening to the phono-text of H.D.'s *Helen* will help us understand the power and perhaps also the danger of the "tunings" between the wireless imagination and the modernist epic.[15]

Published in 1961, H.D.'s *Helen in Egypt* is the last modernist epic composed under the spell of "the wireless imagination." The least familiar and arguably the most elusive of these epics, it is also the most extreme in its creation of an inclusive field of resonance, a rapt attention—a tension—of the ear. Although H.D. was typical of her generation in her fascination with new acoustical technologies, she had more occasion than most to reflect on their impact. As a critic of silent film, she reviewed an early demonstration of the Movietone sound machine; as a translator and poet, she heard several of her works "on the air" from London and New York; and finally, her sound-studio taping of several sections of *Helen in Egypt* significantly altered the course of its composition. A careful reading of the aesthetics, cosmology, and politics of this epic should help us audit some of the effects of the new sense ratios set up by the technological dilation of the ear.

Sound in *Helen in Egypt* is more than melopoeia, onomatopoeia, or echo. It is a mode of primary attention, an orientation, a concentration. Many factors in H.D.'s background encouraged aural acuity, among them the centrality of hymns in Moravian ritual, her family's passion for music and storytelling, and her many years of residence among foreign speakers.[16] Listening in *Helen in Egypt*, however, is more than a preference or a skill. In H.D.'s epic, sound opens directly into memory, desire, and meaning. When Achilles is ferried into the afterlife, what he remembers is not the smell of the smoldering city, the last glimpse of his ship, or the disorientation of his body but "only the sound of the rowlocks" (57). Thetis lures Helen from the temples of Egypt with a promise that a forest tree's "whispering . . . holds subtler meaning / than this written stone" (108). Helen backs her claim that the defeated Trojans still exist by saying not "I see their bodies" but "I hear their voices" (2). The crucial scenes of H.D.'s epic occur on a beach at night, in a candlelit bedchamber, in a "winter-dark" room (157), or in a dim mountain hut, intimate settings that isolate and sharpen our sense of hearing. As in a radio drama, we in H.D.'s audience join her characters in a near-total orientation through sound.[17]

CD3

To a large extent, sound is the scenery of this epic. Each character has a sound motif, and every shift of scene is signaled by a shift in sound, so that, to return to H.D.'s and Pound's telephone punning, we know we are "here" or "not here" by what we do or do not "hear." The action of the epic is arrayed across four distinct acoustical planes: the masculine world of Achilles, which rings, rasps, cracks, and clangs with the machinery of war (39); the feminine world of Helen, which echoes with laughter, murmuring, lyre music, and footsteps in a hall or on a turret; a divine world that manifests through disembodied oracular enticements and summations; and under and throughout it all, the "*beat and long reverberation,* / [the] *booming and delicate echo*" of the sea, the matrix from which sounds emerge and into which they subside (304).[18] As characters from different planes meet, interact, recede, and reminisce, the epic takes its form as a kind of Eisenstein for the ear: an acoustical collage, a superimposition or montage, a fading, clashing, and blending of sounds. In the last stage of composition, after her taping in the Zurich studio, H.D. prefaced each of her sections with a headnote that functions as a kind of voice-over, an introduction to and meditative guide through the mix of sounds to come. Like an avant-garde radio play, H.D.'s epic emerges from the workings of the acoustical imagination.

The separation of hearing from seeing in H.D.'s epic is as startling and powerful as the separation of seeing from hearing in silent film. Such drastic alteration of normal sense ratios produces an eerie, intimate, elusive effect, the effect which led H.D. to prefer silent film to Movietone sound cinema. For H.D., to see as in a silent film or, by extension, to hear as through radio can induce concentration keen enough to coax an audience out of the everyday world into a "super-normal or . . . sub-normal layer of consciousness" ("Mask" 23). While the projection of voice and the projection of image "each alone [leaves us] to our dreams," together they are "too much": too crude, too realistic, too materialistic to provide more than a caricature of day-to-day experience ("Mask" 21). In 1956, the year after she completed *Helen in Egypt*, H.D. ran across reviews of the global release of a movie that realized her worst fears for sound cinema. This film, she complained to Pearson, reduces Helen of Troy—a Spartan, a goddess—to a talking doll, a "cutie" (letter, 31 January 1956).[19] For H.D., concentration of attention in one sense—eye or ear—has the potential to engage a more profound layer of the psyche and generate a trance—an entrancement—which opens into myth, dream, and the unconscious.

One of the best guides to the art of listening in a period of technologized orality is, appropriately enough, the model for one of H.D.'s characters in the epic. After leaving Egypt, Helen visits the philosopher-hero Theseus, who settles her on a low couch near a small stove in the late afternoon dusk to recount her story. This staging replicates the scene of H.D.'s analysis with Freud and demonstrates a point Freud elaborated in his recommendations to physicians. For the same reasons H.D. preferred silent film to Movietone cinema, Freud advised the analyst to place himself behind—and therefore out of sight of—the analysand. Using acoustical technology to elaborate this recommendation, Freud argued that the analyst, deprived of sight clues, "turn[s] his own unconscious like a receptive organ towards the transmitting unconscious of the patient . . . adjust[ing] himself to the patient as a telephone receiver is adjusted to the transmitting microphone. Just as the receiver converts back into sound-waves the electric oscillations in the telephone line which were set up by sound-waves, so the doctor's unconscious is able, from the derivatives of the unconsciousness which are communicated to him, to reconstruct the unconscious, which has determined the patient's free associations" ("Recommendations" 115–16).[20] Like an archaic Greek attending to a bard, like Havelock in Toronto listening to Hitler, like Mother entranced by GE's golden tones, the analyst is an ear in thrall to a voice.[21]

Unlike H.D.'s Imagist poems, which were "written to be seen," *Helen in Egypt*, H.D. told Pearson, must be "dramatized" (letter, 25 February 1955). It needs to be apprehended, whether in print or on the air, as acoustical data. The importance of the phonotext became clear to H.D. through the act of taping sections from the poem. As she reports to Pearson, this was an ecstatic, even a transformative experience. It made a composition in space into an event in time, connected it with the performative traditions of the epic, and restored its address, at least in theory, from a small number of eyes to a collective ear. "Instead of confiding my tale, my song, my saga, confidentially, to the few," she explained to Pearson, "I seemed to be lecturing a multitude" (letter, 3 February 1955). From this point forward, memorizing its lines, murmuring them to herself like a chant or mantra, H.D. insisted on the dual nature of her composition. For her, henceforward, it was in equal parts aural *and* oral, graphotext and phonotext, "inked-in" and "ink-din."[22]

Like all successful epics, H.D.'s work is a revision—or, perhaps better, a reaudition—of a tale familiar enough to constitute a community: "*We all know the story*," the poem begins, "*of Helen of Troy*" (1). H.D.'s rendition of this story is as disembodied as a narrative told over the phone or on the radio. To engage it is to enter the place GE's advertising copy calls "almost . . . another dimension." In this strange territory, the narrator speaks, Helen speaks, Paris speaks, Theseus speaks, Achilles and his mother Thetis speak, not to each other, except in memory, but, it seems, directly to us. Rhythmic, repetitive, intimate, eerily familiar, H.D.'s language repeats—or re-creates —a moment when we were all, first and foremost, oralists. As the conventionally gendered structure of the illustration accompanying GE's advertisement suggests, this moment is connected more to the Mother/Daughter dyad than to Father. The territory of the voice is a preoedipal ghostland or dreamland, at once sensuous and dematerialized, erotic and disembodied.[23] Connections in this territory are no less instantaneous than phone transmissions or radio relays. To think of a person is to reach her; to conceive of a place is to go there; to recall an event is to relive it. To ask if the "real" Helen was on the ramparts in Troy or in the temples of Egypt is, we come to understand, a question from another register of consciousness. Like puns, truth here is a matter not of distinctions but of simultaneities.   CD4

Like ancient oral epics, H.D.'s poem is copious, elaborative, and participatory. It reproduces, that is, the configuration Ong and other commentators identify as the mindset of primary orality. *"There is more to it,"* a headnote proclaims, summing up the story of Paris (112). "There was always another and another and another," Theseus says, setting up his own story (162). Additive rather than analytic, the poem moves by means of formulas and clusters, parallel terms, phrases, and clauses. Its hinges are paratactic rather than hypotactic: "and" and "then," not "however," "because," or "therefore." If the voice-over in a headnote asks a question—as it almost invariably does—the section that follows presents not an answer but a series of echoes that proliferate and complicate the query. *"Who caused the war?"* a headnote inquires (111). A rational question. "Paris . . . Thetis . . . Eris," the section chimes, starting a rhyme that cascades across the rest of the epic. In this clustering of sounds, Paris is at once Eros and Eris, love and strife. He seduces Helen, an act that allies him with Eros, but he also shoots the arrows that kill Achilles, an act that makes him a double of Ares, the brother of Eris, the nymph who sought revenge when Thetis excluded her, alone of all deities, from her marriage feast. "Did Ares bequeath his arrows / alike to Eros, to Eris?" H. D. asks (183) in a spin of sounds that functions as a kind of aural *mise en abîme*, an M. C. Escher for the ear.

The replications of H.D.'s language pluralize meaning by folding the many into the one and exfoliating the one into the many. This simultaneous proliferation and condensation performs a structuring law of H.D.'s epic, a cosmic principle embodied by its heroes and deities, who are, she tells us, "One," even though, she continues, "the many // manifest separately" (78–79). When Osiris is torn into pieces, is he singular or plural? Are Isis, Osiris, and their child Horus three-in-one, one, or many? How about Helen, Achilles, and their child Euphorion, in whom are reborn, H.D. tells us, the slain hero-warriors of Greece? When the souls of these warriors rose in a cloud of sparks from the funeral pyre at Troy to surround the union of Helen and Achilles on the beach in Egypt, were they one or many? Are love and death, L'Amour and La Mort, two signifieds occupying the space of one signifier or one resonant sign (288)? The unstable phonotext of H.D.'s epic, its aural flux and swirl, makes questions such as these—questions of the logical, rational, scientific mind—seem not just unanswerable but, in some fundamental sense, beside the point.

To follow the shifts in H.D.'s language, the close listener must think in a communal, aggregative, undifferentiated manner, one that is closer to orally based thought and expression than it is to forms of consciousness structured by writing (see Ong 31–77). The phonotext of H.D.'s epic is a primer of the empathic, communal, ritualistic imagination, the imagination of primary orality. In this state of mind, families, tribes, and nations cohere like a cluster of bees, a swirl of snow, a galaxy, "an infinite number," in H.D.'s summary, "yet one whole" (43). If "writing restructures consciousness," as theorists of orality and literacy have argued (Ong 78), it is not unreasonable to imagine that the opposite is also true, that a resurgent aural consciousness might be able to bind us back into our lost family, tribe, nation, and cosmos. The modernist epic's glossolalia, echolalia, puns, transegmental shifts and drifts—all the sound effects, the sound defects, of a charged poetic phonotext—are amplified by their tendency to converge at a moment in which everything else seems to rip apart. The technologies that allowed a World War II speech delivered in Germany to resound simultaneously in the streets of Toronto, Paris, London, and New York made the world once again small enough to submit to a single storyteller, a politician, or a poet able to weave a spell into which "all members of the community [could be] drawn" (*Preface* 140).[24]

In the postwar years during which H.D. composed *Helen in Egypt*, a divided Germany, the Cold War, the rapid disintegration of empires, Egypt's struggle for independence, and above all the threat of nuclear warfare seemed to testify to a collectivity torn to pieces.[25] It is not surprising, then, that H.D., like Pound, Eliot, and Williams, turned the resources of the epic toward the task of cohesion. The phonemes that collapse into one another—arrows, Ares, Eris, Paris, Eros—reverse the current of dissolution, pull the fragments back toward the collective, and ask a center to hold. With the swift and startling economy of the first photographs of the earth from the moon, H.D.'s acoustics bring together gods and warriors, Greeks and Trojans, men and women, adults and children, the living and the dead. In the aural overlaps of her epic, we return full circle to Arnheim's utopian dreams for acoustical technologies: "the omnipresence of what people are singing or saying anywhere, the overleaping of frontiers, the conquest of spatial isolation, the importation of culture on the waves of the ether, the same fare for all, sound in silence" (14), even, perhaps, the establishment of a universal language, instantaneous travel through collapsing space, and the achievement of a lasting global peace.

The voice that suggested to Havelock and others the power of orality—the voice that reverberated through the world-community that H.D.'s World War II *Trilogy* called "your (and my) old town square" (3)—belonged, however, not to a generous, shape-shifting, variously manifesting international god-force but to Hitler, a fact that ought to give us pause about the ghost-land of the wireless imagination. Plato ejected the bards of orality from his Republic in the name of values that we critique but nonetheless continue to endorse, among them, rationality, discrimination, and critical distance.

Like the Homeric bard, radio, loudspeakers, and other acoustical technologies initially cast such a powerful spell that listeners, like Mother in GE's golden-toned ad, had to be reminded that what they heard was only a program. When an audience submits to the spell of a speech, a broadcast, a sermon, or, for that matter, a sound-saturated epic poem, the effect is not a spectacle apart but a resonance within, a kind of possession. As Alice Yaeger Kaplan shows in her compelling study of Fascist France, acoustical technologies served—and continue, in other sites, still to serve—as instruments of xenophobia, anti-Semitism, fundamentalist diatribe, and other seductive group-mind ideologies. The technologies Arnheim and others wanted to appropriate for the cause of peace also have been turned to the uses of indoctrination, intimidation, and infantilization.

If the wireless imagination lost sight of the many in its enthusiasm for the one, the specular imagination of the late twentieth century might be said to err in the opposite direction. In our fascination with difference, that is, we too easily lose sight of similarities that bind us together. Both extremes of the continuum are vexed—few would want to have to choose between coercive community, on one hand, and balkanization on the other. As the virtual realities of cyberspace propel us further into yet another technologized cast-of-mind, it is important to remember the overlap between new opportunities and new vulnerabilities, the powerful sway forms of communication exert on the psyche, and the mixed record that emerges from the acoustical ghostland or dreamland of the modernist epic.

NOTES

1. In this concept of the epic, I am indebted to Ingalls and Bernstein.

2. In a survey reported in August 1994 on National Public Radio, only a minuscule percentage of respondents listed their telephones as one of the ten most useful household technologies. Among the earliest acoustical technologies still in use, the telephone is by now so familiar we no longer recognize it as a technology. For very different reactions when telephones were new, see Marvin.

3. The sensation Pound registers as being "heerd" by a receiver, H.D. conceives as a telegraphic relay: "If we had the right sort of brains," she explains in *Notes on Thought and Vision*, "we would receive a definite message from [works of art], like dots and lines ticked off by one receiving station, received and translated into definite thought by another telegraphic centre" (26).

4. H.D.'s tape is available from Watershed Tapes, P.O. Box 50145, Washington, D.C. 20004. For her descriptions of the act of taping, see her January 1955 letters to Pearson at the Beinecke. All materials from the H.D. archives at the Beinecke are quoted with the permission of New Directions and Perdita Schaffner.

5. Exceptions to this generalization include the essays collected in *Continuum* 6.1 (1992), ed. Toby Miller; in "Radiotext(e)," *Semiotext(e)* 6.1, no. 16 (1993), ed. Neil

Strauss; and especially in Kahn and Whitehead, *Wireless Imagination*. Catalogs of prestigious publishing houses such as Routledge bear out the disparity of interest in media of sight and media of sound, for against a plethora of historical, theoretical, and critical studies of film and TV, Routledge publishes only one study of radio, Crisell's brief overview of British radio, *Understanding Radio*.

6. See Perloff, *Radical Artifice*, esp. xii.

7. See Davies, "History," for a timeline of acoustical legends, musical instruments, automata, technologies, and treatises from ca. 1150 B.C. to 1977.

8. For descriptions of early radio, see Czitrom, esp. chap. 3, "The Ethereal Hearth: American Radio from Wireless through Broadcasting, 1892–1940." Frank A. Biocca tells us that in 1922 America was gripped by an audio "purchasing craze," "a veritable epidemic," "bombs bursting in the air." According to the most conservative estimates, by late 1923 the number of radios had jumped by 660 percent, although a number of contemporary writers placed that estimate as high as 2,500 percent, while in 1923 alone the number of stations increased by 1,850 percent. For a typical scene of ritualizing listening, see the advertisement for General Electric radios captioned, "Don't Cry Mother . . . It's *Only* a Program," on the inside front cover of *Life*, January–February 1940, reproduced above. For the design of radio cabinets, see Hill, *Cat's Whisker*.

9. For Pound, see *Literary Essays* 58, 297, and *ABC* 73, 81. For H.D., see *Notes* 26–27.

10. "I Gather the Limbs of Osiris, IV" 179; "I Gather the Limbs of Osiris, II" 130. For more on this topic, see Nänny.

11. See picture of Berliner's angel in Kittler 232. Hermes, the Greek prototype for Mercury, haunts both the *Cantos* and *Trilogy*. For angels, see in particular H.D.'s series of invocations in "Tribute to the Angels," the second part of *Trilogy*.

12. See Davies and Millard for dates and brief definitions of these inventions.

13. As if to underscore their secondary orality, most modernist epics were performed, recorded, and/or taped. Pound read his on his radio broadcasts, H.D. taped hers, and Eliot's and Pound's were both recorded and distributed by Caedmon Records. It is not, however, crucial to my argument that these poems be read aloud.

14. See Havelock, "Radio & the Rediscovery of Rhetoric," chap. 4 of *Muse*.

15. For an elaboration of the term "tuning," see Antin.

16. For the aurality of her Moravian background, see her memoir *The Gift*. Moravian traditions included a trombone choir, in which her grandfather Francis Wolle played, and, in the early days, polyglot hymn-singing. Her uncle, Fred Wolle, established the annual Bach festival in Bethlehem, Pennsylvania, and her mother was for many years a music teacher.

17. See Cory for the use of sound in radio drama.

18. For a sustained description of the masculine and feminine worlds in *Helen in Egypt*, see Friedman 257–61.

19. In "Work of Art," Benjamin makes a similar point in a different vocabulary. For him the advent of sound is linked to the "artificial build-up of the 'personality' outside the studio" which turns "the unique aura of the person" into "the 'spell of the personality,' the phony spell of a commodity" (231).

20. See also Freud's reprise of these instructions in "On Beginning the Treatment."

21. In his essay "Listening," Barthes links the posture of hearing to "an attitude of decoding what is obscure, blurred, or mute, in order to make available to consciousness the 'underside' of meaning" (249, 251). The power of the act of listening to bring subjects into relation seems to hold even when the listener is a crowd lending an ear—or, as the transegmental drift would suggest, "a near"—to the speaker.

22. "I have been happy with the *Helen*," H.D. reported to Pearson, "—the only poems I ever wrote that I have memorized in part, and say over and over" (letter, 24 December 1955).

23. For elaborations of this point in a number of different registers, see Kloepfer on the mother-daughter scenes in H.D.'s *HERmione*, Lawrence on women's voices in cinema, and Kaplan on auditory technology in Fascist France.

24. "Chesterfield is merely the nation's cigarette, but the radio," Adorno and Horkheimer remind us, "is the voice of the nation" (377). Part of the power of World War II broadcasts by Hitler, Mussolini, Roosevelt, Churchill, and DeGaulle was their claim to speak to—and for—one or another vast collective body.

25. For a discussion of the political context into which H.D. inserted her meditations on Egypt, see Edmunds 95–100.

WORKS CITED

Adorno, T. W., and M. Horkheimer. "The Culture Industry: Enlightenment as Mass Deception." *Mass Communication and Society*. Ed. James Curran, Michael Gurevitch, and Janet Woollacott. London: Edward Arnold, 1977. 349–83.

Ahl, Frederick. *Metaformations: Soundplay and Wordplay in Ovid and Other Classical Poets*. Ithaca: Cornell University Press, 1985.

Antin, David. "tuning." *tuning*. New York: New Directions, 1984. 105–42.

Arnheim, Rudolf. *Radio*. Trans. Margaret Ludwig and Herbert Read. London: Faber & Faber, 1936.

Barthes, Roland. "Listening." *The Responsibility of Forms: Critical Essays on Music, Art, and Representation*. Trans. Richard Howard. New York: Hill & Wang, 1985. 245–60.

Benjamin, Walter. "The Work of Art in the Age of Mechanical Reproduction." *Illuminations: Essays and Reflections*. Ed. Hannah Arendt. Trans. Harry Zohn. New York: Schocken, 1973. 217–51.

Bernstein, Michael André. *The Tale of the Tribe: Ezra Pound and the Modern Verse Epic*. Princeton: Princeton University Press, 1980.

Biocca, Frank A. "The Pursuit of Sound: Radio, Perception, and Utopia in the Early Twentieth Century." *Media, Culture, and Society* 10 (1988): 61–79.

Carpenter, Humphrey. *A Serious Character: The Life of Ezra Pound*. New York: Delta, 1988.

Connor, James A. "RADIO free JOYCE: *Wake* Language and the Experience of Radio." In this volume.

Cory, Mark E. "Soundplay: The Polyphonous Tradition of German Radio Art."

Wireless Imagination: Sound, Radio, and the Avant-Garde. Ed. Douglas Kahn and Gregory Whitehead. Cambridge, Mass.: MIT Press, 1992. 331–71.

Crisell, Andrew J. *Understanding Radio*. London: Methuen, 1986.

Culler, Jonathan. "The Call of the Phoneme." *On Puns: The Foundation of Letters*. Ed. Jonathan Culler. New York: Blackwell, 1988. 1–16.

Czitrom, Daniel J. *Media and the American Mind: From Morse to McLuhan*. Chapel Hill: University of North Carolina Press, 1982.

Davies, Hugh. "A History of Recorded Sound." *Poésie Sonore Internationale*. Ed. Henri Chopin. Paris: J. M. Place, 1979. 13–40.

Edmunds, Susan. *Out of Line: History, Psychoanalysis, and Montage in H.D.'s Long Poems*. Stanford: Stanford University Press, 1994.

Eliot, T. S. *The Waste Land and Other Poems*. New York: Harcourt, 1934.

Frank, Joseph. *The Widening Gyre: Crisis and Mastery in Modern Literature*. New Brunswick, N.J.: Rutgers University Press, 1963.

Freud, Sigmund. "On Beginning the Treatment (Further Recommendations on the Technique of Psycho-analysis I)" (1913). *Complete Works of Sigmund Freud* (1911–1913). Ed. and trans. James Strachey. Vol. 12. London: Hogarth, 1958. 123–44.

———. "Recommendations to Physicians Practicing Psycho-analysis." *Complete Works of Sigmund Freud* (1911–1913). Ed. and trans. James Strachey. Vol. 12. London: Hogarth, 1958. 109–20.

Friedman, Susan Stanford. *Psyche Reborn: The Emergence of H.D.* Bloomington: Indiana University Press, 1981.

H.D. *The Gift*. Abr. ed. New York: New Directions, 1982.

———. *H.D.: Collected Poems, 1912–1944*. Ed. Louis L. Martz. New York: New Directions, 1983.

———. *Helen in Egypt*. Audiocassette. Watershed Tapes, 1981.

———. *Helen in Egypt*. New York: New Directions, 1961.

———. *HERmione*. New York: New Directions, 1981.

———. Letters to Norman Holmes Pearson. Beinecke Rare Book and Manuscript Library. Yale University.

———. "The Mask and the Movietone: The Cinema and the Classics III." *Close-Up* 5 (November 1927): 18–31.

———. *Notes on Thought and Vision and the Wise Sappho*. San Francisco: City Lights, 1982.

———. *Trilogy*. New York: New Directions, 1973.

Havelock, Eric A. *The Muse Learns to Write: Reflections on Orality and Literacy from Antiquity to the Present*. New Haven: Yale University Press, 1986.

———. *Preface to Plato*. Cambridge, Mass.: Harvard University Press, 1963.

Hill, Jonathan. *The Cat's Whisker: Fifty Years of Wireless Design*. London: Oresko, 1978.

Ingalls, Jeremy. "The Epic Tradition: A Commentary." *East-West Review* 1 (1964): 42–69.

———. "The Epic Tradition: A Commentary II." *East-West Review* 1 (1964): 173–211.

Kahn, Douglas, and Gregory Whitehead, eds. *Wireless Imagination: Sound, Radio, and the Avant-Garde*. Cambridge, Mass.: MIT Press, 1992.

Kaplan, Alice Yaeger. *Reproductions of Banality: Fascism, Literature, and French Intellectual Life*. Minneapolis: University of Minnesota Press, 1986.

Kenner, Hugh. *The Mechanic Muse*. New York: Oxford University Press, 1987.

———. *The Pound Era*. Berkeley: University of California Press, 1971.

Kittler, Friedrich A. *Discourse Networks, 1800/1900*. Trans. Michael Metteer, with Chris Cullens. Stanford: Stanford University Press, 1990.

Kloepfer, Deborah Kelly. *The Unspeakable Mother: Forbidden Discourse in Jean Rhys and H.D.* Ithaca: Cornell University Press, 1989.

Lawrence, Amy. *Echo and Narcissus: Women's Voices in Classical Hollywood Cinema*. Berkeley: University of California Press, 1991.

Lord, Albert B. *The Singer of Tales*. Cambridge, Mass.: Harvard University Press, 1960.

McGann, Jerome. *Black Riders: The Visible Language of Modernism*. Princeton: Princeton University Press, 1993.

Marinetti, Filippo Tommaso. "Destruction of Syntax—Wireless Imagination—Words in Freedom." *Lacerba* 11 May, 15 June 1913. Translated in Richard J. Pioli, *Stung by Salt and War: Creative Texts of the Italian Avant-Gardist F. T. Marinetti*. New York: Lang, 1987. 45–53.

Marvin, Carolyn. *When Old Technologies Were New: Thinking about Electric Communication in the Late Nineteenth Century*. New York: Oxford University Press, 1988.

Millard, Andre. *America on Record: A History of Recorded Sound*. Cambridge: Cambridge University Press, 1995.

Nänny, Max. *Ezra Pound: Poetics for an Electric Age*. Bern: Franke, 1973.

Ong, Walter J. *Orality and Literacy: The Technologizing of the Word*. London: Methuen, 1982.

Perloff, Marjorie. *The Dance of the Intellect: Studies in the Poetry of the Pound Tradition*. Cambridge: Cambridge University Press, 1985.

———. *Radical Artifice: Writing Poetry in the Age of Media*. Chicago: University of Chicago Press, 1991.

Pound, Ezra. *ABC of Reading*. New York: New Directions, 1934.

———. *The Cantos of Ezra Pound*. New York: New Directions, 1970.

———. "I Gather the Limbs of Osiris, II. A Rather Dull Introduction." *New Age* 10.6 (7 December 1911): 130.

———. "I Gather the Limbs of Osiris, IV. A Beginning." *New Age* 10.8 (21 December 1911): 179.

———. *Literary Essays*. Edited with an introduction by T. S. Eliot. New York: New Directions, 1935.

———. "Three Cantos." *Poetry* 10.3 (June 1917): 113–21. Unrevised version of Canto 1.

Stewart, Garrett. *Reading Voices: Literature and the Phonotext*. Berkeley: University of California Press, 1990.

Terrell, Carroll F. *A Companion to the Cantos of Ezra Pound*. Vol. 1 (Cantos 1–71). Berkeley: University of California Press, 1980.

Whitehead, Gregory. "Out of the Dark: Notes on the Nobodies of Radio Art." *Wireless Imagination: Sound, Radio, and the Avant-Garde.* Ed. Douglas Kahn and Gregory Whitehead. Cambridge, Mass.: MIT Press, 1992. 253–63.

Williams, William Carlos. *Paterson.* New York: New Directions, 1958.

Yeats, William Butler. "Byzantium." *Poems.* New York: Macmillan, 1960. 243–44.

THE RADIO INTELLECTUAL
Specific, General, or Just Wired?

We want to begin our consideration of the position of the specific radio intellectual by offering two texts for comparison. The first is a string of quotations from a very famous intellectual who derides the concept of the general intellectual and offers, in its place, a strategy of specificity and epistemic minimalism:

> The word "intellectual" is foreign to me. I have never encountered any intellectuals. I have known people who write novels, and others who take care of illnesses; some who do economic studies and others who compose electronic music. I have encountered people who teach, people who paint, and people who do I don't know what. But intellectuals, never. (Foucault, "Masked" 194)

> The work of the intellect is to show that what is, does not have to be. (Foucault, "How" 252)

> But, then, what is philosophy today—philosophical activity, I mean—if it is not the critical work that thought brings to bear on itself? In what does it consist, if not in the endeavor to know how and to what extent it might be possible to think differently, instead of legitimating what is already known? There is always something ludicrous in philosophical discourse when it tries, from the outside, to dictate to others, to tell them where their truth is and how to find it, or when it works up a case against them in the language of naive positivity. (Foucault, *Use* 8–9)

The second text is an exchange between a radio announcer and a much less famous intellectual. Unlike the first text, this passage is not an edited discussion intended for written publication in a scholarly European forum under the name Michel Foucault.

Rather, it is a transcription of a "naturally occurring" dialogue on Australian AM radio between Kevin Hume and Toby Miller (K and T, respectively). It might be thought of as an instance of the specific intellectual at work:[1]

1 K: . . . at twelve tuh *six* .hhh now to our *sen*sitive cultural commissar who joins us each tuesday ev'ning on Dri::ve, Toby, Mi?ller .hh putting at least er seven intriguing levels 'v meaning tuh th' mos' commonplace of or'nary be*hav*ior in our pop culture *slot* .hh like)f'r example⟨ getting z:*apped* .hhh or *z:app*ing as it is sometimes caused er called uh a)ref'rence o' course⟨ to er *arcane video* be*hav*ior Tobe)is 'at right?⟨

(.)

2 T: .hh it may well be Kevin but as usual you've caught me totally off guard with your—*cha*rming description of me, sensitive, when did I suddenly get this appellation

3 K: Well it w's—after you::r grov'ling 'nd er before the altar of post *fem*inist *fem*inism:: las' week er where you w'r reproving me fer not being politic'ly correct Tobe s'I thought .hhhh obviously th- here's a man who's er .h chasing after)shall we say⟨ er .hh sensitive new age s::*kirt*.

(2.6)

4 T: I'd like tuh say th't Telecom's cut in here and there's some kinda communic( )ns breakdown

                           [ ]=

5 K: .hh

6 K: =hahk y'k hah

      [ ]

7 T: ( )ing like tha— 'n we all know I'm thee —
authentic f:eminized male 'v thee: — early *nine*ties

                      [   ]=

8 K: (hh) hah

9 K: =hah hah

      [   ]

10 T: Let's get *ser*ious

While, to be sure, Foucault (the more famous of our two sons of knowledge) refuses to offer a general theory of the specific intellectual, he does present a strategy: the denial of what, in ethnomethodological circles, would be called "the ironic stance" (Garfinkel and Sacks 345)—a position of social critique from which others are advised on how to speak or act. For at its worst, this stance can be prophetic, omniscient, and condemnatory. Instead of engaging in such "naive positivity," the specific intellectual works on one or a number of distinct and local fronts, including radio. His or her public intellection is geared toward showing how things could be otherwise, in a historical rather than moral-prescriptive sense. But ultimately, perhaps all that is reconstructed is the intellectual's own sense of self, the "exercise of oneself in the activity of thought." To use Foucault's own terminology, the strategy of the specific intellectual is an "ascetic" one. This is a primer in self-problematization, a means of training oneself to know one's desires — and hence know one's limitations — that prepares the subject for the governance of others (*Use* 9, 30, 72–73).

But, and this is our central question, is this *general strategy* of Foucault's specific intellectual, this nontheory which is still an in-principle ethics, so straightforward when it comes down to the *specific tactics* of an interview on radio? How does it avoid conservative versions of consensus and quietism? What can and should the specific intellectual do when, as happens in our second text, his moral position is challenged to the point where complicity in that particular radio game would — again to use the ethnomethodological term — "membership" him in ways that he finds politically abhorrent? Under these circumstances, is it sufficient to stay purely within an "exercise of oneself," or must some disruption, some unruly display, be projected into the calculus of the public event itself? How can such a tactic work without casting oneself as the ironic, prophetic, moral-prescriptive expert — the very general intellectual Foucault rejects (for what we think are very good reasons)? Put in a broader context: following the complex, polyvalent trends in identity politics over the past twenty years, this (or any) model of the general intellectual is in question. Transparently, today, it matters *who* speaks, *who* listens, and *who* is the subject of that speech. What role can the cultural critic usefully fulfill, given reforms to the model in line with Foucault's notion of the specific intellectual and the transition from the totalization of the modern to the particularity of the postmodern?

In attempting to answer these questions, we consider the necessary industrial and (auto)biographical positionings of the specific intellectual, problems with definitions of the general intellectual, and the question of local tactics that might — for at least the radio occasion we have presented — meet not only Foucault's exacting requirements but also those of the interviewee "under attack": i.e., what to do in a position where the strategy of the pre-Foucauldian general intellectual is a highly attractive proposition.

Industry and Biography

In writing about Foucault, we would normally confine our remarks to the published works, as broadly defined. Too much passion has already been imported into the discussion of him as a biographical personage (Eribon; Macey; J. Miller; for discussion, see T. Miller 177–79). But when Foucault writes about the role of the intellectual, he is already being personal, and in two senses. Firstly, we will always know that he is talking about Michel Foucault, the specific person called on to speak about a whole range of matters. Secondly, the explicit strategy of many of the later interviews is a reconstruction of himself—he says so in as many words—and of little else. And yet in offering "us" *his* strategy—why else would it be published?— Foucault is necessarily put in an awkward and possibly self-defeating position. He questions the very desirability of the category "intellectual," and ironically calls on such people to renounce "their old prophetic function" ("End" 155). Now given that Foucault was a person who wrote, spoke, taught, and acted in such dispersed fields as linguistics, penology, philosophy, sexology, medicine, cinema, economics, history, biology, politics, military studies, ethics, literary criticism, ethnology, somatics, psychology, aesthetics, and the classics, this seems a tendentious claim, at least as a pathway to his own practice. Is "Foucault" an oxymoron then? Rather like the question once put to Shirley MacLaine on Australian television ("Ms. MacLaine, is there *any*thing you don't believe in?"), one might ask Foucault whether there is any form of knowledge about which he would not venture a "specific" opinion.

Yet this is to be churlish, especially when that self-effacing historian of thought is referring to singular, deterministic, and transcendental moves when he disparages "general" models of explanation and prediction that privilege the experience or theory of a single, charismatic caste of person. In place of the shadow thrown by seers and sages, Foucault imagined "the intellectual destroyer of evidence and universalities." Contrary to those who would classify him as a nihilistic hedonist, this should be seen as a questioning of authority, a problematization of the self (as both biographical human subject and institutional intellectual figure) through an incessant displacement of one's own stature as a knowing expert who is "outside" the problems under discussion ("End" 155). Foucault noted the auratic power of a supposedly disinterested overall competence, a long-standing condition of public academic significance. He tied this to its companion in modernity, the human sciences' power of application. The European Enlightenment legacy of university scholarship and laboratory apparatus effectively transformed the figure of the free-floating pundit into a person whose stature was authenticated by the exercise of power and by the division of the social into the good and the bad, the well and the sick, in fields of knowledge that imposed definite bodily effects ("Power" 64). Foucault's critique of this was in keeping not only with his despair in the face of the failure of the classic *meta-récits* to explain and predict, but also with their inordinately powerful and grotesque capacity to seize the lives of populations and remold them as objects of knowledge.

If Pierre Bourdieu is to be believed, Foucault was *only* an intellectual and not an "academic" (xix). For most of his working life, his industrial conditions left him free of the most onerous tasks of university procedures and politics. No job specification (apart from obligatory but short lecture courses) interfered with his writing and his broader intellectual and political commitments (Eribon 209–10, 222–3). But what of our other relevant biographical and industrial circumstance, that of Toby Miller? As with almost all academics, for Miller, the odd public guest appearance — on radio or elsewhere — is and was a kind of time-out, an occasion of flattery rather than work-as-usual. While it is true that appointments and promotions committees do consider public or community service as part of their deliberations, this is usually very low on their list of priorities, behind scholarship, teaching, and committee work. To speak on radio as a weekly guest-commentator on cultural affairs takes Miller (and him less than many others) out of his academic milieu. In a minor way, it makes him a personality. He is called upon as much for his personhood as for his professionally acquired skills.

While both Foucault and Miller, when they appear in interviews or as guests in other media, are expected more than ever to speak about their immediate times and local issues, for the latter the space of the appearance always runs the risk of unprofessionalism. Added to this is a national difference. In France, as we know, leading academics are expected to contribute regularly to public debate. In Australia there are few such figures (we might instance Geoffrey Blainey and Donald Horne). The minimal space available for "intellectual" comment is taken up by almost antiacademic professional news "intellectuals" such as Phillip Adams and P. P. McGuinness. In Australian broadcasting, the academic is not only "personalized" for a rare moment; he or she is also, paradoxically, marginalized as the object of a continuing desire to cull tall poppies.

Whether we like it or not, there is an autobiographical dimension to our analysis. And this is all the more so, since Miller's career (once described in a university scholarship committee as "checkered") has not been straightforwardly and solely academic. This career involves, inter alia, four years in the 1970s as an undergraduate working as a radio newsreader, music announcer, and sporting presenter for the former Australian Broadcasting Commission, now a corporation (ABC), and four years from 1989 as a weekly academic guest on ABC radio doing film reviews and pop culture commentary. From all-round functionary to specialist cultural critic is the move—one that takes him from the general announcer reading lines prepared by others to the general critic, from delivering on-air truths to guaranteeing their authenticity.[2] The interviewer replete with techniques for assuming the position of naive inquiry becomes the interviewed. None of this, as we shall see, is without its relevances and resonances for the exchange between Miller and Hume presented above.

But of course, this individual trajectory is determined by social, economic, cultural, and historical forces. One of the central frames to public culture in Australia is the 1950s invention of the "cultural cringe." This refers to the notion that Australian intellectual life is always already derivative— degenerately so—and narrowly chauvinistic. The description was animated through a series of invidious self-comparisons with Britain, the United States, and parts of continental Europe. The achievement of overseas success, in cinema, science, business, or scholarship, continues to provide a talisman of worth that, once donned, can frequently be used as a reentry certificate to Australia.

This indigenous denigration is periodically reinforced by assaults from outside. Witness Fredric Jameson's recent belittlement of Australians as "the noisiest detractors of 'grand theory'" in cultural studies, guilty of "anti-intellectualism" (29), or Perry Anderson's lack of interest in Confucianism, Maoism, Islam, Aboriginal culture, and the whole of Asian-Pacific life in his "account" of "the principal region of intellectual production" (ix). Domestically, the unease with a self-presentation of Australia as unforgivingly and unremittingly utilitarian but also forged from governmental activity (and hence prepared to establish and sustain thoroughgoing systems of public welfare and broadcasting) leads to a dialogue between notions of applied, policy-oriented work and organic, yet disinterested, criticism (Collins; Head 2–3). The first of these apparent antinomies favors a technocratic model of modernity, in which knowledge can be directly applied to offer solutions to problems. It belongs to the social sciences. The second, Enlightenment, model lives with the humanities. It is atmospheric and moralistic by contrast. These oppositions become very mixed, pseudo-antinomies indeed in Australia, where time is dedicated *inside* the technocratic model to worrying away at practical, developmentalist applications and their cultural correlatives that so easily call up the ugly tropes of land-grabbing excavation and new-world selfishness rather than the more welcome signs of beauty-of-life aesthetics and nation-binding civics.

In his study of Australian media intellectuals, Albert Moran suggests that the practice of *inquiry* characterizes intellectuals. He is particularly concerned with journalists and other media workers, emphasizing the twin sites of appearance for media intellectuals in Australia: the state and the market. The state sustains a broadcasting system of reflection and investigation, via the ABC and the multicultural Special Broadcasting Service, while the market supports sensation and surface via commercial stations—a familiar opposition. ABC radio has been quite crucial to the establishment of extra-university intellectual culture, through talks, drama, orchestral music, and left and feminist politics (109, 114–15). So the Australian radio system—based as it is on a mix of commercial, community, and arms-length governmental stations—provides for a complex interplay of general expertise (signaled by university credentials and a humanities address) and specific/populist knowledge (signaled by approachability and "personality").

Here, we might note a more microtechnological difference between our two sons of knowledge. Consider the dissonance in methods of transcription between the multitude of Foucault interviews, so measured and controlled, so timelessly ironized, as opposed to the instantaneity, the chaos, the very messiness of the Miller-Hume exchange as we have physically represented it here. Of the 397 items in David Macey's Foucault bibliography, 35 are discussions, round tables, and exchanges, and 92 are interviews, 5 from radio and 1 from television (542–65). Many of these published texts involved "corrections" and "revisions" by Foucault; some masked his identity; others united a band of questioners into a single subject (the notorious "collective Historian" in "Questions" n. 73). This may be in keeping with his status as a political participant, and consonant with his nonsystemic brand of historicized philosophizing (Morris and Patton preface 8). But even with these careful problematizations of authority and singularity, the means of communication continue to privilege script over voice. Interviews are rendered proseworthy in a way that is not merely archival but also editorial. The conditions of speech are removed in favor of a rather stately practice of turn-taking, where sentences are completed, subject and predicate need not weep for their partners, and enunciation is pure and clear. By contrast, the conditions of communication confronting the wired intellectual are much less conducive to the archive and the curriculum vitae; closer, perhaps, to small advertising slots, but without access to both parts of the scripted dialogue. This relates in turn to the differential requirements of the wired, specific interviewee. Miller is being spoken to for his knowledge (and on-air fluency), whereas Foucault is in some sense being spoken to for himself; it matters not that "an intellectual argues as follows . . . ," but rather that "the latest from Michel Foucault *is* . . . ." This is not to suggest that the specific intellectual model (for which read, "specific" to the speaking subject(s) "Michel Foucault") is without risk. As Deborah Cook has noted in her discussion of what we should make of the huge body of his interview "writings," this semiauthorized detritus can easily bring forth wild psy-complex analyses that posthumously therapize, or insistent fire breathing within encyclopedic hermeneuts in an endless quest for what Foucault really meant. But she continues to claim a dialogic quality to the interview, arguing that we read Foucault here at an "oral and spontaneous" moment, one in keeping with his own media agenda. He regarded the genre of the interview as simply one more means of handling information, no less worthy than the scholarly book, and if anything to be prized for its ability to reach extra-academic audiences (147). But this again tells us more about the genre's possibilities for the celebrity-academic rather than the artisanal one. Only the former is invited to engage in ascetic self-promotion/problematization in the marketplace. At the same time, the constitution of a talent to engage, as much as a vocabulary to impart, may also be relevant to the more artisanal figure ("But is s/he good talent?" asks the producer).

When ABC personnel spoke to Miller about his tasks as a film reviewer in Brisbane and then as a popular culture commentator in Perth, there was an apparently strong binarism dividing their view of what they wanted. On one hand, an academic was needed to furnish expertise and authority in discussions ranging from TV violence and media ownership to Woody Allen, *auteur et père*. But on the other, these were friendly topics. By contrast with the economy or the Gulf War, they should be approached as part of "the cool down," as "light" components of drive-time programs. As a consequence, Miller was called on to have definite opinions, to present a "personality"—in short, to be both performative and constative of a particular version of the Zeitgeist. So the dim, studious remove of academe would lend credence. And the bright, playful space of individualism was to contribute a humanizing organicism. This meant drawing upon research work, recasting it in short sentences open to interpolation, and always being ready for parody and modal self-mockery.

In terms of modality, one could conceive of this as the difference between a verbal overlay of personal ease and amity—or antagonism—versus an underlying set of principles that references critical social questions, such as power and subjectivity in culture. These binary divisions were really about contending but overlapping discourses of professionalism. The radio intellectual exists at the repeatable site of a rapprochement between a commitment to the protocols of theory and research and a commitment to a small insertion inside two hours of produced audio each day that must sound balanced over a five-day week.

In turn, this calls up the audience hailed by the program, an audience with middle-level cultural capital, interested in local and national politics, and itself part of a labor force characterized by credentialism *and* a sense of radio as distraction/information. This understanding saw Miller decide to concentrate on deploying three relatively discrete forms of talk. The first of these is the form of the knowing subject, who is both a respectable public speaker and an "interesting" on-air voice, engaging in a certain confessional tendency that leavens academic discourse. The second form is the topic, alternating between policy, institutional, textual, and popular understandings. And, finally, a third, hermeneutic form that reduces texts to what might be called a unitary (or at least well-known) indeterminacy by acknowledging the comparative openness of texts, their indefinite capacity to be remade as social objects through the transformative power of interpretation. It overtly stresses the partial, positional nature of the account given, in turn offering *it* up as interpretable. By contrast, the unitary nature of this avowed openness is evident in the decision to pick on a specific subjectivity inside texts, such as gender, class, or race. But this in turn needs to be understood inside the discourse of sound, of radio sound, and of discussion itself, all of which are themselves generic and rule-governed. And we will see these problems at work, below, when we return to the text of the broadcast.

For now though, these are the positionings—albeit in shorthand—of a quite specific public intellectual and of a quite specific theorist/strategist engaged in his off-duty "business." Outside these necessarily biographical-industrial positionings, only two alternatives are easily found. The first is silence, a seminarian academic politics with elitist assumptions about the popular. As with most silences, it is best passed over in emulation of itself. The second alternative is to adopt a position within the field of the pre-Foucauldian "general intellectual." What would this mean—and what has it meant historically as a speaking position?

The Intellectual

The year 1994 marked the hundredth anniversary of the emergence of the intellectual as a derogatory category, used, at first, to describe the Dreyfusards. The word "intellectual" has broadened out from that meaning, so that today we associate it with producing, transmitting, and adapting ideas about nature, culture, and the social (Head 3). Those processes of production are always to do with application. It is a commonplace now that the intellectuals of the modern West have presented themselves as prophets, fully knowledgeable and critical of the social order and ready to advise on processes of self-reform. In keeping with this prophetic self-styling, knowledge is valorized for its utility, for its ability to make the future better than the present through the application of intellect and education as means of producing truth, of codifying and interpreting signs.

The failures of this group of mental workers are now thought to have resided in the formations of power and authority that made them worthy of attention in the first place and in the promises of social improvement that supposedly locked intellectuals again and again into a quid pro quo with other formations of power. This rapprochement has been centered around finding new policies and programs for ordering society through training at universities, the accreditation of professionals, and the generation of ideas and applications. In the United States and Australia that often takes the form of direct advice to government (Etzioni-Halevy 1–3, 17–22).

Where does this position the media intellectual or, more specifically for our purposes here, the radio intellectual? Eva Etzioni-Halevy's useful survey of intellectuals identifies one crucial motif of success: presenting oneself as original, plausible, and consistent (37). This seems, contra Foucault's view, like a classic Enlightenment ground of purportedly nonsignifying meta-critique, a space and style of transcendental excellence, of science rather than its running partners that we term "nature," "culture," or "ideology."

As such, this traditional account has no explanation of the intellectual and the mass media. It can hardly be expected to, precisely because it tries to find a single set of elements common to intellectual activity. Chief among those public elements is the yoke of prophecy. But, as we have noted, in place of the general and the prophetic, Foucault called for the "specific intellectual." Such intellectuals would seek to identify the nature of the historical moment and space in which they were functioning and isolate the "systems of thought" prevalent at that moment. Although this might still seem an overarching or general approach, its specificity would be guaranteed by twin moves: first, the acknowledgment of an event's particularity and, second, a preparedness to work alongside "practitioners" as a means of ensuring a tight connection to outcomes ("What" 282).[3]

The idea is to place oneself as close as possible to the prevailing *episteme* by subjecting the rationality of the times to a historicization that avoids any transcendent logic. Operating close to workers in different fields of intellectual application in order to make oneself "permanently capable of self-detachment," this form of life eschews the seductions of intellectual conversion to one way of seeing. There is no publicly endorsed technology that legitimizes intellectuals seeking "to mold the political will of others." Instead, assumptions should be challenged in order to "dissipate conventional familiarities," rendering the familiar strange, and vice versa. The labor of "re-problematization" marks out the specific intellectual. The next move is the one that undertakes "the formation of a political will," but that shift sees the intellectual as "citizen" rather than expert (Foucault, "Concern" 303, 305–6).

Some earnest interviewers, worrying away at the future of sociology, recently asked Zygmunt Bauman for his disciplinary prognosis. Bauman referred to certain departmental closures in American universities, shedding no tears. In the tradition of Max Weber, he rejected what had been both their founding premise and the formidable promise of modernity—assisting and abetting "the managers of public, economic and political life," whether from the right or the left—because this found them dependent on welfare and warfare bureaucracies (cf. Bennett). In place of this carpetbagging service to the state or revolution or vitamins, intellectuals should be opening up definitions, querying solutions, and offering "commentary on contemporary experience" (Bauman 143). The supersession of sociologists as technocrats by neoclassical economists offers up the space for careful theoretical debate inside the general public sphere by this newly excluded other.

What *is* the nature of debates about the contemporary experience? And what can humanities academics offer, particularly within a broadcasting regime? Most areas of general cultural critique are by definition grandstanding. In order to attain a regular position of public commentary, normal academic labor (such as intense archival research, the special work of creating vocabularies known as "theory," or the cooptive domain of public consultancy) must be surpassed (or perhaps stopped short of).[4] The humanities academy is increasingly turning popular cultural artifacts into high-culture ones through the use of theory. And that relationship produces a sense of populism and elitism conjoined. (We are referring of course to our own field of cultural studies.)

But the relationship can be more than that. Consider Simon Frith's account of the need to connect "the explicitly political identities offered by the democratic process and the experiences of inclusion and exclusion involved in mass consumption." He puts this most pointedly in asking whether cultural resistance is an expression *of*, or a substitute *for*, political action (3).

Such anxieties reach an overly sharp point when doubts are raised about the insufficiently theoretical nature of a "lay cultural populism" that amounts to "a knowing middlebrow consumer guide" (Frith and Savage 107). Is this countenanced and reproduced through a weekly radio slot on the topic? What costs to a life, a body (perhaps even a fire) are endured? How can the requirements of cultural critique match the antiprophetic techniques of the specific intellectual? What local techniques can be mustered in a situation where the radio intellectual is under the double dictates of Foucauldian specificity and a challenge from his host over a generalized identity politics?

The Radio Interview

In the radio fragment transcribed at the beginning of this chapter, Toby Miller is being interviewed by phone, live-to-air on radio, in his role as an academic expert on popular culture.[5] Regular listeners to the program know that Miller and his skeptical, more conservative interviewer, Kevin Hume, often engage in verbal sparring. As the interview begins, regular listeners will also know that Kevin ended the previous session by doubting the authenticity of Toby's profeminist politics. That session ended (right on the regular time, after several signals from Kevin that it was *time* to end) with Toby making the sound "Hm::::?" marked by a very clearly upwardly rising contour instead of the usual closing procedures (Schegloff and Sacks). So as the session in question starts, we can hear this topic being taken up again—a nice instance of a turn-pause lasting a whole week!

The interesting phenomenon here is the gap between turns 3 and 4. By any standards this is a very long conversational gap. Since it occurs at a transition, it is clearly Toby's gap and not Kevin's. Toby is expected to speak here, to do something in response to Kevin's taunt that Toby's profeminism is actually a sexual ploy. At turn 4, Toby jokingly offers a technical hitch as the reason for his silence. But this is clearly not what has happened. In fact, Miller was simply furious and outraged at such an insinuation. He was in danger of replying in terms that are unacceptable on radio. So, being a trained broadcaster, he held his tongue. This gave him time to collect his response, and it also gave Kevin's show a dose of what all professional broadcasters fear: dead air. It worked as a kind of reprisal, but one without content; no explicit position was offered. Once the gap was over, Toby was able to use the "Telecom" explanation as a polite excuse (with his word "communications" conveniently blipped across by a tiny patch of broadcast silence) and get on with his riposte.

We can see that a technical requirement (minimization of gap—one of the major design-specifications of the turn-taking system) has been passed over (though not breached) in favor of a moral requirement. In this case the requirement is for Toby to express his deep-seated community member-ship allegiances and his differences in this respect from Kevin. At the same time Kevin is clearly attempting—in the other direction—to enroll Toby as co-misogynist, inviting him into an admission of co-membership in that community ("here's a man who's chasing after . . . sensitive new age skirt"). Off-air, verbal abuse might be the only available and effective reply, fol-lowed by a termination of the talk. On-air, such a tactic would mean only one thing: Toby is an arrogant intellectual prick! But suitable on-air lan-guage would sound like a compromise, and the station's contract with Toby requires him to continue the talk somehow. Temporary but extended silence has the artful design-consequence that it both generates dead air (as a di-rect and immediate reprisal) and allows the formulation of an overemphatic and parodic riposte that reminds Kevin of the purpose of the program ("we all know I'm the authentic feminized male of the early nineties . . . let's get serious"). As with Toby's earlier "Hm::::?" sign-off, it marks a commu-nity membership difference (despite, and perhaps because of, its resistance to interview conventions). Political differences have been signified both at the level of a substantive irony and through the manipulation of silence, in ways that are both required by and subversive of the norms of radio, ways that utilize the two systems of general knower and specific personality to make their parodic point.

But note that the effect is produced through the techniques of talking, not in the talk itself—at least not in any words that were spoken. The tactic involves communication through noncommunication—not, of course, as a general principle but as a precision-timed move that touches the limits of the conventions of proper radio conduct. Without speech it says, "Any fur-ther, Kevin, and you have to improvise for the next few minutes." And while it is true that Foucault, especially in his earlier writings, is attentive to how discursive techniques work, it is equally true that, by "discursive," he means something much broader than language and communication. In fact he has said this explicitly: "What I am analyzing in the discourse is not the system of its language, nor, in a general way, the formal rules of its construction: for I am not concerned about knowing what renders it legitimate or gives it its intelligibility and allows it to serve in communication. The question which I ask is not that of codes but of events" ("Politics" 14). Foucault's mis-take here is to assume that language serves as communication because of its merely formal (or even functional) codes. Foucault is right, discourse-as-historical-epistemology is a direct alternative to formal linguistic analysis. But formal linguistic rules are not what makes communication possible. There is no need to invoke linguistic rules, then. But to ignore communicational tactics is to ignore an important aspect of events. At the same time, however, our event is much more micrological than any Foucault would deal with. As a historian, this is not what he meant by "in a moment of time and in a point in space" (*Archaeology* 85). So our event is so specific as to be almost of no use to any standard Foucauldian analysis. It shows that Foucault's prescriptions-in-nonprescriptive-guise for the specific intellectual cannot be fully realized until they address the difficult questions of local effectivity. Among these questions is What do you do, live-to-air, when the alternatives are (a) to make yourself into the obnoxious academic snob or (b) to kowtow to an explicitly reactionary politics? And more importantly, how do you do something other than these two things in the space of 2.6 seconds? Put another way: if the space of an omniscient meta-commentary is off the menu today, what is left to guard against quietism? These seem genuine questions about intellectual specificity and, to that extent, to be at least as much as Foucault was asking us to consider. Perhaps more.

Conclusion

The intellectual is not "the representative of the universal," in the sense of being someone with access to an unsplit subjectivity or a proper utopia or a sense of a way forward for the whole of society (Foucault, "Truth" 41). But that does not mean one cannot speak from a given position to voice concerns that are quite general and with techniques that are highly specific, because in some sense the regular slot on a national media organization is specific. It has enormous generic limitations: ten minutes of airtime, overriding technology favoring the presenter's voice, the species-being of a regular time slot, a sense of flippancy about the nature of popular culture discussion, a set of banal exercises in the service of forming an on-air personality, and so on. These are not the stuff of the imaginary free-floating master; they are formative of the rules of what counts as expertise. But part of the quite specific requirements of intellectuals who appear regularly on-air is precisely that they *be* general figures of knowledge, that they assume the capacity to speak about—which is to form—some sort of Zeitgeist. To refer to questions of class, gender, creativity, freedom, and other transcendental abstractions is not necessarily problematic under these conditions. For the actual community of afternoon drive-time listeners expects to encounter these grandiose self-presentations and make use of the materials on offer, in common with the operations that audiences routinely conduct on genres.

For instance, when Miller was a weekly film reviewer with another part of ABC radio, he was regularly expected to evaluate films—not an unreasonable stipulation, in that the program was providing information and opinion to its listeners. But working through that impost, and acknowledging it, one could decide to concentrate on a certain type of issue and draw on it each week. In this case, it was gender. Every review would comment on what could be guaranteed to be central to the—mostly Hollywood— narratives under review. From action-adventure to situation comedy, such texts always incorporated elements of gendered subjectivity that could be easily discussed. This performed a dual function inside the radio station. As part of a national network, it was under instructions from a central authority to employ more women as announcers. At the same time the local management had sufficient autarky to insist that these women stayed away from feminism. An outsider, a male academic, was able to voice material that otherwise seemed too partial and disquieting for ABC executives.

Should we deride these practices as the alliance of capitalist media and utilitarian academia, as does Régis Debray? Or should we view them as a modest, imperfect, incomplete, political, sound intervention? This would be to acknowledge, with Debray, that cultural power is "the power to take up other people's time" (123). Here it is the relatively discretionary time-space continuum of the office radio, car stereo, or kitchen tuner, occupied temporarily and with the aim of addressing the listener on a contingent, site-specific basis; but for Miller it led to numerous requests to speak to agencies such as Rotary International, a group of middle-class businessmen prepared to listen to left ideas when applied to areas of popular culture such as the commodification of sport or the cultural imperialism of American audiovisual trade. This is not cultural grandstanding. Their function as teachers in loco parentis—and something more—manufactures a metonymic role for intellectuals, a space that is occupied by moving toward an apparently "unrestricted" linguistic code (Gouldner 3). In fact, that code is of course more a matter of a meta-language, and meta-languages are characterized by the specificity of their address, their paradoxically occasioned nature.

The slide between an Olympian cultural critique that elaborates from the semiotic system of a given popular culture text to a more productive, site-specific social semiosis is encouraged by the architecture of the drive-time interview. It brings into question the opposition between common sense and intellectualism, where the former is foregrounded as a site of certainty for conserving culture and the latter is assailed as a utopian imaginary of new subjectivities. For Frith and Savage this opens up the prospect of cultural theory's support for the popular to be stylized and appropriated by the populist right (109). That might be true as part of a very general trend, but do we need to worry much about occasional voices? For those voices are at least engaging the humanities with political contestation in a way rarely seen in the postwar era. And this is because sound, image, and interpretation are presented with a meta-meaning inside postmodernity and its turn toward service industries (Eagleton). While the humanities cannot and should not hope to exercise control over the production and dispersal of culture, we might make certain claims to influence aspects of its circulation — and be political-sounding as we do so.

NOTES

1. Transcription conventions are as follows:

.hhh	audible exhalation
(hh)	audible inhalation
:	prolongation of sound
)word(	word spoken quickly
word	word stressed
wor-	word cut off
word—word	short pause between words
?	rising intonation
(.)	untimed pause
(0.0)	timed pause in seconds and tenths
[ ]	beginning and end of overlapped talk
=	continuation points — no pause
( )	word(s) untranscribable

2. The general announcer is known in the trade as a JAFA — Just Another Fucking Announcer.

3. Note here that Foucault's conception of an event is much broader than ours, specifically in relation to the radio event transcribed earlier. In addition, his idea of working alongside practitioners is a very problematic description of what happens in our radio event.

4. We have already mentioned Phillip Adams. In a 1993 *Late Night Live* program on ABC, he asked Meaghan Morris for basic definitions of "postmodernism" and "poststructuralism." Before she could complete her first sentence, he was already making objections based on his preconceived ideas about these terms. We continue to wonder, then, about the space of the guest expert.

5. The fragment in question is also analyzed in McHoul, "Con/versation."

WORKS CITED

Anderson, Perry. *A Zone of Engagement*. London: Verso, 1992.

Bauman, Zygmunt. "Modernity, Postmodernity, and Ethics: An Interview with Zygmunt Bauman." *Telos* 93 (Fall 1992): 133–44.

Bennett, Tony. "Useful Culture." *Cultural Studies* 6 (1992): 395–408.

Bourdieu, Pierre. *Homo Academicus*. Trans. Peter Collier. Stanford: Stanford University Press, 1988.

Collins, Hugh. "Political Ideology in Australia." *Australia: The Daedalus Symposium*. Ed. Stephen R. Graubard. North Ryde, N.S.W., Australia: Angus and Robertson, 1985. 147–69.

Cook, Deborah. "Umbrellas, Laundry Bills, and Resistance: The Place of Foucault's Interviews in His Corpus." *CLIO* 21 (1992): 145–55.

Debray, Régis. *Teachers, Writers, Celebrities: The Intellectuals of Modern France*. Trans. David Macey. London: Verso, 1981.

Eagleton, Terry. "The Crisis of Contemporary Culture." *New Left Review* 196 (1992): 29–41.

Eribon, Didier. *Michel Foucault*. Trans. Betsy Wing. London: Faber & Faber, 1991.

Etzioni-Halevy, Eva. *The Knowledge Elite and the Failure of Prophecy*. London: Allen & Unwin, 1985.

Foucault, Michel. *The Archaeology of Knowledge*. Trans. A. M. Sheridan Smith. London: Tavistock, 1972.

———. "The Concern for Truth." Trans. John Johnston. *Foucault Live: (Interviews, 1966–84)*. Ed. Sylvère Lotringer. Foreign Agents Ser. New York: Semiotext(e), 1989. 293–308.

———. "The End of the Monarchy of Sex." Trans. Dudley M. Marchi. *Foucault Live: (Interviews, 1966–84)*. Ed. Sylvère Lotringer. Foreign Agents Ser. New York: Semiotext(e), 1989. 137–55.

———. *The History of Sexuality*. Trans. Robert Hurley. Vol. 2. *The Use of Pleasure*. London: Penguin Books, 1986.

———. "How Much Does It Cost for Reason to Tell the Truth?" Trans. Mia Foret and Marion Martius. *Foucault Live: (Interviews, 1966–84)*. Ed. Sylvère Lotringer. Foreign Agents Ser. New York: Semiotext(e), 1989. 233–56.

———. "The Masked Philosopher." Trans. John Johnston. *Foucault Live: (Interviews, 1966–84)*. Ed. Sylvère Lotringer. Foreign Agents Ser. New York: Semiotext(e), 1989. 193–202.

———. "Politics and the Study of Discourse." Trans. Anthony M. Nazzaro. Rev. Colin Gordon. *Ideology and Consciousness* 3 (Spring 1978): 7–26.

———. "Power and Form: Notes." Trans. W. Suchting. *Michel Foucault: Power, Truth, Strategy*. Ed. Meaghan Morris and Paul Patton. Sydney: Feral Publications, 1979. 59–66.

———. "Questions of Method." *The Foucault Effect: Studies in Governmentality*. Ed. Graham Burchill et al. London: Harvester Wheatsheaf, 1991. 73–86.

———. "Truth and Power." Trans. Paul Patton and Meaghan Morris. *Michel Foucault: Power, Truth, Strategy*. Ed. Meaghan Morris and Paul Patton. Sydney: Feral Publications, 1979. 29–48.

———. "What Calls for Punishment?" Trans. John Johnston. *Foucault Live:*

(Interviews, 1966–84). Ed. Sylvère Lotringer. New York: Foreign Agents Ser. Semiotext(e), 1989. 279–92.

Frith, Simon. "Contemporary Culture and the Academy: Notes towards a Research Strategy." *Critical Quarterly* 35.1 (1993): 1–7.

Frith, Simon, and Jon Savage. "Pearls and Swine: Intellectuals and the Mass Media." *New Left Review* 198 (1993): 107–16.

Garfinkel, Harold, and Harvey Sacks. "On Formal Structures of Practical Actions." *Theoretical Sociology: Perspectives and Developments*. Ed. John C. McKinney and Edward A. Tiryakian. New York: Appleton-Century-Crofts-Meredith, 1970. 337–66.

Gouldner, Alvin W. *The Future of Intellectuals and the Rise of the New Class: A Frame of Reference, Theses, Conjectures, Arguments, and an Historical Perspective on the Role of Intellectuals and Intelligentsia in the International Class Contest of the Modern Era*. New York: Continuum, 1979.

Head, Brian. "Introduction: Intellectuals in Australian Society." *Intellectual Movements and Australian Society*. Ed. Brian Head and James Walter. Melbourne: Oxford University Press, 1988. 1–44.

Jameson, Fredric. "On 'Cultural Studies.'" *Social Text* 34 (1993): 17–52.

Macey, David. *The Lives of Michel Foucault*. London: Hutchinson, 1993.

McHoul, Alec. "Con/versation." *Pretending to Communicate*. Ed. Herman Parret. Berlin: Walter de Gruyter, 1993. 196–211.

Miller, James. *The Passion of Michel Foucault*. New York: Simon, 1993.

Miller, Toby. *The Well-Tempered Self: Citizenship, Culture, and the Postmodern Subject*. Baltimore: Johns Hopkins University Press, 1993.

Moran, Albert. "Media Intellectuals." *Intellectual Movements and Australian Society*. Ed. Brian Head and James Walter. Melbourne: Oxford University Press, 1988. 109–26.

Morris, Meaghan, and Paul Patton, eds. Preface to *Michel Foucault: Power, Truth, Strategy*. Sydney: Feral Publications, 1979. 7–10.

Schegloff, Emanuel, and Harvey Sacks. "Opening up Closings." *Semiotica* 8 (1973): 289–327.

N. KATHERINE HAYLES

VOICES OUT OF BODIES,

Audiotape and the Production

BODIES OUT OF VOICES

of Subjectivity

Aurality and print: how is the copula between them to be understood? One signifies a sensory response; the other, a writing technology. The mind struggles to make them equivalent. Should we understand them as hearing and seeing, perhaps? In that case the inclination might be to think of print as a medium dominated by sight, ceding the domain of hearing to other media—radio, phonograph, and tape recorder. The identification of print with sight is strengthened by the close connection between orality (voice producing sound) and aurality (ear hearing sound). Since the influential work of Eric A. Havelock, Walter J. Ong, Elizabeth Eisenstein, and Marshall McLuhan, among others, it is almost impossible not to think of aurality and print as designations for cultural epochs that stand in contrast, if not opposition, to one another.[1] Orality is succeeded by print; print, by secondary orality. We know the story, and it is a good story. But I think there is another story to be told, one that would see aurality and writing not as indicating separate domains but as suggesting a bodily response to certain literary possibilities.

This story has long been implicit in the study of poetry, for one can hardly discuss poems without talking about the sound effects associated with them. It was not until Garrett Stewart's groundbreaking work *Reading Voices: Literature and the Phonotext*, however, that the implications of associating aurality with print began to unfold. Stewart begins by asking not how we read or why we read but where we read. We read, he decides, in the body, particularly in the vocal apparatus that produces subvocalization during silent reading. This subvocalization is essential to literary language. The literariness of the language is achieved by surrounding its utterances with a shimmer of virtual sounds, homophonic variants that suggest alternative readings to the words actually printed on the page. Subvocalization actualizes these possibilities in the body and makes them available for interpretation. Several interesting consequences flow from this argument. First, the bodily enactment of suppressed sound plays a central role in the reading process. Second, reading is akin to the interior monologue that we all engage in, except that it supplies us with another story (usually a more interesting one) than that we manufacture for ourselves to assure ourselves we exist. Third, the production of subvocalized sound may be as important to subjectivity as it is to literary language.[2]

We are now in a position to think about what tape recording means for certain literary texts. Audiotape opens the possibility that the voice can be taken out of the body and placed into a machine. If the production of subvocalized sound is essential to reading literary texts, what happens to literature when the voice—not any voice, but one's own voice—comes from the machine? Can the tape recorder be understood as a surrogate body? In that case, does the body become a tape recorder? Is the interior monologue a recording played on the body-as-tape-recorder? What happens if this interior monologue is externalized and made into a tape played on another recorder, mechanical or organic? What happens to the stories we and others tell if the production of these stories is no longer situated in the body's subvocalizations but in the machine? Often histories of technology and literature treat the impact of technology as a theme or subject to be represented within the world of the text. I take a different approach. By focusing on the production of sound within the body and within the machine, I hope to understand how audiotape functioned not only as a theme, a metaphor, or a vehicle for expression but as a mode of relation that produced a certain kind of postmodern subjectivity. Fractured by temporal dislocations and riven by disconcerting metamorphoses, this evolving subjectivity emerges from the instabilities produced when voices are taken out of bodies and bodies find themselves out of voices.

Audiotape and Its Cultural Niche

Born in the early 1900s and coming of age after World War II, audiotape may already be reaching old age, fading from the marketplace as it is replaced by compact disks, computer hypermedia, and the like. The period when audiotape played an important role in U.S. and European consumer culture may well be limited to the four decades of 1950–90. At the end of this period, interest turns to the integration of magnetic tape into other media; at the beginning, the interesting story concerns the new possibilities tape made available for cultural production and representation. It is this story that will occupy us here.

Long after writing dissociated presence from inscription, voice continued to imply a subject who was present in the moment and in the flesh. Audiotape was of course not the first technology to challenge this assumption, and the cultural work it did can best be understood in the context of related audio technologies, particularly telephone, radio, and phonograph. Telephone and radio broke the link between presence and voice by making it possible to transport voice over distance.[3] Prior to audiotape and phonograph, however, these media happened in the present. Speaker and listener, although physically separated, had to share the same moment in time. Telephone and radio thus continued to participate in the phenomenology of presence through the simultaneity that they produced and that produced them. In this sense they were more like each other than either was like the phonograph. By contrast, the phonograph functioned primarily as a technology of inscription, reproducing sound through a rigid disk that allowed neither the interactive spontaneity of telephone nor the ephemerality of radio.

The niche that audiotape filled was configured through the interlocking qualities of the audio technologies that preceded it. Like the phonograph, audiotape was a technology of inscription, but with the crucial difference that it permitted erasure and rewriting. As early as 1888 Oberlin Smith, at one time president of the American Society of Mechanical Engineers, proposed that sound could be recorded by magnetizing iron particles that adhered to a carrier.[4] He was too busy to implement his idea, however, and the ball passed to Valdemar Poulsen, a young Danish engineer who accidentally discovered that patterns traced on the side of a magnetized tuning fork became visible when the fork was dipped in iron powder. When the fork was demagnetized, the patterns were erased. He saw in the imprinting and erasure of these patterns the possibility of a recording device for sound, using iron wire as the carrier. Its immediate commercial use, he imagined, would lie in providing tangible records of telephone conversations. He called the device a "Telegraphone," which he understood to signify "writing the voice at a distance." At the 1900 Paris Exposition he won the Grand Prix for his invention.[5] Despite extensive publicity, he was not able to raise the necessary capital for its development in Europe. By 1903 the patents had passed to the American Telegraphone Company, which raised a huge amount of money ($5 million) selling stock. Five years later they had still not built a single machine. Their main business, in fact, turned out to be raising money for the machines rather than actually producing them. When they did finally turn out a few operational devices in 1911, using the famous model Phoebe Snow to advertise them as dictation machines, the sound quality was so bad that the Dupont Company, after installing them in a central dictation system, ended up suing. The questionable status of the machines was exacerbated when, during World War I, the Telefunken Company of America was accused of using them to encode and transmit secret messages to Germany. From the beginning, audiotape was marked with the imprint of international capitalism and politics as surely as it was with the imprint of voices.

By 1932 steel tape had become the carrier of choice in high-end machines, and the BBC became actively interested in its development, using it to carry the Christmas address of King George V that year. Film tape, created by coating paper or plastic tape with iron oxide and feeding it through a ring-shaped head, appeared on the scene by 1935 (Lubeck 79–111). The great advantage of film tape was that it could be easily spliced, but originally it had such poor sound quality it could not compete with steel tape. The problem of establishing good correspondence between sound frequency and the pattern on film tape (that is, controlling hysteresis) was partly solved by the introduction of high-frequency bias in 1938.[6] By 1941 the sound quality of film tape had improved so that it was competitive with steel tape in studio work. On the consumer market, machines with wire were still common. It was not until after World War II that systematic research was carried out on finding the optimum coating material for film tape, and only in 1948 was the first American patent issued for a magnetic recording machine using film tape and a ring head. The use of film tape expanded rapidly after that, and within a decade it had rendered steel tape obsolete, expanding through the consumer market as well as the professional studios.

By the late 1950s, then, magnetic tape had acquired the qualities that, within the existing cultural formation, gave it the force of paradox. It was a mode of voice inscription at once permanent and mutable, repeating past moments exactly yet also permitting interventions in the present that radically altered its form and meaning. These interventions could, moreover, be done at home by anyone who had the appropriate equipment. Whereas the phonograph produced objects that could be consumed only in their manufactured form, magnetic tape allowed the consumer to be a producer as well. The switches activating the powerful and paradoxical technoconceptual actors of repetition and mutation, presence and time delay, were in the hands of the masses, at least the masses who could afford the equipment.

When these qualities of audiotape are enacted within dramatic and literary productions, a complex interplay is set up between their representational codes and the specificities of the technology. Books and bodies have a long tradition of being imaged in terms of each other. For certain texts after 1950, the body became a tape recorder. When voice, historically linked with presence and therefore with the immanence of the body, was displaced onto tape, the body metonymically participated in the transformations voice underwent in this medium. If voice could be transported through time and spliced in with different sounds, the body-as-tape-recorder could also undergo time delay and mutation. Two texts, written when film tape recorders began to appear on the popular market, illustrate the permutations that result when the body figures as a tape recorder.

In Samuel Beckett's 1958 play *Krapp's Last Tape*, Krapp on his sixty-ninth birthday listens to a tape of himself on his thirty-ninth birthday, made when he has just finished listening to a tape of himself at twenty-nine, or thereabouts. The recorded thirty-nine-year-old voice scorns the illusions of the twenty-nine-year-old and has his pretensions ridiculed in turn by the old man at sixty-nine. This complex temporal layering is further complicated by the different modes in which the three Krapps manifest themselves. The twenty-nine-year-old is the most attenuated presence, a shadowy echo heard only in the paraphrases and judgments that the thirty-nine-year-old pronounces. The middle-aged Krapp has a more vivid sense of presence, existing as a still-vibrant voice on the tape recorder, subject however to the interventions of his successor as the sixty-nine-year-old edits and replays to suit himself. The old man has the strongest sense of presence, produced through the embodied practices of articulation, gesture, posture, and movement of the actor who plays him. Following a logic of displacement and replication, the drama unfolds through a series of binary oppositions that uneasily jostle one another without being resolved or integrated. At the center of these oppositions is a stage image emblematic in its force: an old man sits motionless in a cone of light surrounded by darkness, his ear glued to the tape recorder. The image burns into consciousness the realization that body and voice no longer necessarily go together. Voice can persist through time outside the body, confronting the subject as an externalized other.

Burroughs's *The Ticket That Exploded*, written four years after Beckett's play, envisions even more radical possibilities for the body-as-tape-recorder. "Language is a virus," the narrator asserts, and the text draws extensively on the Buddhist-inspired idea that one's sense of selfhood is maintained through an internal monologue, which is nothing other than the story the self tells to assure itself that it exists. Woven into this story are the fictions that society wants its members to believe; the monologue enacts self-discipline as well as self-creation. The text proposes to stop the interior monologue by making it external and mechanical, specifically by recording it on tape and subjecting the recording to various manipulations. "Communication must become total and conscious before we can stop it," the narrator asserts (51). Yet splicing tape is far from innocuous. Once someone's vocalizations and body sounds are spliced into someone else's, the effects can feed back into the bodies, setting off a riot of mutations. The tape recorder acts both as a metaphor for these mutations and as the instrumentality that brings them about. The taped body can separate at the vertical "divide line," grotesquely becoming half one person and half another, as if it were tape spliced lengthwise. In a disturbingly literal sense the tape recorder becomes a two-edged sword, cutting through bodies as well as through the programs that control and discipline them.

Considered together, the two texts have an interesting symmetry. In *Krapp's Last Tape* the emphasis is on time delay. Over time the voice is taken out of the body and displaced into the machine, leaving the body finally without voice. In *The Ticket That Exploded* the emphasis is on mutation. Through mutation, voices produce the bodies they inhabit. In this context "bodies out of voices" does not indicate silence but its reverse, an interior monologue that infests the body and replicates through it to create physical changes and mutations within it. In part these differences result from the different temperaments and orientations of the two writers. In part they reflect the differences between drama and narrative fiction. Drama produces and is produced through bodies physically present onstage. Sound comes not through subvocalization but directly through the auditory channel. When the body onstage in *Krapp's Last Tape* no longer speaks, the physical location of the voice shifts into the machine. In narrative fiction, by contrast, the suppressed speech of subvocalization generates the bodies that the reader visualizes within the represented world of the text. In this sense the bodies in the text do indeed emerge from voices that are located not in them but somewhere else, in a realm that intersects their world but exists, so to speak, in another dimension.[7] Both texts thus enact the possibilities and constraints of their genres as well as the agendas of their authors. Setting them side by side gives a richer sense of what it means to have voices out of bodies and bodies out of voices than would be possible if only one genre were considered. In the sections that follow, I explore these dynamics in more detail.

Krapp's Last Tape:
When Is a Voice Not a Body?

Krapp's Last Tape was born at the crossroads where radio met tape. When Beckett's radio play *All That Fall* had an even worse reception on its second Paris broadcast than the first received, the recording tapes were sent to Beckett, since the studio did not anticipate using them again. He therefore had in his possession the tape recordings, drawing his attention, we may suppose, to this new medium. Meanwhile, Donald McWhinnie had heard Patrick McGee read a small part in the 1957 BBC production of *All That Fall*. He was so struck by McGee's "curious cracked voice" that he suggested to Beckett that McGee might read portions of *Molloy* and *Malone Dies* on BBC's Third Programme (Knowlson, "Beginnings" 46). The readings were successful, prompting George Devine, then planning the English-language premiere of *Endgame*, to ask Beckett to write a monologue for Patrick McGee as a companion piece. In March 1958 Beckett wrote to McWhinnie, telling him that the proposed monologue would involve a tape recorder. He asked McWhinnie to send operating instructions, so that he could have some sense of how a recorder worked as he crafted his play. These events led Martin Esslin to surmise that "*Krapp's Last Tape* owes its existence both to Beckett's discovery of the fascinations of tape recording . . . and to his discovery of McGee as an ideal embodiment of characters like Molloy" (Esslin 42).

In 1958 magnetic tape was a novelty in Britain, as McWhinnie makes clear in an interview: "We were still operating mainly on discs at the BBC and tape was a comparatively new thing then. . . . When Sam wrote *Krapp's Last Tape*, I don't think he knew for a minute how the mechanics of the thing worked. In fact, when we came to do it [in October 1958] even then we had to say 'how are we going to operate this device?'" (Knowlson, "Beginnings" 46–47). Roy Walker recalls the impact that making a BBC recording had on him during this period: "Anyone who has made a BBC recording and been in on the editing session may emerge feeling that he can no longer call himself his own. Cuts and transpositions can be and are made. Halves of sentences spoken at different times can be amalgamated to let a speaker hear himself say the opposite of what he knows he said. Hearing oneself say something and continue with something else said half an hour earlier can be peculiarly disconcerting. You might have the feeling that if you went quickly out of the studio you might catch yourself coming in" (49). His language locates the disconcerting effect both in the time delay ("sentences spoken at different times can be amalgamated") and in the disjunction between voice and presence ("he can no longer call himself his own"). He sees the tape recorder as a solution to "a problem that baffled the experimental playwrights between the wars," namely how to represent the internal monologue that constitutes consciousness, with all of its ephemerality, multivocality, and obsessive repetitions. Perhaps, he muses, "the epiphenomena of consciousness could be revealed by bringing the recorder on stage. *Krapp's Last Tape* transforms a playback into a play" (49).

As Walker's aphorism hints, the play is structured by the binary opposition between the presence of Krapp onstage and the mechanical reproduction through the tape recorder of his voice in earlier times. Complex patterns of replication and difference are set up between the two voices, resulting in sounds and movements that echo between them in almost musical fashion. The voices themselves sound eerily like an echo, for the actor who plays Krapp also makes the recording. Jean Martin, who played Krapp in the 1975 Paris production, explains that "you must choose either to change the voice of the actor playing the old Krapp or change the voice on the recording made by the younger Krapp. . . . I chose as a solution to keep my normal voice for the Krapp of thirty years ago. And when acting I made the voice of the later Krapp a little older, a little heavier, and a little slower" (Knowlson, *Theatrical Notebooks* 82). The play between the voices is an aural invitation to the audience to speculate on differences and similarities, across time and technology, even before the voices articulate words and sentences. Articulation then gives structure and content to these speculations.

Consider, for example, the five laughs and their orchestration, as Krapp and the tape sometimes laugh together, sometimes not. The first laugh on tape, in which Krapp joins, comes when the voice of thirty-nine-year-old Krapp laughs at his twenty-nine-year-old incarnation. "Hard to believe I was ever that young whelp. The voice! Jesus! And the aspirations!"[8] Surely the voice that the sixty-nine-year-old finds humorous is not that of the twenty-nine-year-old, which he has not heard, but the voice of the thirty-nine-year-old. Thus he laughs partly with the taped voice, partly at him. "And the resolutions!" (l. 106), the taped voice continues, resulting in a second laugh together. But when the voice specifies, "to drink less, in particular" (l. 107), the sixty-nine-year-old laughs alone, knowing that thirty years later he is still timing his drinks in an effort to keep them to a reasonable level. The thirty-nine-year-old, summarizing the tape he has just heard, announces themes that will be echoed in his own tape: a "less engrossing" sexuality; a parent's death; the "flagging pursuit of happiness"; "unattainable laxation"; the sneers of an older man at his younger self (the twenty-nine-year-old, we learn, sneered at his "youth" as a time he had outgrown);

and the "opus . . . magnum." "Closing with a"—the tape laughs briefly alone, in anticipation of the coming joke—"yelp to Providence," precipitating a "prolonged laugh" from both voices (ll. 110–15). Both laugh at their younger selves, and both continue with the same follies and obsessions.

At the root of these obsessions is a series of binary divisions that Krapp has made in his life, setting up a line of Hobson's choices—between the magnum opus and love, between his desire for discipline and his weakness for bananas and drink, between his admiration for the eyes and breasts of women and his fear of becoming entangled with them, between the dark that, at thirty-nine, he thought he understood and the light that creates the zone he inhabits within his den. In the tape recordings he creates another binary, between voice as technological object and body as presence. For the writer who could imagine a limbless body in a jar, its only mobility the stream of thoughts issuing from it, the spectacle of a motionless body, glued to the machine from which a voice is speaking, must have been particularly striking. In his directions to the actor, Beckett divided the instructions between "Motionlessness Listening," "Agitation Listening," and "Nonlistening." He emphasized that Krapp should remain absolutely motionless during his listening, concentrating his (and consequently the audience's) attention on the machine. When he becomes impatient and agitated, activity comes in a quick burst and then, just as abruptly, switches back to motionlessness, as if he too were a machine with a binary on-off switch.[9]

The immobility of Krapp as he listens establishes a powerful tension between the aural and the visible, between presence as technologically mediated voice and presence as embodiment. Pierre Chabert, in his excellent essay "Samuel Beckett as Director," writes about what Krapp's immobility means for the actor: "One of the most exciting aspects of the acting consists in passing the mobility of expression through the immobility of the mask. The voice is inscribed, imprinted on the face" (96). This physical imprinting of sound on the body visually demonstrates that aurality has material effects. The point is heightened by the many aspects of the production chosen for the sound effects they created. In the Schiller-Theater Werkstatt production in Berlin in 1969, for example, Beckett replaced the cardboard boxes that originally held the tape spools with tins, so that when Krapp bangs them on the table or sweeps them impatiently to the floor, they make a metallic crash reminiscent of the tape recorder's metallic parts. Krapp also signals his attention to the sound of words, independent of their meaning. "Spooooool," he intones not once but three times, pronouncing his enjoyment of the sound "the happiest moment of the past half million." Even the laughs show attention to sound as a structuring element in itself, apart from its representational function. Commenting on the productions in which Beckett was actively involved, James Knowlson remarks in his introduction to *Theatrical Notebooks* that "Beckett was far more interested in the rhythm and the shape of the five various laughs as they interrelate one to another than with any imitation of realistic laughs" (xxvii). The emphasis on aurality sets up an implicit ontology in which sound has a physical presence in the world. Sound is being, this dynamic suggests, no less than visible objects are being.

The dynamic authorizes two presences onstage: one a voice situated in a human body, the other a voice situated in a machine. The machine-voice echoes the body-voice but also differs from it, not only because of the medium that produces it but also because of the temporality registered within it. Presence and voice are thus broken apart and put together in new ways. Presence can now mean physicality or sound, and voice can be embodied in either a machine or a body. Over time, the voice in the body is displaced into the machine; over time, the body as lived experience is sedimented into the physical organism but leaves its trace on the technologically reproduced voice as well.

Amidst this play of reproduction and displacement, the binary oppositions that make up Krapp's world take shape. His method of dealing with the world is symbolized by the cone of light thrown over his work table, surrounded by darkness. "The new light above my table is a great improvement," the thirty-nine-year-old voice announces. "With all this darkness round me I feel less alone. (Pause.) I love to get up and move about in it, then back here to . . . (hesitates) me. (Pause.) Krapp" (1. 76–78). He identifies his subjectivity as having a defined locus—the light—which is set off from an environment related to it through the binary opposition of dark and light. The stage setting confirms that this way of constructing his subjectivity has not changed in three decades; the lamp still hangs, the darkness still surrounds. If anything, his strategy of encapsulation has become more pronounced with time, for within the "den" there is now another den, the cubbyhole to which Krapp retreats to take periodic drinks and retrieve the ledger.[10] In the San Quentin production, the lighting was arranged so Krapp's shadow was thrown against the cubbyhole wall, setting up another register across which presence and sound, dissociation and reassembly, could play. The point is further reinforced by the play's verbal and visual imagery: Krapp's white shoes and rusty black trousers; the black electrical cord coming out from the wall and connecting to the white lead of the recorder; the black ball the thirty-nine-year-old Krapp recalls throwing to a white dog; the dark nurse he sees in her white starched uniform, pushing a black perambulator; and the darkness that the middle-aged Krapp imagines he has finally come to terms with rather than rejected, an accommodation he sees as the basis for his master work.

At sixty-nine Krapp records the failure of this work: "seventeen copies sold, of which eleven at trade price to free circulating libraries beyond the seas. Getting known" (ll. 232–36). As Bernard F. Dukore has pointed out, Krapp is constipated intellectually as well as physically; his books do not circulate (147). The failure, of course, is not only of the work but of the life, resulting not so much from the choices he has made as from the construction of his life as a series of choices between binary opposites. If he wants to engage in serious work, he must say farewell to love; if he wants to embrace the darkness, he should turn away from light; if he wants to develop his mind, he should disassociate from the body. Now onstage there is another binary, the voice in the tape recorder and the body that strains motionless to hear it. Beckett conceived of the tape recorder as the "companion of [Krapp's] solitude," functioning both as a site for his projections and as a "masturbatory object" (Knowlson, *Theatrical Notebooks* 181). The emotions that Krapp feels toward the voice—his impatience with its pretensions, his attraction to the girl in the punt—are transferred onto the tape recorder itself. "Tape recorder relationship both fundamental and almost impossible to convey through the acting without descending to the level of the sentimental," Beckett wrote. At all costs, he did not want Krapp's attachment to the machine to be overplayed. He directed the actor to express erotic attachment through "just a few looks and some movements of the hands, his left hand for tenderness . . . as he switches on for example, and both hands to express irritation" (Knowlson, *Theatrical Notebooks* 181). Separated from the body and reattached to the machine, the voice invites a fetishistic reification of technology.

In his final tape, Krapp turns toward the choices he rejected. Now he is fascinated by the seemingly peripheral story of the girl in the punt, not the dramatic announcement of the grand work. The machine-voice recalls how the girl shut her eyes against the sun, isolated within another dichotomy of light and dark. Only when he stands in front of her, creating a mediating zone of shade, does she open her eyes and "let me in."[11] The lyrical beauty of their union in the boat, amidst the gently moving water, suggests a road not taken, a way of being not constructed through the relentless binary logic that has governed Krapp's life. But at the time Krapp must have thought of it as a dead end, for he has just told the girl it is "hopeless and no good going on" (ll. 200–201). In fact, the interlude may be possible for him precisely because it is bracketed by this announcement. Since he has decided the relationship is not going anywhere, he can let down his guard and "be again," as the elder Krapp momentarily yearns to do before he decides he does not want to repeat the past. At that moment he breaks with his tradition of making a recording on his birthday, wrenching the reel containing his tape off the machine and throwing it away in disgust.

No longer interested in inscribing onto tape how his life looks to him now, Krapp turns silently toward the machine. Although his lips move, he will not speak again in the play.[12] The significance of the moment is underscored by Pierre Chabert: "Is not this separation—the voiceless body listening—the image of a form of dispossession, a dispossession of the body by speech, by the voice?" (103). When Krapp rewinds the recording so he can listen again to the voice tell of the girl in the punt, it is not clear whether he is attracted to the story because he thinks of it as the other choice he might have made (in which case he remains within binaries) or whether he glimpses the possibility of escaping from the constructions that have defined him. Whatever significance the story has, it no longer has the power to change his life. For, as the play's title reminds us, this is Krapp's *last* tape. Beckett's directions call for the actor, at certain moments, to glance backward into the dark. These glances, Beckett confided, represent an unconscious search for death. As the play ends and the light fades, only the red eye of the recorder remains visible. Beckett thought of the play as ending at the penultimate moment. When morning comes, Krapp will be dead.

Drama of course requires incorporation to be fully realized; only when the dramatic text is enacted through the particular instantiations of a performance does it come to life. As a performing art, drama not only presupposes but continually enacts the link between body and voice. *Krapp's Last Tape* demonstrates how the shape of a life—and the shape of the genre—can be affected when body and voice no longer imply each other. With narrative fiction the dynamics are necessarily different, for the author no longer has at his disposal the visual production of the body onstage. By the same token, neither is he constrained by forms that can be physically represented onstage. Burroughs had four years more than Beckett to become familiar with the tape recorder, and there is no question that he knew perfectly well how to operate the machine. In fact, he operated it in ways the manufacturer probably never imagined. On intimate terms with the body of the machine, he took seriously the possibilities for the tape-recorder-as-body. Following a logic of reciprocity, he also reasoned that the body can become a tape recorder. The voice can then be resituated in the body, not as a naturalized union of voice and presence but as a mechanical production that has the frightening ability to appropriate the body's vocal apparatus and use it for ends alien to the self. Nowhere are the intense ambiguities of the metaphoric slippage between recorders and bodies explored more powerfully than in Burroughs's *The Ticket That Exploded*, to which we now turn.

The Ticket That Exploded:
Tape Recorder as God's Little Machine

In *The Ticket That Exploded*, the body is a site for contestation and resistance on many levels, as metaphor, physical reality, linguistic construct, and last but hardly least, tape recorder. The tape recorder is central to understanding Burroughs's vision of how the politics of cooptation works. Entwined into human flesh are "pre-recordings" that function as parasites to take over the organism. These pre-recordings may be thought of as social conditioning—for example, an "American upper middle-class upbringing with maximum sexual frustration and humiliations imposed by Middle-Western matriarchs" (139), which not coincidentally matches Burroughs's own experience. A strong sense of sexual nausea pervades the text, and sexuality is another manifestation of pre-recording. Parodically rewriting the fable in Plato's *Symposium* about the spherical beings who were cut in half to make humans, resulting in incomplete beings who spend their days searching for their other halves, the narrator asserts that "all human sex is this unsanitary arrangement whereby two entities attempt to occupy the same three-dimensional coordinate points giving rise to the sordid latrine brawls. . . . It will be readily understandable that a program of systematic frustration was necessary in order to sell this crock of sewage as Immortality, and Garden of Delights, and *love*" (52).[13]

The idea of two entities trying to occupy the same space is further reinforced by the vertical "divide line" crossing the body, the physically marked line in bone, muscle, and skin where the neural canal of the month-old fetus closes to create the beginnings of the torso. The early point at which the divide line is imprinted on human flesh suggests how deeply implicated into the organism are the pre-recordings that socialize it into community norms. In one scene the narrator sees his body "on an operating table split down the middle," while a "doctor with forceps was extracting crab parasites from his brain and spine—and squeezing green fish parasites from the separated flesh" (85). "My God what a mess," the doctor exclaims. "The difficulty is with two halves—other parasites will invade sooner or later. . . . Sew him up nurse" (85). As the doctor intimates, when the body is always already fallen, divided within itself rather than an organic unity, it is subject to occupation and expropriation by a variety of parasitic forms, both cultural and physical.

Chief among these is "the word." It is a truism in contemporary theory that discursive formations can have material effects in the physical world. Without having read Foucault and Derrida, Burroughs came to similar conclusions a decade earlier, imagining the word as the body's "Other Half." "Word is an organism. The presence of the 'Other Half' a separate organism attached to your nervous system on an air line of words can now be demonstrated experimentally" (49). The experiments to which the narrator alludes were performed, among others, by John Cunningham Lilly, who in the late 1950s and 1960s used isolation tanks to test the malleability of human perception.[14] The experiments required subjects to enter a dark tank and float in water kept at body temperature, cut off from all sensory input. The narrator mentions that a common "hallucination" of subjects in sense withdrawal was "the feeling of another body sprawled through the subject's body at an angle" (49). "Yes quite an angle," the narrator ironically remarks, identifying the sensation as the subject's perception of the " 'other half,' " the word virus that invades the organism until it seems as intrinsic to the body as flesh and bone.

For the narrator, the proof of this parasitic invasion and infection is the interior monologue we all experience. "Modern man has lost the option of silence," he asserts. "Try to achieve even ten seconds of inner silence. You will encounter a resisting organism that *forces you to talk*. That organism is the word" (49–50). In a more than trivial sense the Other Half is present in the text from the beginning, for the narrative starts with an account of a journey made by inseparable companions. "We are the only riders," the narrator remarks. "So that is how we have come to know each other so well that the sound of his voice and his image flickering over the tape recorder are as familiar to me as the movement of my intestines the sound of my breathing the beating of my heart" (1). So entwined has the word become into the flesh of the narrator that "my body is convinced that my breathing and heart will stop if his voice stops" (3). Later the narrator remarks that if someone believes that his very life depends on maintaining his interior monologue, in a self-fulfilling prophecy he may indeed die if it stops (160). The text can be understood as a prophylactic designed to defeat this belief.

Burroughs's project is to offer the reader as many ways as he can imagine to stop the monologue, rewrite or erase the pre-recordings, and extricate the subject from the parasitic invasion of the Other Half. Tape recorders are central to this project; "it's all done with tape recorders," the narrator comments (162). One strategy is to "externalize dialogue" by getting "it out of your head and into the machines" (163). He suggests the reader record the last argument he or she had with his or her boyfriend or girlfriend;

the reader's side is recorded on one machine and the friend's on the other. Then the two recorders can argue with each other, leaving the human participants free to stop replaying the conversation in their heads and get on with their lives. The narrator also suggests recording random sounds on a third machine—snippets from a news broadcast, say—and mixing them in, too. The intrusion of the random element is significant; it aims to free the reader not only from personal obsessions but from the culturally constructed envelope of surrounding sounds and words. "Wittgenstein said: 'No proposition can contain itself as an argument,'" the narrator remarks, interpreting this to mean, "The only thing *not* prerecorded in a prerecorded universe is the prerecording itself which is to say *any* recording that contains a random factor" (166).

The intrusion of randomness is important in another way as well, for Burroughs is acutely aware of the danger that he might, through his words, spread the viral infection he is trying to combat. It is important, therefore, that disruptive techniques be instantiated within the text's own language. These techniques range from his famous use of the "cut-up," where he physically cuts up previously written narratives and arbitrarily splices them together, to more subtle methods like shifting between different linguistic registers without transition or explanation.[15] Perhaps the single most important device is the insistent pressure to take metaphors literally—or put another way, the tendency to erase the distinction between words and things. Language is not merely like a virus; it *is* a virus, replicating through the host to become visible as green fish in the flesh and crab parasites tearing at the base of spine and brain. In Burroughs the material effects of language do not need to be mediated through physical discipline to reform the body, as, for example, the prescribed postures and gestures did that constituted instruction in penmanship in the eighteenth and nineteenth centuries. With a writer's license, he makes language erupt directly into the body. The body itself, moreover, is treated as if it physically were a recorder, regulated by the principles that govern magnetic tape in its reproduction, erasure, and reconfiguration.

The pressure toward literalization can be seen in the parts of the narrative that use the conventions of science fiction to figure the invasion of the word as a physical operation (early on the narrator announces, "I am reading a science fiction book called *The Ticket That Exploded*" [5]). In this track the earth has been invaded by the alien Nova mob, so-called because their strategy is to drive the planet to extreme chaos, or "nova." The mob includes creatures such as heavy metal addicts from Uranus, sex addicts from Venus, and other parasitic organisms that can occupy human flesh. "Nova criminals are not three-dimensional organisms—(though they are quite definite organisms as we shall see)—but they need three-dimensional human agents to operate" (57). A single parasitic alien can take over hundreds of humans, stringing together its hosts to form rows of "coordinate points," analogous to lines of print or to phonemes subordinated through grammar and syntax. The reputed leader of the mob is an appropriately bimorphic creature called variously "Mr Bradly Mr Martin," "Mr and Mrs D," or simply "the Ugly spirit." In this instantiation of the Other Half, the word itself is split down the middle.

A counterinvasion has been staged by the Nova police, who use as weapons radio static, "camera guns" that destabilize images by vibrating them at supersonic speeds, and, of course, tape recorders. Recruiting "Mr. Lee" (a pseudonym Burroughs often uses—Lee was his mother's maiden name), the district supervisor tells him that he will receive his instructions "from books, street signs, films, in some cases from agents who purport to be and may actually be members of the organization. There is no certainty. Those who need certainty are of no interest to this department. This is in point of fact a *non-organization* the aim of which is to immunize our agents against fear despair and death. We intend to break the birth-death cycle" (10). One of the criminals they seek is Johnny Yen, whose name suggests sexual desire. "Death *is* orgasm *is* rebirth *is* death in orgasm *is* their unsanitary Venusian gimmick *is* the whole birth death cycle of action," the narrator explains. He proceeds, apparently exasperated, to make his point even more obvious. "You got it?—Now do you understand who Johnny Yen is?—The Boy-Girl Other Half strip tease God of sexual frustration—Errand boy from the death trauma" (53).

In this track, the action can be read as a physical contest between the Nova mob and the Nova police, as when a police operative from Minraud blows a mob crab guard into smithereens. But if the word is a parasite with material effects, the distinction between metaphor and actuality, representation and reality, is moot. Thus another strategy of resistance is the "Rewrite Room," the space from which comes the exposé of Johnny Yen cited above. Johnny Yen is not blown away but rewritten to become a rather enchanting green fish boy, an amphibious life form (a benign bimorphic creature) living in the canals and mating with Ali the street boy in a nonhuman life cycle that destabilizes the human sense of what constitutes the body, life, and death.

This destabilization can be threatening as well as liberating, for the narrative attempts to put into play all the boundaries that define human subjectivity. Body boundaries are often literally disintegrated—for example, by the Sex Skin, an organism that surrounds its victims with a second skin that gives them intense sexual pleasure while dissolving and ingesting them. Positioned against the clear threat of this kind of sexual delirium are tape recorders, potentially liberating but also not without danger. Recording one's body sounds and splicing them in someone else's can free one from the illusion that body sounds cannot exist apart from the interior monologue. But just as Burroughs's words can become parasitic if not self-disrupted, so these sounds have the potential to constitute a parasitic monologue in turn. According to the narrator, the splicing produces a strong erotic reaction. If it is expressed in actual sexual contact, "it acts as an aphrodisiac . . . nothing more. . . . But when a susceptible subject is spliced in with someone *who is not there* then it acts as a destructive virus," ironically becoming the phenomenon it was meant to counteract (20).

As well as disrupting words audibly present, Burroughs wants to create—or expose—new ones from the substrata of the medium itself. He describes experiments based on "inching tape," manually rubbing the tape back and forth across the head at varying speeds. "Such exercises bring you a liberation from old association locks. . . . You will hear words that were not in the original recording new words made by the machine different people will scan out different words of course but some of the words are quite clearly there" (206). The technique gives new meaning to McLuhan's aphorism that "the medium is the message," for it is "as if the words themselves had been interrogated and forced to reveal their hidden meanings it is interesting to record these words words literally made by the machine itself" (206).

Burroughs actually performed the tape recorder experiments he describes from the late 1950s through the late 1970s. He inched tape to create, as he heard it, new words; he recorded radio broadcasts and spliced the tape to achieve an aural cut-up; and he held the microphone to the base of his throat and tried to record his own subvocal speech. As if anticipating Christian fundamentalists who hear Satanic messages hidden in records and tapes (and whose sensibilities he would no doubt enjoy outraging), he also read from his books, including *The Nova Express* and *The Ticket That Exploded,* and spliced the readings in with music played backward. The recordings have been preserved, and some of this archival material has been collected in a phonograph album titled *Nothing Here Now but the Recordings.* Late one night I traveled to the music library at the University of California at San Diego to hear it.[16] Even though the experience of sitting in the nearly deserted high-tech facility, insulated from exterior sound, was eerily conducive to hearing the words Burroughs claims are there, some of the passages are clearly of historic interest only. The section recording subvocal speech, in particular, is virtually unintelligible as patterned sound. Perhaps paradoxically, I found the recording less forceful than his writing as a demonstration of Burroughs's theories. For me, the aurality of his prose elicits a greater response than the machine productions it describes and instantiates.

The power of that writing is evident in the "writing machine" section. The narrator describes an "Exhibition," which includes "a room with metal walls magnetic mobiles under flickering blue light and smell of ozone" (62). The room is situated, of course, inside a tape recorder. Normally narrative fiction leaps over the technologies that produce it (printing press, paper, ink) and represents the external world as if this act of representation did not require a material basis for its production. Burroughs turns this convention inside out, locating the "external" world *inside* the technological artifact. The move constructs a completely different relation between fiction and the material means of its production, constituting the technology as the ground upon which and out of which the narrative action evolves. As spectators clink through turnstiles, "great sheets of magnetized print held color and disintegrated in cold mineral silence as word dust falls from demagnetized patterns" (62). The description hints at the attraction the recorder has for Burroughs. Sound, unlike print, dies away unless it is constantly renewed. Its ephemerality calls forth a double response that finds material expression in the technology. On one hand, magnetic tape allows sound to be preserved over time; in this respect it counters sound's ephemerality. On the other hand, inscriptions can be easily erased and reconfigured; in this sense, it reproduces sound's impermanence. Burroughs was drawn to both aspects of the technology. The inscription of sound in a durable medium suited his belief that the word is material, while its malleability meant that interventions were possible that could radically change or eradicate the record.

At the Exhibition, language is inscribed through "word dust" that falls from the walls as easily as smog particles from the Los Angeles sky. Anticipating the rise of video tape, Burroughs imagines that "picture dust" also falls from the walls. "Photomontage fragments backed with iron stuck to patterns and fell in swirls mixing with color dust to form new patterns, shimmering, falling, magnetized, demagnetized to the flicker of blue cylinders pulsing neon tubes and globes" (62–63). When the Nova police counter-invade the planet, "falling" phrases repeatedly appear, as if they were news bulletins read over and over on the radio: "Word falling—Photo falling—Time falling—Break through in Grey Room" (104); "Shift linguals—Cut word lines—Vibrate tourists—Free doorways—Pinball led streets—Word falling—Photo falling—Break through in Grey Room—Towers, open fire" (104); "cut all tape" (105); "Break through in Grey Room—'Love' is falling—

Sex word is falling—Break photograph—Shift body halves" (105). The Grey Room evidently refers to the mob's communication and control center, perhaps the "board room" where, the narrator tells us, multinationals plot to take over outer and inner space.

In opposition to the linear centralized control of the Grey Room is the chaotic recursivity of the Exhibition. Here there is no clear line between those who act and those who are acted upon. The traffic flow in the room is structured like a recursive loop. As the spectators pass, they are recorded "by a battery of tape recorders recording and playing back moving on conveyor belts and tracks and cable cars spilling the talk and metal music fountains and speech as the recorders moved from one exhibit to another" (64). "Since the recorders and movies of the exhibition are in constant operation it will be readily seen that any spectator appears on the screen sooner or later if not today then yesterday or tomorrow," the narrator remarks parenthetically (64). Thus spectators move along within the room, hearing and watching recordings of themselves played from machines that are also moving along a conveyor belt. Their reactions as they hear and watch are also recorded in turn by other machines, creating an infinite regress in which body and tape, recording and voice, image and sight, endlessly reproduce each other. Within this world, it makes a weird kind of sense for bodies to mutate as easily as spliced tape, for the distinction between reality and representation has been largely deconstructed. "Characters walk in and out of the screen flickering different films on and off" (64); bodies split in half lengthwise; screens show two films simultaneously, half of one on one side, half of the other on the other side; a writing machine "shifts one half one text and half the other through a page frame on conveyor belts" (65). Inscription, bodies, sounds, and images all follow the same dynamics and the same logic.

In a wonderfully oxymoronic phrase, Burroughs calls the place where culture produces its replicating sound and images tracks the "reality studio" (151). "Clearly no portentous exciting events are about to transpire," the narrator says, implicitly mocking the melodrama of his own space-alien track. "You will readily understand why people will go to any lengths to get in the film to cover themselves with any old film scrap . . . anything to avoid the hopeless dead-end horror of being just who and where you all are: dying animals on a doomed planet" (151). Connecting capitalistic financing with cultural productions (as if remembering the American Telegraphone Company), he continues, "The film stock issued now isn't worth the celluloid its printed on. There is nothing to back it up. The film bank is empty. To conceal the bankruptcy of the reality studio it is essential that no one should be in position to set up another reality set. . . . Work for the reality studio or else. Or else you will find out how it feels to be *outside the film*" (151).

As the text draws to a close, the narrator directs the reader's attention to the possibility that the reality studio may indeed be closing down and one will therefore shortly find oneself outside the film, off the recording. A similar message is given in a different medium, when at the end of the penultimate section the print of the text is disrupted by several lines of cursive script, English alternating with Arabic. Each line runs through a permutation of "To say good by silence," with the lines gradually becoming more random and indecipherable as they proceed down the page (203). Perhaps Burroughs is trying to prepare the reader for the panic that sets in when the interior monologue is disrupted and, for the first time in one's life, one hears silence instead of language. For whatever reason, he takes extraordinary care to achieve a feeling of closure unusual in his works from this period. Compared with *Naked Lunch*, the ending here is formally elaborate and thematically conclusive.

Echoing *The Tempest*, the text as it winds down splices in dialogue from Shakespeare's play with visions of contemporary technologies: "i foretold you were all spirits watching TV program—Terminal electric voices end—These our actors cut in—A few seconds later you are melted into air—Rub out promised by our ever-living poet—Mr Bradly Mr Martin, five times our summons—no shelter in setting forth" (174). The splices invite the reader to tease out resonances between the two works. Whereas insect imagery predominates in *Naked Lunch*, in *Ticket* the usual form of nonhuman life is aquatic or amphibian, recalling Caliban's characterization as a "fishy monster." Prospero conjures spirits from the air, and yet his magic has a terrible materiality; he can, we are told, raise bodies from the dead. Most of all he is a supreme technician, blending illusion so skillfully with reality that his art can effect changes in the real world. Burroughs aims for nothing less, using language to disrupt the viral power of the word, creating recordings to stop the playbacks that imprison our future in the sounds of our past. If the tape recorder is, as Paul Bowles called it, "god's little machine," *The Ticket That Exploded* is the tape that reveals its life-transforming possibilities.

"What we see is dictated by what we hear," the narrator of *Ticket* asserts (168). There is considerable anecdotal evidence to support his claim. Whereas sight is always focused, sharp, and delineated, sound envelops the body, as if it were an atmosphere to be experienced rather than an object to be dissected. Perhaps that is why researchers in virtual reality have found that sound is much more effective than sight in imparting emotional tonalities to their simulated worlds.[17] Their experiences suggest that voice is associated with presence not only because it comes from within the body but also because it conveys information about the subject that goes deeper than analytical thought or conscious intention. Manipulating sound through tape recorders then becomes a way of producing a new kind of subjectivity that strikes at the deepest levels of awareness. The effects are multiplied when the sound is of one's own voice. If time delay and mutation alienate the voice from the subject, in another sense they create a new subject ambiguously located in both the body and the recorder. *Krapp's Last Tape* hints that the place of the subject can be taken over by the voice within the machine; *The Ticket That Exploded* explores and complicates this possibility by positioning the alien voice within the subject's body itself. If we were to trace the trajectory suggested here to the end of the period when audiotape held sway, it would lead to a text such as C. J. Cherryh's *Cyteen* trilogy, where the body has become a corporate product molded by "taking tape," that is, listening to conditioning tapes that lay the foundation for the subject's "psychset." The voice that finally issues from the tape recorder sounds not so much postmodern as it does posthuman. But that is yet another story.

NOTES

1. Havelock's work includes *Preface to Plato* and *The Literate Revolution in Greece and Its Cultural Consequences*. The work of Ong includes *The Presence of the Word* and *Orality and Literacy*. Eisenstein traces the cultural changes brought about by the printing press in *The Printing Press as an Agent of Change*. McLuhan's classic work is *The Gutenberg Galaxy*.

2. Havelock argues that modern subjectivity, with its sense of stable ego and enduring identity, was a historical invention that correlated with the transition from orality to writing; see *Preface to Plato*.

3. The literature on these technologies is extensive. For a useful brief discussion, see Kahn and Whitehead, esp. Douglas Kahn, "Introduction: Histories of Sound Once Removed," 1–30.

4. The pioneering papers in the development of magnetic tape recording are collected in Camras. His brief introductions to the sections provide a valuable (if sketchy) history, which I have drawn on here.

5. For the patent description of the Telegraphone, see V. Poulsen, "Method of Recording and Reproducing Sounds or Signals," in Camras 11–17. The model exhibited in Paris differed in some regards from the patent description.

6. A useful review of this work is J. C. Mallinson, "Tutorial Review of Magnetic Recording," in Camras 229–43.

7. Burroughs said on several occasions that he admired Beckett's work very much. Comparing his work to Beckett's, he remarked, "What I want to do is to learn to see more of what's out there, to look outside, to achieve as far as possible a complete awareness of surroundings; Beckett wants to go inward. First he was in a bottle and now he is in the mud. I am aimed in the other direction—outward"

("Art of Fiction" 35). The comment is revealing in many ways, not least for the light it throws on Burroughs's use of science fiction themes and scenarios.

8. As Beckett worked with actors and then directed his own performance, he made changes in the text. Quotations are taken from the revised version incorporating his changes in *Krapp's Last Tape*.

9. Beckett's notes on the play can be found in Knowlson, *Theatrical Notebooks* 180–201.

10. Beckett expected that the sounds issuing from the cubbyhole would also be recorded. Sound and presence do not necessarily go together there, either.

11. Knowlson comments on this passage perceptively in *Theatrical Notebooks* xxiv.

12. According to the stage directions in early performances, Krapp moves his lips. Later Beckett revised the direction to "face frozen to end."

13. Nelson has an excellent discussion of the body in relation to space in Burroughs, including *The Ticket That Exploded* and its companion novels.

14. Lilly describes these experiments in his autobiographical account, *The Center of the Cyclone*. In a characteristically literalizing passage, Burroughs suggested that isolation tanks could literally dissolve body boundaries: "So after fifteen minutes in the tank these Marines scream they are losing outlines and have to be removed — I say put two marines in the tank and see who comes out — Science — Pure science — So put a marine and his girl friend in the tank and see who or what emerges" (*Ticket* 83).

15. The cut-up method is described in many places by Burroughs and others; see, for example, Burroughs, "Cut-up Method," and Odier, *The Job*. Lydenberg lucidly discusses the political and theoretical implications of the practice in *Word Cultures*. In "Collage Theory," Gefin contextualizes the practice in the avant-garde techniques of collage. Friedberg, in "Cut-Ups," traces the cut-up method through the Dadaists.

16. Lydenberg has a good discussion of Burroughs's experiments with tape recordings, including this album.

17. Brenda Laurel and Sandy Stone, private communication.

WORKS CITED

Beckett, Samuel. *Krapp's Last Tape*. Ed. James Knowlson. Vol. 3. *The Theatrical Notebooks of Samuel Beckett*. New York: Grove, 1982.

Burroughs, William S. "The Art of Fiction." *Paris Review* 9.35 (1965): 12–49.

———. "The Cut-up Method of Brion Gysin." *Re/Search* 4–5 (1982): 35–38.

———. *The Ticket That Exploded*. New York: Grove, 1967.

Camras, Marvin, ed. *Magnetic Tape Recording*. New York: Van Nostrand Reinhold, 1985.

Chabert, Pierre. "Samuel Beckett as Director." Trans. M. A. Bonney and J. Knowlson. *"Krapp's Last Tape": A Theatre Notebook*. Ed. James Knowlson. London: Brutus, 1980. 85–107.

Dukore, Bernard J. *"Krapp's Last Tape* as Tragicomedy." *"Krapp's Last Tape": A Theatre Notebook*. Ed. James Knowlson. London: Brutus, 1980. 146–50.

Eisenstein, Elizabeth. *The Printing Press as an Agent of Change: Communications and*

Cultural Transformations in Early-Modern Europe. 2 vols. New York: Cambridge University Press, 1979.

Esslin, Martin. "Samuel Beckett and the Art of Broadcasting." *Encounter* 45.3 (1975): 38–46.

Friedberg, Anne. "Cut-Ups: A Synema of the Text." *William S. Burroughs at the Front: Critical Reception, 1959–1989.* Ed. Jennie Skerl and Robin Lydenberg. Carbondale: Southern Illinois University Press, 1991. 169–73.

Gefin, Laszlo K. "Collage Theory, Reception, and the Cutups of William Burroughs." *Perspectives on Contemporary Literature: Literature and the Other Arts* 13 (1987): 91–100.

Havelock, Eric A. *The Literate Revolution in Greece and Its Cultural Consequences.* Princeton: Princeton University Press, 1982.

———. *Preface to Plato.* Cambridge, Mass.: Harvard University Press, 1971.

Kahn, Douglas, and Gregory Whitehead, eds. *Wireless Imagination: Sound, Radio, and the Avant-Garde.* Cambridge, Mass.: MIT Press, 1992.

Knowlson, James. "The Beginnings of *Krapp's Last Tape.*" *"Krapp's Last Tape": A Theatre Notebook.* Ed. James Knowlson. London: Brutus, 1980. 45–48.

———. *The Theatrical Notebooks of Samuel Beckett.* Vol. 3. New York: Grove, 1982.

Lilly, John Cunningham. *The Center of the Cyclone: An Autobiography of Inner Space.* New York: Julian, 1972.

Lubeck, Heinz. "Magnetic Sound Recording with Films and Ring Heads." *Magnetic Tape Recording.* Ed. Marvin Camras. New York: Van Nostrand Reinhold, 1985. 79–111.

Lydenberg, Robin. "Sound Identity Fading Out: William Burroughs' Tape Experiments." *Wireless Imagination: Sound, Radio, and the Avant-Garde.* Ed. Douglas Kahn and Gregory Whitehead. Cambridge, Mass: MIT Press, 1992. 409–33.

———. *Word Cultures: Radical Theory and Practice in William S. Burroughs' Fiction.* Urbana: University of Illinois Press, 1987.

McLuhan, Marshall. *The Gutenberg Galaxy: The Making of Typographic Man.* Toronto: University of Toronto Press, 1962.

Nelson, Cary. "The End of the Body: Radical Space in Burroughs." *William S. Burroughs at the Front: Critical Reception, 1959–1989.* Ed. Jennie Skerl and Robin Lydenberg. Carbondale: Southern Illinois University Press, 1991. 119–32.

Odier, Daniel. *The Job: Interviews with William S. Burroughs.* New York: Grove, 1969.

Ong, Walter J. *Orality and Literacy: The Technologizing of the Word.* London: Methuen, 1982.

———. *The Presence of the Word: Some Prolegomena for Cultural and Religious History.* New Haven: Yale University Press, 1967.

Stewart, Garrett. *Reading Voices: Literature and the Phonotext.* Berkeley: University of California Press, 1990.

Walker, Roy. "Love, Chess, and Death." *"Krapp's Last Tape": A Theatre Notebook.* Ed. James Knowlson. London: Brutus, 1980. 48–51.

TECHNOLOGIES OF PRESENCE
Orality and the Tapevoice
of Contemporary Poetics

By ear, he sd.
But that which matters, that which insists, that which will last,
that! o my people, where shall you find it, how, where, where
    shall you listen
when all is become billboards, when, all, even silence, is spray-
    gunned? (6)

In this passage from *The Maximus Poems*, Charles Olson delivers an impatient jeremiad to his New England townsfolk, urging them to *listen* in a world where advertising and commercial interests have reified information, where "even silence, is spray-gunned." Elsewhere in his epic poem Olson complains about the wallpaper music piped into public buildings and conveyances, the "musick-racket / of all ownership" that lulls a citizenry to sleep (18). As a corrective, he advocates taking "the way of / the lowest, / including / your legs" (19). Walking and listening keep the individual in touch with the resilient character of quotidian life and force attention on the unique demands of a given moment. Play it "by ear" he urges in a metaphor that unites the ideals of immediacy and acoustics in one imperative.

Olson's concern for the virtues of hearing is part of a pervasive phonocentrism that dominates contemporary poetics. For poets of the 1950s and 1960s, a new oral impulse served as a corrective to the rhetorically controlled, print-based poetry of high modernism. Whereas "voice" for T. S. Eliot and Ezra Pound is a rhetorical construct produced through personae and irony, for postwar poets it becomes an extension of the physiological organism. "Speech," as Robert Creeley says, "is a mouth" (283). Orality signifies unmediated access to passional states, giving testimony to that which only *this* poet could know. We can see this oral imperative in Olson's "Projective Verse" essay, Allen Ginsberg's theories of mantric breathing, Jack Kerouac's "spontaneous prose," Frank O'Hara's "personism," Michael McClure's "beast language," and Denise Levertov's theories of organic form. The recovery of the oral tradition can be felt in movements such as Ethnopoetics, performance and sound poetry that stress not only the sounded qualities of language (their phonetics and pragmatics) but their supposed atavistic origins. Acoustic features play an important role in the poetry of African American writers such as Amiri Baraka, David Henderson, Jayne Cortez, and Sonia Sanchez, who base many of their poems on jazz and blues motifs for which vocalization is an essential component. Each of these tendencies articulates an ideal of immediacy based on the body and its expressive rendering through speech.[1]

Literary historians have explained the origins of this new oralism as a revival of romantic immanence and expressivism in reaction to New Critical ideals of impersonality and distancing.[2] While these aesthetic contexts are relevant, they do not take into account the fact that many of these developments were made possible by technological advances in typography, offset printing, and—most significantly for our purposes—magnetic recording that would seem the very antithesis to any poetics of unmediated presence. In "Projective Verse," Olson could celebrate the advantages of breath and breathing in scoring the line, but he recognized that the notation of such physiological functions was made possible by a machine. The typewriter could provide the poet with the same "stave and the bar" as the musician: "It is the advantage of the typewriter," Olson writes, "that, due to its rigidity and its space precisions, it can, for a poet, indicate exactly the breath, the pauses, the suspensions even of syllables, the juxtapositions even of parts of phrases, which he intends" (22).

Although Pound, William Carlos Williams, and e. e. cummings had exploited the resources of the typewriter in creating a visual page, Olson links the machine directly to phenomenological and cognitive processes for which breath and voice are the vehicles. Likewise, the new technologies of photo-offset printing offered the magazine editor flexibility and speed in layout and design not available to slower, more cumbersome technologies of letterpress printing. If the little magazine revolution of the 1960s was fueled by a neoromantic poetics of testimony and protest, it was enabled by photographic processes that returned the poem to its producer in a most palpable way. Thus the immediacy advocated in the poetics of the period was materialized via forms of electronic reproduction and printing.

When historians speak of "literary culture," they usually mean the history of print technologies of the sort I have just described.[3] Even a committed oralist such as Walter Ong deals only with printed notation in describing forms of "secondary orality" (136–37). With the advances of magnetic recording during the 1930s, however, the tape recorder began to exert its own impact on modernist literature—and I would contend on the concept of voice itself. For the first time, poets could hear their own voices and use that hearing to develop notational and performance strategies. With the rise of poetry readings in jazz clubs, coffeehouses, and college auditoriums in the late 1950s, the tape recorder returned a kind of oral aura to poetry at a point where it had been, as Olson phrased it, removed from "producer and reproducer" ("Projective Verse" 22). The tape recording could render the authenticity of the moment—ambient noise, interlinear commentary, coughs, and catcalls—by which the uniqueness of the event could be measured. Tape recordings of these readings found their way into private and institutional collections, providing a significant oral history of an oral era. In such archives (in the sheer fact of their existence as acoustic records) one can "hear" as well as "see" the profound challenge posed by postmodern art to the authority of ocularcentrism in Western modernism.[4]

I have discussed the uses of tape recordings for literary criticism elsewhere (" 'By ear' "); I would like here to speculate more broadly on the cultural meaning of this technology, for technology exists in a complex web of social articulations that extend far beyond instrumental ends. Rather than merely serving human interests—the neutral recording of acoustic data for purposes of storage and verification—technology helps produce its users. The emergence of magnetic recording during the postwar period transformed the notion of voice from something heard into something overheard such that its invocation by poets as natural or unmediated becomes increasingly problematic. Deconstruction has had a great deal to say about the limits of a phonocentric model of language—its dependence on a voice, metaphysically prior to any inscription—but it has not investigated the relationships between this model and the technologies that "speak" it into being. I would like to make such an investigation by examining what we might call, following Foucault, the "technologies of presence," those systems of production and reproduction within which the voice achieves enough autonomy to regard itself as present unto itself (116).[5] The paranoid versions of these technologies—in Samuel Beckett and William S. Burroughs, for instance—project the tape recorder as an ultimate agent of mind control, a machine capable of replacing human communication with a prerecorded script.[6]

For the poets who took up the cause of orality in the mid-1950s, voice was a contested site in a battle over identity and agency. The rediscovery of formulaic oral traditions by Milman Parry, Albert Lord, and Eric Havelock provided a link between avant-garde literary practices and earlier tribal cultures. These traditions offered an alternative not only to print culture but to the era's tendencies toward standardization and uniformity—"when all is become billboards," as Olson says. In their recuperation of an oralist, phonocentric imperative, poets hoped to suture a social body together by recovering a private body of significant sounds. But "technologies of presence" will always offer a hybrid voice—a voice in a machine—that cannot speak entirely for itself, even though it posits self-presence as its ground. It is this divided character of orality that informs the paranoid testimony of Ginsberg's "Howl," the self-tracking of Kerouac's novels, and the epic apostrophe of Olson's *Maximus*. When the complicity between presence and technology is acknowledged, in the work of William Burroughs, David Antin, Laurie Anderson, or Steve Benson, the tape recorder ceases to be a passive receptacle for a more authentic speech but an active agent in its deconstruction.

Surveillance Culture

Although the idea of storing acoustic information by magnetizing a metallic surface was first patented in 1898 by the Danish inventor Valdemar Poulsen, it was not until the late 1920s that practical applications of magnetic recording were put into practice. With the advent of alternating-current bias that amplified the signal, possibilities for magnetic recording were expanded, first to wire and then to metallic tape. The biggest advance in this technology was the German development of the Magnetophon, first viewed at the 1936 Berlin Radio Fair, which reached levels of acoustic clarity previously unrealized. Linked first to the synchronization of sound in motion pictures and then with the propaganda efforts of the Nazis during the war, the Magnetophon joined with phonographic technology to create the first major break in the long history of print hegemony.[7]

The fact that both forms of sound recording and reproduction were developed as part of the war effort has an important bearing on the voice that was naturalized in the process. Alice Kaplan has discussed the ways that the Nazis exploited the radio, the loudspeaker, and other forms of electronic media to reach a mass audience. She points out that for Nazi propaganda, it was the "*reproduced* voice, rather than the voice itself, that convey[ed] the archaic values demanded by so-called antimodernist fascist rhetoric" (134). The voice of Hitler at mass rallies or heard on the radio was a powerful instrument in the "conversion experience" of many Germans, French, and Italians. Through the tape recording, the führer's voice or that of his operatives could be heard simultaneously in every country within the Axis powers, thus achieving a global presence for a single speaker. Far from retaining the "aura" of the original, these technologies offered an endistanced voice that spoke from no place and yet that was omnipotent. *Je Suis Partout* (I am everywhere) was the title of a major fascist newspaper as well as a recognition of the new media's ability to penetrate all corners of social space. The alienation of voice from speaker contributed to the aestheticization of politics of which Walter Benjamin, in "The Work of Art in the Age of Mechanical Reproduction," warned; the tape recorder's ability to repeat this voice over and over again was no small agent in this process.

With the advent of the Cold War, the tape recorder came to occupy a very different role in the Western cultural imagination. No longer associated with disseminating a voice among the masses, the tape recorder, in the hands of the new postwar surveillance services, could now invade the private space of the individual, gathering information during a period of unprecedented suspicion and secrecy. The expansion of a "surveillance ideology" coincided with the formation of numerous federal agencies, beginning with the Office of Strategic Services (OSS) in 1941 and continuing through the National Intelligence Authority (NIA) in 1946, the Central Intelligence Agency (CIA) in 1947, the Intelligence Advisory Committee (IAC) in 1950, the National Security Agency (NSA) in 1952, the Hoover Commission Task Force on Intelligence in 1955, and the Defense Intelligence Agency (DIA) in 1961, not to mention special congressional committees such as the House Un-American Activities Committee (HUAC) in 1938 and the McCarthy Committee of 1950. These agencies gained greater access to private individuals through new eavesdropping devices made possible through miniaturization and through easing of restrictions on search and seizure prohibitions of the Fourth Amendment. Periodicals celebrated the virtues of the "martini olive" transmitter, the detectaphone (that could listen through walls), and the "spike mike" (that could be implanted in the foundation of buildings). Bugging and listening devices were discovered everywhere, the most powerful example of which was the discovery on 26 May 1960 of a bugging device hidden in the Great Seal of the United States in the U.S. embassy in Moscow.[8]

Surveillance ideology was promulgated through a series of court cases involving the Fourth Amendment prohibition against unreasonable search and seizure. In the days of the Red Scare and the McCarthy Committee, the ability of CIA, the FBI, and other federal agencies to collect information on undesirables was hampered by restrictions, first brought to light in *Olm-*

stead v. United States of 1927, in which the Supreme Court upheld a State of Washington conviction against a bootlegger captured by the use of a wiretap. Since Olmstead's residence was not *physically* violated, the wiretap could not be seen as a form of search and seizure and therefore did not violate Fourth Amendment provisions. Dissenting opinions by Justices Brandeis and Holmes warned of the dangers of such intrusive, if silent, searches and reinforced "the right to be let alone."[9] These warnings were taken up in earnest in the 1934 Federal Communications Act, which stated that "no person not being authorized by the sender shall intercept any communication and divulge or publish the existence, contents, substance, purport, effect or meaning of such intercepted communications to any person."[10] While the 1934 act limited the admissibility of evidence obtained through wiretaps and other surveillance techniques, such evidence could serve in the "fishing expedition" that would lead to an indictment. Throughout the 1950s and 1960s, states and federal agencies tested the limits of Fourth Amendment restrictions, publicly repudiating the electronic invasion of households while privately and institutionally condoning eavesdropping.[11] The upshot was the Omnibus Crime Control and Safe Streets Act of 1968, which sanctioned the use of electronic surveillance once and for all. While the proponents for legalizing eavesdropping based their arguments on the need to defeat organized crime, these techniques of investigation became increasingly useful in the surveillance of antiwar, counterculture activists during the Vietnam era.

The climate of paranoia established during this period has been well documented, finding its cultural representation in works such as George Orwell's *1984*, written in the 1940s, and continuing in the popular imagination through movies such as *Walk East on Beacon* (1952), *Big Jim McLain* (1952), *The Manchurian Candidate* (1962), *The Conversation* (1974), and *Blow Out* (1981). In such films, surveillance destroys the barrier between interiority and exteriority as technology invades all areas of psychic life. The voice that one expects to hear more clearly becomes permeated with conflicting messages — the ideological static bred by surveillance itself — until the "bugged" and the "buggee" exchange places. This dystopic view of surveillance is brilliantly shown in Francis Ford Coppola's 1974 film *The Conversation*, in which Harry Caul (Gene Hackman), the super technician, realizes that whereas throughout his professional career he has been able to listen in on any conversation, his own is now being overheard by forces he cannot identify. In the last scene he begins methodically to dismantle his apartment, searching for the hidden mike. His role, as Kaja Silverman says, is reversed from occupying "a position behind the camera and tape recorder to one in front — from a position 'outside the door' to one 'inside the door' " (97–98). Ironically it was this same obsession with tape-recorded verification that led to the demise of one of the Cold War's most famous orators, a president so much a creation of surveillance ideology that he bugged his own office.[12] No one had been more consumed with ideological infection than Richard Nixon, and so it is all the more ironic—or inevitable, if my example from *The Conversation* can be extended—that he should have been "othered" by the sound of his own voice. The technologies that contained the voice of subversives and opponents also trapped the one running the machine. In a world where presence is increasingly verified by information storage and retrieval, the distinction between producer and consumer of information breaks down.

Surveillance ideology, by treating voice as something overheard rather than heard, creates a secondary level of presence, a simulacrum in which identity is revealed as something having already been recorded. This voice cannot generate information by itself; it is only the conduit for ideological messages that precede articulation. Far from the self-present voice of the new orality, the voice constructed in surveillance ideology is entirely fabricated within the laws of secrecy, covert action, and damage control. It is little wonder that when disclosures of the Watergate cover-up got closer and closer to the White House, Nixon in his public responses to the press spoke of himself in the third person as "The President."

Take a simple tape from all you are (Allen Ginsberg)

By speaking of surveillance ideology in the context of poetry, I do not mean to imply that poets necessarily thematized surveillance in their work or that they were more "investigated" than others of the McCarthy period. The best minds of Allen Ginsberg's generation *were* more likely to be subjects of surveillance, but their voices were raised against larger targets than Ampex or the Bell labs. The connection I would establish between the worlds of surveillance and poetics is that the virtues of orality become increasingly significant in a world where technology is capable of separating voice from speaker, conversation from community. Apprehension of this alienation animates the work of many writers during this period. But far from rejecting the tape recorder as an agent of reification, they embraced it as an accomplice in the recovery of more authentic speech.

Among the Beat writers, the tape recorder held a particular fascination, both as a sign of Cold War surveillance and as an instrument for personal confession. The bulk of Jack Kerouac's *Visions of Cody* (1960) is devoted to a taped conversation between Neal Cassady (Cody) and Kerouac, followed by a satiric "Imitation of the Tape" that serves as a kind of auto-critique.[13]

The stoned, unrehearsed dialogues between the two men offer a verbal immediacy that contrasts to the stifling conformism of middle America. By substituting recorded conversations for fictionalized dialogue, Kerouac celebrates the dynamic possibilities of "lived speech" as a palliative for the deadened newspeak of square society. And in William Burroughs's *The Ticket That Exploded* (1962), the tape recorder is viewed as a panoptical vehicle for total mind control, capable of entering the body through the ear and transforming informational diversity and difference into bureaucratic master codes. "We don't know who is doing it or how to stop them," one of Burroughs's agents says. "Everytime we catch up with someone . . . we capture a tape recorder" (20). Against such communicational invasion, Burroughs splices and intercuts diverse acoustic materials to create his novel, much as he collaged printed materials together in *Naked Lunch*. In an afterword to the novel Burroughs points to the defamiliarizing function of such techniques: "take a political speech on television shut off sound track and substitute another speech you have prerecorded hardly tell the difference isn't much record sound track of one danger man from uncle spy program run it in place of another and see if your friends can't tell the difference it's all done with tape recorders consider this machine and what it can do" (205). Burroughs's reference to the popular television series *The Man from U.N.C.L.E.* suggests that not only are all television programs the same but that surveillance culture has provided its own forms of self-representation (and parody) to neutralize its more insidious practices.

One poet who thoroughly considered what "this machine" could do to recover the voice was Allen Ginsberg. In *The Fall of America* he traverses the United States in a Volkswagen, speaking his observations into a tape recorder and singing the requiem of Walt Whitman's democratic vistas. The book was written in 1966 during the first major escalation of the Vietnam War, and Ginsberg was among the first to register the enormous impact of global telecommunications on that conflict. One poem in that volume, "Wichita Vortex Sutra," captures the bizarre contradictions between distant Indochina and middle America. Ginsberg is literally in a vortex of recorded speech as he drives (or is driven) from Macpherson, Kansas, to Wichita, where he is to give a poetry reading. He describes himself being surrounded by high tension wires, telegraph poles, and invisible radio waves:

> News Broadcast & old clarinets
> Watertower dome Lighted on the flat plain
> car radio speeding acrost railroad tracks —

Kansas! Kansas! Shuddering at last!
PERSON appearing in Kansas!
angry telephone calls to the University
Police dumbfounded leaning on
their radiocar hoods
While Poets chant to Allah in the roadhouse Showboat!
Blue eyed children dance and hold thy Hand O aged Walt
who came from Lawrence to Topeka to envision
Iron interlaced upon the city plain —
Telegraph wires strung from city to city O Melville!
Television brightening thy *rills of Kansas lone*
I come. (394)

Ginsberg views himself as a "lone man from the void," like Whitman, who has been sent to identify himself as a "PERSON" in Kansas. His isolation is contrasted to a world of electronic sound—news broadcasts, crank telephone calls protesting his appearance on college campuses, police in their "radiocars," and television signals. It is against this electrical interference that the salutary voices of Whitman and Herman Melville are remembered, voices forged in a different America and a different auditory sensorium.

As Ginsberg rolls through middle America, he records the voices of radio announcers broadcasting the daily body count of the dead in Southeast Asia. Newspaper headlines, billboards, and other forms of highway signage add to the general information blitzkrieg as Ginsberg strives to retain a voice capable of prophecy:

"We will negotiate anywhere anytime"
said the giant President
Kansas City Times 2/14/66: "Word reached U.S. authorities that Thailand's leaders feared that in Honolulu Johnson might have tried to persuade South Vietnam's rulers to ease their stand against negotiating with the Viet Cong.
American officials said these fears were groundless and Humphrey was telling the Thais so."
AP dispatch
The last week's paper is Amnesia. (400)

Quoted material from newspapers, far from clarifying the ambiguities of the historical moment, creates further confusion. The speech of Johnson or Humphrey, filtered through Associated Press journalese, fails to convince either the Thai leaders who want further assurance of American support of South Vietnam or the poet who wants the opposite. Against the double-talk of Washington or the newspaper Ginsberg poses the prophetic voice of Whitman's Democratic Vistas. In a world so riven by undirected sound, Ginsberg yearns for a sign or an icon that participates directly in the physical character of its source. He finds it, partially, in the Chinese character for truth as defined by Ezra Pound: "man standing by his word."

> Word picture: forked creature
> Man
> standing by a box, birds flying out
> representing mouth speech
> Ham Steak please waitress, in the warm café. (401)

Ginsberg wants a voice that has not already been heard, one equivalent to Pound's image that captures in an instant what the canned voice of the media cannot provide. The voice as "word picture" would be as immediate as birds flying out of a box or a request from a lunch menu. For Ginsberg the orality of the tapevoice stands in direct opposition to the reproduced heteroglossia of in-corporated sound. Newsmedia, press reports, advertising, and police radio transmissions are all implicated in an information blockage against which the low-tech, Volkswagen-driven minicassette recorder stands as alternative. Prophecy no longer emanates from some inner visionary moment but from a voice that has recognized its inscription within an electronic environment, a voice that has seized the means of reproduction and adapted it to oppositional ends. "I sing the body electric," Whitman chants, but the literal possibility for such a song had to wait for Ginsberg and his generation.

what am i doing here (David Antin)

That generation included a loosely knit group of poets living in New York's Lower East Side during the 1950s and 1960s for whom the tape recorder became an increasingly important element in composition. Paul Blackburn, LeRoi Jones (Amiri Baraka), Jerome Rothenberg, David Antin, Armand Schwerner, Robert Kelly, and Jackson Mac Low linked tape recording to European avant-garde experimentation. Within the group could be found an interest in projectivist and "Deep Image" theories, applications of John Cage's chance operations, religious and ritual uses of the voice, and Russian Futurist and Dadaist theater. The tape recorder participated actively in all of these areas.

Perhaps no one believed more fervently in the advantages of the tape recorder than Paul Blackburn. He brought his small, portable machine to readings at Le Metro, Les Deux Magots, Dr. Generosity's, and St. Mark's Church. He conducted his own poetry show on WBAI radio, thus bringing the new writing out of the clubs and bars of the Lower East Side and making it available to a wider audience. Furthermore, he turned on his tape recorder during informal drinking sessions with poet friends at his apartment, and the desultory conversations that resulted offer their own interest for the literary record. Beyond this, he used the machine to record world-historical events like the moon landing or the Kennedy assassination reports and collaged them informally among poetry readings, telephone conversations, and spontaneous raps. Blackburn is important to our concerns for a number of reasons, not the least of which is his synthesis of Mediterranean lyric culture (in its Poundian transformations) with new electronic recording media. He was the first American poet to use the tape recorder as an archival vehicle for poetry, much as Alan Lomax and other rural ethnologists had used it for recording folk music. But Blackburn's omniscient tape recorder was more than a vehicle for retrieval; it became a dimension of his material text, as immediate as pen and paper had been for previous generations. And because it was invariably onstage with the poet, the tape recorder became synonymous with the body of the performer.

It is in the work of Blackburn's friend, David Antin, that we see magnetic recording subjected to a directly countertextual imperative. Antin's work since the early 1970s marks a decisive break with the oralist and tribal ideas of Olson and Ginsberg and points to a new, problematized attitude toward the voice. In his "talk" pieces, Antin inverts the traditional, phonocentric relationship between text and voice by speaking first and writing it down later. He enters the gallery or auditorium, takes out his portable tape recorder, turns it on, and begins speaking. The "talk" is conducted without text or notes and gives the appearance of being spontaneously delivered. The talk is over when Antin turns off his tape recorder. Later he transcribes the talk into his own, highly idiosyncratic notation, which utilizes unjustified left and right margins, lowercase letters, gaps between phrases, and little or no punctuation. Although I have referred to the printed version as a transcription, it is in no sense a replica of the talk itself. Rather, Antin freely edits and modifies the talk so that it becomes a representation, not a mimesis, of speech.

However spontaneous these works may appear, they do follow certain patterns. The title often establishes the general territory that subsequent anecdotes, stories, and examples elaborate. When Antin gives the same talk piece in several venues, he uses the same materials and sequencing of stories, much as a standup comedian will repeat a pattern of jokes. And there is a good deal of borscht belt humor in Antin's work. He relies extensively on timing—the incremental building of a metaphor, or the deferral of the punch line—and combines it with the subtle creation of himself as a schlemiel in a world of slick impresarios. These verbal strategies and postures have their antecedents in classical rhetoric as much as in Henny Youngman, and Antin often exploits the fuzzy boundaries between the two realms. Antin draws on the dialectical method of Socrates, not the spatial logic of Aristotle or Quintilian, and like Socrates he asks questions for which he already has the answers.

As other commentators have noted, many of Antin's talk pieces are about themselves.[14] It is less often recognized that they are also about the status of voice in an age of electronically reproduced information. In his three books, *talking at the boundaries*, *tuning*, and *what it means to be avant-garde*, each talk is framed by brief prefatory and concluding remarks concerning the actual circumstances leading up to and following the talk. These remarks introduce the event organizers, art patrons, and gallery curators who make the talk possible. Within the talk itself, however, are other self-reflexive comments regarding audience expectations that often initiate the larger subject of the talk. For the subject of the talk is very much the deixis of the talk environment, the manipulation of positional relations between a putative speaker and his listeners.

A good example of Antin's self-conscious manipulation of deixis occurs in "whos listening out there," delivered on radio station KPBS, a National Public Radio affiliate in San Diego. Since most of his talk pieces during the early 1980s had been delivered in public spaces, the challenge of addressing a potentially large but absent audience offered a chance to explore another dimension of his technique. In his printed version, Antin adds a preface that describes the format of the radio show on which he appeared. This particular program featured a first half-hour devoted to readings of poems by Dante Gabriel Rossetti and Christina Rossetti, read by the show's moderator and other guests. These recitations, "burnished by elocution lessons," are the very antithesis of Antin's oral style and procedure. They represent a late nineteenth-century notion of dramatic recitation in which ornate rhetoric is enhanced by histrionic vocal inflections.

In his performance on the radio, Antin explains to his host,

> *i didnt read anymore   that i talked as the occasion*
> *required   but i dont think he really believed me*

until he saw me setting up my cassette recorder
i explained it was my habit to record my talks
to find out what id said   but he pointed out that
the station engineer regularly recorded the show
and that the quality would surely be better   so i
put away my tape recorder and prepared to listen. (268)

This offhand remark — or, as we shall see, this representation of an offhand remark — sets up a dialectic of technology and orality around which many of his talks are based. The technological expertise of professionals (in this case, the station engineer) is posed against the naiveté of the oral poet who relies on his voice and his improvisatorial skills. In the talk itself, Antin utilizes the anonymity of his audience to explore the ways that radio fictionalizes the presence of its auditors. He assures his audience that although he is not reading from a script,

"you people out there you shouldnt be afraid either"
       i wont say anything so surprising that youll have to turn
the set off   and i know that you have confidence in that
    at least you generally have confidence in that   otherwise you
wouldnt have your radio on. (270)

This assurance does exactly the opposite of what it proposes by calling into question the pact between radio listener and announcer. By addressing himself directly to the listener's fears that something out of the ordinary will *not* happen, he causes that something to happen. Such an intervention is what speech act theorists would call a violation of appropriateness or felicity and occurs when the contract between addressor and addressee is broken.[15] At such moments attention is distracted from the progressive line of argument onto the utterance itself; communication becomes recursive performance. And while much of modernism is engaged with breaking criteria of appropriateness, Antin situates its problematic within the orbit of technology.

In order to further illustrate the fictions of appropriateness that radio makes possible, Antin stages a fanciful image of himself for the listeners:

                    you cant see me running
    my hand   nervously through my greying hair   .   .   .

    .   .   .   .

    resting my lean   almost gaunt chin in the cup of my right
    hand   regarding with mild amusement from my one good eye
       the somewhat bemused expressions on the faces of my two

companions in this radio booth   who might have expected
        some greater degree of decorum from a lean and tweedy
    english-looking gentleman with a black eyepatch. (270, 272)

Needless to say, such a portrayal does not correspond to the "real" David
Antin any more than the news received from authoritative voices of the
media corresponds to events on which it reports. But the fictive pact which
audition presupposes is circular. Just as his audience cannot know him, so
Antin cannot know his listeners. In order to imagine his interlocutors, he
creates a sequence of possible auditors drawn from his neighbors. The bulk
of the talk piece is taken up with re-imagining some of these local figures:

        so maybe its mr canton im talking to "hello mr canton
    are you out there?"   mr canton was a red faced frenchman
        tall and straight   from montreal and he rented a room
        further on down the bluff. (276)

On one hand, such apostrophes personalize the address, turning an anonymous vocal medium into an intimate one. These characters really *could* be
listening, since their personalities are so vividly rendered. Yet each story
concludes with Antin's recognition that each of his potential auditors is
out of range in some way: Timmy, who is living "too far north to pick up
our transmission," or Cindy, who doesn't listen to "anything but music on
the radio," or Mrs. Harris, whose "hearing [is] beginning to go," or even
Mr. Canton, who has probably died by this time. So the potential for hearing, offered by the personalized address, is withdrawn in each case as if to
illustrate how limited each construction of presence really is.

    The dialogue between technology and voice in Antin parallels a de-
bate between professionalism and amateurism. A dominant theme in many
of his talk pieces is the authority of technicians, museum curators, doctors, and scientists, critics whose claims to knowledge are legitimated by
the discursive fields they occupy and not by innate competence. Against
the professional, Antin posits the amateur, the autodidact, the untutored
citizen who, like himself, is simply trying to find answers to fundamental
problems. By posing himself as the humble seeker-after-truth, Antin most
resembles his Socratic ideal.

    In "whos listening out there," this debate over professionalism is pre-
sented via a lengthy anecdote about doctors and their claim to be members
of a scientific rather than a service community. The anecdote concerns a
cocktail party that he and his wife attend consisting largely of doctors who

spend much of the evening bemoaning the threat to medicine from the rising costs of malpractice insurance. Antin and his wife intercede in this debate, asking embarrassing questions about medical ethics and making nuisances of themselves. Antin argues that by regarding themselves as scientists, doctors exempt themselves from responsibility for mistakes, living according to a professional ideal beyond the reach of blame. In reality, they should regard themselves as part of a service economy in which, like plumbers and contractors, they have clients who have legitimate interests in the success of their work. In Antin's view,

> a patient comes to a doctor with a complaint   not
> with a disease and what the doctor offers him is a disease   a
> disease is the doctors prospective gift to the patient   which is
> then followed by other gifts   since one gift leads to another
> a course of therapy   drugs surgery   who knows   and
> these are more securely attached to the disease than the complaint
> as the doctor is more securely attached to the treatment and
> to the disease than he is to the complaint or the patient. (281)

The problem is not that doctors are incompetent but that they invest their work with an image of their professional calling to the exclusion of the patients' needs. To this extent, the anecdote about doctors extends the earlier discussion about radio audiences. In a discourse situation in which there is no feedback (e.g., the patient is only the recipient of a "gift" of a disease; the listener has no basis on which to validate his/her image of the announcer), the effectiveness of a diagnosis is based on the authority vested in the voice. The way to illustrate the limitation of this discourse situation is to imagine it as a radio in which an announcer could address specific listeners and in which listeners could attach a body to speech.[16]

However critical Antin is of professionals, he constantly reveals himself to be a competent amateur. In fact his talk pieces show him to be an authority on many things, from mathematics to foreign languages to carpentry to baseball. Antin restages the Platonic dialogue in which the naive dialectician speaks, often deferentially, to "real" professionals—rhetoricians, rhapsodes, and critics—who claim to know but who have no practical experience of the objects of their knowledge. By speaking rather than by writing, Socrates is revealed to be closer to the truth because he argues directly, unhindered by a script. For the contemporary talk poet, writing (or printing) is the transcription of speech, a second degree of performance rendered as such by the use of spacing and indentation in the printed text.

The validation for Antin's distrust of professionals is provided at the end of his talk piece when he reveals that the engineer who had promised to make a tape of the broadcast somehow neglected to record it. But the piece was not lost:

> the next day i got a call from the artist
> reesey shaw who told me that she and her husband
> david had been listening to me on the radio the
>   night before   david was experimenting with
>   recording and reesey wanted to know if id like
> a tape of the show. (296)

This last frame draws together all of the themes discussed in "whos listening out there." The ineptness of the professional is countered by the artist and amateur who, because of her investment in what is being said, makes a tape and offers it to the poet. Thus, the hermeneutic circle has been entered the right way, through a tape loop in which voice is understood not as something preserved but as something always already reproduced, something made in unmaking itself as truth.

Playing the Body Electric (Laurie Anderson)

Despite Antin's interest in the frames of voice, he nevertheless believes in one individual's ability to wrest truth from illusion. His use of electronic media is distinctly low tech, the appropriation of technology to serve certain minimal goals (transcription) and validate authorial presence through the presentation of a voice grounded in debate. At the same time Antin realizes that any proposition of a "more real voice" is constructed in highly specific discursive contexts. Hence he tailors his talks to the audience at hand (or, in my example, the lack of audience). That the audience is seldom given an opportunity to respond limits the dialogical possibilities of the talk but does not alter Antin's faith in poetry's public character.

In the work of Laurie Anderson (at least in her videos and records) there is no audience and therefore no claim to dialogue. Technology becomes both the subject (in the ontological as well as thematic sense) and means of reproduction. In a recent sampler of her videos (*Collected Videos*), Anderson is shown at home, surrounded by synthesizers, mixers, tape recorders, electric keyboards, and microphones on which she constructs her performances. She moves from one electronic gadget to another, describing each one affectionately as she flips switches or speaks into mikes — a parody, perhaps, of the 1950s domestic worker displaying her new labor-saving kitchen.

But if her self-presentation as technician is ironic, her skill at using these devices is evident in all of her work.

Through her use of synthesizers—synclavier, harmonizer, and contact mike—Anderson creates a cyborg voice, partly her own and partly that of technology itself. Unlike earlier performance artists (and this would include Antin), the identity of voice with presence can no longer be presumed. As Craig Owens says, Anderson's uses of these filters "amplify, distort and multiply her actual voice in such a way that it can no longer be identified as hers" (122). Instead, voice is an index to certain ideological messages for which the body serves as a conduit. And while she projects a vision of technological dystopia akin to that of William Burroughs or Thomas Pynchon, she retains a critical perspective on the state and corporate apparatus from which these messages extend. "Language," as she quotes from Burroughs, "is a virus from outer space."

By speaking of her voice as a cyborg projection, I am inflecting Anderson's critical perspective with specifically feminist implications. Rather than recruit nature or biology as woman's realm against the deadening effects of technology, Anderson explores, in terms strikingly similar to Donna Haraway's, her constructed nature within both areas. By utilizing her body and voice as instruments for manipulating electronic signals, Anderson treats herself as a conductor of sound, a vessel in the most literal sense: a stretched-skin whose internal spaces resonate and vibrate. And in her more recent work she uses video and audio synthesizers to lower her voice and distort her features into a male clone of herself, a comic straightman who writes her lyrics and sings her songs. Although in her performances Anderson speaks through a phallic microphone, the voice that emerges is a multiple, choric construction.

The full implications of this cyborg presence are explored in Anderson's 1983 work, *United States*. In this six-hour opera, Anderson projects a technological wasteland where the relationship between Big Science (fusion, nuclear weapons research, and star wars) and Big Signs (infomatics and telecommunications) mediates all relationships.[17] Much of *United States* (both the performance and the geopolitical entity) is based on processed information such as phone messages, computerized voices, tape loops, advertising jingles, and technojargon. These are voices without origin, detached from bodies, yet by their anonymity they are capable of controlling their listeners. Anderson seems to be asking how these simulacral voices gain their power if they have no agency. In one section ("Language of the Future"), for example, she tells the story of being in an airplane that loses an engine and begins a sudden, precipitous descent:

A voice came over the intercom and said:

Our pilot has informed us that we are about to
attempt
a crash landing. Please extinguish all cigarettes.
Place your tray tables in their upright, locked
position.

Your captain says: Please do not panic.

Your captain says: Place your head
in your hands.

Captain says: Place your head
on your knees.

Captain says: Put your hands on your head.
Put your hands on your knees!
(heh-heh)

This is your Captain.
Have you lost your dog?
We are going down.
We are going down, together. (Part I)

In her recorded version of this section, Anderson reads the voices of flight attendant and captain in the same deadpan manner, creating an even more sinister quality to her narrative. The calm, reasonable words of the flight attendant merge with the voice of the captain, whose assurances turn demonic when he plays Simon Says over the intercom: "Place your hands on your head. / Put your hands on your knees!" By confusing the voices of the traditionally feminine flight attendant with the masculine voice of authority, Anderson exposes how gender is ventriloquized within technological instrumentation. The adequacy of voice to message cannot be based on anything said but on the auditor's willingness to accept the technological mise-en-scène. "Jump out of the plane," the voice commands; "There is no / pilot. / You / are not / alone." The source of such messages is difficult to locate since it, like Anderson's voice, is electronically mixed. If there is no pilot—no source for voice—then the subject is truly "not / alone" in her paranoia.

Many of Anderson's vignettes in *United States* concern an addressee who, like the passenger in the airplane, is the passive recipient of potentially violent and threatening imperatives. The same Orwellian tapevoice that we find in 1950s surveillance ideology reappears here; the phone rings, and a voice on the other end says,

Please do not hang up.
We know who you are.
Please do not hang up . . .
We've got your number. (Part I)

And in a brilliant piece of concrete poetry, Anderson renders the circuit from phone to phonetap:

```
    R         ING
    R         ING
W   ARE       IN              LINE
WE  ARE     A PING   YOUR   LI  E
WE  ARE    TA PING   YOUR   LI  E
WE  ARE    TAPPING   YOUR   LINE.
```

Here the larger dimensions of the phone message become clear as more letters are added: from "We are in line" to "We are taping your lie" to "We are tapping your line." Each message increases the metaphor of invasion, from the ring of the phone to the beginning of the voice to the phonetap itself. At each stage, information is added through a digitalized matrix of letters and spaces—one letter added to a space, a space filled by a letter. "This / is the language / of the on-again / off-again / future. And / it is Digital."

But this paranoid scenario does not end in some anonymous printout. The next sequence features Anderson playing a tape recording of a violin solo through a "pillow speaker" hidden in her mouth. By modulating the shape of her lips, the violin solo is shaped and modified, thus offering an analog alternative to the digitalized network of the printed script. Her voice circumvents the "on-again / off-again" world of commands and responses, figured in the intercom voices of the airplane or the surveillance message, and sends back its own message shaped by the internal workings of the body.

The same confusion of genders that we see in "Language of the Future" appears again in "O Superman (For Massenet)," in which the nurturing voice of "Mom" blends into the Voice of Authority associated with corporate America. "O Superman" begins with the most pervasive form of invasive tape recording, the phone message:

Hi. I'm not home right now. But if you want to leave a message,
just start talking at the sound of the tone.

Hello? This is your mother. Are you there? Are you coming home?
Hello? Is anybody home. (Part II)

Having established that no one is home, the mother's solicitous query
quickly takes on ominous overtones:

Well you don't know me
but I know you
And I've got a message to give to you.
Here come the planes.

.   .   .   .

And the voice said:
this is the hand, the hand that takes.
This is the hand. The hand that takes . . . Here come the planes.
They're American planes made in America. Smoking or non-smoking?
   (Part II)

As Henry Sayre points out, in this section Anderson uses the harmonizer
to lower her voice, linking the identities of technological authority and
masculinity (150). And just as female performer and male voice are united
through technological manipulation, so the maternal caller (Mom) is linked
to the sinister "hand that takes." The recipient of this message—presumably the daughter—must accept Mom's message and ask for comfort, not
in filial terms but in those offered by corporate rationality:

So hold me Mom, in your long arms,
in your automatic arms,
your electronic arms,

.   .   .   .

your petrochemical arms,
your military arms . . . . (Part II)

Critics of Laurie Anderson have objected to a certain depthlessness and
redundancy in her performances, yet such criticisms ignore the ways that
she implicates such depth models as part of her critical project.[18] *United
States* deals with the voice as a vessel for technological rationality—of "electronic arms," "smart bombs," and "friendly fire"—where the rhetoric of
nurturance and comfort is electronically imprinted onto the voice of authority. Such rhyming of rhetorics—of "mom" and "bomb"—occurs in the

larger media, to be sure, but finds its local occasion in the tapevoice of the phone machine, where absence is signaled by a simulacrum of presence.

Released from inexplicable code (Steve Benson)

As we have seen in the case of Ginsberg and Olson, the creation of a new lyric, performative voice was the first stage in contesting surveillance culture. The use of typewriter and tape recorder in rendering presence was a way of adapting the means of reproduction to productive uses. In the process, poets unwittingly discovered the role of technology in producing a poetics of presence. For Ginsberg, the spontaneous recording of his own voice into the tape recorder becomes the aural equivalent of the romantic diary, retaining a quotidian threatened by the "narcotic tobacco haze of capitalism" (as he says in "Howl"). Antin also privileges the immediacy of voice as the site of real-time experience. It is important for both Ginsberg and Antin that the tape recorder maintain a low profile as the agent for transcription, not for direct intervention. With Laurie Anderson and, as I will point out, Steve Benson, the tape recorder becomes an active agent in composition, modulating the voice, permitting its duplication, and assisting in its fragmentation. In place of lyric testimony, Anderson creates a hybrid, electronically modified voice, in which gender identity has been confused and technological complicity in gender hierarchies is foregrounded. Steve Benson uses the tape recorder to achieve many of the same results as Anderson in calling the self-sufficient speaker into question, yet he does so by some of the more process-oriented ethos of poets such as Ginsberg and Frank O'Hara.

Benson shares with many of his language-writing colleagues a distrust of the expressive voice that dominated much 1950s and 1960s writing, but he utilizes the latter's interest in real-time experience to create what Barrett Watten calls "dissonances of scale that call the speaker into account" (111). He does this by orchestrating interruptions in his performances that require him to improvise on the spot. Since 1977 he has used the tape recorder as a collaborator in this process. In various performances Benson wears headphones into which a tape is being played and to which he produces a spontaneous commentary. Whereas Laurie Anderson thematizes technology's intrusion into the quotidian, Benson *produces* the quotidian by his edgy, often uncertain response to the interrupting material. By an odd reversal of terms, technology allows him a greater degree of presence by forcing the speaker to respond, to interact, and to distract himself from the printed page. At the same time, since the audience is a party to only one portion of his performance—that being improvised—it must fill in or re-create the silent "other" voice available only to the one wearing the headphones.

A brilliant example of Benson's performance style can be seen in "Echo," a work that involves the recursive properties of a text endlessly recorded, played back, and responded to. Because "Echo" is first and foremost a performance, its transcription into a book (*Blindspots*) represents less the final product than a stage in what is a potentially infinite process of recording and rereading. The structure of the work is deceptively simple. Benson begins by reading a poem called "Echo." He then improvises a desultory rap with reference to the poem he has just read. He records this rap and then rewinds the tape, during which time he reads sections from a notebook or journal.[19] He then plays back the previously recorded tape through headphones and responds to it orally. By occasionally switching the public address speakers on and off, he controls the amount of prerecorded tape that the audience can hear, thus confusing the border between private and public hearing. The "new" version incorporating both improvised and prerecorded materials is simultaneously being recorded, and when he is finished, Benson rewinds this new tape, while once again reading from journals. He then plays the new tape—now containing all of the previous material—back through earphones and, once again, responds to it. In the performance from which the published version is based, the "original" tape is subjected to three re-readings, although in principle the number could be extended indefinitely.

While these complex procedures may resemble chance-generated techniques of Jackson Mac Low or John Cage, they differ in the degree of affective response they require. Benson is not trying to circumvent intentionality through randomness but to show one sort of intentionality thwarted by another. Nothing is random in the performance, since every new element is based on something that has already appeared. The audience witnesses a person trying to stay on top of an accretional information overload that threatens to overwhelm him. As a result, much of the text is devoted to rhetorical "filler"—the parenthetical language of everyday speech: "and the sort of I don't know I mean I wonder you know if listening to that you get the experience of a kind of a *haze* or you know does like there's nothing like Kirby was saying the 'it'" (32). It is this aimless quality of daily speech—the "it-ness" of real time—that interests Benson; he wants to find the intersection of a presence already heard (and recorded) with a presence immediately coming-into-being.

As an illustration of Benson's accretional mode, we might look at the opening lines of the four recorded variations. The first rap comes in direct response to the poem, "Echo":

1. That was, like many things, not really so much something that I
         would want to deem an abstraction
   or
   something that necessarily came across
   began to appear with a purpose to belong in some idea . . . (32)

2. It was, like many things
            I decided that, the most
      casual and appropriate plan would be to
                            sort of, step out of
   some kind of a black forest that I'd imagine myself to be in
   and without any particular purpose or a sense of trying to make
                     a case for my belonging, in the situation
            I would find some use for myself (35)

3. *It was , like many things*

            I decided that, the most
                            So—if   if there isn't a
      casual and appropriate plan would be to
                     model that attaches to that kind of
                            sort of, step out of
            practice of heading into
   some kind of a black forest that I'd imagine myself to be in
            white noise (39)

4.   **I decided that, the most**
      that we knew what that was and that if we got started
                     if there isn't a

      casual and appropriate plan would be
   into it we would inevitably be sort of propelled along as a
      model that attaches to that

                     step out of
            a madness, but in fact there wasn't
   practice of heading into

            a black forest that I'd imagine myself to be in
   anybody there other than some other people who basically were
   white noise. (47)

From a meditation on the poem "Echo," Benson, in part 2, imposes a mythic narrative onto his composition—"a black forest" inspired perhaps by the story of Echo and Narcissus. In part 3 he acknowledges that the "dark forest" that he hopes to escape is, in fact, a narratological model, a transformation of the writer's mimetic imperative into a social construct. In this section the emphasis is on his choice of certain semiotic elements to hold off "white noise," the obliteration of significant sound. In the fourth section the dark forest of self-reflection is revealed as potential "madness," and the white noise is revealed as the sound of "other people."

Of course to impose such a linear, developmental model on this work does violence to the performative experience. The tapevoice, its complexity notated by roman, italic, and bold typefaces, challenges the improviser's abilities to make sense. The overall recording of the performance displays Benson's nervous attempt to find "the right word" or to generate the "apt response" to a splintering informational field. It is, as his references to the "dark forest" indicate, a latter-day equivalent to Dante's journey into the *selva oscura*. At times he becomes aware of the tension between the desire to keep the present moving forward and the desire to write it down: "It's odd how I think / I *do* sort of tend to generate certain themes / and so you know immediately there's the impulse to / escape, to try to write it down" (41). But this impulse, as he says, "*preposterously* informs the present with a / manic reaction against what in fact was originally / improvised" (41). What Benson seems to be saying in such passages is that the impulse to treat the text as stabilizing the present is a vain endeavor, since all utterances are an improvisation within specific discursive limitations. By imposing several restraints on his ability to "go on," Benson achieves a Beckett-like stoicism in the face of temporal diffusion and disorder. But unlike Krapp, whose tapes provide a mnemonic for reflection, Benson re-creates the past by re-taping the present.

Echo and Narcissus: The Tapevoice Returns

Echo is the nymph whose fate it is to fall in love with Narcissus, a figure who can only love his own image. Her attempts to declare her love are complicated by the fact that she can only repeat his words. She is the tapevoice who is forced to speak by respeaking the language of others. Her voice is the simulacrum of voice, a speech without origin. By using the myth of Echo, Benson seems to be asking whether a truly reflective voice is possible in a technological age. Is Echo's private voice different from her public speech, or is it always a mirror of Narcissus's? In Vygotskyian terms, does her inner speech merely replicate the public sphere, or does thought constitute a fundamentally different mode of knowledge, and can that be represented? Benson tries to answer some of these questions by manipulating the tape recording such that each repetition of information contains a supplement of new material. Or to put it another way, each generation of new information always contains a residue of the past. Echo does not repeat herself in a solipsistic circle; she also generates a new subjectivity out of her debate with the other. As she announces in the title poem,

> You are trying to *be* the sunset. You are trying to make a
> person out of me. A person you might know.

> Know me but do not meet me. Hold me up to this tree
> and see the light I shed. (29)

Echo's crisis is that of the posttechnological cybervoice: how to generate authentic speech while recognizing one's inscription in prior voices. The fixed gender roles of Echo and Narcissus are broken down in the interplay between I and you, poet and beloved, poet and reader. By manipulating the frames between poem and tape, improvised voice and tapevoice, Benson situates his readers in the position of Echo, suspended "between" voices — our own and that of the addressee — just as Benson, wearing his headphones and pacing anxiously between one side of the performance space and the other, is between layers of tape.

Benson's attempt to create a modern, technological version of Ovid's tale represents an extreme version of presencing, one in which poetry is generated by submitting to the machine's reification of the voice. Although an earlier writer like Burroughs demonizes submission to the tape recorder of surveillance, Benson sees in such vulnerability a way of opposing the machine's panoptical control. By using the tape recorder to create contingency (rather than store it), Benson reestablishes an uneasy relationship to his own voice. And in the four decades since the "golden age" of surveillance, Ginsberg, Antin, and Anderson have provided, through the tape recorder, an alternative to the "waning of affect" lamented by Fredric Jameson and other postmodern theorists. Rather than search for forms of presence in peasant shoes or the windowless monad of aesthetic autonomy, these writers have heard in the tapevoice, to adapt Wallace Stevens, "ghostlier demarcations, keener sounds."

NOTES

1. Marjorie Perloff points out that when poets of the 1950s and 1960s speak of "common speech," it is not that of the common man, as invoked by poets from Wordsworth to Eliot, but "the making present, via the breath, of internal energy . . . *this* speech, *my* speech" (*Radical Artifice* 34). Perloff traces the growing

skepticism with this personalist ethos to the importance of masscult phenomena like television talk shows and political sound bytes in which the illusion of "common speech" is presented as actual, in which Baudrillard's "hyperreal" replaces the rhetoric of feeling, depth, and affectivity.

2. The best standard accounts are Altieri, *Enlarging*; Breslin; and Molesworth.

3. The important exception is the collection of essays on sound, radio, and magnetic recording edited by Kahn and Whitehead, *Wireless Imagination*. The editors rightly recognize that modernism was formed around a visualist imperative. Their anthology is an attempt to show the vitality and range of experimentation utilizing new acoustic technologies in everything from futurism and dada to the cut-up novels of William Burroughs.

4. On postmodernism as antiocularcentric, see Jay.

5. My interest in extending Foucault's thesis regarding the production of sexuality through specific social and ideological practices comes from Lauretis 35–38.

6. On Burroughs's use of the tape recorder, see Robin Lydenberg, "Sound Identity Fading Out: William Burroughs' Tape Experiments" in Kahn and Whitehead 409–37.

7. On the history of magnetic recording, see Angus; Engel; "Sound"; and Thiele.

8. On surveillance technology, see Brenton; Donner; Lapidus; Long; Miller; and Packard.

9. *Olmstead v. United States*, 277 U.S. 438, 48 S. Ct. 564, 72 L.Ed. 944 (1928).

10. Qtd. in Lapidus 17.

11. "Despite repeated refusals of Congress to legalize eavesdropping, over sixty executive agencies were reported to have extensive electronic monitoring hardware which they used in investigations. The Internal Revenue Service of the Treasury Department conducted a seven-week course for agents in electronic eavesdropping, installing microphones, and monitoring calls. The Department of Justice in 1962 created an Organized Crime Division and authorized investigations to be made by use of electronic equipment" (Lapidus 12).

12. Nixon was by no means the first president to bug his office. Franklin Roosevelt installed a secret recording device, although as McCullough says, it was removed by Truman when he took office (403).

13. I have discussed *Visions of Cody* and its use of the tape recorder in *San Francisco Renaissance* 73–76.

14. On Antin's talk pieces see Altieri, "Postmodernism"; Davidson, "Writing"; Perloff, " 'No More Margins' "; and Sayre.

15. See Austin, and Levinson 24–27, 229–31, 238–40.

16. This scenario is at the core of Horkheimer and Adorno's criticism of radio in "Culture Industry." The difference between a telephone and a radio, Adorno contends, is that "the former [allows] the subscriber to play the *role* of the subject" while the latter is democratic: "it turns all participants into listeners and authoritatively subjects them to broadcast programs which are all exactly the same" (122). Antin challenges the unidirectional format of radio by permitting the listener to "play the role of subject." But it is still a "role" that the listener plays, since she/he is really not permitted a response. What Adorno fails to see (or at least could not

have anticipated when the essay was written in the 1940s) is the degree to which certain forms of radio (talk shows, consumer channels, and call-in formats) provide the listener with a more interactive role.

17. Parts of *United States* can be heard on a Warner Brothers recording, *Big Science* (1982), and seen in a book, *United States* (1984). References to the text will refer to the book, although since it is not paginated, reference will be made to individual sections listed in the book's contents page.

18. For a résumé of critical responses to *United States* along with an interview with Laurie Anderson, see Dery.

19. In a performance of "Echo" at 80 Langton Street in San Francisco, Benson says that in reading from his journals he tries to "negate every sentence and turn the sentence into saying the opposite of what it seemed to be saying." In conversation Benson elaborated on this remark, saying that such negations and transformations represent ways of keeping the performance situation alive and mobile. Instead of providing "filler" while the tape is rewinding, these journal readings provide another occasion for response.

WORKS CITED

Altieri, Charles. *Enlarging the Temple: New Directions in American Poetry during the 1960's.* Lewisburg, Pa.: Bucknell University Press, 1979.

———. "The Postmodernism of David Antin's *Tuning.*" *College English* 48 (1986): 9–26.

Anderson, Laurie. *Collected Videos.* Los Angeles: Warner Reprise, 1990.

———. *United States.* New York: Harper, 1984.

Angus, Robert. "History of Magnetic Recording: Part I." *Audio* 68.8 (1984): 27–33, 96–97.

———. "History of Magnetic Recording: Part II." *Audio* 68.9 (1984): 33–39.

Antin, David. "whos listening out there." *tuning.* New York: New Directions, 1984. 269–96.

Austin, J. L. *How to Do Things with Words.* Cambridge, Mass.: Harvard University Press, 1975.

Benjamin, Walter. "The Work of Art in the Age of Mechanical Reproduction." *Illuminations: Essays and Reflections.* Ed. Hannah Arendt. Trans Harry Zohn. New York: Schocken, 1968. 217–51.

Benson, Steve. *Blindspots.* Cambridge, Mass.: Whale Cloth Press, 1981.

———. Reading at 80 Langton Street. Audiotape. University of California, San Diego. Archive for New Poetry L-714, 1981.

Brenton, Myron. *The Privacy Invaders.* New York: Coward-McCann, 1964.

Breslin, James E. B. *From Modern to Contemporary: American Poetry, 1945–1965.* Chicago: University of Chicago Press, 1984.

Burroughs, William S. *The Ticket That Exploded.* New York: Grove, 1967.

Creeley, Robert. "The Language." *The Collected Poems of Robert Creeley, 1945–1975.* Berkeley: University of California Press, 1982. 283.

Davidson, Michael. " 'By ear, he sd': Audio-Tapes and Contemporary Criticism." *Credences* n.s. 1.1 [1981]: 105–20.

————. *The San Francisco Renaissance: Poetics and Community at Mid-century*. Cambridge: Cambridge University Press, 1989.

————. "Writing at the Boundaries." *New York Times Book Review* 24 February 1985: 1, 28–29.

Dery, Mark. "Signposts on the Road to Nowhere: Laurie Anderson's Crisis of Meaning." *South Atlantic Quarterly* 90 (1991): 785–801.

Donner, Frank J. *The Age of Surveillance: The Aims and Methods of America's Political Intelligence System*. New York: Knopf, 1980.

Engel, Friedrich Karl. "Magnetic Tape: From the Early Days to the Present." *AES: Journal of the Audio Engineering Society* 36 (1988): 606–16.

Foucault, Michel. *The History of Sexuality*. Vol. 1. Trans. Robert Hurley. New York: Vintage, 1980.

Ginsberg, Allen. *Collected Poems, 1947–1980*. New York: Harper, 1984.

Haraway, Donna J. "A Cyborg Manifesto: Science, Technology, and Socialist-Feminism in the Late Twentieth Century." *Simians, Cyborgs, and Women: The Reinvention of Nature*. New York: Routledge, 1991. 149–81.

Horkheimer, Max, and Theodor Adorno. "The Culture Industry: Enlightenment as Mass Deception." *Dialectic of Enlightenment*. Trans. John Cumming. New York: Seabury, 1972. 120–67.

Jameson, Fredric. "The Cultural Logic of Late Capitalism." *Postmodernism: Or, the Cultural Logic of Late Capitalism*. Durham: Duke University Press, 1991. 1–54.

Jay, Martin. *Downcast Eyes: The Denigration of Vision in Twentieth-Century French Thought*. Berkeley: University of California Press, 1993.

Kahn, Douglas, and Gregory Whitehead, eds. *Wireless Imagination: Sound, Radio, and the Avant-Garde*. Cambridge, Mass.: MIT Press, 1992.

Kaplan, Alice Yaeger. *Reproductions of Banality: Fascism, Literature, and French Intellectual Life*. Minneapolis: University of Minnesota Press, 1986.

Lapidus, Edith J. *Eavesdropping on Trial*. Rochelle Park, N.J.: Hayden Book, 1974.

Lauretis, Teresa de. *Technologies of Gender: Essays on Theory, Film, and Fiction*. Bloomington: Indiana University Press, 1987.

Levinson, Stephen. *Pragmatics*. Cambridge: Cambridge University Press, 1985.

Long, Edward V. *The Intruders: The Invasion of Privacy by Government and Industry*. New York: Praeger, 1967.

McCullough, David. *Truman*. New York: Simon, 1992.

Miller, Arthur R. *The Assault on Privacy: Computers, Data Banks, and Dossiers*. Ann Arbor: University of Michigan Press, 1971.

Molesworth, Charles. *The Fierce Embrace: A Study of Contemporary American Poetry*. Columbia: University of Missouri Press, 1979.

Olson, Charles. *The Maximus Poems*. Ed. George F. Butterick. Berkeley: University of California Press, 1983.

————. "Projective Verse." *Selected Writings of Charles Olson*. Ed. Robert Creeley. New York: New Directions, 1966. 15–26.

Ong, Walter J. *Orality and Literacy: The Technologizing of the Word*. London: Methuen, 1982.

Owens, Craig. "Amplifications: Laurie Anderson." *Art in America* 69 (1981): 120–23.

Packard, Vance. *The Naked Society*. New York: McKay, 1964.

Perloff, Marjorie. " 'No More Margins': John Cage, David Antin, and the Poetry of Performance." *The Poetics of Indeterminacy: Rimbaud to Cage*. Princeton: Princeton University Press, 1981. 288–339.

———. *Radical Artifice: Writing Poetry in the Age of Media*. Chicago: University of Chicago Press, 1991.

Sayre, Henry. *The Object of Performance: The American Avant-Garde since 1970*. Chicago: University of Chicago Press, 1989.

Silverman, Kaja. *The Acoustic Mirror: The Female Voice in Psychoanalysis and Cinema*. Bloomington: Indiana University Press, 1988.

"Sound." *Encyclopedia Britannica: Macropoedia*. 1992.

Thiele, Heinz H. K. "Magnetic Sound Recording in Europe up to 1945." *AES: Journal of the Audio Engineering Society* 36 (1988): 396–408.

Watten, Barrett. "Total Syntax: The Work in the World." *Total Syntax*. Carbondale: Southern Illinois University Press, 1985. 65–114.

PART TWO

Performance/

GROUNDINGS

Ritual/Event

THE MUSIC OF
John Cage's
VERBAL SPACE
"What You Say . . ."

> Syntax, like
> government, can only be obeyed.   It is
> therefore of no use except when you
> have something particular to command
> such as: Go buy me a bunch of carrots. (Cage, "Diary" 215)

As early as 1939, when he was in residence at the Cornish School of Music in Seattle, John Cage investigated the application of electrical technology to music. His first (perhaps *the* first) electroacoustic composition was *Imaginary Landscape No. 1*, a six-minute radio piece for muted piano, cymbal, and two variable-speed record turntables, designed to accompany the production of Jean Cocteau's play *Marriage at the Eiffel Tower*. The piece was performed by Cage, his wife, Xenia, and two friends in two separate studios; mixed in the control room; and beamed the short distance to the theater.[1] *Imaginary Landscape No. 1* looks ahead to any number of Cage compositions involving radio, magnetic tape, and computer technologies. And yet the irony is that, having produced so many complex intermedia works using the most varied acoustic materials, by 1970 or so Cage started to write a series of "mesostics," performance works that made use of only a single instrument—the human voice—and a single medium—language.

"My first mesostic," Cage writes in the foreword to *M*, "was written as prose to celebrate one of Edwin Denby's birthdays. The following ones, each letter of the name being on its own line, were written as poetry. *A given letter capitalized does not occur between it and the preceding capitalized letter.* I thought I was writing acrostics, but Norman O. Brown pointed out that they could properly be called 'mesostics' (row not down the edge but down the middle)" (*M* 1).

Here is the Edwin Denby mesostic of 1970, called "Present":

rEmembering a Day i visited you — seems noW
as I write that the weather theN was warm — i
recall nothing we saiD, nothing wE did; eveN so
(perhaps Because of that) that visit staYs.

This first attempt, as Cage suggests, was clearly not quite satisfactory. The four-line text, with its justified left and right margins, does not have much visual interest, the capital letters merely appearing in a linear sequence. More important, the Denby mesostic does not have much aural or musical complexity, its prose format being that of normal writing of the sort we all do when we write a note to a friend on an occasion like a birthday. True, the mesostic rule (Cage was later to call this a 50 percent mesostic, since the given letter capitalized can occur between it and the following capitalized letter, whereas a 100 percent mesostic does not allow for occurrence of the letter either preceding or following its appearance) is observed, but hearing this particular text read, one would not especially notice the structuration of language by the EDWIN DENBY string, although — a harbinger of things to come — the *Y* word, "staYs," rhymes with the *D* word, "Day."

The difficulty at this stage was that Cage was still using normal syntax. In another early mesostic, titled "On the windshield of a new Fiat for James K[losty] (who had not made up his mind where to go) and Carolyn Brown," we read:

asK

Little

autO

Where it wantS

To take

You. (*M* 94)

Unlike the Denby mesostic, this one is "written as poetry," in that each capital letter gets a line to itself (and as a 100 percent mesostic, its "wing words" are of necessity very short), but again, the poem's syntax and sound are almost those of ordinary conversation. Thus, although the Klosty mesostic is visually more of a "poem" than is the Edwin Denby one, the poetic problem has not yet been resolved.

Cage was quite aware of this quandary. When, in the early 1970s, the French philosopher Daniel Charles posed the question, "*Aren't your lectures, for example, musical works in the manner of the different chapters of Walden?*" Cage replied, "They are when sounds are words. But I must say that I have not yet carried language to the point to which I have taken musical sounds. . . .

I hope to make something other than language from it." And he adds, "It is that aspect, the *impossibility of language*, that interests me at present." Again, in a later exchange, when Charles remarks, "*You propose to musicate language; you want language to be heard as music*," Cage responds, "I hope to let words exist, as I have tried to let sounds exist" (*For the Birds* 113, 151).[2]

Making language as interesting as music, Cage was to learn, depended on the dismantling of "normal" syntax. Much as he loved James Joyce, Cage felt that even *Finnegans Wake* was conventional in this respect: "Reading *Finnegans Wake* I notice that though Joyce's subjects, verbs, and objects are unconventional, their relationships are the ordinary ones. With the exception of the Ten Thunderclaps and rumblings here and there, *Finnegans Wake* employs syntax. Syntax gives it a rigidity from which classical Chinese and Japanese were free. A poem by Basho, for instance, floats in space. . . . Only the imagination of the reader limits the number of the poem's possible meanings" (*M* 2). In the former case, the words themselves are made strange, Joyce being, of course, a master of word formation, punning, metaphor, and allusion, but the syntax is left intact; "Joyce," Cage remarks elsewhere, "seemed to me to have kept the old structures ('sintalks') in which he put the new words he had made" ("Writing" 133). The alternative (Basho's) is to use "ordinary" language but to explode the syntax, a process Cage regularly referred to as the "demilitarization of the language." "Speaking without syntax," he explains in a note on "Sixty-Two Mesostics Re Merce Cunningham," "we notice that cadence, Dublinese or ministerial, takes over. (Looking out the rear-window.) Therefore we tried whispering. Encouraged we began to chant. . . . To raise language's temperature we not only remove syntax: we give each letter undivided attention setting it in unique face and size; *to read* becomes the verb *to sing*" ("Notes" 97). But he admits in the foreword to *M* that "my work in this field is tardy. It follows the poetry of Jackson Mac Low and Clark Coolidge, my analogous work in the field of music, and my first experiments, texts for Song Books. . . . Concrete and sound poets have also worked in this field for many years, though many, it seems to me, have substituted graphic or musical structures for syntactical ones" (2).

Cage is quite right to refer to his work in this field as tardy. As early as 1960, Jackson Mac Low had written a sequence called *Stanzas for Iris Lezak* based on chance operations. "Call me Ishmael," for example, takes the first three words of *Moby-Dick* as its acrostic string and finds the words that begin with the thirteen consecutive letters *C-A-L-L-M-E-I-S-H-M-A-E-L* in the novel's first few pages, as determined by chance operations.[3] These operations also determined their lineation, so that we have five three-line stanzas, with the pattern 4–2–7 words per line, respectively:

Circulation. And long long
Mind every
Interest Some how mind and every long

Coffin about little little
Money especially
I shore, having money about especially little

Cato a little little
Me extreme
I sail have me an extreme little

Cherish and left, left,
Myself extremest
It see hypos myself and extremest left,

City a land. Land.
Mouth; east,
Is spleen, hand, mouth; an east, land. (89)

When Cage began to write mesostics, he adopted Mac Low's acrostic procedures, but with an important difference. Whereas in the example above,
Mac Low lets chance operations generate the entire text, Cage, as we shall
see, uses these operations to generate the word pool to be used and the rules
to be followed, but he then fills in lines with wing words, generated, as
he repeatedly put it, "according to taste."[4] The result is an idiom markedly
different from Mac Low's, especially in its vocal quality, Cage preferring
softer, blending sounds to the harshly stressed monosyllabic nouns, separated by strong caesuras, that we find in "Call Me Ishmael."

A similar difference may be observed between Cage and concrete poets
such as the Brazilian Noigandres group (Augusto de Campos, Haroldo de
Campos, and Decio Pignatari), with whom he shared many aesthetic principles and who have assiduously translated and disseminated his writings.
In concrete poetry—say Augusto de Campos's *Luxo* or Pignatari's *Beba coca
cola*—the visual image predominates, the actualization of performance not
giving the listener the full effect of the figure the poem makes, a figure de-
pending on complex patterns of typography, spacing, color contrasts, and
so on. In Cage, by contrast, it is the aural that dominates. Indeed, however
visually striking Cage's verbal scores may be, the mesostic column creating an interesting pattern and the punctuation marks of the original often
strewn around the page, as in *Roaratorio*, poetic density depends primarily

on sound, as actualized in performance. Cage was, after all, a composer even when the materials he worked with were linguistic rather than musical.

The influences Cage cites in *M* could thus take him only so far. A decade of experimentation followed. While the earliest mesostics, such as the "25 Mesostics Re and not Re Mark Tobey" (*M* 186–94), were written in Cage's own words (the first "MARK" mesostic reads "it was iMpossible / to do Anything: / the dooR / was locKed"), and while what we might call the middle ones were "writings through" such great literary texts as *Finnegans Wake* or Ezra Pound's *Cantos*, in his last years Cage turned increasingly to making mesostics out of texts not in themselves consciously poetic.[5] In Tokyo in 1986, for example, Cage performed a mesostic piece called "Sculpture Musicale," which used as its source text for the mesostic string only that title and the following words of Duchamp's: "sons durant et partant de différents points et formant une sculpture sonore qui dure." A second Tokyo piece submitted to writing-through Cage's own "Lecture on Nothing," even as his "Rhythm, etc." (1988) takes a passage from *A Year from Monday* ("There's virtually nothing to say about rhythm . . .") and uses the four sentences of this passage as the mesostic string.

Discussions of Cagean mesostic have usually ignored this evolution from mesostic strings based on single proper names, repeated throughout (as in the case of the name JAMES JOYCE in the *Roaratorio*), to strings derived from larger statements or paragraphs, whose individual words are part of the standard lexicon. The turning point from the "proper name" string to what we might call the "sentence" string may well have come with the writing, in the early 1980s, of the performance piece "James Joyce, Marcel Duchamp, Erik Satie: An Alphabet." In this complex work, the hypothetical "conversation" between the three artists is presented, partly by means of found text, artfully collaged from their writings, and partly by Cage's own discourse, structured by the proper names of the three artists, repeated as mesostic strings according to chance operations. In "A Conversation about Radio in Twelve Parts" with Richard Kostelanetz, conducted a few years later, Cage expressed dissatisfaction with *Alphabet* because its "scenes [are] in a very simple way differentiated from one another. They don't overlap so that it's as simple as a work by Stravinsky, but within each part there's a great disparateness with the next part; so that the act of listening is very uncomfortable." "All those scenes," he explained, "have beginnings and endings. It's a multiplicity of beginnings and endings. That's what annoys me. I don't mind it as something to read; but as something to hear" (293–94).

What Cage means, I think, is that proper-name mesostics, derived not from a writing-through but from sentences made up for the occasion, have a tendency to form independent strophes of four to six lines, strophes divided by a sharp pause and hence not sufficiently "interpenetrating" phonemically. For example:

from his Jumping
the older one is Erik SAtie
he never stops sMiling
and thE younger one
iS joyce, thirty-nine

he Jumps
with his back tO the audience
for all we know he maY be quietly weeping
or silently laughing or both you just Can't
tEll[6]

Here the syntactically straightforward narrative perhaps too easily yields the requisite mesostic letters: *J-A-M-E-S* and *J-O-Y-C-E*; if, say, an *O* were needed as the final mesostic letter, Cage could substitute "knOw" for "tEll" without it making much difference. Then, too, the stanza break follows the normal syntactic break: "the younger one is Joyce, thirty-nine. // He jumps," thus producing the "differentiat[ion] from one another" Cage criticizes.

The solution was to use a seemingly inconsequential prose text as the source, not only for his own writing-through but for the mesostic string as well. Cage called this form of mesostic an autoku: " 'Ku' I take from haiku. . . . An autoku uses its entire source as the string down the center of the mesostic, providing, at the same time, all the wing words" ("Time" 266). In this variant of mesostic, there is, in other words, a rule to follow, but that rule is so hidden that "beginnings and endings" cannot call attention to themselves. Moreover, the discourse of ordinary prose—a passage from an interview, a newspaper paragraph, or a statement from a lecture— could now be decomposed and recharged so as to uncover the mysteries of language. "You see," Cage told Niksa Gligo in an interview, "language controls our thinking; and if we change our language, it is conceivable that our thinking would change" (Kostelanetz 149). For this purpose, "empty words" are more useful than "full" ones. "Full words," Cage explains to Richard Kostelanetz, "are words that are nouns *or* verbs *or* adjectives *or* adverbs," whereas "empty words" (what we call function words or deictics) are "connective[s] or pronoun[s]—word[s] that refer to something else" (141).

As an example of such an "empty word" mesostic, I have chosen the autoku "What You Say . . ." from 1986, a writing-through of an informal statement on aesthetics made by Jasper Johns in an interview with Christian Geelhaar. This is the first of two companion texts based on Johns's commentary on his work, the second being "Art Is Either a Complaint or Do Something Else," which is taken from a series of statements cited by Mark Rosenthal in his *Jasper Johns: Work since 1974*. Cage discusses this mesostic piece with Joan Retallack, in an interview originally published in *Aerial* (1991), together with "Art Is Either a Complaint." As Cage explains the piece, "it's all from words of Jasper Johns, but they're used with chance operations in such a way that they make different connections than they did when he said them. On the other hand, they seem to reinforce what he was saying . . . almost in his way. And why that should surprise me I don't know because all of the words are his. (*laughs*) But they make different connections" ("Second Conversation" 107).[7]

Consider the "different connections" in "What You Say . . . ," which draws on a statement Johns makes at the very end of the Geelhaar interview:

> What you say about my tendency to add things is correct. But, how
> does one make a painting? How does one deal with the space? Does
> one have something and then proceed to add another thing or does
> one have something; move into it; occupy it; divide it; make the
> best one can of it? I think I do different things at different
> times and perhaps at the same time. It interests me that a part can
> function as a whole or that a whole can be thrown into a situation
> in which it is only a part. It interests me that what one takes to
> be a whole subject can suddenly be miniaturized, or something, and
> then be inserted into another world, as it were.[8]

Notice that Cage's reproduction of Johns's response is already a kind of writing-through, the sentences being arranged as line lengths and centered so as to give the whole an accordion-like visual shape. At the Los Angeles performance I attended (at UCLA, 4 September 1987, in conjunction with the opening of the exhibition of the Samuel Beckett–Jasper Johns collaboration *Fizzles*), "What You Say . . ." was preceded by the reading of three short mesostics on the name JASPER JOHNS, one of them having appeared in *Empty Words* (1979) under the title "Song":

```
            not Just
                gArdener
        morelS
            coPrini,
        morEls,
        copRini.

            not Just hunter:
        cutting dOwn
        ailantHus,
            cuttiNg down
        ailanthuS. (10)
```

Notice that this mesostic belongs to Cage's earlier "concrete poetry" phase, the lines built primarily on catalogs of nouns, and the game being that each of two words (or phrases) per stanza can supply the poet with the necessary capital letters (e.g., the *S* and *E* of "morels"). These are primarily eye devices. By the time Cage wrote "What You Say . . . ," his aim was to "musicate" the language, letting it do the sorts of things he had hitherto done with musical sounds. Indeed, at the UCLA performance the piece was performed by a dozen or so readers, according to the following program notes:

> For any number of readers able to read in one breath any of the 124 "stanzas" (a "stanza" is a line or lines preceded and followed by a space).

> Each reader, equipped with a chronometer, and without intentionally changing the pitch or loudness of the voice quietly reads any 4 "stanzas" at any 4 times in each minute of the agreed-upon performance time.

> The readers are seated or stand around the audience or both within and outside it.[9]

Whether performed chorally or by Cage himself (and I have heard it done both ways), the "frame" is now no longer the decision how many times to repeat a given proper name like JAMES JOYCE but the "agreed-upon performance time." Cage's initial experiments with magnetic tape in the late 1940s and early 1950s, Margaret Leng Tan has pointed out, "emphasized the fact that duration (time length) is synonymous with tape length (space) and it is the application of this principle which forms the basis for the space-time proportional notation used in the *Music of Changes* and the *Two Pastorales* of 1951" (51). The same principle, Cage came to see, could be applied to language texts. In the case of "What You Say . . . ," duration would seem to be determined by the need to provide one line for each of the 512 letters in Johns's paragraph. But in fact "What You Say . . ." is much longer than 512 "lines" because of the spacing (silence) Cage introduces between word groups, with extra rests replacing the missing letters—missing because "for several letters there were no words: the v of have (twice); the v of move; the j of subject; and the z of miniaturized. Spaces between lines take the place of the missing letters" ("What," in *Formations* 53).

The selection of words from the source pool, Cage explains in his note to "What You Say . . ." (53), is based on MESOLIST, "a program by Jim Rosenberg," extended for this particular piece by a second program made by Andrew Culver, which expanded "the number of characters in a search string . . . to any length; this extended MESOLIST was used to list the available words which were then subjected to IC (a program by Andrew Culver simulating the coin oracle of the *I Ching*)." Although I have not seen this program, it seems clear that even though the MESOLIST-derived "chance operations" do govern the sequencing of the words that contain the requisite letters for the mesostic string, the variable length of the search string made it possible for Cage to create precisely the semantic and phonemic juxtapositions that suited him. In this particular case, he had to begin with a line containing the *W* of the first word, "What," followed by the *h*, the *a*, and so on, and the first *W* word designated by MESOLIST is the last word of Johns's statement—"were." But although chance operations dictated the selection of "were" as the first capitalized word to be used in "What You Say . . . ," it was Cage's own choice to place, in the opening line, the whole phrase, "as it Were." Indeed, as we shall see, in this instance as elsewhere, Cage's poetic composition is nothing if not *designed*. As he put it in the foreword to *Silence*, "As I see it, poetry is not prose simply because poetry is in one way or another formalized. It is not poetry by reason of its content or ambiguity but by reason of its allowing musical elements (time, sound) to be introduced into the world of words" (x).

The world of words, in this case, consists of 7 "ordinary" sentences (3 of which are questions), containing 127 words, 99 of which are monosyllables. This is already an unusual linguistic situation, but—what is even odder—there are only 7 words in the entire passage that have more than 2 syllables.[10] And further, the majority of monosyllables and disyllables are deictics or function words: "it" appears 7 times; "thing," 6 times; "one," 5 times; "something," 3 times; "how," "what," and "whole," 2 times each. In this context, the word that stands out is the 5-syllable "miniaturized" in the next to last line.[11]

The sentence structure is as elementary as is the word pool. "How does one" with the variant "does one" appears four times; "it interests me that," twice; and simple parallel structure occurs in "move into it; occupy it; divide it; make the best one can of it." Johns's statement, at least as lineated here, thus has a naive or childlike sound structure, especially since the artist hesitates or withdraws statements, as in "I think I do different things at different times and perhaps at the same time," or when he declares that "a whole subject can suddenly be miniaturized, or something." Finally, the paragraph concludes with the qualifier, "as it were."

Why would Cage, who has previously written-through the incredibly rich word pool of *Finnegans Wake* or the hieratic rhythms of Pound's *Cantos*, select such an ordinary, flat discourse to write-through? After all, Johns's statement is just an unrehearsed response to a question from an interviewer. This is, of course, Cage's point. "There is no such thing as an empty space or an empty time. There is always something to see, something to hear" (*Silence* 8). Even in his off-the-cuff remarks about his art making, Johns, so Cage posits, is saying something significant, is posing basic questions about painting. And moreover, Johns's own vocal patterns, with which Cage was of course deeply familiar, produce a sound curve to which Cage's own sound curve is designed to respond. Indeed, the composer-poet's role, in this scheme of things, is to bring Johns's "something," his particular signature—the visual made verbal and vocal—out into the open, by "de-militarizing" the syntax so as to controvert the chosen statement's linearity
CD5 and permit its components to realign themselves. Let us listen.

"What You Say . . ." opens with the final "as it Were" of Johns's paragraph and comes full circle to "wEre" on its last page. Here is the beginning:

as it Were

anotHer world

A whole or
The best one can of it

suddenlY
sOmething

move

miniatUrized.

Perhaps the first thing to perceive here is the elaborate sound structure, a structure especially notable in Cage's own reading of the text in which each line, spoken slowly, is followed by a silence the length of a short syllable.[12] The first three lines are linked by stress pattern (two stresses per line), anaphora of short *as* and internal rhyme ("Were"/"world"/"or").

In line 4, the sound shifts to short vowels, embedded in *t*s and *th*s; the lightly stressed monosyllabic line "The best one can of it," being related to the first three by the repetition of "it," the internal rhyme of "an" (in "another") and "can," and of "-tHer" and "The" (*t*s and *th*s, incidentally, constitute fifty-two or roughly one-tenth of the poem's phonemes). Lines 5 and 6—"suddenlY / sOmething"—are again related by stress pattern and alliteration, and "move," with its open vowel followed by a voiced spirant, opens the way for the alliterating *m* of the passage's longest (and perhaps least musical) word, "miniatUrized," a word that appears again and again, furnishing the different letters of the "What You Say . . ." string.

But there is also a curious clinamen in this passage. Line 7, "move," is not part of the mesostic string at all, "WHAT YOU" being complete without it. The source text reads, "does one have to do something; move into it." Cage might have put "move" on line 6 with the semicolon, or he might have left the word out completely, since the search string can be, as Cage points out, of any length. Yet "move," physically moved over to the right here, has an important effect. The domain of art, the text suggests, is "as it Were / anotHer world / A whole or / The best one can of it." This other world is "suddenlY / sOmething," and it is, in Cage's elliptical construction, "move"—which is to say, moving, on the move, in movement, in a move toward, the "miniaturization" of "subject" that is art.

But of course the text itself we are reading (or hearing) is precisely this miniaturization, this creation of "suddenlY / sOmething." Lift the ordinary out of the zone of saying, Cage seems to say ("The best one can of it") and "it" will become "something." Just as Johns would paint ordinary numbers (0 to 9) or the letters of the alphabet (*A* to *Z*) or a clothes hanger or beer can, so Cage will take words as uninteresting as "as," "it," "or," "of," and "a"; place those words in particular spatial configurations, white space (silence) being at least as prominent as the spoken and written language itself; and create a minimalist *ars poetica* (see fig. 1).

That Cage's work continues to go unrecognized as poetry by those who produce books such as the *Norton Anthology of Poetry*, as well as those who read and review them, has to do with our general inability to dissociate "poetry" from the twin norms of self-expression and figuration. "What You Say . . . ," it is argued by Cage's detractors (and they are legion), is, after all, no more than a reproduction of someone else's text: the "I" is not Cage's, and in any case, there is no psychological revelation of a personal sort. Moreover, in the passage we have just read there is not a single metaphor (except for that dead metaphor "world") or arresting visual image. Indeed, Cage's diction, so this line of reasoning goes, is merely trivial, isn't it?

Figure 1. Jasper Johns, *Figure 5* (1955). Encaustic and collage on canvas, 44.5 cm x 35.6 cm (17 ½″ x 14″). Collection of the artist.

This is to ignore the crucial role played by the context in which words occur, by their temporal and spatial arrangement, and especially by their sound. Take, for example, the common phrase "make the best one can of it" in Johns's paragraph. Eliminate the initial "make" and the phrase becomes the strange "The best one can of it," made even stranger by its insertion in the text between "A whole or" and "suddenlY." Yet the realignment produces a new meaning: "a whole or / the best" may now be read as adjectives modifying "world," and "the best one can" may be construed as a noun phrase. Certainly a "can" is a kind of whole. Aural performance, in any case, activates any number of meanings, especially since the spacing (the visual equivalence of silence) ensures very slow reading, whether one or more persons are reading simultaneously. "SuddenlY / sOmething / move / miniatUrized"—one word per line, a rest between lines—the audience is forced to listen carefully, to pay attention to the sound of each unit.

The strategy of "What You Say . . ."—and this is where the mesostic mode, with its dependence on a fixed word pool, can work so effectively— is to recharge individual words by consistently shifting their context and hence their use. Take the word "whole," used three times in Johns's statement: "It interests me that a part can function as a *whole* or that a *whole* can be thrown into a situation in which it is only a part. It interests me that what one takes to be a *whole* subject can suddenly be miniaturized" (my emphasis). In Cage, this "normal" syntax gives way to astonishing variations. "Whole" appears twenty-eight times, each of its letters appearing in the mesostic string of the text. Along the way it yields stanzas such as

oF it

a whole sUbject
aNd then
a whole Can be
whaT you say about
It

Occupy it

a whole caN
hAve
different timeS and
tAkes
can be throWn
and perHaps at the same time

Or
how does one deaL with
diffErent times and. ("What," in *Formations* 62)

Here the mesostic string is "FUNCTION AS A WHOLE." But the poem itself questions this "function"; the "whole sUbject" is in apposition to a mere "it"; "a whole Can be" "whaT you say about / It," "a whole caN / hAve / different timeS and / takes," it can be "throWn / and perHaps at the same time." On the next page "wHole" furnishes Cage with the *H* mesostic letter and thus becomes a "hole."

Now let us look again at the source text, which reads, "What one takes to be a whole subject can suddenly be miniaturized." Cage's own text enacts precisely this statement: what we "take to be a whole" dissolves into a number of possibilities. Not only can this "whole" be "miniaturized," but it "caN / hAve / different timeS and / tAkes"; there is no essential truth behind the word: "a whole Can be / whaT you say about / It." A neat illustration, as it were, of Wittgenstein's proposition that "the meaning of a word is its use in the language."

Again, consider the couplings and uncouplings given to the word "tendency," which appears only once in Johns's statement, in the opening sentence: "What you say about my tendency to add things is correct":

hoW

about my tenDency

thrOwn into a

thEn

and then be inSerted

my tendency tO

move iNto it.

What tendency, we wonder, is this? "ThrOwn into a / thEn"? "My tendency tO / move iNto it"? It sounds risky. Two pages later, we read

How does one

It

my teNdency to

have somethinG

deAl

where "deal" may be either noun or verb, either indicative or imperative, the "teNdency to / have somethinG" therefore being quite mysterious. Further down on the same page, the plot thickens:

i Think

a situatiOn in which

you sAy about

one Deal with

tenDency

As it were.

Let's make a deal and take care of the situation in which the tendency in question arises, as it were. Two pages later, we find the stanza

```
                    moVe
                     It
                                      make
                   i Do
                  movE
                  whIch
                    Tendency
                   My
              situAtion in which
            i thinK
               onE
        can funcTion as.
```

The instructions are to "moVe / It" (reinforced by the verb "make," another one of what we might call outriders in the text, "make" not being part of the mesostic chain, which here is "[DI]VIDE IT MAKE T[HE BEST OF IT]"), to which the response is "i Do / movE," and now "tendency" is explicitly linked to "situation," a "situAtion in which / i thinK / onE / can funcTion as." Function as what? Johns's "tendency to add things" now takes on a darker cast, his tendency producing a situation in which the artist only thinks he can function. When "tendency" reappears some time later in the performance, it is "thAt / teNdency to / oF it," where the "tendency" can be interpreted in a variety of ways. Or again, it becomes a "whoLe / tendencY to / whAt one / occuPy." The last three pages of "What You Say . . ." accelerate the repetition, "tendency" appearing six more times:

```
(1)                            to bE
                      my tendenCy
                           That
                         spaCe

(2)                          doeS one
                             fUnction as a
                           tenDency

(3)                          mY tendency
                  is correct

(4)                        it intErests me
                           tenDency
                     it
```

(5)	anD perhaps
	whaT one takes to be
tendency to add tHings is	
havE	

(6)	caN
	One
	Tendency to
sometHing.	

This is Cage at his most Steinian, charging language by means of permutation, words like "tendency" taking on a different aura with every repetition. What makes these pieces so remarkable is that they are, to use Joyce's term, "verbivocovisual." Visual, to take it backward, in that the spacing and mesostic chain produces its own meanings, so that "tenDency," with that "ten" separating out, is not the same as "tendenCy," and the construction of larger units will depend on word placement and spacing. "Verbi," in that Cage is always constructing new meanings, in this case giving new connotations to a "tendency" Johns mentions only casually. But it is the "voco" (musical) element that perhaps dominates here. For given the nature of the writing-through process, there are only so many words at the composer's disposal, and these words — "what," "world," "perhaps," "another," "something," "interest," and "function" — appear again and again, becoming familiar counters. "Miniaturized," for example, has nine lives, supplying the mesostic string with necessary letters (aurally phonemes) at frequent intervals, even as its z, as Cage notes, cannot be used.

As such, Cage's sound structure has a decisive semantic import. Unlike most actual art discourse, the mesostic written-through lecture or essay cannot just continue, cannot move from point to point, from thesis statement to exemplification or analogy, in a logical way. Rather, the discourse must "say something" about aesthetic, using no more than its baseline of 127 words, whose rule-governed permutations take us from "as it Were" to "a wholE can / peRhaps / wEre."

That it does "say something" is, of course, the work's great feat. "What You Say . . . ," what Cage's work "says," takes us back to the famous (perhaps too famous) theorem of "Experimental Music" that the "purposeless play" of art means "waking up to the very life we're living, which is so excellent once one gets one's mind and one's desires out of its way" (*Silence* 12). Purposeless play is not a matter of making "just any experiment." It does not mean that anything goes, that anyone can be an artist, that any random conjunction of words or sounds or visual images becomes art. What it does mean, as a reading of "What You Say . . ." teaches us, is that the ordinary (in this case, Jasper Johns's not terribly edifying comment about his painting habits) can provide all that the artist needs to make "something else." Indeed, the challenge is to take the ordinary—words such as "it" and "one" and "function" and "situation"—and "miniaturize" it into "something."

And that is of course what Johns himself does in his paintings. When he remarks, "Does one have something and then proceed to add another thing or does one have something; move into it; occupy it; divide it; make the best one can of it?" we should note the allusion to his own famous warning to "avoid a polar situation." For of course there is no meaningful opposition between "add[ing] another thing" or "hav[ing]something [and] mov[ing] into it"; the either/or proposition is falsely posed. Johns is playing similar games when he says, "I think I do different things at different times and perhaps at the same time." At one level, the tautology is absurd. But as we learn from Cage's "What You Say . . . ," such tautologies are integral to the process whereby we learn that there *is* no essential truth about art making, no way of saying for sure what art is or what the artist does.

"I think," Cage remarked a few months before his death, "a very impressive quality [of Johns's painting] is the absence of space. Something has been done almost everywhere. So it leads very much to the complexity of life."[13] The verbal equivalent of this absence of space can be seen in a passage like the following:

Or does one

function As

another WorlD

Do

Time

and tHen proceed to

dIvide it

oNe

a paintinG. ("What," in *Formations* 54)

In the source-text interview, Johns speculates on the ways "a whole subject" might "be inserted into another world." Cage shows how such insertion is performed by presenting himself as "one" who can actually "function *As* / another WorlD." And just as Johns's painting is characterized by an "absence of space" (which is to say, unused space), so Cage's performance poem is characterized by an absence of time, in that each word, each morpheme, each phoneme must do double duty. Look, for example, at the way *d*s, *o*s, and *n*s are modulated in the "miniaturizing" sequence "Or—does—one—function—another—world—do—proceed—to—divide—one—painting."

When Cage began to experiment with mesostics, he worried that he had not yet hit on a way of "carry[ing] language to the point to which I have taken musical sounds." The solution, it seems, was to learn to "Do / Time / and tHen proceed to / dIvide it." But even this stanza, taken out of context, may seem too assertive, too dogmatic to suit those like Cage and Johns who want to avoid polar situations. And so the poem makes a tentative circle back to the "as it Were" of the opening:

> a wholE can
>
> peRhaps
>
> wEre

where the last two lines introduce internal rhyme—"peR" / "wEre"—only to qualify repetition by the intrusion of that little particle "haps," which repeats the *p* sound but combines it with a prominent spirant so as to produce dissonance. "A wholE can / peRhaps / wEre": the difference, as Gertrude Stein would put it, is spreading.

NOTES

1. In *Roaring Silence*, Revill notes that "it was also in the *Imaginary Landscape* that Cage first employed his system of rhythmic structure. The simple figures that constitute the piece fit into a scheme of four sections consisting of three times five measures which are separated by interludes which increase in length additively from one to three measures; the piece ends with a four-measure coda" (65–66).

2. The English version, *For the Birds: John Cage in Conversation with Daniel Charles*, was published by Marion Boyars in 1981. The actual interviews were begun in 1968 but were submitted by Charles to Cage for revision and commentary and were not published until 1976 under the title *Pour les oiseaux*.

3. For a detailed account of these operations, see Mac Low 71–85.

4. See, for example, Cage, *Roaratorio* 173.

5. Cage was not satisfied with his writing-through of Pound's *Cantos*. "Now that I've done so [i.e., written-through them]," he remarks in an interview, "I must say that I don't regard them as highly as I do the *Wake*. The reason is that there are about four or five ideas that keep reappearing in the *Cantos*, so that in the end the form resembles something done with stencils, where the color doesn't really change. There's not that kind of complexity, or attention to detail, as there is in Joyce"; see Kostelanetz 152. No doubt Cage also objected to Pound's studious elimination of the very words Cage himself liked best—prepositions, conjunctions, articles, and pronouns—and, in addition, Pound's parataxis of nouns and noun phrases made a writing-through extremely difficult. Much more suitable for his purposes was Allen

Ginsberg's "Howl"; I have written of Cage's brilliant deconstruction of that poem in "A Lion in Our Living Room" 219–22.

6. On the piece as a whole, see my " 'duchamp unto my self.' "

7. For Cage's account of the evolution and design of "Art Is Either a Complaint or Do Something Else," see "Second Conversation" 109–14. Unlike "What You Say . . . ," this piece is based on separate statements made by Johns, appearing in different contexts.

8. For Johns's actual statement, see "Interview" 197.

9. These program notes were not included in the printed version in *Formations*, evidently because there is no way the instructions could be followed during a silent reading of the text. What status, then, does the printed text have? It is, we might say, a score that must be activated, an incomplete verbal-visual construct that needs to be "audiated."

10. I am not counting "different" or "interests" because in standard American speech (and certainly in Jasper Johns's southern idiolect) both words are pronounced as having only 2 syllables: "dif-rent" and "in-trests." The 7 words are "another" (used twice), "tendency," "occupy," "suddenly," "inserted," "situation," and "miniaturized."

11. Again, syllable count is not the same in the oral performance as in the written. When spoken, "miniaturized" usually has 4 syllables: "min-ya-tyuw-riyzd."

12. Cage's reading of this and related mesostics is, in many ways, inimitable, his soft, neutral California speech rhythms giving the pattern of sounds and silences of the lineated text an edge not quite duplicable when anyone else reads the "score."

13. Cage, "Second Conversation."

WORKS CITED

Cage, John. "Art Is Either a Complaint or Do Something Else." *Aerial* 6/7. Washington: Edge, 1991. 1–35. Repr. in revised form in *Musicage: Cage Muses on Words, Art, Music*. Ed. Joan Retallack. Hanover, N.H.: Wesleyan University Press, 1996. 3–42.

———. "Diary: How to Improve the World (You Will Only Make Matters Worse) Continued, 1971–72." *M: Writings '67–'72*. Middletown, Conn.: Wesleyan University Press, 1973. 195–217.

———. *Empty Words: Writings '73–'78*. Middletown, Conn.: Wesleyan University Press, 1979.

———. *For the Birds: John Cage in Conversation with Daniel Charles*. Salem, N.H.: Marion Boyars, 1981.

———. "James Joyce, Marcel Duchamp, Erik Satie: An Alphabet." *X: Writings '79–'82*. Middletown, Conn.: Wesleyan University Press, 1983. 53–101.

———. *M: Writings '67–'72*. Middletown, Conn.: Wesleyan University Press, 1973.

———. "Notes on Compositions III, 1967–78." *John Cage: Writer: Previously Uncollected Pieces*. Selected and introduced by Richard Kostelanetz. New York: Limelight, 1993. 93–108.

———. *Roaratorio: An Irish Circus on Finnegans Wake*. Ed. Klaus Schoning. Munich: Atheneum, 1985.

———. "Second Conversation with Joan Retallack." *Aerial* 6/7. Washington: Edge, 1991. 97–130. Repr. in revised form as "Cage's Loft, New York City: September 6–7, 1990," in *Musicage: Cage Muses on Words, Art, Music*. Ed. Joan Retallack. Hanover, N.H.: Wesleyan University Press, 1996. 43–79.

———. *Silence: Lectures and Writings*. Middletown, Conn.: Wesleyan University Press, 1961.

———. "Time (Three Autokus) (1986)." *John Cage II*. Ed. Heinz-Klaus Metzger and Rainer Riehn. *Musik-Konzepte* II (Munich 1990). 264–304.

———. "Toyko Lecture and Three Mesostics." *John Cage: Writer: Previously Uncollected Pieces*. Selected and introduced by Richard Kostelanetz. New York: Limelight, 1993. 177–82.

———. "What You Say . . . ." *John Cage II*. Ed. Heinz-Klaus Metzger and Rainer Riehn. *Musik-Konzepte* II (Munich 1990). 267–77. Repr. in *Formations* 4.1 (Spring–Summer 1987): 52–67.

———. "Writing for the Second Time through *Finnegans Wake*." *Empty Words: Writings '73–'78*. Middletown, Conn.: Wesleyan University Press, 1979. 133–76.

Johns, Jasper. "Interview with Jasper Johns." *Writings, Sketchbook Notes, Interviews*. New York: Museum of Modern Art, 1996. 188–97.

Kostelanetz, Richard. *Conversing with Cage*. New York: Limelight, 1987.

Kostelanetz, Richard, and John Cage. "A Conversation about Radio in Twelve Parts." *John Cage at Seventy-Five*. Ed. Richard Fleming and William Duckworth. Lewisburg, Pa.: Bucknell University Press, 1989. 270–302.

Mac Low, Jackson. "Selected Poems from *Stanzas for Iris Lezak* in Roughly Chronological Order (May–October 1960)." *Representative Works, 1938–1985*. New York: Roof, 1986. 71–105.

Perloff, Marjorie. "'A duchamp unto my self': 'Writing through' Marcel." *John Cage: Composed in America*. Ed. Marjorie Perloff and Charles Junkerman. Chicago: University of Chicago Press, 1994. 100–124.

———. "A Lion in Our Living Room: Reading Allen Ginsberg in the Eighties." *Poetic License: Essays in Modernist and Postmodernist Lyric*. Evanston: Northwestern University Press, 1990. 199–230.

Revill, David. *The Roaring Silence: John Cage, a Life*. New York: Arcade, 1992.

Rosenthal, Mark. *Jasper Johns: Work since 1974*. London: Thames and Hudson, in association with the Philadelphia Museum of Art, 1988.

Tan, Margaret Leng. "'Taking a Nap, I Pound the Rice': Eastern Influences on John Cage." *John Cage at Seventy-Five*. Ed. Richard Fleming and William Duckworth. Lewisburg, Pa.: Bucknell University Press, 1989. 34–58.

FROM PHONIC TO SONIC

The Emergence of the Audio-Poem

The 1950s saw the development of what might be termed a third phase in Western sound poetry. Prior to this time, in a period roughly stretching from 1875 to 1928, sound poetry's second phase manifested in several diverse and revolutionary investigations into the nonsemantic, acoustic properties of language. In the work of the Russian Futurists (Khlebnikov and Kruchenykh), the intermedia activities of Kandinsky, the *bruitist* poems of the Dadaists (Ball, Schwitters, Arp, Hausmann, and Tzara), and the *parole in libertà* of the Italian Futurist F. T. Marinetti, the *phonematic* aspect of language finally became isolated and explored for its own sake. (Previous sporadic pioneering attempts had been made by several writers, including Aristophanes, Rabelais, the seventeenth-century Silesian mystic Quirinus Khulman, Molière, Petrus Borel [ca. 1820], Lewis Carroll [1855], Christian Morgenstern [ca. 1875], and August Stramm [ca. 1912].) This second phase is convincing proof of the continuous presence of a sound poetry tradition throughout the history of Western literature. The first phase, perhaps better termed the paleotechnic era of sound poetry, is the vast, intractable territory of archaic and primitive poetries, the many instances of chant structures and incantation, of syllabic mouthings and deliberate lexical distortions still alive among many North American, African, Asian, and Oceanic peoples.

We should bear in mind also the strong, persistent folkloric strata that manifests in the world's many language games, the nonsense syllabary of nursery rhymes, mnemonic counting aids, whisper games and skipping chants, mouth music, and folk-song refrains, which serve as important elements of composition in work as chronologically separate as Kruchenykh's *zaum* poems (starting ca. 1913) and Bengt af Klintberg's use of cusha-calls and incantations (1965). Among the Russian Futurists both Khlebnikov and Kruchenykh openly acknowledge their debt to popular forms.

CD6

F. T. Marinetti (1876–1944), the core architect of the Italian Futurist movement, introduced his *parole in libertà* (words in freedom) in 1912 as an attempt at a radical syntactic explosion, the liberation of the word from all linear bondage and a consequent revision of the page as a dynamic field of typographic and, by implication, sonographic forces. In place of the ruling psychological paradigm, Marinetti substitutes "the lyric obsession with matter" (87). His list of abolitions includes syntax, all adjectives and adverbs, conjunctions, and punctuation (84–85). In performance Marinetti laid heavy stress on onomatopoeic structures arrived at by the deliberate distortion of words. "Lyrical intoxication allows us, or rather forces us, to deform and reshape words; to lengthen and shorten them; to reinforce their center or their extremities by increasing or diminishing the number of vowels and consonants" (Clough 50). Writes Marinetti, "In my *Zang-tumb-tumb* the strident onomatopoeia *ssiii*, which reproduces the whistle of a tugboat on the Meuse, is followed by the muffled *fiiii fiiii* coming from the other bank. These two onomatopoeias have enabled me to dispense with a description of the breadth of the river which is thus measured by contrasting the consonants *s* and *f* " (Clough 50). Less interesting morphologically than the work of Kruchenykh (for in *parole in libertà*, sound is still anchored in a representationality), Marinetti's work attempts to find a more basic connection between an object and its verbal sign than Saussure's oppositive, arbitrary relation, a connection predicated on the efficacy of the sonic as a direct, unmediated vector. The most significant effect of *parole in libertà* has been its enduring impact on the possibilities of the poem's extended visual notation. Indeed, the Futurist revolution in typography is one of its indisputably enduring achievements. Marinetti himself claimed that Futurist typography allowed him "to treat words like torpedoes and to hurl them forth at all speeds: at the velocity of stars, clouds, aeroplanes, trains, waves, explosives, molecules, atoms" (Clough 52). Clearly, Marinetti sees his typographic revolution as a breakthrough in the printed representation of kinetic forces.

Writing in 1920 A. Soffici describes the purported qualities of Futurist lettering: "The letters themselves are beautiful; in fact their beauty as an ideographic sign remains after it has become stereotyped in the alphabetic series. They have an extraordinary power of suggestion; they evoke past civilizations, dead languages. Their beauty may be enhanced by pictorial practices which, however, do not go beyond the means and instruments of the type-setter. Changes in size, arrangement and colour give the requisite movement to a page which may, with justification, be called a work of art" (qtd. in Clough 52). Marinetti's famous "Bombardamento di Adrianopoli" is a stunning typographic text of great visual excitement. Employing different letter sizes, its linear, diagonal, and vertical presentations create a nongravitational text available for vocal realization. It marks one of the earliest successful, conscious attempts to structure a visual code for free, kinetic, and voco-phonetic interpretation.   CD7

It can be safely claimed that the sonological advances of the Futurists have been eclipsed unfairly by the historical prominence granted the Dada sound poets. Hugo Ball (1886–1926) claims to have invented *verse ohne worte* (poetry without words), which he also termed *lautgedichte*, or sound poem. In a diary entry for 23 June 1916 Ball describes the compositional basis for his new poetry: "The balance of vowels is weighed and distributed solely according to the values of the beginning sequence" (70). In a diary entry (just above a quotation from Novalis, "Linguistic theory is the dynamic of the spiritual world") Ball elaborates the performative implications of his poetry: "Nowhere are the weaknesses of a poem revealed as much as in a public reading. One thing is certain: art is joyful only as long as it has richness and life. Reciting aloud has become the touchstone of the quality of the poem for me, and I have learned (from the stage) to what extent today's literature is worked out as a problem at a desk and is made for the spectacles of the collector instead of for the ears of living human beings" (54).[1] The sacerdotal, even shamanistic underpinnings to Ball's *lautgedichte* are clearly evident in the program notes accompanying his first sound poetry performance at Zurich's Cabaret Voltaire. "In these phonetic poems we totally renounce the language that journalism has abused and corrupted. We must return to the innermost alchemy of the word, we must even give up the word too, to keep poetry for its last and holiest refuge" (Ball 71). In an earlier entry, dated 18 June 1916, Ball acknowledges his own genealogy through Marinetti:

We have now driven the plasticity of the word to the point where it can scarcely be equalled. We achieved this at the expense of the rational, logically constructed sentence. . . . We have loaded the word with strengths and energies that helped us to rediscover the evangelical concept of the "word" (logos) as a magical complex image. . . . With the sentence having given way to the word, the circle around Marinetti began resolutely with "parole in libertà." They took the word out of the sentence frame (the world image) that had been thoughtlessly and automatically assigned to it, nourished the emaciated big-city vocables with light and air, and gave them back their warmth, emotion, and their original untroubled freedom. We others went a step further. We tried to give the isolated vocable the fullness of an oath, the glow of a star. And curiously enough, the magically inspired vocable conceived and gave birth to a *new* sentence that was not limited and confined by any conventional meaning. Touching lightly on a hundred ideas at the same time without naming them, this sentence made it possible to hear the innately playful, but hidden, irrational character of the listener; it wakened and strengthened the lowest strata of memory. (68)

This problematic conjunction of religious utterance and linguistic innovation is first addressed by Eugene Jolas. In his anthology *Vertical: A Yearbook for Romantic-Mystic Ascensions* Jolas insists "language must become vertical. The character of conjuration implied in the mystic faculty must be established by the poet who attempts to give voice to the superconscious. Mystics often invented their own secret language. But the new religious poetry cannot use a language the psycho-pathology of which is obvious. Words of the ecclesiastical tradition fail to impinge on the modern consciousness" (95). Jolas goes on to suggest the potentially positive contribution of technological vocabulary to revolutionizing sacred language. "Mystic language must be revolutionized. It may be possible that the much insulted vocabulary of technology may furnish us new symbols. Aeronautics, which is one element of ascension, should be able to renew the vertical speech. The vast changes in our conception of the universe made by modern physics will doubtless help to metamorphose the sacred language" (95).[2] In actual fact, the form of Ball's poems is not markedly different from earlier attempts at the end of the nineteenth century by poets such as Christian Morgenstern ("Kroklokwafzi" appeared in 1905) and Paul Scheerbart (whose well-known poem "Kikakokú" was published in 1897). All present a morphological experience with an absent, yet potential "meaning," and their poems can be accurately described as specimens of virtual semantics.[3] This treatment of the sound poem as a text in another language formed the basis of the material used in the several "African Nights" presented at the Cabaret Voltaire. The tendency found further development by another Dadaist, Tristan Tzara, in a pseudo-ethnopoetry realized most successfully in his *Poèmes nègres*, loose and often pseudo-translations from the African, which Tzara then used for sound scores.[4]

CD 8-10

The collective activities of Janco, Ball, Huelsenbeck, Tzara, and Arp at Zurich's Cabaret Voltaire culminated in the simultaneist poem, a high-energy, performance-oriented cacophony of whistling, singing, grunting, coughing, and speaking. Partly based on the earlier work of Henri Barzun and Fernand Divoire (Ball 57), the simultaneous poem stands as an early example of intermedia.[5] Defying accurate categorization as either theater, music, or poetry, the Dada simultaneities emphasize the improvisatory and aleatoric possibilities of multivocal expression. Ball theorizes on the first presentation of the *poème simultane* on 29 March 1916 allegorizing both voice and noise. "The 'simultaneous poem' has to do with the value of the voice. The human organ represents the soul, the individuality in its wanderings with its demonic companions. The noises represent the background—the inarticulate, the disastrous, the decisive. The poem tries to elucidate the fact that man is swallowed up in the mechanistic process. In a typically compressed way it shows the conflict of the *vox humana* [human voice] with a world that threatens, ensnares, and destroys it, a world whose rhythm and noise are ineluctable" (57). Despite Ball's conflictual narrative of human versus machinic, the prime acoustic effect of the simultaneity is to break down language into vocal, predenotational texture, arriving at effects strikingly similar to the later electroacoustic manipulations of Henri Chopin.

Raoul Hausmann is perhaps the most historically significant of Dada sonosophers because of his significant advances in the techniques of notation. In 1918 Hausmann developed his "optophonetics" utilizing typographic variations in size to indicate proportionate variations in pitch and volume. Writing in the *Courrier Dada* Hausmann argues, "The poem is an act consisting of respiratory and auditive combinations, firmly tied to a unit of duration. . . . In order to express these elements typographically . . . I had used letters of varying sizes and thicknesses which thus took on the character of musical notation. Thus the optophonetic poem was born. The optophonetic and the phonetic poem are the first step towards totally non-representational, abstract poetry" (qtd. in Richter 121). It is important to realize the technological contingency of this development. Like Marinetti's *parole in libertà*, optophonetics draws directly on the advanced possibilities made available by early twentieth-century type design and display type.[6] Moholy-Nagy emphasizes this collusion between aesthetic and commercial criteria as early as 1947:

CD11

> Fortunately, the tremendous demands of business advertising have forced the typographer as well as the commercial artist to some imaginative solutions which can be understood as a successful preparation for the complex task of the new communication. . . . Catalogs of merchandise, illustrated advertising, posters on billboards, front pages of tabloid newspapers move towards inventive visual articulation. . . . Apollinaire's ideograms and Marinetti's poems served, perhaps, not so much

as models, but as tradition-breakers which freed experimenters to create a quick, simultaneous communication of several messages.[7]

In 1921 Theo Van Doesburg, founder of de Stijl, published three "letter-sound images" with the following accompanying statement: "To take away its past it is necessary to renew the alphabet according to its abstract sound-values. This means at the same time the healing of our poetic auditory membranes, which are so weakened, that a long-term phono-gymnastics is necessary" (qtd. in Jaffé 186). Adopting a broadly similar platform, the Lettrist poets of the 1940s offered a full-scale lexical revolution based on similar alphabetic revitalizations. Isadore Isou and Maurice Lemaître, founders of the group, drew up a *Lexique des Lettres Nouvelles* comprising over 130 entries designed as an alphabet of sound to be employed in vocal performance. This preverbal, protodenotational arrest of the sign continued in the work of François Dufrêne, a former Lettrist who left the original group to pursue his own "ultra-lettrism." His *cri-rhythmes* eschew entirely the alphabetic dimensions of the Lettrist *Lexique*, using instead an intensely somatic base in subphonemic and graphically unnotatable units.

CD12

Even in the transrational *zaum* of the Russian Futurists, the word persists as a desired destination. Kruchenykh's first *zaum* poem ("Dyr bul shchyl") was written in December 1912, three months before his definition of the form appeared in the manifesto *Declaration of the Word as Such*. Much *zaum* was Babelian rather than transrational, written consciously to imitate the sounds of foreign languages (Markov 20)—an estrangement but hardly a shattering of the word as such. Kruchenykh describes his proto*zaum* writings (gathered in *Pomada* 1913) as written with words "that do not have a definite meaning" (Markov 44). The focus of Kruchenykh's attack is not the word but the word's subordination to meaning. In his famous assertion that the "word is broader than its meaning," Kruchenykh uncouples the binding relation of signifier to signified but strives to expand the word rather than effect its demolition. For Kruchenykh, poetry is the conscious attempt to return language to its arational ground, involving the open sacrifice of meaning as a constituent of the poem (or, rather, meaning in its restricted, semantic sense) and the deployment of various "poetic irregularities" such as clipped words, lexical hybrids, neologisms, and fragmentations (Markov 128).

CD13

Kruchenykh traces the genealogy of *zaum* back to religious glossolalia, the speaking in tongues practiced by religious mystics such as Sishkov of the Khlysty sect of flagellants (Markov 202).[8] Kruchenykh's ultimate attachment to the word (as a flexible organization of phonematic material capable of translogical, but nonetheless emotional, communication) is evident in several places. In his article "Novye puti slova" (The new ways of the word), Kruchenykh claims, "One can read a word backward, and *then one gets a deeper meaning*" (Markov 128; emphasis mine). Earlier in the same article we find the following hortation: "One should write in a new way, and the more disorder we bring to the composition of sentences, the better." The mandate is clear: a lateral disorganization of the word and sentence is preferable to their complete abandonment. In a similar spirit Khlebnikov speaks of new meanings achieved through bypassing older forms of meaning, of meanings "rescued" by "estrangement." In his article "Vremya mera mira" (Time is a measure of the world), Khlebnikov endorses the aesthetic value of the word against its depreciating epistemic value: "The word, though it is no tool for thinking anymore, will remain [as a medium] for art" (Markov 301). Against the contemporary claims of Baudoin de Courtenay that *zaum* is not language but a species of "phonetic excrement," the evidence presented suggests that in both Kruchenykh's and Khlebnikov's writings an attraction to the word — as a teleological aura — persists in the condition of the sememe's own near-excommunication.[9]

Sound poetry prior to the developments of the 1950s is still largely a word-bound practice, for while the work of the Dadaists, Futurists, and Lettrists served to free the word from semantic mandates, redirecting a sensed energy from themes and "message" into matter and force, their work nevertheless preserved a morphological patterning that still upheld the aural presence of the word. It could be said that what sound poetry achieved, up to the era of the tape recorder, was a full-scale revisioning of the word as a desired destination when purified of its cultural bondage to meaning. As part of this complex transformation of the semantic paradigm, the materiality of the sign emerged as a central, almost primitivistic preoccupation.[10] This transcendental lamination of value onto the materiality of the verbal sign specifies the limits of sound investigation up to the 1950s.

François Dufrêne's special achievement is to have renounced successfully the aura of the semantic and pushed the limits of the poetic centripetally, entering the microparticulars of morphology so as to investigate the full expressive range of predenotative elements: grunts, howls, shrieks, and hisses. For Dufrêne it is energy, not meaning, that constitutes the essence of communicated data. The *cri-rhythmes* are, first and foremost, a conscious deformation of linguistic form beyond the phonemic boundaries of the Dadaists. The complexities of Dufrêne's total poetic should be enumerated. Posited a priori within bodily performance as physical expenditure, his poetry appears to be incontrovertibly predicated on a biological paradigm and thus, unavoidably, entangled in a metaphysics of presence. Additionally, there is the severe problem of the limitation of his art to the idiosyncratic athleticisms of the individual body. Are not these performative demands a perverse resurgence of that Romanticism that linked lyric extremity to power? Fellow sound poet Henri Chopin expresses this problem aptly when declaring (of himself), *"Le poème c'est moi."* However, Dufrêne's *cri-rhythmes* further invite a crucial question: does the human cry mark an unmediated presence or trace a physiological outlay? Undoubtedly Dufrêne's investigation of human sound in isolation and liberated from both phonematic structures and recognizable sign functions, together with his revisioning of the poem *as the practice of an outlay* mark important stages in establishing the agencies for a general libidinal emancipation through human voice. Yet equally the *cri-rhythme* opens to breath's other possibility. "What death transfigured, my sorrow reached like a cry" (Bataille, *Impossible* 63). Cries are nonsemantic physical expenditures, the waste products of an anguish. Conceived as a dyadic movement—of inspiration and respiration—breath can be fissured in accordance with an ambiguity implicit in its own constitution. On one hand, breath is life-giving, an inspiration, productive of a presence at once physical and metaphysical. However, breath's other law involves the negative economy of involuntary expenditure. This ambivalence within the conceptual constitution of the *cri-rhythme* is stated well by Lyotard in his comments on periodic rhythm. "The decay of epic or the decline of tragedy, assuming this to be the case, implies the end of periodic rhythm as such. Time then ceases to be organized as respiration according to a process of inhalation and exhalation which inserts a moment of life between two silences or zero points" (Lyotard 2). Dufrêne's work, then, involves a gestural poetics of severe ontological ambivalence: assertive, parousial, and Romantic, but at the same time fragile, interstitial, and wasteful. As a new way to blow out old candles, *cri-rhythmes* expose a further, economic, pelegrosity, namely, the risk to self with the latter committed to an unavoidable expenditure. Dufrêne's poetry entails that general economy of inescapable discharge specified by Bataille.[11] Unlike Ball, who in his pursuit of the "innermost alchemy of the word" opts for the alchemical, Dufrêne installs his poetic of the cry within the nonlogical emissions of the sacrificial. Regardless of these complexities, the *cri-rhythmes* certainly satisfy the criteria set down by Julia Kristeva for an authentic literary practice as the exploration and discovery of the possibilities of language as an activity that frees us from given linguistic networks and accordingly takes its place CD14   in the larger cultural struggle against all forms of preconditioning.

The demise of both the tribal and the groupuscule as socially subversive forces through the tumult of the 1940s may help to explain the depreciation of the paleotechnic sound poem. Though advancing a counteraesthetic to the dominant, the sound poets of the first half of the twentieth century lacked a radical political base and embraced an extended aesthetic appeal (presented as oppositional) to a belated Romanticism, rather than offering a cogent critique of contemporary conditions. With the 1950s, however, came the gift of an external revolution. The popular availability of the tape recorder to sound poets made audiotechnological advancement of the art form a reality. Tape provided the revolutionary capability to finally transcend the biological limits on human bodily expression. Considered as an extension of human vocality, the tape recorder permits the poet to move beyond her or his own physical limitations. With the body no longer an ultimate, inflexible parameter, voice becomes a point of departure, not a teleologically prescribed point of arrival. The tape recorder creates a secondary orality predicated on a graphism (tape, in fact, is another system of writing, where writing is described as any semiotic system of storage), thereby liberating the sound poem from the athletic sequentialities of the human body. Cutting, in effect, becomes the potential compositional basis in which vocal segments can be arranged and rearranged outside the binding unidirectionality of real-time performance. The tape recorder also shares micro/macrophonic qualities, permitting a more detailed appreciation of the human vocal range. Technological time can be superadded to authentic body time to achieve either an accelerated or a decelerated experience of vocal time. Both space and time are harnessed to become less the controlling and more the manipulable factors of audiophony. There exists, then, through recourse to the tape recorder as an active compositional tool, a possibility of "overtaking" speech by the machine. Electroacoustic sound poetry mobilizes a technicism to further decompose the word; it permits, through speed changes, the granular structure of language to emerge and make itself evident. The phonetic poem (from Aristophanes to Isou), although involving nonsemantic registrations of the voice, showed more limitation in the scope of its negation, for it accepts the physical limitations of the human speaker as its own governing parameters. The tape recorder, however, allows speech—for the first time in its history—a physical and ideological separation from voice. British sound poet Bob Cobbing underlines the paradoxical potential of tape: "Strangely enough, the invention of the tape-recorder has given the poet back his voice. For, by listening to their voices on the tape-recorder, with its ability to amplify, slow down and speed up voice vibrations, poets have been able to analyse and then immensely improve their vocal resources. Where the tape-recorder leads the human voice can follow" (qtd. in Kostelanetz 386). Cobbing's anticipations are significant, for by avoiding a negative stance toward technology, he is able to envision a positive feedback to a human, nontechnological ground, a recuperation back into acoustic performance.

The advantages of tape began to be realized in the 1950s. Henri Chopin (b. 1922) made a decisive break from the phonetic base to sound poetry and began to develop his self-styled *audio-poèmes*, utilizing microphones of high amplification to capture vocal sounds on the threshold of audition. The *audio-poème* constitutes a much more radical break with the tradition of Western poetics than anything before. Ball, Marinetti, Khlebnikov, and Isou all maintained a paradigmatic ne plus ultra at the thresholds of the vowel and the consonant. Upon this extenuated tradition Chopin unleashed a Copernican revolution. His early work (ca. 1955) comprised a decomposition and recomposition of vowels and consonants. Words are slowed down, speeded up with multiple superimpositions, whilst additional vocalic texture is provided by a variety of respiratory and buccal effects. Still adhering to verbal elements as their constituents, these poems can be best described as technological assaults on the word.[12] Later Chopin discovered and used the "micro-particle" as the compositional unit of his work, abandoning the word entirely. This marks the birth of *poésie sonore*, which Chopin categorically distinguishes from *poésie phonetique*. Chopin's first *audio-poème*, *Pêche de Nuit*, was created in 1957. Using a core verbal text made up of an onomatopoeic listing of fish names, Chopin destroyed all verbal recognition by subjecting the verbal text to six speed changes and an additional forty-eight superimpositions of the initial reading of the text. According to Larry Wendt, "[The] words were lost for the sound: the ballet of captured fish had inspired a dance of microvocalic particles and buccal instances. It had the sound of life squirming in all of its articulated movements" (2).[13]

Because his "vocal micro-particulars" are realizable solely through the agency of contemporary tape technology, Chopin's art is the first ever poetry to be entirely dependent on the tape recorder. "Without this machine," claims Chopin, "sound poetry would not exist" (qtd. in McCaffery 48). It is an irrevocable marriage to a technological determinism that, Chopin argues, guarantees a radically nonaesthetic grounding for his electroacoustic poetry. The *audio-poème* finds "its sources in the very sources of language and, by the use of electro-magnetics, [owes] almost nothing to any aesthetic or historical system of poetry" (qtd. in McCaffery 48). Chopin locates his text-sound compositions in the technophysical tension between microsonics (their amplification and exteriorization) and the heuristic desire to explore one vital question: What would constitute a body without writing? The body has always been a lodestar for analogical operations, seducing models and metaphors into its blank, nonanswering space. Bataille, for one, situates the body outside technology in a basal opposition to nihilism. "The fundamental right of man," he writes, "is to signify *nothing*" (qtd. in Richmond 138). Bataille's suggestion is that totality is grasped in a gesture of the *non sens*. Chopin proposes a homologous notion of *the body without signification*. For Bataille and Chopin alike, it is the sociocultural denial to the body of a blank, meaningless space that supports a nihilism, not vice versa. The body is *nothing* when trapped within its systems of representations but becomes everything when posited outside meaning. For Chopin, technology is the primary instrument with which to realize that nonrepresentational, nonsemantic state. Chopin's theoretic body emerges at the point where discursive realization is either abrogated or else collapsed into the intractable anticoncept of a postlinguistic corporeality. CD15

The skeleton was an object of intense fascination to the Renaissance, and its cultural emergence as doubly emblem and icon coincides with the scientific understanding of the human body's complex articulations. Donne's poem "A Valediction: Of my Name in the Window" as well as a startling anticipation of Marcel Duchamp's *Large Glass* is also a meditation on the proposed analogy between graphic and skeletal articulation:

> Or if too hard and deepe
> This learning be, for a scratch'd name to teach,
>   It, as a given deaths head keepe,
>   Lovers mortalitie to preach,
> Or thinke this ragged body name to bee
>   My ruinous Anatomie. (22)

In contrast, Chopin explores less the articular than the glandular aspects of human anatomy: the sounding of pulses and resonances of cavities in a speleography of sound that refuses to accommodate the spatial paradigm of bones transfixed on an ossiographic and baroque template.[14] Subjected to Chopin's creativity, technology functions first and foremost as a heuristic, amplificatory prosthesis. His is an exploratory poetry of interior intensities, an art that unfolds the Romantic interior self, at once demythologizing human interiority (as the *hegemonikon*, the scholastic site of the soul) and debunking traditional, anatomical prohibitions.[15] Chopin works to detect and revitalize the fragmentary, discontinuous waste products of both respiration and orality. It is the shit of speech that attracts him, the ignored expenditures that physically vehiculate the logocentric amalgam. Paying attention to the body's heterological sonic phenomena—in sum the body's noise—Chopin transforms them into a powerful, expressive vocabulary. In short, Chopin manipulates the tension between the microsonic and its amplification and exteriorizing. By seeking out the microparticulars of speech, Chopin makes manifest an art of the insensible made sensible through the magnifying powers of the tape recorder.

Chopin's notorious splicings and layerings organize the temporal appearance of the sonic like a writing. However, it would be inaccurate to represent him as an exponent of a strictly secondary orality. Admittedly, Chopin has recorded his works and used technology to realize an impressive and definable audiographics. Such work bears all the characteristics of a graphism: iterability, retrievability, and replication. However, Chopin's primary concern in his use of tape is to extend the parameters of performance. If the quotidian impact of audiotechnologies has been the permanent separation of speech from a present subject (via radio, the telephone, and the gramophone), then we must credit Chopin for repossessing vocality as a new nonsemantic lexicon, a material modified, purified of the Logos and then returned to a performative, gestural poetics. Chopin's *poèsie sonore* involves two distinct orders of technological manifestation. Firstly, the microphone is employed as a physical insurgent, an anatomical probe utilized as the sonic equivalent of fiber optics, a search tool of the inaudible. Secondly, the tape recorder functions in a mise-en-scène, a theatrical setting for the demonstration of its own capabilities of public occasion. Into this recontextualized technology (as performance) Chopin enters as conductor to demonstrate the mind's control over processed human sounds, via an expert orchestration of tonalities and volumes, returning sound as an audible writing, an audiographic imprint capable of controlled appearance and sequencing.[16] The method is patently anatomical *and* theatrical. We are reminded first of Vesalius *and then* of Jules Verne: the former's detailed surgical engravings that first revealed to the Eurocentric imagination a body with organs; the latter's narratives of inner, microscopic journeys.

Like no other poet before him, Chopin reclaims technology back from its invisible circuitries to the visible in human performance. The implications of this appropriation need not be hyperbolized. There is no crisis of the audiated sign but rather a plasticity in potential sufficient to accommodate the paradox. Having freed those heterological aspects that are necessarily constituent to speaking (the sound of the lips, the teeth, and glottal movements) and having liberated them from all semantic paradigms, effectively proposing the body's other sounds as worthy of audition, Chopin returns his repertoire of expenditures back to a public, performative domain. These are my sounds, normally inaudible now audible through electronic enhancement. Moreover these sounds are not only what you hear but what you see. Me. Henri Chopin. *Le poème c'est moi.* Returning this way to the rhetorical discourse of the Sun King minus both Versailles and Logocentricity.[17] But this recuperation of a self does not involve a necessary aggrandizement of the force of the subject. On the contrary, because of the scope of Chopin's work, his commitment to both technographic and performative paradigms, the subject position is rendered, if not unstable, then optional. It can be argued that Chopin's art continues that line of subversive decontextualizing first announced in this century by Duchamp's Ready-mades, intervening—with technological assistance—into the hidden processes of bodily functions, to decontextualize their acoustic waste products and resituate them inside the spectacle of public performance. The transgression here connects to Bataille's important observation that our shit, when inside of us, is perfectly acceptable but becomes heterological when it makes its excremental appearance in the world. Chopin, like Bataille, argues against the body's own physical interdictions as a censorial barrier.

Chopin's achievement comes as the result of his tenacious explorations of the virtual ratios of body to both technology and poetics. Whereas Olson's proprioception is withheld as a theoretical direction toward a reader's relation to equally theorized organs, Chopin stages these organs performatively as the active agents of noise, tone, and rhythm.[18] Chopin implodes the proprioceptive, redirecting Olson's projective narrative of organ tissues outering through voice inside an actual journey through the body, an inner exploration of corporeal cavities and a nonjournalistic recording of detectable, sonic phenomena.

Larry Wendt correctly describes Chopin's practice as a "caveman technology in action" (3), a paleotechnic *détourne* of electroacoustic apparatuses.[19] Chopin's relation to prescribed technological functions is one of abuse. His interest is in circumventing a designated use and exploring the possibilities of extended, "unofficial" functions. Wendt reports that Chopin

found the sound of his own spoken declamation to be disappointing. However, by interfering with the recording head and tape path through which a recording of his own spoken words would pass, he found interesting timbres in his voice which he was unaware of before. On a little bit better quality tape recorder, he found that changing the tape speeds and performing simple techniques such as defeating the erase heads with match sticks for multiple superimpositions, [Chopin] could produce a whole orchestra of vocal effects. (1–2)

An obvious parallel here is John Cage's prepared piano, used in his *Sonatas and Interludes* (1946–48). In a manner similar to Chopin's prepared recorder, Cage intervenes into the structure of the piano, inserting screws, metal bolts, plastic spoons, and rubber bands so as to alter the sound of the instrument. It is this transgression of designed function that situates Chopin's art within the wider issues of the politics of poetic form and the sociocultural domain of tactics. In addition we are made aware that the very concept of "technology" is incommensurate to its applications.[20]

The technosciences affect the arts in multiple ways with technologies that impoverish and ones that fecundate. In hyperspatial technology, especially, the hegemony of the digital and binary come close to eradicating the simple fact that the cognitive is contextualized within actual human bodies. "Poetry," claims Chopin, "is the 'physical word' . . . the word that is simply movement. . . . Get rid of all those bits of paper, whole, torn, folded, or not. It is man's body that is poetry, and the streets" (qtd. in McCaffery 48). In the light of Chopin's audiography we should emphasize a less obviously civic placement and add an important supplement to his Heraclitan poetics. The radical achievement is to have rescued the mouth's acoustic possibilities from anatomic limitations and resituated them in a technological, prosthetic synthesis. Chopin rejects not only all graphic rules and economies, those "vague tonal notations of sighs and groans" (McCaffery 48), but also the several sonic limitations imposed upon the human mouth. More dangerous than the ideality of meanings are the procrustean restrictions of the phoneme and syllable. "The mouth," he reminds us, "is a discerning resonator, capable of offering several sounds simultaneously as long as these sounds are not restricted by the letter, the phoneme, or by a precise or specific word" (qtd. in McCaffery 48). Chopin here effectively exposes a covert ideological issue within sound and orality itself. The stale binary of sound/writing is claimed to be far from basal. For sound per se is the complex target for variant and oppositive appropriations. Beyond the sonic complexities of his pieces we are led into questioning the cultural constructedness of the phoneme and syllable themselves, leading us to interrogate their status as linguistically positive phenomena.[21] Chopin is rarely brought into theoretical contestation with Charles Olson, but we might venture a beginning in such a direction by concluding not with "the HEAD, by way of the EAR, to the SYLLABLE / the HEART, by way of the BREATH, to the LINE" but with the CAVITIES, by way of the THROAT, to the SOUND / the BODY, by way of TECHNOLOGICAL EXTENSION to the STREETS.[22]

NOTES

1. It is tempting to identify Ball's creative motivations with those of fellow Dadaist Richard Huelsenbeck, to which Ball refers enthusiastically: "His [Huelsenbeck's] poetry is an attempt to capture in a clear melody the totality of this unutterable age, with all its cracks and fissures, with all its wicked and lunatic genialities, with all its noise and hollow din" (56).

2. It is of interest in this respect to recall that Gertrude Stein's first experience of flight presented her with a view of the ground as a cubist painting. Significantly, Jolas commits himself solely to the lexemes and verbal imagery that constitute a technological discourse but does not engage the hypothetical strategies of vertical performance.

3. To substantiate this claim, here are the texts of both Ball's and Scheerbart's poems for comparison:

Kikakokú!
Ekoralaps!

Wîso kollipánda opolôsa.
Ipasatta îh fûo.
Kikakokú proklínthe petêh.
Nikifilí mopa Léxio intipáschi benakáffro—próposa
pî! própsa pî!
Jasóllu nosaréssa flípsei.
Aukarótto passakrússar Kikakokú.
Núpsa púsch?
Kikakokú bulurú?
Futupúkke—própsa pî!
Jaóllu   .   .   .   (Paul Scheerbart)

gadji beri bimba
glandridi lauli lonni cadori
gadjama bim beri glassala
glandridi glassala tuffm i zimbrabim
blassa galassasa tuffm i zimbrabim (Hugo Ball).

Grammatical indicators are present in both pieces. In Scheerbart interrogative and exclamatory markers function alongside capitalized "words" to provide guides to emphases and intonational changes, two prerequisites of virtual semantics. As readers we are deprived of semantic but not grammatical access. In Ball's poem the effect of repetition is to suggest a presidential grammar in operation.

4. Tzara first expressed an interest in African art in a short article, "Note 6 sur l'art nègre," which first appeared in the magazine *Sic* (September–October 1917) and reappeared with minor alterations in his collection *Lampisteries* 87. For a detailed discussion, see Paterson 45–62.

5. Barzun's theory of simultaneity can be found in his "Voix, Rythmes, et Chants Simultanés." The work drew immediate objections from Apollinaire and led to controversy over "the visual and auditory claims to the term 'simultaneity.'" As Weaver puts it, "[The] use of several voices in addition to the gramophone did not

prevent Barzun's work from being a succession. Apollinaire put forward as a contrast his calligrammes 'in which simultaneity existed in the mind, even in the letter, since it is impossible to read them without immediately conceiving the simultaneity of what they express' " (107). For more on Barzun's theories, see Bergman. Though not listed in the *OED*, the first use of the term "intermedia" is credited to Samuel Taylor Coleridge by American Fluxus artist Dick Higgins. The term was reapplied by Higgins in 1965 "to describe art works which lie conceptually between two or more established media or traditional art disciplines" (qtd. in McCaffery 65). Examples of Higgins's own intermedia can be found in his *Some Poetry Intermedia*.

6. For an excellent analysis of twentieth-century typographic practice and its relation to the developments of modernism, see Drucker. Lacking the advanced capabilities of movable type in Russia, Kruchenykh achieves effects comparable to those of Hausmann and Marinetti by the manual use of rubber stamp letters. In the 1920s Hausmann invented the "optophone," described by Lucy Lippard as "a photo-electric machine for transmitting kaleidoscope forms into sound, a continuation of his new interests in electronic music and his early preoccupation with bruitist poetry, one of Dada's goals having been, as Hugo Ball put it, the 'devastation of language' " (qtd. in Lippard 57).

7. From *Vision in Motion* [1947], qtd. in Kostelanetz. Moholy-Nagy was also the first critic to perceive an antecedent to Hausmann's optophonetic notation in Apollinaire's "Calligrammes": "The ideograms [*sic*] of Apollinaire were a logical answer to this dull typography, to the levelling effects of the gray, inarticulate machine typesetting. He not only printed the words, but *through the emphasis of position and size differentiation of the letters, he tried to make them almost 'audible'*" (95; emphasis mine).

8. Markov alleges that the source of Kruchenykh's glossolalic theories is the article by D. G. Konovalov, "Religious Ecstasy in Russian Mystical Sectarianism," an "article he [Kruchenykh] never mentions" (202). Konovalov's work has also eluded the scrutiny of both George B. Cutten and Felicia Goodman in their respective studies of glossolalia. A Futurist book, *Zaumnaya gniga*, published in 1915, brought attention to a new *zaum* poet, called Alyagrov, known subsequently under his real name of Roman Jakobson (Markov 334).

9. In an article appearing soon after the publication of Kruchenykh's *Declaration of the Word as Such*, de Courtenay contended that *zaum* was "the result of a linguistic and an aesthetic chaos in [the] creators' heads." Stressing the need for words to be attached to referents, de Courtenay argues that *zaum* "words" are neither words nor speech but "phonetic excrement." For a detailed presentation of de Courtenay's argument, see Markov 223. In contrast, Victor Shklovsky argues that *zaum* is a personal and private, if not a transrational, language in which words lack definite meanings but nonetheless produce direct emotional affects (Markov 284).

10. Attention was first called to the primitive nature of *zaum* in 1914 by the critic Kornei Chukovsky. Chukovsky proposes *zaum* to be of the nature of a protolanguage, hence not a language of the future. Having castigated the Futurists as being, in reality, anti-Futurists, Chukovsky goes on to conclude that the genuine Futurist of world literature is Walt Whitman. For more details, see Markov 220.

11. Bataille's important theory of expenditure is outlined in *La Parte Maudite*, translated as *The Accursed Share*.

12. One work from this period, for example, is based on the words "sol air" with additional nonsemantic sounds, such as buccal and breathing effects, all of which are superimposed up to fifty times.

13. *Pêche de Nuit* was quickly followed by *Vibrespace*, *Espace et Gestes*, and *La Peur*.

14. The skeleton, as well as being infrastructural, is also the permanent part of the human body remaining after mortification and corruption, a value that did not go unnoticed during the Renaissance.

15. An interesting discussion of the *hegemonikon*, together with its cardiac and thoracic sitings, can be found in O'Neill.

16. Typical of Chopin's theatrics is to place the volume and speed controls of his pieces in a separate area of the auditorium and then send eccentric, gestural signals to the sound technician regarding volume, pitch, and channel changes.

17. The only person to have traced the implications of Chopin's performance to a site in power is the Italian sound poet Enzo Minarelli. Minarelli cites Walter Ong to support the thesis that "one cannot utter a sound without exercising a power" (Zurbrugg and Hall 13). Both Minarelli and Ong locate power in the identical social vocality by which Althusser establishes the force of interpellation as constituting the self. Minarelli, however, lauds this embrace of power through sound, contextualizing it within the aesthetics (if not the politics) of Marinetti and the Italian Futurists. In a passage in which it is impossible not to recall Luigi Russolo's art of noise, Minarelli writes of "that power which Henri Chopin always understood from his very first experiments, disregarding language as it is ordinarily understood, in order to liberate a meaningful art of noise — *un rumorismo significante* — skilfully combined with electronics, the other primary element in his sound poetry" (13). Minarelli concludes that Chopin realizes in his poetry both "a project and 'a power'" (13).

18. Olson describes proprioception as "the data of depth sensibility / the 'body' of us as object which spontaneously or of its own order produces experiences of 'depth' Viz SENSIBILITY WITHIN THE ORGANISM BY MOVEMENT OF ITS OWN TISSUES" and later in the same essay "the 'body' itself as, by movement of its own tissues, giving the data of depth" (*Proprioception* 17–18).

19. I take the term *détourne* from the French Situationist Guy Debord, who defines *détournement* as "the reuse of preexisting artistic elements in a new ensemble" and cites its "particular power" as coming from "the double meaning, from the enrichment of most of the terms by the coexistence within them of their old senses and their new, immediate senses" (55). For examples of *détournement*, see Knabb and Sussman. Debord's earlier association had been with the Lettrist International and French sound poet Gils Wolman (inventor of the *megapneume*), who maintained early associations with the Situationist International in the late 1950s. There is, however, no record of Chopin's opinions on the SI.

20. We can trace in visual poetry a parallel effect in the systematic xerox-disintegrations developed by bp Nichol and myself in the late 1960s. By the systematic reproduction of a copy, then a copy of that copy ad infinitum, there results a progressive distortion of textual clarity to a point where, if sufficient generations are produced, the initial text is unrecognizable. Like the audiopoem, systematic xerox-disintegrations foreground a paradox within a specific technological appa-

ratus, inducing the paradoxical failure of the machine's designed function through a systematic, "proper" application of those same functions.

Certeau describes the tactic as "a calculus which cannot count on a 'proper' (a spatial or institutional localization) nor thus on a borderline distinguishing the other as a visible totality" (xix). Being denied the spatial advantage of a base, tactics assume the form of nomadic and necessarily provisional actions. Certeau continues, "A tactic depends on time — it is always on the watch for opportunities that must be seized 'on the wing.' Whatever it wins, it does not keep. It must constantly manipulate events in order to turn them into 'opportunities'" (xix). For the deployment of tactics in some contemporary poetry, see my "Insufficiencies of Theory to Poetical Economies."

21. The phoneme is defined by Pei (citing Bloomfield) as the "minimal unit of distinctive sound-feature." The syllable is "a group of phonemes consisting of a vowel or continuant, alone or combined with a consonant or consonants, representing a complete articulation or complex of articulations, and constituting the unit of word formation." In addition the "PHONETIC syllable is identifiable with the CHEST PULSE," the latter being defined as a "sudden expiratory movement of the chest muscles, the outward impulse of breath so produced" (200, 268–69, 37). Olson's exploitation of the profound linkage of syllable and breath is well known and develops the valorization of the syllable we find advanced by Friedrich Schlegel in the sixth lecture of his *Philosophie der Sprache*:

> Properly syllables, and not letters, form the basis of language. They are its living roots, or chief stem and trunk, out of which all else shoots and grows. The letters, in fact, have no existence, except as the results of a minute analysis; for many of them are difficult, if not impossible, to pronounce. Syllables, on the contrary, more or less simple, or the complex composites of fewer or more letters, are the primary and original data of language. For the synthetical is in every case anterior to the elements into which it admits of resolution. The letters, therefore, first arise out of the chemical decomposition of the syllables. (Schlegel 461)

22. See Olson, "Projective Verse" 19. In conclusion I will mention two other artists, younger than Henri Chopin, both of whom situate their art in order to exploit, or complicate, this technological aporia. In his *Sound Poems for an Era of Reduced Expectations*, Larry Wendt employs voice, prerecorded tape, and cheap computers. It is a stunning amalgam of human voice and junk technology created from the insight that technological determinism leaks its own fecal residue in the form of obsolete equipment. The extinction of acoustic phenomena through development predicated on a performativity paradigm creates the fissures into which Wendt tactically intervenes.

Quebec poet Pierre-André Arcand, in his "livre sonore," returns the scriptive gesture to purely sonic dimensions, profoundly questioning the role of the book as the center of all possibilities of writing. Arcand describes his "idiophonic" instrument as "a metal box, filled with fragmented words (book object). It sings, speaks, makes noises and rhythms when the microphone is rubbed on its open cover. The microphone is handled as if it were a pen. In order to create and record sounds" ("Traffic Somewhere between Media" 209). Examples of the *livre sonore* are contained on two compact discs by Arcand: *ERES + 7* (1992) and *ERES + 16* (1995), both produced by Obscure Editions, Quebec.

WORKS CITED

Arcand, Pierre-André. "Traffic Somewhere between Media." *Performance au Canada, 1970–1990.* Ed. Alain-Martin Richard and Clive Robertson. Quebec: Editions Intervention, 1991. 209.

Ball, Hugo. *Flight out of Time: A Dada Diary.* Ed. John Elderfield. Trans. Ann Raimes. New York: Viking, 1974.

Barzun, Jacques. "Voix, Rythmes, et Chants Simultanés—Esthétique de la Poésie Dramatique." *Poème et Drame* 4 (May 1913): 6–13.

Bataille, Georges. *The Accursed Share: An Essay on General Economy.* Trans. Robert Hurley. 3 vols. New York: Zone Books, 1988–91.

——. *The Impossible.* Trans. Robert Hurley. San Francisco: City Lights, 1991.

Bergman, Par. *"Modernolatria" et "simultaneita": Recherches sur deux tendances dans l'avant-garde litteraire en Italie et en France à la veille de la première guerre mondiale.* Doctoral thesis. Uppsala University, 1962. Uppsala: Svenska bokforlaget/Bonniers, 1962.

Certeau, Michel de. *The Practice of Everyday Life.* Trans. Steven F. Rendall. Berkeley: University of California Press, 1984.

Clough, Rosa Trillo. *Futurism: The Story of a Modern Art Movement, a New Appraisal.* New York: Philosophical Library, 1961.

Debord, Guy. "Détournement as Negation and Prelude." *Situationist International Anthology.* Ed. and trans. Ken Knabb. Berkeley: Bureau of Public Secrets, 1981. 55–56.

Donne, John. *The Complete Poetry and Selected Prose.* Ed. Charles Coffin. New York: Modern Library, 1952. 21–23.

Drucker, Johanna. *The Visible Word: Experimental Typography and Modern Art, 1909–1923.* Chicago: University of Chicago Press, 1994.

Higgins, Dick. *Some Poetry Intermedia.* Barrytown, N.Y.: Unpublished Editions, 1976.

Jaffé, Hans L. C. *De Stijl.* Trans. R. R. Symonds and Mary Whitall. New York: Abrams, 1967.

Jolas, Eugene, ed. *Vertical: A Yearbook for Romantic-Mystic Ascensions.* New York: Gotham Bookmart, 1941.

Knabb, Ken, ed. and trans. *Situationist International Anthology.* Berkeley: Bureau of Public Secrets, 1981.

Kostelanetz, Richard, ed. *The Avant-Garde Tradition in Literature.* Buffalo: Prometheus, 1982.

Lippard, Lucy, ed. *Dadas on Art.* Englewood Cliffs, N.J.: Prentice-Hall, 1971.

Lyotard, Jean-Francois. *Peregrinations: Law, Form, Event.* New York: Columbia University Press, 1988.

McCaffery, Steve. "Insufficiencies of Theory to Poetical Economies." *The Ends of Theory.* Ed. Jerry Herron et al. Detroit: Wayne State University Press, 1996. 257–71.

McCaffery, Steve, and bp Nichol, eds. *Sound Poetry: A Catalogue*. Toronto: Underwhich Editions, 1978.

Marinetti, Filippo Tommaso. *Marinetti: Selected Writings*. Ed. R. W. Flint. Trans. R. W. Flint and Arthur A. Coppotelli. New York: Farrar, Straus and Giroux, 1972.

Markov, Vladimir. *Russian Futurism: A History*. London: MacGibbon & Kee, 1969.

Olson, Charles. *Additional Prose: A Bibliography on America, Proprioception, and Other Notes and Essays*. Ed. George F. Butterick. Bolinas, Calif.: Four Seasons Foundation, 1974.

————. "Projective Verse." *Selected Writings of Charles Olson*. Ed. Robert Creeley. New York: New Directions, 1966. 15–26.

O'Neill, Ynez Violé. *Speech and Speech Disorders in Western Thought before 1600*. Westport, Conn.: Greenwood, 1980.

Paterson, Elmer. *Tristan Tzara: Dada and Surrational Theorist*. New Brunswick, N.J.: Rutgers University Press, 1971.

Pei, Mario. *A Glossary of Linguistic Terminology*. New York: Columbia University Press, 1966.

Richman, Michele H. *Reading Georges Bataille: Beyond the Gift*. Baltimore: Johns Hopkins University Press, 1982.

Richter, Hans. *Dada: Art and Anti-Art*. Trans. David Britt. New York: Abrams, 1965.

Schlegel, Friedrich von. *The Philosophy of Life and Philosophy of Language in a Course of Lectures*. Trans. A. J. W. Morrison. London: Henry G. Bohn, 1847.

Sussman, Elisabeth, ed. *On the Passage of a Few People through a Rather Brief Moment in Time: The Situationist International, 1957–1972*. Cambridge, Mass.: MIT Press, 1989.

Tzara, Tristan. "Note 6 sur l'art nègre." *Sic* 21–22 (1917): unpaginated. Repr. in "Note sur l'art nègre." *Lampisteries; Precedees des sept manifestes dada*. [Paris]: Pauvert, 1963. 87–88.

Weaver, Mike. "Concrete Poetry." *Lugano Review* 5–6 (1966): 100–125.

Wendt, Larry. "Henri Chopin and Sound Poetry." *Furnitures* 10 (1993): 2.

————. *Sound Poems for an Era of Reduced Expectations*. Toronto: Underwhich Editions, 1981.

Zurbrugg, Nicholas, and Marlene Hall, eds. *Henri Chopin*. Morningside: Queensland College of Art Gallery, Griffith University, 1992.

RUDE BWOYS, RIDDIM,
Systems of Political Dissonance in
RUB-A-DUB, AND RASTAS
Caribbean Performative Sounds

night number one was in BRIX/TON:
SOFRANO B sounn sys/tem

was a-beatin out a riddim/wid a *fyah*,
commin doun his reggae-reggae *wyah*;

it was a sounn shakin doun you spinal col/umn,
a bad music tearin up you *flesh*;
an th'rebels-dem start a-fightin,
th'yout dem jus tunn *wild*.

... sounn commin doun NEVILLE KING'S music iron;
th' riddims jus bubblin an back-firin,
ragin and risin, when suddenly th' music cut

    Linton Kwesi Johnson, *Dread beat and blood*

A nation's emergence is always predicated on the
construction of a field of meaningful sounds.
    Houston A. Baker Jr.,
Modernism and the Harlem Renaissance

Abeng is an African word meaning conch shell. The blowing of the conch
called the slaves into the canefields in the West Indies. The *abeng* had
another use: it was the instrument used by the Maroon armies to pass their
messages and reach one another.
    Michelle Cliff, *No Telephone to Heaven*

As Houston A. Baker Jr. has claimed, each emerging nation has its
genesis not only in material cultural practice but in sound: "Just as
infants babble through a welter of phones to achieve the phonemics of a native language, so conglomerates of human beings
seeking national identity engage myriad sounds in order to achieve
a vocabulary of *national* possibilities" (71). In the process of nation
formation, a repertoire of sounds emerges. These may be "natural"
sounds (the sea or croaking lizards), industrialized sounds (truck

gears or gunfire), percussive sounds (Burru drumming), human vocalizing sounds (a wail, a laugh, a dialect phoneme, a vocal cadence or timbre, or a melody), or a variety of these sounds collected, generated, and remixed through sound technologies (sound systems, recording studios, radios, phonographs, cinemas, or TVs). Yet each of these sounds as it reaches a moment-of-audition is a historicized performance, "having taken meaning and shape . . . [and sound] in a socially specific environment," providing a sound track for current ideologies and praxis (Bakhtin 276). In a decolonized situation, and especially in the Caribbean, where the official languages of the colonizing nation have been creatively "versioned" by creole speakers, natural sounds, the sounds of cultural resistance, and the disruption of normative sounds through sound *mediats* (technological manipulations) articulate a desire for self-determination. For the purposes of this discussion, I examine 1972, the year of Michael Manley's election as prime minister of Jamaica, as an important moment in Jamaica's attempt at decolonization. At this crossroads, the sound repertoires of impoverished slum dwellers, Rastafarians, Rude Boys, performance poets, and a grandstanding politician with a democratic socialist cause established a geopolitical sound signature.

Looking at this noise-filled moment in Jamaican history raises questions often avoided by studies theorizing sound formations in avant-garde art: How is poetry formed out of the material conditions of cultural production? How does sound perform a national identity? How does sound establish a zeitgeist, a cooperative zeal across class lines, a desire for economic and cultural "progress"? What is the role of sound in nation formation, the effort in a decolonized state to organize for self-governance and provide protection for the state's sovereignty from more powerful and encroaching countries? After "the nation" has replaced the colonizing power, how does sound perform revolutionary protest against the conservative programs of the bourgeoisie and the "ethico-political and epistemological agenda[s] of nationalism" (Radhakrishnan 757)? How might a study of sound redefine paradigms for thinking about cultural history, tracing intercultural and transnational flows rather than accentuating national boundaries? How does sound technology promote hybridity? How does an emphasis on the avant-garde in other studies of sound poetry resist the obvious, that sound artists are everywhere now that inexpensive sound equipment allows any person on the street to capture cultural noise and dub, sample, version, or subvert it with cut-'n-mix technology?

Edward Kamau Brathwaite, as one of the initial organizers of CAM, the Caribbean Arts Movement (1966–1972), emphasized the Caribbean poet's primary relationship to the performative sounds of his culture: "The poetry, the culture itself, exists not in a dictionary but in the tradition of the spoken word. It is based as much on sound as it is on song. That is to say, the noise that it makes is part of its meaning, and if you ignore the noise (or what you would think of as noise, shall I say) then you lose part of the meaning. When it is written you lose the sound or noise and therefore you lose part of the meaning" (*History* 17). As critics we have little apparatus for discussing mediated cultural or poetic "noise," especially when this noise arises from systems of colonial and postimperialistic exploitation. As Douglas Kahn states in the introduction to *Wireless Imagination: Sound, Radio, and the Avant-Garde*, "The literature on the arts of recorded and broadcasted sound, and of conceptual, literary, and performative sound, is scant at all levels, from basic historical research to theoretical modelings" (1). Theorists who attempt to discuss connections between history, orature, performative literature, and sound technology tend to focus on modernist, postwar, avant-garde, or postmodernist experimentalism. We have studies of Velimir Khlebnikov's *zaum* language; F. T. Marinetti's Futurism, fascism, and *La Radia*; John Cage's noise productions; Antonin Artaud's radio talk; William Burroughs's cut-'n-mix sound montages; Dada; Man Ray's phonetic poetry; Kurt Schwitter's sound sonatas; Eugen Gomringer's concrete poetry; Caetano Veloso's vocal drama; Warren F. Motte's fractal poetry, or Oulipo; L=A=N=G=U=A=G=E poetry, and so forth.[1] Yet these studies privilege either European/North American experiments with sound technologies or Western art music, which Kahn has called " 'musicalized' . . . sound stripped of its associative attributes" and its "sociopolitical realities" (3).

Developed and exploited during a global period of decolonization and postimperial expansionism, sound technologies and the cultural soundings they relay obviously participate in sociopolitical realities, institutional workings, and transnational negotiations, including systems of ideological and economic oppression. One might even argue that the transatlantic trade routes that distribute marketed sounds are part of a foundational "network of economic, social, and political relations" established during the era of plantation slavery and reinforced by current global capitalism (Gilroy 54–55). At the same time as technology allows the flow of sounds across national boundaries, from one geopolitical soundscape to another, hegemonic discourses and sound fields are destabilized by the improvisational sound repertoires of emerging nations. While Third World sounds can be appropriated by mass market (World Beat music), sounds from imperialistic discourses can be recontextualized by Third World sound technicians. Accordingly, as Iain Chambers notes, the "local cultural refashioning" and creolization of the empire's mother tongue disturbs the tempo of colonial history. The resulting hybrid art is a mix of vernacular performances previously separated by "aesthetic, social, and geographical distinctions" (85). Thus, in discussing the sound productions of Jamaica, a "relatively small and poor island on the periphery of, but within the communication system of, the most affluent, powerful and technologically developed capitalist nation" (Stone, *Class* 98), tied in innumerable ways to exploitative economies, it is important to emphasize the significance of the innovative sound experiments of a nation existing in harm's way. Rather than *musicalizing* sounds, theorists, or First World listeners, remind themselves of the sociopolitical and economic roots of Jamaican urban sounds and the transcultural "work" these sounds accomplish.

This emphasis has implications not only for studies of Jamaican urban music and for a more sociopolitical critique of avant-garde phonotexts but also for debates about postcolonial discourse and diaspora. As R. Radhakrishnan complains, "Poststructuralist appropriation of the diaspora aestheticizes it as an avant-garde lifestyle based on deterritorialization" and celebrates *difference* without adequately acknowledging actual diasporic conditions (764). Brathwaite reminds critics of the historical factors contributing to the creative but "cracked, fragmented, ambivalent" cultural norms of a creolized society: "mercantilism, slavery, materialism, racism, superiority/inferiority syndromes, etc." ("Contradictory Omens" 6). Elaborations on one of the most frequently used terms in current discussions of "borderland subjectivities and epistemologies" (Dirlik 355), "hybridity," especially as popularized by Homi K. Bhabha, often depend on Western theories of subjectivity rather than on creolization processes or economic forces of neocoloniality. Akin to Jamaica's national motto, "Out of Many, One People," this vision of amalgamation ignores continuing struggles for hegemony, the question of access to nation-building resources, and traditions of intentional subversion that Sylvia Wynter terms "indigenization," or the purposeful appropriation of cultural forms by colonized peoples (see Brathwaite, "Contradictory Omens" 14, 58, 62).

In this discussion of Jamaican soundspace, the term "hybridity" is used to designate a cultural process that has been continually conditioned by economic forces and racialism; the creative creolization or "unplanned, unstructured but osmotic relationship" between cultures in the post-plantation Caribbean (Brathwaite, "Contradictory Omens" 6); the multiple forms and mix of performative traditions made possible by sound technology; and the "cultural politics of high-tech miscegenation" (Cooper xii), the intercultural mixings proliferated by global transmissions of reggae, dub, and other New World sounds from the "black Atlantic."[2] This view credits the slum-yard sound system operators as powerful and unacknowledged agents in creating improvisational paradigms of artistic production, cultural historiography, identity, hybridity, nationalism, postcolonialism, liberation politics, and transnational exchanges currently debated in postcolonial literary studies but often omitted in studies of the avant-garde phonotext.

In *Subculture: The Meaning of Style*, Dick Hebdige discusses the power of deejay improvisation and sound system technologies (mobile discos with heavy amplification and a cut-'n-mix recording style) in Caribbean political sound-scripting and aesthetic innovation:

> The "sound system," perhaps more than any other institution within . . . West Indian life, was the site at which blackness could be most thoroughly explored, most clearly and uncompromisingly expressed. To a community hemmed in on all sides by discrimination . . . the sound-system came to represent, particularly for the young . . . a black heart beating back to Africa on a steady pulse of dub . . . carried along on a thunderous base-line, transported on 1000 watts. Power was at home here—. . . it hung on the air—invisible, electric—channelled through a battery of home-made speakers. (38–39)

In the urban slums of West Kingston, Jamaica, where the Caribbean sound system operators and their most internationally known "sounds" (ska, rock steady, reggae, deejay toasts, and dub poetry) originated, the sound system blues dances provided a site for noisy exchange and laughter, sensuality (rub-a-dub), and murderously overamplified sound (sounn shakin doun you spinal col/umn). Yet the sound system events also aired the dialect of the urban soundscape; the deejay's political scatting and discursive montage; the Rastafarians' syncopated, apocalyptic preaching; the Rude Boys' cool dread; and the "riddims" of African-influenced Burru drummers, as opposed to the sanctioned Afro-Saxon sounds of metropolitan Kingston. In a decolonized situation, all citizens do not have equal access to the sound repertoires, ideologies, and technologies generating the nation-state. As Brathwaite notes, communication problems limit access: "power cuts, poor transmission, faulty sets, tv in fact limited to certain income groups; follow-up in newspapers, on radio, uncertain and possibly inaccurate; with many people in fact unable to read; and some areas inaccessible to broadcast and news van" ("Contradictory Omens" 23). Thus the overamplified sound system dances provided an alternative space for urban soundings where the ideologies and innovations of the underclasses were accessible to all listeners within hearing distance.

Destabilizing totalizing narratives of any singular cultural "sound system," deejays juxtaposed sound material arising from disparate periods of economic organization (plantation, decolonization, and neocolonization), sites of institutional power (American capitalism and British imperialism), and colonial cultures (American rhythm and blues [R&B] and Afro-Latin rhythms of the Spanish colonies). Early sound system men of West Kingston collected their first "sounds" (45 rpm recordings), hard-to-come-by R&B tunes, while working as Jamaican migrant workers in the orange groves of Florida and the sugarcane fields of the American South in the 1950s through 1970s. To protect the exclusivity of their sounds against rival sound systems, operators scratched off record labels or renamed the sides with phony labels, freeing the commodified American R&B sounds from notions of originary authorship or corporate ownership and making them available for appropriation, versioning, and incorporation into the improvisational repertoire of a new Jamaican national identity (see Davis 37; Hebdige, *Cut-'n-Mix* 64). At the heavily amplified sound system blues dances, Jamaican culture was articulated as a "dialectic of various temporalities—modern, colonial, postcolonial, 'native'—that cannot be a knowledge that is stabilized in its enunciation: 'it is always contemporaneous with the act of recitation. It is the present act that on each of its occurrences marshalls in the ephemeral temporality inhabiting the space between the "I have heard" and "you will hear"'" (Bhabha, "DissemiNation" 303). From the interstices between "I have heard" and "you will hear," from the marginalized position of the urban rebel, the deejay provided sociopolitical commentary that reverberated a distance of two miles or more from the open-air slum yards or rented halls. In this pastiche of sounds, in this moment of performative hybridity, "what [was] spoken in private [was] now expressed for the whole society to hear and react to" (Saakana 123–24; see Whitney and Hussey 10).

During the volatile 1970s, "*fyah!*" was the ubiquitous message on the deejay sound chain, a righteous fire that would burn down Babylon (North American and British capitalists *and* the bourgeois classes and police forces of the Caribbean). Several of the sound system men of West Kingston, such as Sir Coxsone Downbeat (Dodd), Prince Buster, Duke Reid the Trojan, Lee "Scratch" Perry, and King Tubby, had by this time become record producers. Graduating from the one- or two-track studios of the early years to multitrack systems that allowed deejays to record their improvisations ("talk overs," "toasts," or "dubs") with the coopted basic rhythm tracks of old R&B tunes or reggae, operators captured the *dread* atmosphere of the times by adding reverb, delay echo, phasing, slide faders, a thumping bass line, other urban sound effects (gunshots, screams, bomb blasts, car horns, or synthesized distortions), dropping tracks in and out, and sampling North American cultural sounds. Deejays also asserted Afro-Caribbean cultural identity by sampling the sounds of "churchicals," spirituals, gospel songs, Pukkumina or Revivalist hymns, work songs, ring tunes, digging songs, nursery rhymes, gossip, riddles, proverbs, and the sardonic humor of street-corner "groundings."[3] By this time the *dread* Rastafarian and Rudie sounds had created the heavy "rootsy" music, rock steady, and reggae, and sound system deejays, such as King Stitt, Clancy Eccles, Sir Lord Comic, U-Roy, I-Roy, Dennis Alcapone, Scotty, Count Matchuki, and Prince Far I, were sampling Rasta and Rudie talk against Babylon into their live performances and recorded dubs.

CD16&17

The sounds that had been blasted into Jamaican consciousness by the sound system amplifiers, mobile record-selling trucks with loudspeakers, car radios, or cheap transistors exploded into international consciousness with Bob Marley's 1973 polemical reggae album *Catch a Fire*. Perry Henzell's movie *The Harder They Come* (1972), starring Jimmy Cliff and depicting a Rudie rebel in West Kingston's soundscape, appeared at Kingston's Carib Cinema and was later released internationally. According to Brathwaite, the premier of this Jamaican film "marked a dislocation in the socio-colonial pentameter, in the same way that its music and its stars and their *style*, marked a dislocation in the hierarchical structure in the arts of the Caribbean. At the premier, the traditional 'order of service' was reversed. Instead of the elite . . . the multitude took over. . . . For the first time at last . . . a nation language voice was hero. In this small corner of our world, a revolution as significant as Emancipation" (*History* 41). At the same time the masses demanded access to the artistic versioning of their lives by storming the Carib Cinema, they took to the streets to protest economic oppression by island class antagonisms, racialism, and political agendas. During the 1972 Jamaican elections, aware of the disgruntled sounds emanating from the underclass, Michael Manley, leader of the People's National Party (PNP), incorporated mobile sound systems, reggae "roots" bands (including Bob Marley and the Wailers), and the *fyah* of Rasta sounds into his national campaign for a conversion of Jamaica to a democratic socialist state. Although Manley would later turn conservative and support capitalism in the 1980s, during the 1970s sound systems dances and records produced out of West Kingston, Manley's political machinations, and the performative poetry of the literary elite generated the Jamaican identity in the shared performance of hybridized "righteous" sounds.

The hybrid sound repertoires of the urban poor and island sound technologies also resonated during the Manley election years in numerous literary anthologies of West Indian poetry, journals (especially *Savacou* [Jamaica] and *BIM* [Barbados]), individual poetry collections, performances, and discussions held by the members of CAM. These artists, who had for some time been interested in Caribbean orature and musical rhythms, frequently incorporated reggae, dub-style toasting, and Rastafarian or Rudie dread into their written/performative works. The introduction of urban soundings into political and artistic realms produced transformational waves in Jamaican identity and Caribbean sound production.

As a democratic socialist and labor organizer for sugar worker unions in the 1950s, Manley had realized early the motivational power of these sound repertoires of the underclass, sound system technologies, spectacle, and feel-it-in-your-body politics. In *A Voice at the Workplace: Reflections on Colonialism and the Jamaican Worker*, Manley states,

> To get to speak to sugar workers in Jamaica requires an enormous investment in time in that it means meetings in little villages all over the countryside. I had my car equipped with a loud-speaker bolted to the roof with an amplifier, microphone, and most importantly, a turntable for records. Having always believed that life need not be dreary, I personally chose all the calypsoes, rock-and-roll numbers, the "yank" tunes and other popular music which were in vogue at the time. We did not have tapes in those days so I used to park the car first, and start playing records. When a crowd had gathered and the young boys and girls had established their presence and identity by dazzling displays of dancing, we would settle down to the serious business of speech making. (93)

The loudspeaker functioned as an *abeng* (a conch shell used by maroon armies during plantation times): it was a call to power, a call for workers oppressed by sugar plantation systems developed during slavery to congregate in a moment of politicized community. Manley's 1972 campaign would likewise mobilize the masses of West Kingston and rural Jamaica by using mobile sound systems to amplify "protest" reggae songs and slogans such as "Power to the People," "We Shall Overcome," and "Under Heavy Manners" at political rallies to echo back to the crowd its own incendiary *ire-ation* and *Jah*-inspired pleas for black brotherhood and love.

Because of his experiences as a union organizer, Manley realized that it was "no longer possible for either party to operate effectively without the ability to mobilize the mass of the Jamaican people" (Stephens and Stephens 469; see Davis 88). His most effective campaign strategy was to adopt the symbols, slang, and protest sounds of the masses. Manley—who during a visit to Ethiopia had invited Emperor Haile Selassie I, Ras Tafari, the divine subject of Rastafarianism, to make a state visit to Jamaica in 1966 — appealed to the masses by displaying at political spectacles a staff, or "Rod of Correction," given to him by Selassie to "right all wrongs" (Chevannes 257). Crowds shouted, "Joshua, Joshua," as Manley took the platform. According to Payne, by employing biblical oratory, Old Testament wrath, and Rastafarian iconography and using the *sound* experiments of the masses, Manley tapped into the socialist sentiments already pulsing in Jamaican groundations and performance.

In a time of extreme censorship of the reggae sounds of West Kingston, when Hugh Shearer's Jamaica Labour Party (JLP) government had sanctioned police raids on sound system dances, discontinued "blasphemous and seditious" Rastafarian radio programs, effectively banned all pro-PNP songs from radio stations JBC and RJR, and "practically exiled" rootsy forms of reggae (including Bob Marley and the Wailers) "from the airwaves" (Owens 97), the Jamaican soundspace was a crucial site of contest. An article titled "Dance Beaters" appearing in the Jamaican Black Power newspaper *Abeng* (19 July 1969) acknowledged the sound system dance space as a "cultural and political threat" to Babylon, as a site of "African militancy" and assembly where "Man and Man are not only seeking Saturday night fun but are reasoning and organizing among themselves": "Every week-end armed policemen move into dance halls between midnight and one o'clock to harass Black Man and disorganize our assembly. . . . Apart from shooting and making arrests some policemen wreck the sound systems and raid the bar for beers or rum before crashing another spot." Protesting the state's campaign to criminalize West Kingstonian dances, the *Abeng* article celebrates the difficulty of suppressing sound: "The sounds are now too widespread for them to jump the gun which has set off the complete yanking of our enemies."

As Carl Stone notes, the limited reading proficiency in West Kingston made newspapers a "middle-class medium" and radio "the medium of the masses" ("Ideology" 317). Even though protest sounds from West Kingston were forcibly silenced from radio, these reggae, Rastafarian, and urban Rudie soundings rumbled through the Jamaican soundscape, emanating from the renegade mobile sound systems of the yard and the free or low-cost PNP Musical Bandwagon, which attracted an average crowd of 20,000 (Waters 132). Angered by the censorship and attracted by Manley's Ethiopianism, Bob and Rita Marley joined the Bandwagon for several weeks, as did other "roots" bands and deejays: "The island's best singers," Davis writes, "weighed in behind the PNP: Delroy Wilson's 'Better Must Come' was the campaign's theme song; Clancy Eccles' 'Rod of Correction,' Max Romeo's 'Let the Power Fall on I,' Junior Byles' 'Beat Down Babylon' and 'Hail the Man' by Ken Lazarus all proclaimed the rise of a Jamaica yearning for equal rights" (88–89). As Anita M. Waters notes, these Bandwagon events were advertised not as political rallies but as concerts, "with pictures of the artists' faces around the announcement and a photograph of a crowd at bottom. Michael Manley's photograph appeared among those of the singers" (131). Manley himself recorded a dub version of Clancy Eccles's reggae hit "Power for the People" in which Eccles sings the chorus while Manley talk-sings the "politics of participation" and "collective consultation" the PNP would institute (Waters 122).[4] Although several of the Bandwagon performers would also criticize Manley's government in such songs as Junior Byles's "When Will Better Come?," at the moment of the political rally the sounds of the sufferer coalesced with the official discourse of nation formation and the socialist agenda (see Hebdige, *Cut-'n-Mix* 44).

The sound system dances and Manley's Bandwagon "broke through the official structures of social discourse and breached the state ideological quarantine" by "constructing an alternative site for free political communication" (Gray 74). Deejays of the election era sampled sounds that resonated with their own origins. African drumming styles used for centuries by plantation slaves for work rhythms, celebrations, spirituality, and revolt expressed revolutionary tension, a tension felt in the reggae-based dub rhythm tracks. As Rohlehr argued in defending the publication of Rastafarian poetry in a 1972 issue of *Savacou*,

> Each new weight of pressure has its corresponding effect on the music, and the revolution is usually felt first as perceptible change in the bass, the basic rhythm, the inner pulse whose origin is in the confrontation between the despair which history and iniquitous politics inflict, and the rooted strength of the people. When such innovation takes place in the ground-beat, the whole trivial stream of popular appeasing which increases the dread and tension in the whole society, because the beat *dominates* the city: the rhythm of the basic bass is the grounded heart-beat of the city [*sic*]. So when the rhythm goes dread, the whole city feels the tension. ("Afterthoughts" 228)

Pithy creole proverbs echoing the dread tension of the drums and bass threatened the bourgeoisie (I-Roy's "Heart Don't Leap" [1971]: "Don't be like Humpy Dumpy, sit at top have great fall"). By the 1970s Rastafarians responded to capitalism by pressuring Jamaicans to "face the reality of a black underclass dispossessed in a lop-sided polity structured and operated to enrich a traditional few" (Stone, *Class* 90). Using African vowel rounding, omission of verbs and subject-opposition, "I-and-I," and the voice to replicate the sounds of Nyabinghi drums, Sir Lord Comic chanted down Babylon, asking "What profit it a man to gain the whole world, an lose his own soul?" ("Jack of my Trade" [1970]). As Obika Gray notes, the Rastafarians mixed Marcus Garvey's rhetoric of Black Power, Marxist representations (the hammer and sickle often adorned Rastafarian buildings), and biblical rhetoric to provide a powerful sound system for lumpenproletariat anticapitalist dissidence (Barrett 143). Rude Boys (Rudies)—"anybody against authority," including "anarchic and revolutionary youths of the slums," "gangsters and mercenaries pressed into goon squads by the two political parties," [5] and "Rasta-inspired" Rudies who "rejected traditional colonial religion and morality"—also rebelled by inverting capitalism's official codes of dress, conduct, speech, and sound. Gray explains, "To the speech affectations of the middle-class, the youth responded with a variation of working class speech. Indeed, not unlike the Rastafarians, they developed a form of speech which probably gave better expression to their cultural experience by allowing unorthodox linkages among emotion, language, and sound" (74). To the threatening Rudie slang delivered in sardonic lighthearted patter or somber monotonous voice-as-drum, the deejay bricoleurs added the sound effects of revolution—screams, gunfire, and bomb blasts—and a menacing reggae rhythm track, "so 'heavy' that listeners would be left in no doubt as to its real meaning" (Hebdige, *Cut-'n-Mix* 81).[6]

At the same time Manley drummed up support for nation-forming democratic-socialist agendas by exploiting the sound system innovations of the underclass, the roots sounds of West Kingston reverberated in the highly politicized Pan-Caribbean productions centered in Britain. Taking their cue from Rastafarian and Dread Deejay toastmasters, dub poets such as Oku Onuora, Mikey Smith, Paul Keens-Douglas, Mutabaruka, and the British-based Jamaican sound poet Linton Kwesi Johnson chanted a memorized "roots" poetry—poetry that acknowledged African ancestry; decried the diaspora, enslavement, and neocolonialist exploitation; and provided reminders of current West Indian unrest—to a backing reggae sound track. Oku Onuora explained dub poetry's ability to "mash up" the colonizer's poetic traditions, language, and ideologies: "It's dubbing out the little penta-metre and the little high falutin business and dubbing in the rootsical, yard, basic rhythm that I-an-I know. Using the language, using the body. It also mean to dub out the isms and schisms and to dub consciousness into the people-dem head. That's dub poetry" (Oku Onuora at a seminar, "Dub Poetry," Jamaica School of Drama, 17 January 1986, qtd. in Cooper

80–81).[7] Popular with urban Jamaicans, British West Indians, and British subculture youth, dub poets attained the status of "pop stars," appearing in performance with Marley, Peter Tosh, and the Calypsonian Sparrow, while Johnson's sound poems made the pop music charts in Britain (see Brathwaite, *History* 45; Berry xxv).

Profoundly influenced by sound systems and dub poetry, members of CAM who had previously incorporated creole languages and calypso material into their literary works participated during the Manley election years in a "quest for oneness" with down-pressed Jamaicans. Endorsing the decision to include the poetry of Rastafarian Bongo Jerry in an issue of *Savacou*, Rohlehr explained how the Caribbean literary elite were increasingly tuning in to Jamaican sounds and protest politics (*BIM* 1972): "This can be seen in the new confidence with which the various creoles are being used, and the omnipresent themes of grounding, identification with society's poverty, and accepted responsibility for its guilt" ("West Indian" 85). Recognizing in the innovations of West Indian sound system operators and cut-'n-mix politics the "repetition and pulsation of the national sign," members of CAM, in varying degrees of affiliation with Rastas and Rudies, versioned urban dissidence in their literary works.

The improvisational sound repertoires emanating from postindependence Jamaica produced important versions of West Indian identity in the mother country in 1972, the year that marked the end of mass West Indian immigration. After the 1971 Immigration Act forbidding further black West Indian immigration came into force in 1972, the Caribbean community, Anne Walmsley explains, "gradually became less one of immigrants or exiles, more one of black British" (330). In seeking to maintain ties with Caribbean forms of expression and agendas of nation formation while confronting the oppressions of black Britain, the literary elite and popular sound performers further hybridized disc jockey dread. During the Manley election years, sound system deejays addressing militant West Indian immigrants in Britain, dub poetry performances in London clubs, reggae hits on British and international pop charts, radio broadcasts, lectures, public poetry readings, and literary publications served as a "constant reminder to the postimperial West [and especially the 'mother country'], of the hybridity of its mother tongue, and the heterogeneity of its national space" (Bhabha, "Interrogating Identity" 203).

Prior to 1972, members of CAM often discussed the Caribbean collective identity asserted in Jamaican soundwork. CAM members recognized the potential of Jamaican sound both to "redefine their pseudo-classical notions of literature" (Brathwaite, *History* 49) and to address their political imperatives. In 1968, according to Walmsley, CAM members aligned themselves with the performance poets of Kingston, including Rasta Bongo Jerry, in response to the JLP's ban on Black Power literature and its expulsion of Walter Rodney. At one session Locksley Comrie gave an account of the "new literary activity among the young Rastafarian and black radical writers in Kingston," and John La Rose and Andrew Salkey read examples of deejay-influenced sound poetry, including the poems of Bongo Jerry, whom Brathwaite would later publish in *Savacou*. Bongo Jerry's work, Brathwaite argued in *History of the Voice*, provided the "roots and underground link" between the experiments of sound systems and those of the literary establishment (49). Defending the publication of Jerry's poems in *Savacou* against the Tobago poet Eric Roach's complaints that the poetry was "bad, fanatical, boring, and naive" (qtd. in Walmsley 226), Rohlehr acknowledged Jerry's acumen and praised his "technique of knitting words and phrases together, which the Sounds System Disc Jockeys employ all the time" ("West Indian Poetry" 87). Noting the immediacy of Jerry's sound performance, he compared the fusion of music, sermon, and drumbeat in "Mabrak," a version of the reggae meditation "Satta Amasa Gana," with Jerry's poem of the same name (a Rastafarian term for the black lightning that will wreak vengeance against Babylon): "A friend of mine who was at the [*Savacou*] reading had this to say: 'In *Mabrak* is a different kinda thing happening. Power within the people. . . . Not prophecy and lyricism and spectral doom but *menace* and *cool* and *menace*'" ("West Indian Poetry" 138–39). In "Mabrak" Bongo Jerry demanded that West Indians respond to neocolonialism by deprogramming blacks brainwashed by the white noise of colonial knowledge. A revolution must be predicated on sounds:

MABRAK

Lightning
is the future brightening,
for last year man learn
how to use black eyes.
(wise!)

Mabrak:
 NEWSFLASH!
"Babylon plans crash"
Thunder interrupt their programme to
announce:

BLACK ELECTRIC STORM
IS HERE . . .

MOSTOFTHESTRAIGHTENINGISINTHETONGUE—so . . .

SILENCE BABEL TONGUES; recall and
recollect BLACK SPEECH.

Satirizing the rhetoric of "newspeak" and the Bible, using a rhyming deejay
style, and indicating sound performance through graphic spacing, Bongo
Jerry targets the sounds of white Babylon.

For the West Indian literary community, caught during the early 1970s
between modernist literature and the explosive dissonance of urban sound
systems, the desire to narrativize a suppressed Caribbean history and construct a nation-forming aesthetic forced middle-class writers to acknowledge their ambivalence about the militant heroes of Dread City. Versioning
dread sounds, Andrew Salkey, Anthony McNeill, Dennis Scott, Edward
Kamau Brathwaite, Mervyn Morris, and other Caribbean poets of the
Manley election years used traditional tropes of martyrdom to portray the
possible delusions of Rastafarian beliefs, the liberating energy of Ras's
dreams, and their own affiliations with or anxiety over the ominous "sufferer's beat." These poets attempted to understand how the consciousness
of the emerging Jamaican nation would be formed, to a great extent, by the
quests of the dispossessed. As Salkey writes in *Jamaica* (1973), an epic-length
poem utilizing *mento* rhythms:

> Down Temple lane,
> the drums were beating brass
> in the shattered drinkers' heads;
> the drums blared like sudden eyes,
> lunatic, *ganja* eyes,
> bongo eyes;
> heads, hips, and hands
> smashed Caliban! (61)

This stanza conveys a vision of the Rastas as both subversive and deluded.
Like possessed Shango dancers or smashed Calibans, the drinkers curse
their colonizers with drumming sounds, yet they are also shattered by drink,
ganja, and lunatic visions.

In the sound poems of Anthony McNeill's *Reel from "The Life Movie"*
(chapbook insert for *Savacou*, 1972) and Dennis Scott's *Dreadwalk: Poems,
1970–78*, Old Ras is portrayed both as a wounded saint, unacknowledged

"king" of the dungle, and as a schizophrenic "sacrificial figure . . . at Babylon's crossroads" (Rohlehr, "West Indian Poetry" 84). McNeill's "Saint Ras" contrasts Ras's "city of dreams" with the world of capitalistic exploitation. As Lloyd W. Brown notes, from a Saxon or Afro-Saxon point of view, Ras's "every stance seemed crooked" and self-deluded (178). In McNeill's "Ode to Brother Joe," similarly, Brother Joe's Rastafarian beliefs cannot protect him from harassment by the law:

CD18

the drums start
Hail Selassie I
Jah Rastafari
and the room fills with the power
and beauty of blackness,
a furnace of optimism.

But the law thinks different.
This evening the Babylon catch
Brother Joe in his act of praise
and carry him off to the workhouse.

Who'll save Brother Joe? Hail
Selassie is far away
and couldn't care less,
and the promised ship

is a million light years
from Freeport.

Incorporating the reggae cadences of Brother Joe's "tough sermon," McNeill ends the poem with the harsh realization that the prison's "door is real and remains shut." In "for the D Don," a tribute to Don Drummond, the schizophrenic Rastafarian trombonist of early ska recordings, however, the poet discovers that his unity with down-pressed Jamaicans and his own spiritual redemption depend on his compassion for the deprivations of the slum yard and his understanding of the protest *sounds* of the masses. He pleads for "all seekers together, one heart" to "lock consciousness with wrong":

May I learn the shape of that hurt
which captured you nightly into
dread city, discovering through
streets steep with the sufferer's beat;

teach me to walk through jukeboxes
& shadow that broken music
whose irradiant stop is light. . . .
in the evil season sustain
o heaviest spirit of sound.

Divided by class, education, and religious skepticism, the poet and Rastafarian musician are joined in political consciousness by a sound bridge.

Dennis Scott also identifies with Rastafarians, yet even as he borrows
dread rhythms, his speakers are estranged by class from the slum yards
and threatened by the apocalyptic times. The poet ultimately identifies
with the demands of Rudie subculture by using ghetto sounds to express
his own pain. In "Squatter's Rites," Old Ras, "king" of his "drowsy hill,"
dies ignobly in squalor, yet his son, a reggae musician, pays tribute to the
squatter's tenacious spirit: ". . . at night, when the band played / *soul*, the
trumpet / pulse beat / down the hill / to the last post, / abandoned, / leaning in its hole / like a spectre / among peas, corn, potatoes." The pulse of
Ras's noble soul carries on in the trumpet beats. Scott rarely portrays sound
system productions as benign tributes to Old Ras, however. In "And it's
true," the speaker drives "to the beat of a jukebox song": "The speakers are
rattling, / the chords are wrong." The speaker clearly perceives menace: "I
know what they're saying. It is: / Doesn't he hear the drums singing of fire /
that will burn down the Dungle?" In "Apocalypse dub," the apocalypse
rider, described as a Rastafarian, feeds in the gutter behind the speaker's
house. When the speaker's companion, afraid, shuts the window and turns
up the radio, they hear the cheerful voice of the deejay: "the DJ said greet-
ings to all you lovely people. / But in the street the children coughed like
guns." In "No sufferer," the speaker marks the distinction between his private suffering and the material suffering of the ghetto while still claiming
kinship with the sufferahs, his body and mind fusing with Dread City:

. . . I have my version—
the blood's drum is
insistent, comforting. . . .
And there are kinds of poverty we share,
when the self eats up love
and the heart smokes
like the fires behind your fences, when my wit
ratchets, roaming the hungry streets
of this small flesh, my city

:in the dreadtimes of my living

. . . acknowledge I.

The poem's plea, the Rasta prayer "acknowledge I," a request for unity with Jah, marks the speaker's claim to urban "roots" soundscapes and asks for unity with the Rastafarians.

More than any other West Indian poet during the Manley election years, Edward Kamau Brathwaite sought a synthesis of the sound structures available in modernist poetry, the Caribbean creole continuum, and folk orature, blues, spirituals, jazz, ska, calypso, reggae, and African and Caribbean drumming. Going beyond private affiliations to write into history the trauma of the Caribbean, these sounds foregrounded the strength of a culture that sustained itself through subversive sounds. However, Brathwaite has claimed that Caribbean poets breaking into nation language first got a sense of the literary possibilities of these oral sounds from the experimentalism of T. S. Eliot: "It was Eliot's actual voice—or rather his recorded voice . . .—reading 'Prelude,' 'The Love Song of J. Alfred Prufrock,' *The Waste Land* and *The Four Quartets*—not the texts—which turned us on. In that dry deadpan delivery, the riddims of St. Louis (though we didn't know the source then) were stark and clear for those of us who at the same time were listening to the dislocations of Bird, Dizzy, and Klook" (*History* 13). Brathwaite sampled into his own poems both Eliot's deadpan style and stark riddims and the sound innovations of New World African emancipation. Although he would later make a careful study of grassroots sounds by collecting Rastafarian publications, publishing Rasta poems in *Savacou*, and analyzing reggae recordings, Brathwaite turned on to Jamaican protest sounds during the early CAM debates on nation language. In a 1968 letter to Andrew Salkey, he expressed his excitement: "Little pamphlets, broadsheets, broadsides, good journalism, interesting poems. And what I like about these boys: they are cool/ They are gentle and quiet. They seem to be listening; watching; waiting. We may have the Revolution with this generation or the next or the next. But there is certainly a change; a difference" (qtd. in Walmsley 262). Brathwaite admired the politicized use of nation language, which rang out like a "howl or a machine-gun or the wind or a wave . . . like the blues . . . English and African at the same time" (*History* 13), and credited his own poem, "Wings of a Dove" (1967), with demonstrating to CAM members that a poem in this language "could be 'serious' and employ not only semantic but *sound* elements" (*History* 33).

Titled after a traditional Pukkumina ritual song versioned in Carlos Malcolm's ska recording "Wings of a Dove," Brathwaite's poem samples a

Rastafarian/Pukkumina chant, "Lumba," a reggae tune by Mystic Revelation of Rastafari, and "Dry Bones" spirituals to catch the anticapitalist fervor of a "prophet and singer" in a Jamaican shantytown (Rohlehr, *Pathfinder* 337). In attacking Eric Roach's criticism of Rasta poems, Rohlehr explained the importance of sound elements in Brathwaite:

> If I remember rightly Mr. Roach once told me that he did not understand the dimension of "Wings of a Dove" until he heard it read. He also said that he now knew why Caribbean leaders imprisoned people like the reader of the poem. I had found his second statement rather strange then, though I no longer do now. Mr. Roach seemed somehow to be afraid of the sheer energy of the poem, a work whose dramatic magnitude I myself never quite grasped until I heard Ras Mortimo Planno, a Rastafarian, read it. I understand then, why Mr. Roach was afraid. ("West Indian Poetry" 134)

As the poem starts, Brathwaite's Rastaman seems to share the pathos of some of Salkey's, McNeill's, and Scott's depictions:

> Brother Man the Rasta
> man, beard full of lichens
> brain full of lice
> watched the mice
> come up through the floor-
> boards of his down-
> town, shanty-town kitchen,
> and smiled. Blessed are the poor
> in health, he mumbled,
> that they should inherit this
> wealth.

However, in a recorded performance of this poem, Brathwaite accompanies his first slow cadences with the drumming of his hands against the lectern, an introduction of the dread tension of the drum-as-black-consciousness. This insistent beat is emphasized in the repeated plosives of "Brother," "beard," "brain," and "Blessed" and in the hollow percussive sounds on rhythms of "down-/town, shanty town." His voice is as somber as a bass chord. These sounds heighten the sardonic application of the beatitudes to the Rastaman's circumstances. Brother Man's own quiet sounds revise the biblical texts that promise glory in the afterlife to impoverished sufferers.

As Brathwaite moves the Rastaman through the "streets of affliction," Brother Man incorporates reggae into his growing ire-ation against Babylon. Dazed by his ganja and the eyes of the mice that blaze with revolutionary fire, Brother Man chants:

And I
Rastafar-I
in Babylon's boom
town, crazed by the moon
. . . hear my people
cry, my people shout.

The "boom" signifies the wealth of the bourgeoisie, the sounds of the Nyabinghi drums, and bomb blasts of retribution, while the militant cry rises up from the depths of the Dungle:

Down down
white
man, con
man, brown
man, down
down full
man, frown-
ing fat man. . . .

leh we
laugh dem, mock
dem, stop
dem, kill
dem. . . .[8]

In Brathwaite's performance the rapid drumming and harsh syncopation, the amplitude, and the nursery rhyme simplicity rise up to mock and intimidate the brown-neo-colonizers, who are then compared to John Crows (vultures) that wheel above the Dungle and "fly flip flop / hip hop / pun de ground." The consumerism of the rising classes is chanted down in the rapid-fire drumming of the dry bones spiritual:

Watch *dem* ship *dem*
come to *town* dem

full o' *silk* dem
full o' *food* dem . . .

date *dem* drink *dem*
an consume *dem*[9]

The reggae complaints against the brown men slow into the beats of Rudie dread for the final lines of the poem, in which the speaker calls righteous fire. Serving as a deejay, Brathwaite creates in "Wings of a Dove" a poem that uses Jamaican protest sounds to convey the dread awareness of capitalistic and racial oppression.

During the early 1970s and the 1972 election, a postindependence Jamaican identity emerged in the "roots" sounds of the urban ghetto, sound system experiments, political campaigning, and pan-Caribbean sound poetry. Unfortunately, by the late 1970s Manley's plan for democratic socialism went belly-up, resulting in a flight of capital and protest from the Right, the Left's castigation of its "mild reforms of the status quo" (Kaufman 187), and rioting by the masses who painted walls with the slogans "IMF = Is Manley's Fault," "Joshua = Judah," and "Manlie." After the failure of his reform, Manley abandoned his plans for a democratic socialist state and established a distance between the rhetoric of the nation-state and the soundings of the underclasses. However, reggae performers, dance-hall musicians, dub poets, and dub-literary crossovers have continued to use deejay style, sound system techniques, and multitrack technologies to attack imperialism, injustice at home, political subterfuge, and turncoat politicians.[10]

Caribbean dub performance should lead members of the international literary establishment to question any aesthetic that privileges literary production over the productions of popular movements. As Cooper argues, "In neo-colonial societies such as ours, the very acknowledgment of certain distinctly Jamaican 'noises' as 'art' implies a transgressive ideological position that redefines the boundaries of the permissible, legitimising vagrant texts that both restructure the canon and challenge the very notion of canonicity" (15). By hearing in Jamaican sound system experiments an *abeng* that mobilizes the masses, creates a sense of national identity, and tests ideologies of nation formation, critics can understand the sound system as "cultural progenitor" and the deejay or recording engineer as postcolonial bricoleur.[11]

As literary critics give a hearing to Jamaican sound texts and other postmodern protest sounds,[12] we can begin to question how we might play a part in practices that continue to affect world economies and ideologies. Mutabaruka, who often samples in the most bourgeois, pretentious, or trivial sounds from North American culture, chants down imperial practices in "The People's Court," a dub poem from *Blakk Wi Blak . . . k . . . k . . .* (1991) that indicts Michael Manley, Seaga (Manley's successor, dubbed *CIAga*), and the United States for not listening to the urban sounds of Jamaican dissatisfaction. Playing on the U.S. television program *The People's Court*, as well as on a tradition of mock courtroom scenes in deejay improvisation, Mutabaruka, as Judge "Betta Mus Com," threatens "Politician Sanky Singh" (Seaga) and "Politician Change Mimind" (Manley) with "1000 years for contempt of court":

CD20

> in my court, only me talk
> cause i **am** vex . . .
> u are brought here for trick-
> ing black people . . .
> because of your misman-
> agement spending money . . .
> u keep borrowing money
> from the i.m.f.
> and the world bank
> in the people's name
> continuing de oppression of
> black people by the same
> colonialist
> why u can't learn
> no so called third world
> country has been able to break loose
> from these money hogs . . . .

Mutabaruka demands that Seaga, Manley, and North Americans recall and act on the economic and historical "roots" of Jamaican dissidence rather than simply appropriating its soundings for *politrickin* or entertainment. Change Mimind claims, "when u not in power your / honor it is easy to say dis / and that, / but when you have power is / a different sanky you / have to sing." Judge Betta Mus Com might remind Manley that the sounds he dispensed with after the failure of democratic socialism were sounds imported and creatively versioned by Jamaican migrant workers, who listened to the jive talk of North American deejays while learning firsthand, in the orange groves of Florida and the sugarcane fields of the American South, the exploited place of the black Jamaican worker in New World economics.

NOTES

1. See Kahn's introduction to *Wireless Imagination* and Hardison, esp. 151–211 and 238–78.

2. See Gilroy for a discussion of intercultural borrowings from Caribbean sound systems and the "soul and hip hop styles of black America" (82). He mentions, in particular, the British Asian attempts by groups such as Apache Indian and Bally Sagoo to mix reggae styles with Punjabi music, producing a "raggamuffin" style. For a discussion of Chicano rock and roll fusions with black musical traditions, see

Lipsitz. We may add the Fugees as an example of a contemporary North American group that collaborates with Caribbean musicians, producing a fusion of diasporic aesthetics and themes.

3. See Hebdige, *Cut-'n-Mix* 63, 83–84; Wallis and Malm 277; White 18; and Barret 123. In *Catch a Fire* White describes deejays showing up at open-air dances "dressed in gold lamé waistcoats, black leather Dracula capes, imitation ermine robes, Lone Ranger masks and rhinestone studded crowns" (18), while Hebdige describes deejays posturing as "criminals, gangsters, and legendary bad men" (*Cut-'n-Mix* 63).

4. Kaufman quotes Manley's lyrics in *Jamaica under Manley*: "A background reggae rhythm builds up with a chorus chanting 'Power for the people, if they need it; Power for the people, let them have it.'" Then Manley chants, "'I warn this country we are heading for an explosion because the faith of the people is running out. [Power for the people, if they need it; Power for the people, let them have it]. . . . Only a just society can be viable because it is only justice that endures in human affairs'" (71).

5. For a study of Jamaican political posses, see Gunst.

6. For example, Big Youth's "and di blood goin' flood an di blood goin' run / Blood up town an' blood downtown. / An' di blood roun' town." Transcribed by Hebdige, *Cut-'n-Mix* 86.

7. Transcripts of excerpts done by Mervyn Morris. Habekost and Johnson-Hill analyze dub poetry or Rastafarian performance poetry.

8. Brathwaite's *Atumpan* contains his performances of poems from *X/Self* and *The Arrivants*. As Rohlehr notes, this section versions "Lumba," a reggae tune by Mystic Revelation of Rastafari (*Pathfinder* 337).

9. Although the up-beats are not accentuated by italics in *The Arrivants*, Brathwaite provides them in *History of the Voice* 33.

10. See, for example, reggae performers such as Black Uhuru, Burning Spear, Culture, Bunny Wailer, Third World, Judy Mowatt, Marcia Griffiths, Rita Marley, Eek a Mouse, and Yellow Man; dancehall and ragga musicians Shabba Ranks, Ninja Man, Super Cat, Buju Banton, Bounty Killer, and Beenie Man; dub poets and toasters Sister Carol, Cheryl Byron, Anita Stewart, Mutabaruka, Linton Kwesi Johnson, and Benjamin Zephaniah; dub-literary crossover Jean "Binta" Breeze; and sound poet John Aagard.

11. See Damon for an argument that the poetic vanguard is often composed of socially marginalized writers; "cultural progenitor" is Saakana's term in *Jah Music*.

12. See Rose; Rose and Ross; Potter; and Sexton.

WORKS CITED

Baker, Houston A., Jr. *Modernism and the Harlem Renaissance*. Chicago: University of Chicago Press, 1987.

Bakhtin, M. M. *The Dialogic Imagination*. Ed. Michael Holquist. Trans. Caryl Emerson and Michael Holquist. Austin: University of Texas Press, 1981.

Barrett, Leonard E., Sr. *The Rastafarians: Sounds of Cultural Dissonance*. Boston: Beacon, 1988.

Berry, James, ed. *News for Babylon: The Chatto Book of West Indian-British Poetry*. London: Chatto & Windus, 1984.

Bhabha, Homi K. "DissemiNation: Time, Narrative, and Margins of the Modern Nation." *Nation and Narration*. Ed. Homi K. Bhabha. New York: Routledge, 1990. 291–322.

———. "Interrogating Identity: The Postcolonial Prerogative." *Anatomy of Racism*. Ed. David Theo Goldberg. Minneapolis: University of Minnesota Press, 1990. 183–209.

Brathwaite, Edward Kamau. *Atumpan*. Introduction by Carolivia Herron. Audiocassette. Watershed Tapes, 1989.

———. "Contradictory Omens: Cultural Diversity and Integration in the Caribbean." Monograph no. 1. Mona, Jamaica: Savacou Publications, 1974.

———. *History of the Voice: The Development of Nation Language in Anglophone Caribbean Poetry*. London: New Beacon, 1984.

Brown, Lloyd W. *West Indian Poetry*. London: Heinemann, 1984.

Chambers, Iain. *Migrancy, Culture, Identity*. New York: Routledge, 1994.

Chevannes, Barry. "The Literature of Rastafari." *Social and Economic Studies* 26 (1977): 239–62.

Cliff, Michelle. *No Telephone to Heaven*. New York: Dutton, 1987.

Comic, Sir Lord. "Jack of My Trade." *Keep on Coming through the Door: Jamaican Deejay Music, 1969–1973*. Trojan Records, 1991, 1988. Originally recorded 1970.

Cooper, Carolyn. *Noises in the Blood: Orality, Gender, and the "Vulgar" Body of Jamaican Popular Culture*. Durham: Duke University Press, 1995.

Damon, Maria. *The Dark End of the Street: Margins in American Vanguard Poetry*. Minneapolis: University of Minnesota Press, 1993.

"Dance Beaters." Kingston, Jamaica, *Abeng* 19 July 1969.

Davis, Stephen. *Bob Marley*. Garden City, N.Y.: Doubleday, 1985.

Dirlik, Arif. "The Postcolonial Aura: Third World Criticism in the Age of Global Capitalism." *Critical Inquiry* 20 (1994): 328–56.

Gilroy, Paul. *The Black Atlantic: Modernity and Double Consciousness*. Cambridge, Mass.: Harvard University Press, 1993.

Gray, Obika. *Radicalism and Social Change in Jamaica, 1960–1972*. Knoxville: University of Tennessee Press, 1991.

Gunst, Laurie. *Born Fi' Dead: A Journey through the Jamaican Posse Underworld*. New York: Holt, 1995.

Habekost, Christian. *Verbal Riddim: The Politics and Aesthetics of African-Caribbean Dub Poetry*. Amsterdam: Rodopi, 1993.

Hardison, O. B., Jr. *Disappearing through the Skylight: Culture and Technology in the Twentieth Century*. New York: Penguin, 1989.

Hebdige, Dick. *Cut-'n-Mix: Culture, Identity, and Caribbean Music*. New York: Methuen, 1987.

———. *Subculture: The Meaning of Style*. London: Methuen, 1979.

I-Roy. "Heart Don't Leap." *Keep on Coming through the Door: Jamaican Deejay Music, 1969–1973*. Trojan Records, 1991, 1988. Originally recorded 1971.

Jerry, Bongo. "Mabrak." *Savacou* 3/4 (December 1970–March 1971): 13–15.

Johnson-Hill, Jack A. *I-Sight, the World of Rastafari: An Interpretive Sociological Account of Rastafarian Ethics*. Metuchen, N.J.: American Theological Library Association and Scarecrow Press, 1995.

Kahn, Douglas. "Introduction: Histories of Sound Once Removed." *Wireless Imagination: Sound, Radio, and the Avant-Garde.* Ed. Douglas Kahn and Gregory Whitehead. Cambridge, Mass.: MIT Press, 1992. 1–29.

Kaplan, Alice Yaeger. *Reproductions of Banality: Fascism, Literature, and French Intellectual Life.* Minneapolis: University of Minnesota Press, 1986.

Kaufman, Michael. *Jamaica under Manley: Dilemmas of Socialism and Democracy.* Westport, Conn.: Lawrence Hill, 1985.

Lipsitz, George. "Cruising around the Historical Bloc: Postmodernism and Popular Music in East Los Angeles." *Cultural Critique* 5 (Winter 1986–87): 157–77.

McNeill, Anthony. *Reel from "The Life Movie." Savacou* 6. Mona, Jamaica: Savacou Publications, 1972.

Manley, Michael. *A Voice at the Workplace: Reflections on Colonialism and the Jamaican Worker.* Rev. ed. Washington, D.C.: Howard University Press, 1991.

Mutabaruka. "The People's Court." *Blakk Wi Blak ... k ... k ....* Shanachie 43083, 1991.

Owens, J. V. "Literature on the Rastafari: 1955–1974." *Savacou* 11–12 (1975): 86–105.

Payne, Anthony J. *Politics in Jamaica.* New York: St. Martins, 1988.

Potter, Russell A. *Spectacular Vernaculars: Hip-Hop and the Politics of Postmodernism.* New York: State University of New York Press, 1995.

Radhakrishnan, R. "Postcoloniality and the Boundaries of Identity." *Callaloo* 16 (1993): 750–71.

Rohlehr, F. Gordon. "Afterthoughts." *BIM* 14.56 (January–June 1973): 227–32.

———. *Pathfinder: Black Awakening in the Arrivants of Edward Kamau Brathwaite.* Tunapuna, Trinidad: College Press, 1981.

———. "West Indian Poetry: Some Problems of Assessment." *BIM* 14.54 (January–June 1972): 80–88 and 14.55 (July–December 1972): 134–44.

Rose, Tricia. *Black Noise: Rap Music and Black Culture in Contemporary America.* Hanover, N.H.: Wesleyan University Press, 1994.

Rose, Tricia, and Andrew Ross, eds. *Microphone Fiends: Youth Music and Youth Culture.* New York: Routledge, 1994.

Saakana, Amon Saba. *Jah Music.* London: Heinemann, 1980.

Salkey, Andrew. *Jamaica: An Epic Poem Exploring the Historical Foundations of Jamaican Society.* London: Bogle-L'Ouverture, 1973.

Scott, Dennis. "And it's true." *Dreadwalk: Poems, 1970–78.* London: New Beacon, 1982. 36.

———. "Apocalypse dub." *Dreadwalk: Poems, 1970–78.* London: New Beacon, 1982. 37.

———. "No Sufferer." *Uncle Time.* Pittsburgh: University of Pittsburgh Press, 1973. 53.

———. "Squatter's Rites." *Uncle Time.* Pittsburgh: University of Pittsburgh Press, 1973. 42–43.

Sexton, Adam, ed. *Rap on Rap: Straight-Up Talk on Hip-Hop Culture.* New York: Delta Trade, 1995.

Stephens, Evelyne Huber, and John D. Stephens. "The Transition to Mass Parties and Ideological Politics: The Jamaican Experience since 1972." *Comparative Political Studies* 19 (1987): 443–83.

Stone, Carl. *Class, Race, and Political Behaviour in Urban Jamaica*. Mona, Jamaica: Institute of Social and Economic Research, University of West Indies, 1973.

———. "Ideology, Public Opinion, and the Media in Jamaica." *Perspectives on Jamaica in the Seventies*. Ed. Carl Stone and Aggrey Brown. Kingston, Jamaica: Jamaica Publishing, 1981. 308–29.

Wallis, Roger, and Krister Malm. *Big Sounds from Small Peoples: The Music Industry in Small Countries*. New York: Pendragon, 1984.

Walmsley, Anne. *Caribbean Artists Movement, 1966–1972: A Literary and Cultural History*. London: New Beacon, 1992.

Waters, Anita M. *Race, Class, and Political Symbols: Rastafari and Reggae in Jamaican Politics*. New Brunswick, N.J.: Transaction, 1985.

White, Timothy. *Catch a Fire: The Life of Bob Marley*. New York: Holt, 1989.

Whitney, Malika Lee, and Dermott Hussey. *Bob Marley: Reggae King of the World*. New York: Dutton, 1984.

CANTE MORO

I would like to touch on the topic of "The New American Poetry" where it opens onto matters we would not necessarily expect it to entail—not necessarily "new," not necessarily "American," not even necessarily "poetry." What I would like to touch on is the New American poetry's Spanish connection: García Lorca's meditation on the "dark sounds" of *cante jondo*, deep song, the quality and condition known as *duende*. I will discuss that in relation to an array of dark sounds that bear on a cross-cultural poetics intimated by the inclusion of Lorca's "Theory and Function of the *Duende*" in *The Poetics of the New American Poetry*, edited by Donald M. Allen and Warren Tallman, an espousal of not only cross-cultural but intermedia fertilization and provocation, which I will relate to the work of a number of writers.

The title "Cante Moro" goes back to a recording that came out twenty-five years ago, a recording by Manitas de Plata, probably the flamenco musician best known to listeners in the United States at that time. At one point during one of the pieces on the album, "Moritas Moras," after the opening run of singing by José Reyes, a member of the group says, "Eso es cante moro," which means, "That's Moorish singing." Calling deep song *cante moro* summons the past rule and continuing cultural presence of the Moors in Spain; it acknowledges the hybrid, heterogeneous roots not only of *cante jondo* but of Spanish culture generally, of, in fact, culture, collective poesis, generally. A Gypsy doing so, as in this instance, allies outcast orders, acknowledging hybridity and heterogeneity to entwine the heterodox as well—heterodox Gypsy, heterodox Moor. *Cante moro* bespeaks the presence and persistence of the otherwise excluded, the otherwise expelled.

Let me begin by saying a bit about Lorca. Of the twenty-five writers in the anthology *The Poetics of the New American Poetry*, Lorca is one of the anomalies, perhaps *the* anomaly—the only nonanglophone poet and one of only two non-Americans included. It is fitting he should give the volume its heaviest cross-cultural, cross-pollinating touch. He himself was drawn to the marginalized, the anomalous, those relegated to the outskirts of sanctioned identity and culture. A large part of his importance to Spanish poetry is the respect he accorded the vernacular culture of southern Spain. He sought instruction in the mixed cultural inheritance of Andalusia, in the music of outcast Gypsies, in reminders of the expelled Moors. The book that made him famous is *Gypsy Ballads*, published in 1928. There is a correspondence between what Lorca was doing in Spain and what was going on in this country among black writers during the Harlem Renaissance of the 1920s and 1930s. The tapping of vernacular resources was a defining feature of the Harlem Renaissance, and it is no accident that one of its most prominent poets, Langston Hughes, was one of the first translators of *Gypsy Ballads* into English. Lorca in fact had direct contact with Harlem and the Harlem Renaissance writers while studying at Columbia in 1929 and 1930. The work that came out of that stay, *Poet in New York*, contains a section called "The Blacks," which celebrates Harlem. The recently published translation of that work by Greg Simon and Steven F. White includes letters Lorca wrote to his family from New York. In one of them he tells of meeting the Harlem Renaissance novelist Nella Larsen, author of *Quicksand* and *Passing*, and of the party she gave for him at her house at which "there were only blacks." Of the music they played and sang he writes, "Only the *cante jondo* is comparable" (*Poet* 214).

In his essay on *duende* Lorca is working with the black aesthetic of Spain. One of the things he does early in the essay is quote the Gypsy singer Manuel Torre as having said, "All that has dark sounds has *duende*." That, at least, is how it is translated by J. L. Gilli in the version that appears in *The Poetics of the New American Poetry* (91). Christopher Maurer, in the more recent translation that appears in *Deep Song and Other Prose*, renders it, "All that has black sounds has *duende*" (43). Maurer also points out, in a footnote, that when Lorca met Torre in 1927, Torre, evoking the Gypsies' fabled origins in Egypt, said to him, "What you must search for, and find, is the black torso of the Pharaoh" (140). He meant that you have to root your voice in fabulous origins, find your voice in the dark, among the dead. The word *duende* means spirit, a kind of gremlin, a gremlinlike, troubling spirit. One of the things that marks the arrival of *duende* in flamenco singing is a sound of trouble in the voice. The voice becomes troubled. Its eloquence becomes eloquence of another order, a broken, problematic, self-problematizing eloquence. Lorca also quotes Torre as having told a singer, "You have a voice, you know the styles, but you will never triumph, because you have no *duende*" (*Deep Song* 42). So *duende* is something beyond technical competence or even technical virtuosity. It is something troubling. It has to do with trouble, deep trouble. Deep song delves into troubled water, troubles the water. As a character in Leon Forrest's novel *Two Wings to Veil My Face* puts it, "Still waters don't run deep enough."

Lorca tells a story of the Andalusian singer Pastora Pavón, also known as La Niña de los Peines. He tells of her singing in a little tavern in Cádiz one night before a group of flamenco aficionados. He says that when she finished singing, she was met with silence. Her voice, though technically perfect, and her virtuosity, though impressive, did not move anyone. "When Pastora Pavón finished singing," Lorca writes, "there was total silence, until a tiny man, one of those dancing manikins that rise suddenly out of brandy bottles, sarcastically murmured 'Viva Paris!' as if to say: 'Here we care nothing about ability, technique, skill. Here we are after something else'" (*Deep Song* 45). Which is not to say that you get there by not having skill. You get there by not being satisfied with skill. It is the other side, the far side of skill, not the near side. Then Lorca goes on to say,

> As though crazy, torn like a medieval weeper, La Niña de los Peines got to her feet, tossed off a big glass of firewater and began to sing with a scorched throat, without voice, without breath or color, but with *duende*. She was able to kill all the scaffolding of the song and leave way for a furious, enslaving *duende*, friend of sand winds, who made the listeners rip their clothes with the same rhythm as do the blacks of the Antilles when, in the "lucumí" rite, they huddle in heaps before the statue of Santa Bárbara. (45–46)

It is interesting that Lorca makes the Old World–New World connection, a black connection, a connection between *duende*, black song in Spain, *cante moro*, and black song in Cuba, the music of the Yoruba-Catholic mix known as *lucumí*. That is one of the reasons Lorca is relevant to new American possibilities, to an American newness that is about mix, the meeting of different cultural styles and predispositions. He was interested in Old World predecessor mixes like those in Andalusia, whose further inflections in the Americas he recognized and embraced.

Lorca does not so much define *duende* as grope after it, wrestle with it, evoke it through strain, insist on struggle. He says, for example, that "one must awaken the *duende* in the remotest mansions of the blood" (44). He says that "the *duende* loves the rim of the wound" and that it "draws near places where forms fuse together into a yearning superior to their visible expression" (50). He writes, "Each art has a *duende* different in form and style but their roots all meet in the place where the black sounds of Manuel Torre come from—the essence, the uncontrollable, quivering, common base of wood, sound, canvas, and word" (52). One of the ongoing challenges of Lorca's essay is how to bring *duende*, which he discusses mainly in relation to music, into writing, how to relate it to writing. I would like to touch on four American poets whose work intersects with Lorca's. Three of the four poets were included in the anthology edited by Donald M. Allen, *The New American Poetry, 1945–1960*: Jack Spicer, Robert Duncan and Amiri Baraka. The fourth, Bob Kaufman, was not included, though he should have been.

First, Jack Spicer, who was based in the San Francisco Bay area, a San Francisco poet. Though he began writing in the 1940s, he felt that his real work began with *After Lorca*, which was published in 1957. It is a book of poems and prose pieces, poems that are presented as translations of poems by Lorca, translations in a very loose sense, loose translations. Some of them are translations in an even looser sense, in that they are translations of Lorca poems that do not exist. Interspersed among these translations are the prose pieces, which are written as letters addressed to the dead García Lorca. Lorca was killed during the Spanish Civil War, executed by Franco's troops, which is another reason he has attracted a lot of attention—as a symbol, a sign of the times, times we continue to live in. He is a poet of cultural openness, cultural mix, cut down by the emergence of fascism. A lot of writers have identified with Lorca and the position, implicit and explicit, he took against fascism. Remember that the Gypsies he celebrated so were one of the targets of fascism, that a million Gypsies were killed in concentration camps.

Lorca was killed in 1936 near Granada. Spicer, a very playful writer, albeit a bit grim, begins *After Lorca* with an introduction attributed to "Federico García Lorca / Outside Granada, October 1957" (*Collected Books* 12). The gremlin, the imp, is very active in what he is doing. Also, he is picking up on something that is very important in Lorca's discussion of *duende*, which is that, among other things, it is a conversation with the dead, intimacy with death and with the dead. "The *duende*," Lorca says, "does not come at all unless he sees that death is possible. The *duende* must know beforehand that he can serenade death's house and rock those branches we all wear, branches that do not have, will never have, any consolation" (*Deep Song* 49–50). The disconsolate character and tone of Spicer's work agrees not only with this but with the fact that one of the phrases that recur a great deal in *cante jondo* is *sin remedio*, "without remedy." You will also hear the assertion *no hay remedio*, "there is no remedy." Pepe de la Matrona, who has one of the darkest, gruffest voices you will ever hear (more an extended, variegated growl than a voice), sings a song called "Remedio No Tengas," which means "You Would Have No Remedy." *Duende* often has to do with a kind of longing that has no remedy, not simply loss, unrequited love and so forth, but what Lorca calls "a longing without object" (*Deep Song* 112). He talks about this in relation to *Gypsy Ballads*, to a poem that has to do with a woman named Soledad Montoya, who, he says, "embodies incurable pain": "The Pain of Soledad Montoya is the root of the Andalusian people. It is not anguish, because in pain one can smile, nor does it blind, for it never produces weeping. It is a longing without object, a keen love for nothing, with the certainty that death (the eternal care of Andalusia) is breathing behind the door" (112).

So Spicer opens *After Lorca* with an introduction written by Lorca, at that time some twenty years dead. In it Lorca says that several of the pieces in the book are translations of poems he has written since his death, though he does not say which. In the essay on *duende* he writes, "A dead man in Spain is more alive as a dead man than any place else in the world" (*Deep Song* 47). Spicer seems to have taken him at his word. Impish play and disconsolate spirit — "The dead are notoriously hard to satisfy," we read (*Collected Works* 12) — repeatedly embrace each other in an introduction whose antic humor gathers troubling undertones. The words "execution" and "executed," used in reference to Spicer's technique, resonate with and are darkly inflected by the circumstances of Lorca's death. Likewise the joke with which the introduction ends: "But I am strongly reminded as I survey this curious amalgam of a cartoon published in an American magazine while I was visiting your country in New York. The cartoon showed a gravestone on which were inscribed the words: 'HERE LIES AN OFFICER AND A GENTLEMAN.' The caption below it read: 'I wonder how they happened to be buried in the same grave?' " (12).

Another poet who was engaged with Lorca's work, another San Francisco poet, is Robert Duncan, an associate of Spicer's. In his book *Caesar's Gate: Poems, 1949–50* there is a preface Duncan wrote in 1972, the year the book was published, and in that preface there is a section called "Lorca." The book includes a poem called "What Have You Come to Tell Me, García Lorca?" and in the preface Duncan recalls the 1940s and 1950s, when he was reading Lorca. He writes for several pages about Lorca's importance to his development, and he mentions Spicer as well. He discusses the historical predicament, the historical moment that was Lorca's fate, the Spanish Civil War and the rise of fascism. He discusses *duende*. He also discusses Lorca as a gay poet, a troubled, conflicted gay poet who was important to him and Spicer as gay poets. Not that he advanced a gay poetics but that they saw in him and his work some of the trouble, for him, of being gay—a certain depression and self-censure, a censuring of his own homosexuality. He writes this about *duende*:

> In his lecture "Theory and Function of the *Duende*," Lorca tells us: "The dark and quivering *duende* that I am talking about is a descendant of the merry demon of Socrates." The madness, then, however it may relate to the practice of deliberate alienation which Lorca's intimate friend from student days, Salvador Dalí, had brought into Surrealist circles of Paris from their Spanish conversations, and which led to the work of Breton and Eluard in *L'Immaculée Conception*, contemporary with Lorca's *Poeta en Nueva York*, with Breton's essay on the simulation of verbal deliriums from various categories of insanity—this madness is not ultimately a surrealist simulation drawn from a clinical model in a program of systematic alienation but, past that state, means to return to the divine madness of daemonic inspiration, the speaking more than one knew what, that Plato tells us his Master, Socrates, thought to be at once the power and the dementia of the poet in his art. (xxi–xxii)

He speaks of *duende* as a "mode of poetic dissociation" and of "disturbed meanings." The poet speaks in tongues, multiply, troublingly: "Freed from reality, the trouble of an unbound reference invades the reader's sense of what is at issue" (xxii).

So *duende*, for Duncan, is "the speaking more than one knew what," the taking on of another voice, and that is very much what *duende* is in *cante jondo*. It is a taking over of one's voice by another voice. This wooing of another voice, an alternate voice, that is so important to *duende* has as one of its aspects or analogs in poetry that state of entering the language in such a way that one is into an area of implication, resonance, and connotation that is manifold, many-meaninged, polysemous. One has worked beyond oneself. It is as if the language itself takes over. Something beyond the will, the conscious design or desire of the poet, is active, something that goes beyond univocal, unequivocal control. That is what Duncan means by "the trouble of an unbound reference"—an inordinacy, a lack of adequation that is to language what *sin remedio* is to a longing without object. Bound reference, univocal meaning, is no solution to the riddle of language.

Amiri Baraka cites Lorca as an influence in his statement on poetics in *The New American Poetry*. There is an early poem of his called "Lines to García Lorca," which he prefaces with an epigraph taken from an African American spiritual: "Climin up the mountain, chillun, / Didn't come here for to stay, / If I'm ever gonna see you agin / It'll be on the judgment day."

By doing so he not only acknowledges Lorca's interest in African American music and culture but furthers the analogy, the sense of rapport, between African American spirituality and Andalusian spirituality. Gypsies, though they do not appear explicitly in this poem, come in elsewhere in Baraka's early work to embody a mobile, mercurial noninvestment in the status quo. One of the things going on in "Lines to García Lorca" is the implicit connection between that mercuriality, that nomadism, and the lines "Didn't come here for to stay," behind which lies a well-known, resonant history of African American fugitivity and its well-known, resonant relationship to enslavement and persecution. Thus the resonant apposition of the poem's opening lines, "Send soldiers again to kill you, García. / Send them to quell my escape." At the end of the poem Lorca's voice, "away off," invested with fugitive spirit, laughs:

> But, away off, quite close to the daylight,
> I hear his voice, and he is laughing, laughing
> Like a Spanish guitar.

The way in which fugitivity asserts itself on an aesthetic level, at the level of poetics, is important as well. The way in which Baraka's poems of this period move intimates fugitive spirit, as does much of the music that he was into. He writes of a solo by saxophonist John Tchicai on an Archie Shepp album, "It slides away from the proposed" ("Four for Trane" 160). That gets into, again, the cultivation of another voice, a voice that is other than that proposed by one's intentions, tangential to one's intentions, angular, oblique — the obliquity of an unbound reference. That sliding away wants out. Musicians like Tchicai and Shepp were called "outside" players. Robin Blaser called Spicer's work "the practice of outside" (269). Let me, though, let another poem of Baraka's, "History as Process," say it and show it. Lorca does not explicitly come in, but the Gypsies do, and so does the guitar:

1.

The evaluation of the mysteries by the sons of all
experience. All suffering, if we call the light a thing
all men should know. Or find. Where ever, in the dark folds
of the next second, there is some diminishing beauty we might one
day understand, and scream to, in some wild fit of acknowledged
Godliness.

Reality, is what it is. This suffering truth
advertised in all men's loveliest histories.

The thing, There As Speed, is God, as mingling
possibility. The force. As simple future, what

the freaky gipsies rolled through Europe
on.

(The soul.)

2.
What can I do to myself? Bones
and dusty skin. Heavy eyes twisted
between the adequate thighs of all
humanity (a little h), strumming my head
for a living. Bankrupt utopia sez tell me
no utopias. I will not listen. (Except the raw wind
makes the hero's eyes close, and the tears that come out
are real.)

One hears the pronouncements, the propositions. One also hears the slips, the slides, the shifting ratios—rhythmic, predicative, quick.

The last of the four poets is Bob Kaufman. His work was not included in *The New American Poetry*, even though it was very important to the Beat movement. He was very involved in the development of the Beat movement in San Francisco, in North Beach, and is said to have coined the term "beatnik." Some people consider him the prototypical Beat poet. Steve Abbott has called him "the hidden master of the Beats" (1). He was a poet of African American and Jewish descent to whom Lorca's work was very important. He refers to Lorca in a number of poems, echoing lines from his work, sometimes quoting or paraphrasing them outright. In "Lorca," for example, we find the line "Give Harlem's king one spoon" (4), harking back to Lorca's *Poet in New York*, where "The King of Harlem" begins with the lines, "With a wooden spoon / he dug out the crocodiles' eyes" (29). What spoke most to Kaufman was Lorca's valorization of African American presence. In his lecture on *Poet in New York* Lorca argued that "the blacks exercise great influence in North America," that "they are the most delicate, most spiritual element in that world" (186). The "great central sun" (35) he encourages black people to seek in "The King of Harlem," to continue seeking, is, among other things, the covert centrality of an otherwise marginalized people, a "sun" that cross-linguistically puns on "soul" ("el gran sol del centro").

Kaufman's apocalyptic, ironically patriotic prose-poem "The Ancient Rain" generously samples, as we would say nowadays, "The King of Harlem" and "Standards and Paradise of the Blacks." Its embrace of Lorca's endorsement of new American possibilities, new American mixes, resounds in telling counterpoint not only with Kaufman's noninclusion in *The New American Poetry* (only one nonwhite poet's work was included) but with the negligible attention accorded him and his work in the numerous writings on the Beat generation as well:

> At once I am there at the great sun, feeling the great sun of the center. Hearing the Lorca music in the endless solitude of crackling blueness. I could feel myself a little boy again in crackling blueness, wanting to do what Lorca says in crackling blueness to kiss out my frenzy on bicycle wheels and smash little squares in the flush of a soiled exultation. Federico García Lorca sky, immaculate scoured sky, equaling only itself contained all the distances that Lorca is, that he came from Spain of the Inquisition is no surprise. His poem of solitude walking around Columbia. My first day in crackling blueness, I walked off my ship and rode the subway to Manhattan to visit Grant's tomb and I thought because Lorca said he would let his grow long someday crackling blueness would cause my hair to grow long. I decided to move deeper into crackling blueness. When Franco's civil guard killed, from that moment on, I would move deeper in crackling blueness. I kept my secrets. I observed those who read him who were not Negroes and listened to all their misinterpretation of him. I thought of those who had been around him, those that were not Negro and were not in crackling blueness, those that couldn't see his wooden south wind, a tiltin' black slime that tacked down all the boat wrecks, while Saturn delayed all the trains. (80–81)

"Crackling blueness," out of "Standards and Paradise of the Blacks," is the sky cracked by lightning, the imminence of thunder and rain, wrath and redemption, "the bitter freshness of . . . millenary spit," as Lorca puts it. It is also the raspy, cracked voice of *duende*, the ominous, black vocality of the blues and of *cante jondo*.

Those, then, are four instances of American poets making use of the work of Lorca. They relate to the question of how one's writing can draw on that of predecessors, the sense of tradition, a lineage one creates for oneself and that one seeks out in the work of others. Influence without anxiety call it. As a writer one has to find one's tradition, create one's tradition, and in doing that one creates lines of affinity and kinship that can cut across national boundaries, ethnic boundaries, and so forth. They also relate to the question of how one's writing can be informed and instructed by other artistic media, how one can create or pursue lines of kinship and conversation with nonliterary media. That's one of the useful senses the phrase "cultivation of another voice" I used earlier has. A different medium is a different voice, an alternate vocality. Lorca's sense of *duende* comes out of his engagement with music, the Andalusian music he was obviously moved and inspired by. Attentiveness to those other, alternate voices that speak to you—painting, sculpture, whatever—can make you susceptible, impinge on you in ways that alter your own voice.

My work has a pronounced relationship to music. I was always struck by Louis Zukofsky's definition of poetry as a function whose lower limit is speech and whose upper limit is song. He uses the integral sign from calculus to suggest that we are integrating that lower limit, speech, and that upper limit, song. Poetry is an integral function. But even before I came across Zukofsky's formulation of it, I heard poetry as a musical deployment of language, the music peculiar to language, language bordering on song, speech bordering on song. From doing a lot of listening I have gotten certain ideas about music, a thematics of music, but also an impulse toward a musicality in the writing. Years ago I wrote a poem for John Coltrane, "Ohnedaruth's Day Begun," in which there is this passage:

> I grope thru smoke to glimpse New
> York City, the Village Gate, late
>   '65. I sit at the bar drinking scotch between
>   sets, some kid comes up and says he'd
>   like to hear "Equinox."
>
>   We play "Out of
> This World" instead, the riff hits
> me like rain and like a leak in my
>   throat it won't quit. No reins whoa
>   this ghost I'm ridden by and again
>   I'm asking
> myself what "climb" will Nut ask of
>   me next? . . . (73)

This has to do, among other things, with a surge, a runaway dilation, a quantum rush one often hears in Trane's music, the sense that he's driven, possessed—*ridden*, as it is put here, which recalls the African possession religions in which worshipers are spoken of as horses and the gods, the spirits, are spoken of as horsemen, riders. To be possessed is to be mounted and ridden by a god. You find that imagery in *vodoun* in Haiti, in *candomblé* in Brazil, in *lucumí* or *santería* in Cuba. Possession means that something beyond your grasp of it grabs you, that something that gets away from you—another sense in which fugitivity comes in—gives you a voice. Like Lorca, who, remember, refers to *lucumí*, I think of this as related to *duende*.

That is one place in my work where ideas having to do with *duende* come in. Another place is *Bedouin Hornbook*, which even more extensively and graphically has to do with music. It is prose, written mainly in the form of letters addressed to an angel by a musician/composer, N. *Duende* is a term that comes up a number of times in these letters. One instance is this one, toward the end of a letter that accompanies the tape of a composition that N. has written:

> The name of the piece is "Opposable Thumb at the Water's Edge." Its basic theme I'd put this way: Graspability is a self-incriminating thirst utterly native to every hand, an indigenous court from which only the drowned hope to win an acquittal. The piece makes use of two triadic phrases which I call utility riffs: "whatever beginnings go back to" and "an exegetic refusal to be done with desire." These generate a subtheme which could be put as follows: Thirst is by its nature unquenchable, the blue lips of a muse whose refusals roughen our throats with *duende*. (43)

Unquenchable thirst is a longing without object. Blue, the color of its ostensible object, plants a disconsolate kiss.

The CD accompanying this book includes several tracks that relate to these matters. The first is a piece by the singer Lorca writes about in his essay on *duende*, Pastora Pavón, La Niña de los Peines. It is a piece called "Ay Pilato" and is a type of song known as a *saeta*. The *saeta* is a form of song heard in Andalusia during Holy Week, the week before Easter. A procession takes place through the streets, a procession that includes musicians—sometimes playing nothing but muffled drums but often including horns, brass instruments. The procession carries an image either of the Virgin or of Christ, sometimes both. At each point where the procession stops, there is a singer on a balcony overlooking the street. The procession stops right beneath the balcony, and the singer sings to the image they carry. *Saeta* means arrow. The song is piercing, heartrending. We hear the singer singing from a position of being pierced. What we also hear is a Gypsy-Moorish-Arab substrate piercing—breaking through from underneath—CD21   the occasion's Christian surface.

Another *saeta*, the first one I ever heard, is by Miles Davis, taken from his album *Sketches of Spain*. Miles was very attracted to flamenco. On the *Kind of Blue* album there is a cut called "Flamenco Sketches," and on a later album, the famous *Bitches Brew* that came out in 1970, there is a cut called "Spanish

Key," all of which lends itself to the Andalusian/African American rapport we have seen Lorca and others get at. In late 1959 Miles teamed up with pianist/composer/arranger Gil Evans and recorded *Sketches of Spain*. One of the five pieces on the album is a *saeta*, with Miles, on trumpet, playing the role of the *cantaor*, the singer on the balcony. They even simulate the procession, opening and closing the cut with march music. One hears that tremulous, piercing sound Miles gets out of the trumpet, which there have been various attempts to describe. One critic called it the sound of a man walking on eggshells, and there is the story of a little girl who said he sounded like a little boy crying in a closet. CD22

The next piece does not relate as explicitly to Andalusia, but it still has to do with the things I have been discussing. It is John Coltrane with Miles Davis's group, from the last concert tour that Trane made as part of Miles's band. It was recorded in Stockholm in 1960. The solo he plays on Miles's composition "All Blues" has the quality of reaching for another voice, stretching the voice, passionately reaching; it has the quality of *duende* that Lorca talks about as a tearing of the voice, a crippling of the voice that paradoxically is also enabling. I have discussed, in an essay called "Sound and Sentiment, Sound and Symbol," the connection between limping and enablement in relation to the African god Legba, one of the gods of *vodoun*, *candomblé* and *lucumí*. Legba is the god of doorways, gateways, entrances, thresholds, crossroads, and intersections. Legba is crippled, the limping god who nonetheless dances. That conjunction of limping disability with the gracefulness of dance is one of the things I hear coming through in Trane's solo. This also relates to a forking of the voice, so that we hear the intersection of two lines of articulation—doubling the voice, splitting the voice, breaking the voice, tearing it. There is a dialogical aspect to African American and African music that is very strong. It comes across in call and response, the antiphonal relationship between lead singer and chorus, preacher and congregation. It comes across in the playing of musicians like John Coltrane who use the upper and lower registers of the instrument as though they were two different voices in dialogue with each other, in a sometimes quarrelsome conversation, or in competition with each another. In this instance Trane gets into doing some things with overtones, multiphonics, that make it sound almost as if he is playing two different horns, trying to play in two different octaves at the same time. It makes for an unruly, agonistic sound in which it seems that the two lines of articulation are wrestling, that they are somehow each other's contagion or contamination. It is appropriate that that solo should come in a piece called "All Blues." CD23

This business of the pursuit of another voice, an alternate voice—in *Bed-*

ouin Hornbook N. calls it the pursuit of a meta-voice—is very much a part of the African American musical tradition and very much a part of the African musical tradition. The dialogical quality in music of this disposition can be heard in a number of different idioms and forms. The blues is certainly one of them. One of the striking things about the blues tradition is the way the instrument becomes that other, alternate voice. Everyone talks about the speechlike qualities of instruments as they are played in African American music. Built into that is some kind of dissatisfaction with—if not critique of—the limits of conventionally articulate speech, verbal speech. One of the reasons the music so often goes over into nonspeech—moaning, humming, shouts, nonsense lyrics, scat—is to say, among other things, that the realm of conventionally articulate speech is not sufficient for saying what needs to be said. We are often making that same assertion in poetry. That is one of the reasons that in poetry we seek out that "trouble of an unbound reference" Duncan talks about. That is one of the reasons this music has been so attractive, so instructive, such an inspiration to poets.

In the music of Mississippi Fred McDowell one can hear the interaction between his voice and the guitar, a slide guitar, the way that the line between speech and song is very fluid, frequently blurred. That is very much a part of the tradition. There is an album called *Singing Preachers*, which features preachers whose sermons would taper off into singing, speech into song, and vice versa, back and forth. Notice that in "Everybody's Down on Me" Fred McDowell starts off talking and that he works that talk into song, but notice also what he says, the minilecture, the sermonette he gives as to what this recourse to *sound*, a sound peculiar to the slide guitar, a raucous, unruly wail, is about, what it comes out of. He is talking about being betrayed, and he is saying that you need an unruly, outrageous sound when you feel there is no other way you can get satisfaction. What you can say, what can be stated within the limits of conventionally articulate speech, is not enough. What you need is this *sound*. Notice too how he starts stumbling, how he stumbles as he tries to talk about that sound, stumbles until the sound itself comes to his rescue. Notice how the sound itself rescues crippled speech, which, again, is the eloquence of Legba, the limping eloquence, the limping enablement of Legba.

CD24   Another context in which to think about this recourse to an alternate voice, this movement into a voice beyond one's voice, into a meta-voice, is shamanism, the shamanic roots of music evoked by the Cuban writer Alejo Carpentier in his novel *The Lost Steps*. It was published in the 1950s and has to do with the journey of a composer/musician into the jungles of South America in search of the origins of music, something of an ethnomusicological expedition. Carpentier was, among other things, a musicologist. He did research, for example, into the African roots of Cuban music and culture, into *lucumí* and so forth, and his first novel, *Ecue-Yamba-O!*, has to do with that. The recourse to another voice, the need for an alternate voice, is something he goes into in several passages in *The Lost Steps*. In the depths of a South American forest the narrator witnesses a shamanic rite performed over the body of a hunter who was killed by a rattlesnake bite. He takes this to be the origin of music; he sees the shamanic confrontation with death as the birth of music:

> The shaman began to shake a gourd full of pebbles — the only instrument these people know — trying to drive off the emissaries of Death. There was a ritual silence, setting the stage for the incantation, which raised the tension of the spectators to fever pitch.
>
> And in the vast jungle filling with night terrors, there arose the Word. A word that was more than word. A word that imitated the voice of the speaker, and of that attributed to the spirit in possession of the corpse. One came from the throat of the shaman; the other from his belly. One was deep and confused like the bubbling of underground lava; the other, medium in pitch, was harsh and wrathful. They alternated. They answered each other. The one upbraided when the other groaned; the belly voice turned sarcastic when the throat voice seemed to plead. Sounds like guttural portamenti were heard, ending in howls; syllables repeated over and over, coming to create a kind of rhythm; there were trills suddenly interrupted by four notes that were the embryo of a melody. But then came the vibration of the tongue between the lips, the indrawn snoring, the panting contrapuntal to the rattle of the maraca. This was something far beyond language, and yet still far from song. Something that had not yet discovered vocalization, but was more than word. (184)

He later speaks of this as his having seen "the word travel the road of song without reaching it," and later still of "its verbal exorcism turning into music when confronted with the need for more than one intonation" (200, 217).

Think about that in relation to La Niña de los Peines, whose voice breaks and seems intent on some higher octave, some higher voice. Think about it in relation to the John Coltrane solo, where, working with multiphonics, he voices discontent with the given intonation, bent on going beyond it. Think about it in relation to antiphony, the call-and-response, dialogical impulse that can be heard even in music played by a lone performer, the interplay between voice and instrument especially within the blues tradition, in the music of someone like Fred McDowell. One of the reasons for the development of slide guitar was the need to get a more human (but not quite human) sound out of the guitar, out of the instrumental line—human-but-not-quite-human speech as well as human-but-not-quite-human cry.

In another piece by Fred McDowell, "Jesus Is on the Mainline," one of the striking things is the way he lets the guitar speak, actually lets it take parts of his lines. He will begin singing a line only to break off and let the guitar finish it, suggesting a continuum, a complementarity, between human voice and instrumental voice, an interchange between speech and song, verbal articulation and nonverbal articulation. If you have read Ishmael Reed's novel *Mumbo Jumbo*, you may remember the episode where he talks about an ancient Egyptian musician named Jethro, whose sound he describes as a kind of muddy, delta sound, blurring—muddying—the distinction between the Nile delta and the Mississippi delta. Fred McDowell's guitar has the kind of sound Reed is talking about.

CD25

Another example of multivocality is from an album with the shamanic title *I Talk with the Spirits*, recorded in the 1960s by Rahsaan Roland Kirk, who plays flute on it throughout. In a piece called "The Business Ain't Nothin' but the Blues," Kirk hums while playing, which is something other flute players sometimes do as well. Yusef Lateef is one of the first I ever heard do it. The technique has become something of a standard in the repertoire of jazz flutists. On the current scene, James Newton is a flutist who uses it a lot. Interestingly, it was not something that Eric Dolphy, who was a great flutist, did that much with, but that's another story. Rahsaan, though, hums and even speaks as he plays. Again, the play of voices, a move into multiple voices, is analogous to speaking in tongues. One hears a braiding of vocal and instrumental lines. I have even heard saxophone players hum while playing. Pharoah Sanders does it from time to time, and I have also heard Dewey Redman do it. There is a piece in Amiri Baraka's book *Tales* in which he writes, "The dialogue exists. Magic and ghosts are a dialogue, and the body bodies of material, invisible sound vibrations, humming in emptyness, and ideas less than humming, humming" (91).

CD26

One of the things I have been discussing is cross-culturality, sensing rapport across cultural lines, picking up on rhymes between cultures, dialogue between cultures. A piece that shows the multivocal technique we just heard from Rahsaan—humming while playing the flute—in another context is a love song from Luristan, in Iran. It is performed by a singer accompanied by a flutist playing a reed flute known as a *nay*. The *nay* has quite a special place in the mystical traditions of that part of the world. Rumi, for example, writes of the *nay*: "Hearken to the reed-flute, how it complains, / Lamenting its banishment from its home" (1). He goes on to say that the reed was cut from rushes and that what we hear in the sound of the *nay* is the remembrance of that cutting, that the very sound calls to mind the cutting that brought it into being and which it laments. The sound subsists on that cutting. The *nay* not only mourns but embodies separation. Fittingly, the song from Luristan contains the lines "I am burning, / I have the taste of separation." This is typical of the poetry and music of Iran. In this song the flutist hums while playing the *nay*. In Iran this technique is known as *zem-zemeh*. In this piece the splitting of the voice, the cultivation of a multiple voice, seems to embody at the instrumental level the "taste of separation" that is complained about in the lyrics. So there again one hears humming, the additional voice and vibration it brings in, the buzz it elicits. CD27

Think about that buzz, that vibration, that multiply-aspected vocality, in relation to poetry, to the cultivation of multiple meaning in poems, the play of polysemous articulation. A poem's order of statement is what has been called a buzz of implication, something you can hear in even a very brief passage. Take, for example, these lines of Robert Kelly's in a book called *Songs I–XXX*:

> I was not a tree,
> I hung in my bones like a man in a tree,
> the tree talked. I said nothing. (53)

The play of assertion against a recanting of assertion amounts to a buzz. The changes it registers concerning the status of treeness, the status of the speaker, and the status of speaking make the passage what Rahsaan took to calling his band: a vibration society. The words buzz, whisper among themselves, vibrate with such implicit assertions as that the tree that talks is a skeleton, that the man is not his bones, that bones are gallows, and so forth. I think of this also in relation to the cultivation of resonance in African music. In Zimbabwe, for example, they not only place the mbira, the so-called thumb-piano, inside a calabash gourd, which they call a resonator, but they also attach cowrie shells to the outside of the gourd. The shells rub against the gourd and make a raspy, buzzing sound when the mbira is played. The African predilection for a burred, "dirty" sound, which the Camerounian musician/musicologist Francis Bebey, among others, has commented on, is reluctant to let a tone sit in some uncomplicated, isolated, supposedly pure sense of itself. Poems likewise buzz with meanings, implications, and insinuations that complicate, contaminate, "dirty" one another.

A piece that brings us full circle, back to Andalusian/African American resonances, is Sonny Rollins's "East Broadway Rundown." The bass player, Jimmy Garrison, takes a solo, playing the bass like a big guitar (which it is), playing it, more specifically, like a Spanish guitar—playing the flamenco riffs that came to be one of his trademarks. When Sonny Rollins comes in, what takes place is an interesting interchange that has remained a suggestive, poetic image for me over the years. Rollins removes the mouthpiece from his saxophone and plays it, sans horn. So, again, we have separation, severance, amputation. *Bedouin Hornbook* opens with the idea of music as a phantom limb, a phantom reach with/after something you have but do not have. It is a kind of re-membering, a mended dismemberment. This is one of the pieces that put that idea, that figure, into my head—a bassist playing flamenco while a horn player makes a voice, a high, falsetto voice, out of breakage, an alternate voice out of separating the mouthpiece from

CD28 the horn.

I will finish by mentioning some further extensions and elaborations of *cante moro*. One of the interesting things that has been happening lately with flamenco in Spain is the assertion of its ties to the Moors, to some of the Arab musics of North Africa. This includes collaborations between flamenco musicians and North African performers of a type of music whose roots are in Muslim Spain, a type of music still known as Andalusian throughout the Maghreb. Two recorded instances are José Heredia Maya and the Andalusian Orchestra of Tetuan's *Macama Jonda* and Juan Peña Lebrijano and the Andalusian Orchestra of Tangier's *Encuentros*. In the 1970s and 1980s Lole Montoya, of the group Lole and Manuel, recorded a number of songs in Arabic, traveling to the Sono Cairo studios in Egypt in 1977 to record a song made famous by the legendary Om Kalsoum, "Anta Oumri." Also interesting are the connections some of the younger flamenco musicians have made with New World extensions of the African-Iberian mix. A group called Ketama blends flamenco with Cuban rumba, Brazilian samba, and so forth. They have also collaborated with a kora player from Mali, Toumani Diabate. One of their influences is a musician named Manzanita, whose 1978 album *Poco Ruido y Mucho Duende* presented him accompanied by, as its liner notes explain, "dos mùsicos de color en razón a su sentido improvisatorio y a su 'feeling,' muy próximo al gitano" ("two black musicians because of their improvisatory sense and their 'feeling,' very close to that of the Gypsy"). The two musicians are bassist David Thomas, from the United States, and percussionist Pepe Ebano, from Cuba. Another of Ketama's influences is singer Camarón, who in the late 1970s expanded his instrumental accompaniment to include trap drums, keyboards, and electric bass. Finally, a few years ago a group called Pata

Negra released an album called *Blues de la Frontera*. As is clear from the title, they play a flamenco-blues mix. It builds on the rapport that has long been noted between the two. I remember hearing a radio documentary on Jimi Hendrix. One segment was a tape from a recording session, maybe a jam, and Hendrix was talking to the other musicians and said, "What I want is a Muddy Waters/flamenco sound." The other musicians said, "Yeah!" Everyone knew exactly what he meant. No problem.

WORKS CITED

Abbott, Steve. "Hidden Master of the Beats." *Poetry Flash* 155 (1986): 1.

Allen, Donald M., ed. *The New American Poetry, 1945–1960*. New York: Grove, 1960.

Allen, Donald M., and Warren Tallman, eds. *The Poetics of the New American Poetry*. New York: Grove, 1973.

Baraka, Amiri. "Four for Trane." *Black Music*. New York: Morrow, 1967. 156–61.

———. "History as Process." *Black Magic: Sabotage, Target Study, Black Art: Poetry, 1961–1967*. Indianapolis: Bobbs-Merrill, 1969. 38.

———. "Lines to García Lorca." *New Negro Poets USA*. Ed. Langston Hughes. Bloomington: Indiana University Press, 1964. 55.

———. "Words." *Tales*. New York: Grove, 1967. 89–91.

Blaser, Robin. "The Practice of Outside." *The Collected Books of Jack Spicer*. Ed. Robin Blaser. Los Angeles: Black Sparrow, 1975. 271–329.

Carpentier, Alejo. *The Lost Steps*. Trans. Harriet de Onís. New York: Noonday, 1989.

Davis, Miles. "Saeta." *Sketches of Spain*. Columbia CS 1480.

Davis, Miles, and John Coltrane. "All Blues." *Miles Davis & John Coltrane Live in Stockholm 1960*. Dragon DRLP 90/91.

Duncan, Robert. *Caesar's Gate: Poems, 1949–50*. Berkeley: Sand Dollar, 1972.

Forrest, Leon. *Two Wings to Veil My Face*. Chicago: Another Chicago Press, 1988.

Kaufman, Bob. *The Ancient Rain: Poems, 1956–1978*. New York: New Directions, 1981.

Kelly, Robert. "Song XVII." *Songs I–XXX*. Cambridge, Mass.: Pym-Randall, 1968. 52–53.

Kirk, Rahsaan Roland. "The Business Ain't Nothin' but the Blues." *I Talk with the Spirits*. Limelight LS82008.

Lorca, Federico García. *Deep Song and Other Prose*. Ed. and trans. Christopher Maurer. New York: New Directions, 1980.

———. *Poet in New York*. Ed. Christopher Maurer. Trans. Greg Simon and Steven F. White. New York: Noonday, 1988.

"Love Song." *Folk Music of Iran*. Lyrichord LLST7261.

McDowell, Mississippi Fred. "Everybody's Down on Me" and "Jesus Is on the Mainline." *I Do Not Play No Rock 'n Roll*. Capitol ST-409.

Mackey, Nathaniel. *Bedouin Hornbook*. Callaloo Fiction Ser. 2. Lexington: University Press of Kentucky, 1986.

———. "Ohnedaruth's Day Begun." *Eroding Witness*. Urbana: University of Illinois Press, 1985. 70–74.

———. "Sound and Sentiment, Sound and Symbol." *Callaloo* 10 (1987): 29–54. Repr. in *Discrepant Engagement: Dissonance, Cross-Culturality, and Experimental Writing*. Cambridge: Cambridge University Press, 1993. 231–59.

Pavón, Pastora. "Ay Pilato." *La Niña de los Peines*. Le Chant du Monde LDX 274859.

Reed, Ishmael. *Mumbo Jumbo*. Garden City, N.Y.: Doubleday, 1972.

Rollins, Sonny. "East Broadway Rundown." *East Broadway Rundown*. Impulse! A-9121.

Rumi, Jalaluddin. *Teachings of Rumi: The Masnavi*. Trans. E. H. Whinfield. London: Octagon Press, 1979.

Spicer, Jack. *The Collected Books of Jack Spicer*. Ed. Robin Blaser. Los Angeles: Black Sparrow, 1975.

ADDITIONAL DISCOGRAPHY

Camarón. *Calle Real*. Phillips 814–466–1.

———. *La Leyenda del Tiempo*. Phillips 63–28–255.

Ketama. *Ketama*. Hannibal HNBL-1336.

———. *Songhai*. Hannibal HNBL-1323.

———. *Y Es Ke Me Han Kambiao los Tiempos*. Mango 539.879–1.

Lebrijano, Juan Peña, and the Andalusian Orchestra of Tangier. *Encuentros*. Ariola 1–207240.

Lole and Manuel. *Casta*. CBS S-26027.

———. *Lole y Manuel*. CBS S-82276.

———. *Nuevo Día*. Movieplay 15.2320/3.

Manitas de Plata. *Manitas de Plata: Flamenco Guitar*. Vol. 2. Connoisseur Society CS-965.

Manzanita. *Poco Ruido y Mucho Duende*. CBS S-83188.

Maya, José Heredia, and the Andalusian Orchestra of Tetuan. *Macama Jonda*. Ariola I-295400.

Pata Negra. *Blues de la Frontera*. Hannibal HNBL-1309.

Pepe de la Matrona. *Pepe de la Matrona*. Vol. 2. Hispavox 150–055.

Singing Preachers. Blues Classics BC-19.

FRED MOTEN

SOUND IN FLORESCENCE

Cecil Taylor *Floating Garden*

Phrase

No reading[1] of the words mark a ritual, annular enactment—a fall: the sentence was broken here; a caesura—even, one could say, of the caesura—has occurred. You could bridge the gap with one of many simple denotations supposed to get to the ensemble of what I want you, now, to hear, but that would have already been unfaithful to the truth and attention carried in the name of what, now, I would have you hear. But this will not be a meditation on the idiom of *Chinampas*.[2] No reading because the understanding of literary experience which (a) reading implies is exceeded in the enactment of what *Chinampas* is and what *Chinampas* demands: improvisation. And so I have been preparing myself to play with Cecil Taylor, to hear what is transmitted on frequencies outside and beneath the range of reading. These are *notes* composed in the interest of that preparation. *Phrases*.[3]

CD29

> "Charles Lloyd, asked to comment on a piece of his music by a radio inter-
> viewer, answered, 'Words don't go there.'" (Lange and Mackey x)

Words don't go there. Is it only music, only sound, that goes there? Perhaps these notes and phrases will have mapped the terrain and traversed (at least some of) the space between here and there.

Words don't go there: this implies a difference between words and sounds; it suggests that words are somehow constrained by their implicit reduction to the meanings they carry—meanings inadequate to or detached from the objects or states of affairs they would envelop. What's also implied is an absence of inflection; a loss of mobility, slippage, bend; a missing accent or affect; the impossibility of a slur or crack and the *excess*—rather than loss—of meaning they imply.

Where do words go? Are they the inadequate and residual traces of a ritual performance that is lost in the absence of the recording?[4]

Where do words go? Where, into what, do they turn in Cecil's rendering: a generative disintegration, an emanation of luminous sound? The interinanimation of recording, verbal art, and improvisation—which *Chinampas* is and enacts—places performance, ritual, and event within a trembling—which *Chinampas* escapes—between words' florescence and the constitutive absence of the book.[5] Nevertheless that trembling raises certain questions: for instance, that of the relationship between words and their phrasing.[6] Changes, like that from word to growl, occur here taking the word to where it does not go but neither to any origin as pure sound nor to the simple before of the determinations of meaning. This change and movement might be at the phonemic level, might mark the generation of or from a lost language and/or a new thing that is, in spite of its novelty, never structured as if the before that is absent and indeterminate had never been or does not still remain there. What is the nature of this "sexual cut . . . [or] insistent previousness evading each and every natal occasion," this "*[l]imbo* [that] reflects a certain kind of gateway or threshold to a new world and the dislocation of a chain of miles," that is evident in Cecil's words and improvisations of words?[7] Is the only rigorous model one that necessitates the elimination of any previousness, any new world? Where do words go?

Where do words go? Where, to what, do they turn in Cecil's rendering? A blur, like the typescript on the cover of the album,[8] meaning lifted by design, slurred by packaging, the rhythmic architecture of text, texture, textile *for example the Mande rhythm cloth, where patterns are juxtaposed against each other, several different types of seemingly different patterns that come together and make the ensemble garment. It's acutely apparent on the poetry record where the overdubs, the voices just sliding around and between each other because (sings melody from Pemmican), but because I don't know much music, or I don't know musical terms, it's difficult for me to articulate what it is that I'm hearing.* Good, you have to define for yourself, all the . . . (Richards)[9]: perhaps the blur signifies that everything is (in) Cecil Taylor, is improvisation or, more precisely, that the improvisation of a notion (or, perhaps more faithfully, a phenomenology) of the ensemble heretofore weakly signaled in the sharp edges of words like "everything" is in effect. Note that (in) is always parenthetical, between the opposing words of that structure, between acts or wars, like Woolf and Jones, homologous with the phenomenon of erasure; ~~everything~~ is (in) erasure, the mark of an imaginary structure of homology, the additive and aggregative imposture of a nonsingularist, nontotalitarian ensemble. But, with these provisos, the phrase, the broken sentence, holds (everything).

Cecil's phrase will not be read.

Performance, ritual, and event are of the idea of idiom, of the "anarchic principles" that open the unrepresentable performance of Cecil's phrasing.[10] What happens in the transcription of performance, event, ritual? What happens, which is to say what is lost, in the recording? I am preparing myself to play with Cecil. What is heard there? What history is heard there? There is one which is not just one among others **I'm really quite happy, or becoming more comfortable with the conception that Ellington, after all, is the genius I must follow, and all the methodological procedures that I follow are akin, more closely aligned to that than anything else (Richards)**: the history of (an) organization, orchestra/tion, *construction*. The essence of construction is part of what that phrasing is after; the poem of construction—geometry of a blue space, geometry of a blue ghost— is the poem that is of the music **So, actually, last year for the first time since the seventies I felt more like a professional musician. I never want to be, nor do I consider myself one.** *You say you don't consider yourself a professional musician?* **I would hope never to be a professional musician.** *So, if one has to, how would you classify yourself?* **Ha, Ha, Ha . . . I've always tried to be a poet more than anything else, I mean, professional musicians die. (Phone rings) / Then the music, the imagination from the music led into the words . . . So that the music is primary, but everything is music once you care to begin to apply certain principles of organization to it. So that I imagine there is . . . people have told me they see a certain relationship between the word and the music (Richards).** A poetry, then, that is of the music; a poetry that would articulate the music's construction; a poetry that would mark and question the idiomatic difference that is the space-time of performance, ritual, and event; a poetry, finally, that becomes music in that it iconically presents those organizational principles that are the essence of music. The thing is, these organizational principles break down; their breakdown disallows reading, improvises idiom(atic difference) and gestures toward an anarchic and generative meditation on phrasing that occurs in what has become, for reading, the occluded of language: sound.

Let Cecil's "musicked"[11] and illegible[12] words resonate and give some attention to their broken grammar, the aural rewriting of grammatical rule that is not simply arbitrary but a function of the elusive content he would convey: what's going on is either in an interstice or of the ensemble, either between professionalism and its other—music and poetry—or in the holism of a kind of everyday ritual. Cecil's poetry: the geometry of a ghost? The physics of remembrance? The architecture of the archétrace? Is there a continuity to be written here, or is the continuity in the cut of the phrase? I am preparing myself to play with Cecil Taylor: what is the proper form of my endeavor? Perhaps the transcription of an improvisational blurrrring of the word; perhaps an improvisation through the singular difference of the idiom and its occasion; perhaps an *a*calculation of that function whose upper limit is reading and whose lower limit is transcription—an improvisation through phrases, through some virtual head and coda. Cecil says to his interlocutor, "I'm listening" (Richards). Perhaps he will have said this to me or to the word: I'm listening, *go on.* Then perhaps the ensemble of the word, Cecil and I will have veered off into the silence that is embedded in the transformation, the truth that is held in the silence of the transformation, a truth that is only discernible in transformation.

Rhythm

Sound: suspended brightness, unrepresentable and inexplicable mystery of

music is the improvisation

of organization

ritual is music: principled (*archic*) (spatial) organization that constitutes a kind of nonverbal writing: transparent or instrumental, uninflected by the transformations of a buzz-growl extension, bending whistle, hummm—

> . . . there are and we experience the fact that there are *several* philosophical idioms and that this experience alone cannot not be lived by a philosopher, by a self-styled philosopher, by whoever claims to be a philosopher, as both a *scandal* and as the very *chance* of philosophy.[13]

but an improvisation (an*archic*) of those principles that sees through infinite divisibilities and irreducible singularities, sites of communications never to be received, rites of affliction, tragedies, bodily divisions, spatial/social arrangements that constitute a kind of philosophical writing enacted and reenacted in the annular rememberment and dismemberment of community, *nation and race*, the imposition and maintenance of hierarchical relations within these units, the vexed and impossible task of a reconciliation of one and many via representation: Here it is if I could work through expressive singularity, the im/possibility of direct communication, the ideas of writing as visible speech and writing as independent of speech. Here it is if idiom becomes the site where an improvisation of/through these might occur: not in the name of an originary creativity or a grounded and telic liberty, but of a free, which is to say anarchic and atelic, generativity; a re-conceptualization or out-from-outside reinstrumentalization of idiom that allows an improvisation through rather than a deconstructive oscillation within the *aporia* of philosophy.

Improvisation through the opposition of reading and transcription—pre-condition and effect of preparation to play with Cecil: the preparation is the playing, the trace of another organization; it starts like and away from a reading and ends like and beyond transcription but is neither homage to indeterminacy nor objectifying rendering nor reduction to a narrow sense of "writing"; not about the hegemony of the visual in reading, nor the sus-picion of a singular vision; at the same time not about the etiolation of a capturing picture.

In reading, Cecil's performance—the prefatory dance, the gestures at the instrument that produce/emit sound—along with his sound—indepen-dent, though it is, of the reduction of the word to verbal assertion—are too easily subordinated to the visual/spatial and the pervasive ocularcentrism, structured around a set of obsolete temporal, ethical, and aesthetic deter-minations, which ground it. Nevertheless, Cecil's poetry, the geometry of a blue ghost, is full of spatial and directional renderings. These are impro-vised in his sounding of them which I will not read and cannot transcribe.

Though the visual/spatial binds, its occlusion distorts the undifferentiated but unfixed ensemble (ensemble) the remembrance of the aural gives. The echo of what is not but nothing other than unremembered is a wound in Derrida (for example), confounding the dream of another universality, con-flating that dream with the vision of an old song, old-new language, homely sound, naive or idiomatic writing. Here it is remedied in Cecil moving out from the outside, out from the paradoxes of idiom to offer up idiom's re-sounding, one that avoids philosophical nationalism without devolving into transparent instrumentality, one that is not a reconceptualization but an improvisation of idiom in its relation/opposition to ritual via suspended luminescence, floating garden. That improvisation is activated in a sound that holds information in the implicit graphics of its rhythm, a spatial ori-entation affecting a spatial representation that is sound become dispersive sensuality. So, in a kind of holosensual, holœsthetic reversal, one hears music in Cecil's visual-spatial description and sees gestures and spaces in an aurality that exceeds but does not oppose visual-spatial determination.

In Cecil float/drift/linger/cut are fresh in the improvised parlance of another architecture, another geometry. The recording gives the trace *of* performance in the product or artifact, is a constative vessel of information maintaining the question of the product as determinate sign; yet it also marks a temporal/ethical problem that can be solved only by way of a radical movement through certain questions: of the trace *as* performance, of sound, of the rending of the opposition of aurality and spatiality, of the opposition of speech and writing within verbality, of the question of the gestural in literary style, of the question of silence and the absence of the break. . . .

"Rhythm is life, the space of time danced thru" (Taylor) the cut between event and anniversary wherein lies sound, writing, ritual, all improvised. Two passages (David Parkin's and Claude Lévi-Strauss's) to the crossing of rhythm and ritual:

> Ritual is formulaic spatiality carried out by groups of people who are conscious of its imperative or compulsory nature and who may or may not further inform this spatiality with spoken words. (Parkin 16)

> The value of the ritual as meaning seems to reside in instruments and gestures; it is a *paralanguage*. The myth on the other hand, manifests itself as *metalanguage*; it makes full use of discourses, but does so by situating its own significant oppositions at a higher level of complexity than that required by language operating for profane ends. (Lévi-Strauss, qtd. in Parkin 11)

In these passages ritual is primarily defined by distinctions between itself and forms of aural/verbal activity—most importantly, myth—in which ritual is seen as impoverished or by distinctions between itself and other forms of nonverbal activity that, in their mundaneness, remain untransformed by any ceremonial aura. Parkin focuses on the *silent* communication of propositions in ritual as that which matches or even exceeds verbal assertion through spacing, position or the visual-graphic architectonics that oscillate between fixity and contestation. *such communication quietly echoes the staging of some neo-conservito-classically boppish set of sets of sets of sets as in* Rodney King—*anniversarial reenactment of what Langston Hughes theorized as the origin of real bop's name, the sound whenever a cop busts a (black) guy in the head—for instance: proposition made in the step—never not of the dance—and in the gesture, arms rising, falling: passionate reimposition of a social hierarchy supplemented by various epithets, commentaries, phrases-in-dispute which we all know: the beat of da Lench Mob, "gorillas in the mist," what is the origin of hip hop's name* According to Lévi-Strauss, however, words *do* go there, arriving under the motive force of "a higher level of complexity" than that afforded by the instrumental or gestural in ritual. If one thinks, though, of a poetry reading—which may very well be (for) a "profane end"—one confronts that which requires that we take into account the ways ritual consists of physical action (in time) that may *be*, as well as emit or transmit, the kind of meaningful aural expression that improvises through the distinction between the paralinguistic and the metalinguistic. And if words that had been thought of as the elements of a purely constative expression are radically reconnected to their essential sonic performance by eccentric physical action, by an excess of the physical (trill-making vibration of tongue or vowel-lengthening squint) that deforms the word conceived of as a mere vessel of meaning, then that requirement becomes even more urgent. The attempt to read ritual as it is manifest in the sound of such words or the attempt to transcribe myth transformed by gesture and meaningful positionality might be better thought in terms of the improvisation of ritual, writing, sound, idiom, event.

The spatiotemporal constitution of ritual raises ambiguities as well. On the one hand ritual is durative. The structure and dance of its positions are ongoing, part of an annulus that seems unopposed to the uninterrupted process of the everyday against which it would be defined. But what of the punctuality of the endlessly/daily repeated event? This punctuality is, too, of ritual, and ritual thus lends punctuality the aura of ceremony: the *special* occasion. There is, then, a temporal contradiction in the opposition of ritual and nonritual, one that activates in both terms a juxtaposition that is manifest as the traumatic/celebratory and obsessional rhythmic breakage of the everyday and that implies a directionality of time—a spatiotemporal constitution—that transforms rhythm into a double determination: of position or movement, on the one hand, and syntagmic order on the other. Thus Parkin's focus on "the use made . . . of directionality—of axes, cardinal points, concentric zones and other expressions of spatial orientation and movement" (16) and his interest in the random and contingent effects of contestation as a kind of reading-in-performance, a shifting and reshifting of spatial conventions and temporal order determined by a radical break as when, for instance, the community *cuts* the body in an interinanimation of affliction and renewal, the fragmentation of singular bodies and the coercive reaggregation of community.

Escaping the in/determination of the opposition or sacrificial synthesis of rites of affliction and renewal requires working through the logocentrism of Lévi-Strauss, the ocularcentric, spatiotemporal determinism of Parkin, and their interrelation in a discursive field grounded in a notion of singularity that I want to move through in my preparation. In Cecil's, the spoken words, the speaking of the words, are not an arbitrary feature but are instead constitutive of that which is not but nothing other than (the improvisation of) ritual, writing, ritual as a form of writing. There, the words are never independent of gesture but the gesture is never given priority over the words-as-sound. For gestures (and spatial direction) are given there as the sounded, re-sounded (which is to say transformed, bent, extended, improvised) and resounding (which is to say generative) word.

> We then can define writing broadly as *the communication of relatively specific ideas in a conventional manner by means of permanent, visible marks.* (Boone 15)

Here Elizabeth Hill Boone moves in the direction of a redefinition of writing in anthropology in general and in the study of Mesoamerican and Andean graphic systems in particular. That movement is critical of notions of writing as the "visible speech" that marks a technospiritual difference between cultures capable of graphic-verbal presentation and those before or outside of the historicotemporal frame of the advanced or enlightened. That direction would lead to a more inclusive definition of writing, one that is able to acknowledge the rich constative capacities of nonverbal graphic systems, one that explicitly acknowledges the insistently unbridgeable gap that separates the spoken word from any visual representation. This direction, seen in conjunction with Parkin's attempt to think through the constative/performative opposition that grounds Lévi-Straus's notion of the difference between myth and ritual, would also lead to an indelible connection between ritual, on the one hand, and writing, on the other hand, if writing is defined in the broader way that Boone lays out. Ritual and nonverbal graphesis would both be seen as constative and both would be subject to prejudices that end in the denial of that constativity. There is another similarity between Boone's and Parkin's projects that we'll arrive at shortly (the primacy of the visual-spatial), but these are enough to allow us to follow, for a bit, one of the paths this connection implies.

What kind of writing Is *Chinampas*?[14] Cecil presents no graphic system — if *Chinampas* is writing, it is so in the absence of visuality. Under what conditions, then, could *Chinampas* be called "writing"? Perhaps within an understanding of writing more broadly conceived as nonverbal, as well as verbal, systems of graphic communication. Yet, since what we have there is non-graphic *verbal* communication, the legitimacy of its claim to writing is not self-evident. Nevertheless ideas of and about graphic systems are presented in *Chinampas*, sound blurrring vision in the improvisation of another writing; and image, position, and direction are so encoded—the visual-spatial so embedded—in the poem that what we have is something more complex even than some newly included Outside of writing. Rather, *Chinampas* is out from the outside of writing as it is conventionally defined or redefined in what have become conventional redefinitions. Writing is, in *Chinampas*, a visual-spatial-tactile improvisation of system that activates the aural resources of the language. The poem is an improvisation of writing not to be appropriated by, not proper to, an older and somehow more inclusive graphesis: it is not a valorization but an improvisation of the nonverbal; not an abandonment but a (re)sounding of the visual-spatial.

A possible formulation based on the inclusive redefinition of writing: it's not that Cecil creates visible speech; rather his is an aural writing given an understanding of writing that includes nonverbal graphic resources. This would almost presuppose that Cecil is interested in grounding the aural in an originary writing (the "older and somehow more inclusive graphesis" referred to above) that corresponds—as spatial, rhythmic organization—to ritual. Ritual here is implicitly conceived as Parkin explicitly describes it: a form of nonverbal graphic (visual/spatial) communication for which spoken words are merely supplemental. We could say, then, that Cecil's refers to an originary writing that is neither hieroglyphic nor pictographic but geometric, positional, directional. In that referent, if not in Cecil's reference, spoken words are not only nonoriginary; they are not even seen in terms of a reversal of traditional, conventional views of language in/and its relation to writing.

But this formulation doesn't go there. Rather, what is required is a further reconfiguration of Parkin, one that moves beyond the idea of constative ritual and beyond the idea of ritual as a form of graphic, nonverbal writing to the extent that in such writing priority is given to, originarity is assumed for, the visual-spatial constellation of gesture, position, movement. That reconfiguration is opened by Cecil's aural improvisation of, rather than (un)silent adherence to, an originary writing-as-ritual and his infusion of the diagrammatics/diagraphesis of ritual with sound. For spoken words, especially when infused with the buzz hummm of the metavoice,[15] are not a neutral (as Parkin implies) but a *dangerous* supplement to ritual-as-writing.

Thus, on the one hand, "words don't go there" marks the inadequacy of verbal representation of sound while at the same time signaling the excessive, out-from-the-outside motion and force with which sound infuses the verbal. Words don't go there; words go *past* there. Bent. Turned. Blurrrred.

The picture is text, the image is writing, *sounded and not visible* though of a brilliant luminescence in the ensemble of the graphic, the (non)verbal, the aural. That ensemble is what the floating garden is: word lifted from stone or cloth; *quipu* (an article composed of colored and knotted strings used in Andean cultures to recall various categories of knowledge that are specified by an interpreter; an article whose aesthetic is related to the tactile and to the tactile's relation to rhythm)[16] or rhythm cloth; text/ile, tactile. There meaning is held not unlike a talking drum holds meaning in tone and rhythm; meaning held, for instance, in "eighty-eight tuned drums," independent of any simple, sentence-relational form, given only in phrasing and bent words. In that phrasing Cecil's moves, crucially, past whatever in/determination, whatever singularity, the paradoxical interinanimation of ritual and idiom puts forward as if it were or could be The Event.

> Perhaps something has occurred in the history of the concept of structure that could be called an "event," if this loaded word did not entail a meaning which it is precisely the function of structural—or structuralist—thought to reduce or suspect. Let us speak of an "event," nevertheless, and let us use quotation marks to serve as a precaution. What would this event be then? Its exterior form would be that of a *rupture* and a redoubling.
>
> . . . up to the event which I wish to mark out and define, structure—or rather the structurality of structure—although it has always been at work, has always been neutralized or reduced, and this by a process of giving it a center or referring it to a point of presence, a fixed origin. *The function of this center was not only to orient, balance, and organize the structure—one cannot in fact conceive of an unorganized structure—but above all to make sure that the organizing principle of the structure would limit what we might call the play of the structure. By orienting and organizing the coherence of the system, the center of a structure permits the play of its elements inside the total form. And even today the notion of a structure lacking any center represents the unthinkable itself.*
>
> Nevertheless, the center also closes off the play which it opens up and makes possible. *As center, it is the point at which the substitution of contents, elements or terms is no longer possible.* At the center, the permutation or the transformation of elements (which may of course be structures enclosed within a structure) is forbidden. At least this permutation has always been *interdicted* (and I am using this word deliberately). *Thus it has always been thought that the center, which is by definition unique constituted that very thing within a structure which while governing the structure, escapes structurality. This is why classical thought concerning structure could say that the*

center is, paradoxically, within the structure and outside it. The center is at the center of the totality, and yet, since the center does not belong to the totality (is not part of the totality), the totality has its center elsewhere (Derrida, *Writing* 278–80; my emphasis).

The event of which Derrida speaks, the putting of the structurality of structure, the center itself, into play, is the moment "when language invaded the universal problematic, the moment when, in the absence of a center or origin, everything became discourse . . . a system in which the central signified, the original or transcendental signified, is never absolutely present outside a system of differences." Derrida writes of an event, a rupture, which is also a circle, a circle of thinker-writers but also a circle "unique" in its description of "the form of the relation between the history of metaphysics and the destruction of the history of metaphysics." Here he places the event within a narrative. Part of what I would argue is that this placement of the event within narrative is The Event of the event, the rupture or caesura of the event that occurs within a paradoxical duration or contextualization or montagic-dialectical temporal mapping of the event. This self-rupture of singularity is precisely the geometric precondition of the circularity that Derrida diagnoses and to which he succumbs: the self-deconstructive singularity of the event is the axis on which the circle turns — the one which is not central, the center which is not one. Restructuring could be seen, then, as the process by which structure is placed into play, which is to say into narrative, into the circularity and tension of a narrative that is composed of and that turns on elements or events.

Now we might easily be speaking of the song form as that de/centered structure that Cecil radically reformulates, if not abandons, precisely by re-thinking its status as the singular site of order in improvised music.[17] For the point here is that in his aesthetic Cecil deals in what has truly been the unthinkable of the event-determined circularity of the history/narrative of the West and its thinking: the structure or totality that is un(de)composed by a center or its absence, by the event or The Event and their absences. This is a possibility given in ensemble tone, in the improvisation through a certain tradition of temporization and tympanization, through that tradition's injunction to keep time in a simple way, on the beat (of the event), in that simplest (mis)conception — excusable because of the terminology (and we could all see why Plato would be misled by James Brown in the first place) — of the one. Am I saying that Cecil or The Godfather or The Music in general is not trapped within the circle that is (the history of) metaphysics as the slide away from the ensemble it would propose? Am I saying that there is access to the outside of this circle or that, somehow, we (who? we.) are always already outside it. Yes. I'm talking about something free of the circle, free of the *event*ual tension/tensing of (this) narrative. Other things are also free.

What is immediately required is an improvisation of singularity, one that allows us to reconfigure what is given beneath/outside the distinction between the elements of the structure and its total form. Because what I'm after is an asystematic, anarchic organizing principle (I note the oxymoron), a notion of totality and (ensemble-)tonality at the conjunction of the pantonal and "that insistent previousness evading each and every natal occasion." But wait: the point here is not to make an analogy between the deconstruction of the center and the organization of the jazz ensemble: it's to say that that organization is of totality, of ensemble in general. Among other things, this music allows us to think of tonality and the structure of harmony as it moves in the oscillation between voice and voicing, not in the interest of any numerical determination (the valorization of the multiple or its shadow), not in the interest of any ethico-temporal determination (the valorization of the durative or of process), but for a kind of decentralization of the organization of the music; a restructuring or, if you will, a reconstruction. Cecil is working through a metaphysics of structure, working through an assumption that equates the essence or structurality of structure with a center. What I'm interested in in Cecil is precisely the refusal to attempt a return to the source: one that is not, on the one hand, forgetful of what is lost or of the fact of loss; one that is forgetive, on the other hand, in the Falstaffian sense of the word—nimble and full of fiery and delectable shapes, improvisatory and incantatory when what is structured in the mind is given over to the mouth, the birth, as (that which is, finally, way more even than) excellent wit.

In "Structure, Sign and Play" Derrida goes on to quote Lévi-Strauss's *The Raw and the Cooked*:

> But unlike philosophical reflection, which aims to go back to its own source, the reflections we are dealing with here concern rays whose only source is hypothetical. . . . And in seeking to imitate the spontaneous movement of mythological thought, this essay, which is also both too brief and too long, has had to conform to the requirements of that thought and to respect its rhythm. (Qtd. in *Writing* 286–87. See also Lévi-Strauss, *Raw* 14.)

Lévi-Strauss and his differentiated echo in/as Derrida go on to think this complex copresence of the question of center and origin in terms of myth and music:

Thus the myth and the musical work are like the conductors of an orchestra, whose audience becomes the silent performers. If it is now asked where the real center of the work is to be found, the answer is that this is impossible to determine. Music and mythology bring man face to face with potential objects of which only the shadows are actualized.

Here the musical becomes a sign for the absence of center by way of an all too facile assumption of some correspondence between myth and music. What happens when we begin to think music in its relation to ritual? Myth and text (myth as the written text of the music, betraying a musical rendition of a certain logocentric assumption in Lévi-Strauss) operate in Lévi-Strauss as the agents of a structural fixity whose submission to the law of supplementarity Derrida would always enforce. In this sense, for Derrida, there is a correspondence between myth/text/totality that is troubled by a form of musical organization like Cecil's. Now we are dealing in precisely that absence of the center that Lévi-Strauss and Derrida both read and comment on. Both deal, Derrida more knowingly or self-consciously, with the tension in their work between structure — that which is unthinkable without a center — and the absence of center. This tension is productive; it constitutes or produces something, namely, philosophy. But I'm interested precisely in the unthinkable of philosophy in Cecil's work. For the unthinkable, as we can easily show, is not structure in the absence of the center (for we see all the time that this absence is constitutive of structure; this is what Derrida shows); rather, the unthinkable is structure or ensemble thought independently of any tension between itself and some absent origin. The unthinkable is a tone. That tone is to be thought neither as or in its absence (atonality) nor as/in its multiplicity or plenitude (pantonality): it is rather an ensemble tone, the tone that is not structured by or around the presence/absence of singularity or totality, the tone that is not iterative but generative.[18] (Note that Lévi-Strauss insists on a certain iconicity, insists that discourse on myth must itself become mythic, must have the form of which it speaks. Certainly Derrida follows this formulation to the extent that the old-new language may only be spoken of from within, that it constitutes its own true metalanguage, thereby driving Tarski and his definition of truth as the relation between object- and meta-language crazy such that the old-new language is not only its own metalanguage but its own truth.)

Cecil's is a voice in the interruption of race and nation, just as it is a voice in the interruption of the sentence and, indeed, in the interruption of the word itself. He works the anarchic irruption and interruption of grammar, enacting a phrasal improvisation through the distinction between poetry and music in the poetry of music, the programmatic manifesto that accompanies the music, that becomes music and turns music into poetry. These things occur "between regions of partial shadow and complete illumination" in the cut.

Cecil's also bears the trace of (the peculiar) institution and its organization —its deconstruction and reconstruction. This in connection to the continuous or anniversarial, the institutional-durative: marriage-birth-death-seasonal change; the temporal difference within ritual that corresponds to ritual's temporal difference from, on the one hand, myth and, on the other hand, the mundane since rituals "involve a liminal phase, a betwixt and between element and so presuppose an initial phase of separation and one of reaggregation" (Parkin 16). But let's enact and reenact the *separation* of separation and reaggregation: rather, let's linger, float in the limbo of that cut, in order to mark nothing akin to an initial phase or prior singularity, but, instead, to mark "the insistent previousness evading each and every natal occasion." The trauma of separation is marked here, but not the separation from a determinate origin: rather the separation from the improvisation through origin: the separation from ensemble. How could we have heard the sound of justice called in/by the long duration of the trauma if it hadn't been improvised?

Phrase

I've seen video of Ellington arranged at the piano surrounded by his instrument as they played without—which is to say outside—music, their arrangement signifying (their knowledge of the) arrangement: Ellington would sing the parts, forging the preparation of the music beside writing, the orchestra's change of motion driven, given, proportional to his motive force, the force which feeds: motif.[19] So is Cecil. The instrument, for both, is (the) ensemble wherein lies the chance of a voicing beyond the chord or the cluster (which is to say beyond the simple in/determinations of harmony) even (or, more precisely, especially) in its originary Western philosophical manifestation: that between thinking and being.

Parmenides is, as far as we know, the first among many to "recognize" an essential connection between thinking and being: his poem is the originary text of that harmony, the originary written moment at which the shadow of what must be conceived of as a more fundamental formulation, a more elemental and singular form, is revealed. One wonders what the relation is between the writing of the poem—within which the trace of a sound remains to be discerned or at least reconstructed from its shards—and that harmony. One wonders whether the harmony on which Western metaphysics is founded is not itself founded on—or most clearly manifest at—the intersection of music and poetry that, itself, seems to signal a prior and barely available unity of the two in *mousike*: the singularization of the muses' art, the distillation of the ensemble of the aesthetic.

Only the trace of *mousike* is available to us and only by way of a tracing of the history of its dissolution. Under the heading "Music and Poetry," *The New Princeton Encyclopedia of Poetry and Poetics* makes a brief survey of that history, moving from "the Egyptian 'hymn of the seven vowels,' [which] appears to have exploited the overtone pitches present in the vowels of any language," to the first disjunctions (through which Cecil improvises) between systems of linguistic pitch, on the one hand, and systems of quantitative meter, on the other; from the technicistic origins of alphabetic writing-as-musical notation to the hegemonic excess of the visual-written and the differentiation of the arts it helps to solidify; from elemental *mousike* to its division/reaggregation as poetry and music to its fourfold fragmentation into poetic and musical performance and musical and rhetorical theory within which can be located that opposition between *praxis* and *theoria* that is never not connected to the harmony of thinking and being that constitutes philosophy's origin and end.[20] What becomes clear is a historical movement from the priority of sonic gesture to the hegemony of visual (which is to say theoretical) formulation. The written mark—the convergence of meaning and visuality—is the site of both excess and lack; the word-supplement—only theorizable in the occlusion of its sound—endlessly overshoots its destination; words don't go there. Perhaps it is now possible to give a more satisfactory understanding of this claim, one that is concerned not only with where words do go, but with the nature and position of the "there." First, though, it is necessary to think the effect of that dual spatialization/visualization of the word—its placement within an economy determined by movement, instrumentalization, position, and theorization—which troubles any distinction between ritual and myth.

"*Chinampa*—an Aztec word meaning floating garden."[21] This image moves toward what is made even closer by the conjunction of the image (of the title or name) and the sound (of the saying of what it marks or holds). It signals a suspension that is free or that frees by virtue of the contagion of its movement: when one sees a floating garden or is confronted with the sound that stems from the word-image, one lingers above or below surface and in what is open there. The surface or topography on which a spatiotemporal mapping depends is displaced by a generative motion. One imagines the possibilities inherent in that floating, the chance of a dropping off or an extension of certain of those sounds that require a vibrating surface: the *n*, *m*, *p* are put in motion, deepening and rearranging the sound of the word.[22] This loosening is part of Cecil's method: of the word from its meaning, of the sounds from the word in the interest of a generative reconstruction, as if all of a sudden one decided to refuse the abandonment of the full resources of language, as if one decided to follow no longer the determining, structuring, reductive force of law.

There is a piece of musicpoetry by Cecil titled "Garden" whose words have been collected in *Moment's Notice*, a set of texts that mark the hope or call of a destination for words and for writing.[23] Reading "Garden" raises questions concerning its difference from *Chinampas*, one of which I'd like to address in closing. It is, perhaps unavoidably, a question of spacing or position, a question always shadowed by immaterial visualization: what is the *floating* garden? Perhaps this: the garden that floats is the one that lingers in another, improvisational sense of the aesthetic ensemble that is no simple return to an imagined and originary singularity. Instead the floating garden marks the unprecedented present within which the aesthetic is "ongoingly" reconfigured and reconfiguring, bent and bending; within which the illusion of any immediacy of sound is re/written and the overdetermined and deferred fixity of writing is un/written by the material and transformative present of sound.

It's like when Coltrane, having been shown a transcription of his solo on "Chasin' the Trane," was unable to sightread that which he'd improvised. The beautiful distance between sound and the writing of sound requires a kind of faith that could only be measured, for instance, in Cecil's inability to read

Chinampas #5′04″

ANGLE of incidence
    being matter ignited

one sixtieth of luminous intensity

                                        behind wind

        beginning spiral of two presences

                                     shelter

      ~~light drum~~
angle of incidénce   observant of   sighns

be's core based fiber conducting impulses flattened spirals of spirit
           prompting letter per square centimeter of   *three dimensions*
swept cylinder and cone
               cutting shape   of drying bodiesNow pulverized
                                      having fed on
cactí

   arranged service of *con*stant spiral elements of floating *cocineal* and
                            kaaay and kaay and kaay and
                     agité an-agité and kaay
                          and kaay and   yyeeagiye yoa,
                                  ya yoa
deposits of hieroglyphic   regions
womb of continuing   *light*
preexisting blood per square centimeter of aBlaack bhody
a curve having rotation in three dimensions
     cutting spiral elements at a constant angle

behind wind
the inexpresssssible inclusion
of one within another
   a lustrous red, reddish brown or black natural *fill* compact or attacked
   POINT fixed on circumference
curve about red
does in fact alter regions of contact as a *rooase*
               on the outside circumference   flushed toward slant
intersecting new reference point
moves clockwise
representing a frequency's
      distribution
each bend of ordinan equals the sum in singular
                                 youas youas youas
proceeding enclosure engulfing unending spiral
                          undulation

there floating amidst aliana and overhead
               romela romelaya romela romelaya a ceeia

invisible expressions of warmed *snake*wood soothed by exudation of sloed balsam scent
is arielroot elixir   is knowing circle crossed at oiled extremity
in center of wing burring

creates fire in air
serpent is preexisting light   light   yeah

the meter maintained is ôpen yet a larger *whorl*
describing orbit of earth
eaters incisors   as omniscient
pochee aida aida huelto   aida aida huedo
uniting of three astral plains/planes corresponding to a serpent synthesis

altering the sliii'de
                    disengage'd ecliptic traveling
                                        due north

                            skip through at least two successive meridians
diagonal shear
uniting as macrocosm five heads degrees of   tangiBle *ahhb jects*
graded ascension of floor levels
        suspended voice
                                            vibrations
held within concretized mur'eau de perfume breath
                            again *floating*
'tween lighted mooon///soar
and silent cross of bird sensing cold   at base
invisible to source of satyrial/siderial turn   Between regions of partial
shadow and complete illumination.

omnipotence
omnipotence the florescence of the perpendicular
omnipotence
the floresce of the perpendicular pentamorphic
the florescence of the perpendicular pentamorphic
perpendicular pentamorphic

(kiss, silences, rhythm)

.   .   .

NOTES

1. If this were ever sounded, I would not want the appearance of the cut to be marked by another voice. Just another voicing, which would not be reducible to a difference of voices, and which would be marked only by the palpability of the cut—no glance, no sound outside, just a pause, **and don't stop the tape recorder.**

The question remains: whether and how to mark (visually, spatially, in the absence of sound, the sound in my head) digression, citation, extension, improvisation in the kind of writing that has no name other than "literary criticism."

2. I am going to write (about) the piece's first section in Taylor 1988.

3. In the absence of reading, either or both of *these terms* might be just as reducible or virtual as *word* or *sentence*. Part of what I would like to relate is the way Cecil's (*work art ritual performance music poetry*), the way that which is of Cecil, renders all of *these terms* unavailable. Nevertheless, I must retain them, at least for a minute, otherwise I Can't Get Started. I hope it strikes no one as jarring or silly if I refer to Cecil Taylor by his given name. I refer any of you who are offended to Christopher Smith: "Within the jazz community, certain artists are named in such a 'short-hand' fashion: 'Monk' (Thelonius Sphere Monk); 'Bird' (Charlie 'Yardbird' Parker); 'Dizzy' (John Birks 'Dizzy' Gillespie). In its own way, it is a gesture of respect" (52). In the spooky-action-at-a-distance or strange nontranslation or unbridged transference between (the absence of) the surname and (the advent of) *le surnom* (see Dutoit), one asserts oneself—perhaps presumptuously—as a member of that community, that ensemble, in preparation (Cecil says), improvisation (is), self-analysis.

4. Or, more precisely, the double absence: the disappearance of the performance that is not recorded; the loss of what the recording reduces or occludes by embodying an illusory determinacy and representativeness.

5. Implied here is that glow, aura, *sfumato*, hazy luminescence that smears the edge, the containment, of the image or the letter. Halogen, neon, Las Vegas—though I'm pretty sure Cecil's never played my hometown—are in my head along with a recent recording of Cecil's, *In Florescence*.

6. Or, more precisely, a double phrasing: words' syntagmic ordering and the arrangement and enactment of their internal sonic resources.

7. See Mackey, *Bedouin Hornbook* 34; Harris 26.

8. Gracefully designed by Mike Bennion.

9. Richards's notes consist largely of an interview with Taylor. The recording is of a performance by the Cecil Taylor Unit given on 7 November 1987, just nine days before the recording of *Chinampas*. Richards dates his notes May 1988.

10. "Idiom" demands a break. It demands some extended quotation, first from the *Compact Edition of the Oxford English Dictionary*, then from Derrida's "Onto-Theology." Idiom, according to the *OED*: "peculiarity, property, peculiar phraseology"; "the form of speech peculiar or proper to a people or country"; "the variety of a language which is peculiar to a limited district or class of people"; "*the specific character, property, or genius of any language*"; "*a peculiarity of phraseology approved by the usage of a language and having a signification other than its grammatical or logical one*" (my emphasis). Idiom, according to Derrida: "I shall say simply of this word 'idiom,' that I have just very rapidly thrust forward, that for the moment I am not restricting it to its linguistic, discursive circumscription, although, as you know, usage generally folds it back towards that limit—idiom as linguistic idiom. *For the moment, while keeping my eye fixed especially on this linguistic determination which is not all there is to idiom, but which is not just one determination of it among others, I shall be taking 'idiom' in a much more indeterminate sense, that of prop(ri)e(r)ty, singular feature, in principle inimitable and inexpropriable. The **idion** is the proper*" (my emphasis). Let me add a couple of propositions

to which I'll return: race ("a peculiar or characteristic style or manner—liveliness, sprightliness or piquancy," according to the *OED*) and idiom, in their determination by a conceptual apparatus made up of uninterrogated differences, classes, and sets, are interchangeable; T(race) and phrase constitute an improvisation of race and idiom, one activated within a certain understanding of totality or ensemble in which idiom is defined as the t(race) of a general idiom that is nothing other than the generativity (i.e., what is produced by and is the possibility of the production of) idiom.

11. Here's an echo of Baraka's oft-repeated claim that poetry is "Musicked speech." The particular manifestation of the phrase to which I refer is to be found in Melhem.

12. Or, more precisely, doubly illegible words: the sonic/visual blurring of the words; the fundamental absence of the written text.

13. Derrida, "Onto-Theology" 3.

14. Here I'm in debt to Boone.

15. See Mackey, "Cante Moro."

16. See Rappaport 284.

17. See Cecil's comments on Bill Evans, in Hentoff.

18. Imagine a tone, bearing within it the structure of a phenomenology of totality and singularity that would reveal some opening of the possibility of ethical agency. It would have to provide a *sense*—neither cognitive nor visionary, more than cognitive, more than visionary—of a whole not bound by the interminable oscillation of systemic relation and nonrelation. Such a whole would move beyond the endless and always assymetrical tension between individual and society or self and other; finally, it would move beyond any ontological formulation of and in difference that displaces the ensemble and leaves us at the site of a discursive contestation of infinite curvature where our reality never escapes the forces power exerts over responsibility and in/determination exerts over improvisation.

Ensemble—the improvisation of and through totality and singularity in and as both phenomenological description and morphological prescription—must, therefore, faithfully reclaim the honor of the whole, an honor that is real only within the complex, radical, and realist attention and devotion we pay to particularity, a devotion that must move through the enlightenment tradition's allegiance to singularity and its conflation of singularity and totality—phenomena certain tendencies within poststructuralism both critique and extend in the analysis and affirmation of singularity's always already multiple essence that is embedded in ontological and epistemological questioning. Indeed, the theory of ensemble is enabled by and is an extension and improvisation of the tradition of a singularist and differentiated thinking of the ensemble, most particularly as that tradition—at its highest level of intensity and internal tension—begins to be articulated through calls for its dissolution or continuance in the impossible language prompted by the incommensurable conjunction of community and difference. In short, the possibility of a nonexclusionary totality is opened by the most radical critiques—those of identity politics in addition to those of poststructuralism—of any prior totalization.

The point, here, is that those critiques that pay descriptive and prescriptive attention to singularity and totality while responsibly confronting the horrific effects of singularist totalization must be acknowledged and assimilated. But the fact that they offer no meaningful articulation of the ensemble—that which allows our aspirations for equality, justice, freedom—means they must be improvised. The various discourses that are informed by identity politics open the possibility for such improvisation in their directions toward other philosophical or antiphilosophical modes of thought and representation. But it is precisely in the thought of the other, the hope for an other subjectivity and an other ontology, that the metaphysical foundations and antilibertarian implications of the politicophilosophical tradition to which identity politics attempts to respond are replicated and deepened. Improvisation—and thus the possibility of describing and activating an improvisational ensemble—is thereby foreclosed. I am interested in something out from the outside, other than the other or the same, something unbound by their relation or nonrelation. That is what I think *Chinampas* is.

19. Thanks, again, to Boone (for quoting Stillman Drake) 9.

20. See Winn. Please take note that this entry in this definitive encyclopedia says very close to nothing of the life and shape of the synthesis of music and poetry in "the New World" or in non-Western societies. Cecil's concern with precisely these registers is certainly a constitutive feature of his improvisation through the determinations of the dominant understanding of that synthesis. In his work the trace of *mousike*, the ghostly affect and effect of a certain *free* mode of organization, gives us to imagine a thought not grounded in the architectonics and dynamics of difference that harmony both marks and conceals. It is as if the real/phantasmatic duality of the encounter with the other opens that which demands an improvisation through the condition of its possibility.

21. See back cover of Taylor, *Live in Vienna*.

22. Note one such possible formulation: *Chiapas*. There a generative rearrangement is also under way; more power to it and the ones who carry it off.

23. Check the sentence (written by Art Lange and Nathaniel Mackey, the editors of *Moment's Notice*) that follows Charles Lloyd's expression of doubt concerning the capability of words to arrive at music: "Writers influenced by jazz have been variously rising to the challenge of proving him wrong."

WORKS CITED

Boone, Elizabeth Hill. "Introduction: Writing and Recording Knowledge." *Writing without Words: Alternative Literacies in Mesoamerica and the Andes*. Ed. Elizabeth Hill Boone and Walter D. Mignolo. Durham: Duke University Press, 1994. 3–26.

Compact Edition of the Oxford English Dictionary. Oxford: Oxford University Press, 1971, 1988.

Derrida, Jacques. "Onto-Theology of National-Humanism (Prolegomena to a Hypothesis)." *Oxford Literary Review* 14 (1992): 3–23.

———. *Writing and Difference*. Trans. Alan Bass. Chicago: University of Chicago Press, 1978.

Dutoit, Thomas. "Translating the Name?" *On the Name*. By Jacques Derrida. Ed. Thomas Dutoit. Trans. David Wood, John P. Leavey Jr., and Ian McLeod. Stanford: Stanford University Press, 1995. lx–lxvi.

Harris, Wilson. "History, Fable, and Myth in the Caribbean and Guianas."
Explorations. Ed. Hena Maes-Jelinek. Mändelsträp, Denmark: Dangaroo, 1981.
20–42.

Hentoff, Nat. Liner notes to *Nefertiti, the Beautiful One Has Come.* By Cecil Taylor.
New York: Arista/Freedom Records, 1975. FLP 40106 LP. First published in
Down Beat 25 February 1965, 16–18.

Lange, Art, and Nathaniel Mackey, eds. *Moment's Notice: Jazz in Poetry and Prose.*
Minneapolis: Coffee House, 1993.

Lévi-Strauss, Claude. *The Raw and the Cooked.* Trans. John Wightman and Doreen
Wightman. New York: Harper & Row, 1969.

———. *Structural Anthropology.* Vol. 2. London: Allen Lane, 1977.

Mackey, Nathaniel. *Bedouin Hornbook.* Callaloo fiction ser. 2. Lexington:
University Press of Kentucky, 1986.

———. "Cante Moro." In this volume.

Melhem, D. H. *Heroism in the New Black Poetry.* Lexington: University Press of
Kentucky, 1990.

New Princeton Encyclopedia of Poetry and Poetics. 3rd ed. Ed. Alex Preminger, T. V. F.
Brogan, et al. Princeton: Princeton University Press, 1993.

Parkin, David. "Ritual as Spatial Direction and Bodily Division." *Understanding
Rituals.* Ed. Daniel de Coppet. London: Routledge, 1992. 11–25.

Rappaport, Joanne. "Object and Alphabet: Andean Indians and Documents in
the Colonial Period." *Writing without Words: Alternate Literacies in Mesoamerica and
the Andes.* Ed. Elizabeth Hill Boone and Walter D. Mignolo. Durham: Duke
University Press, 1994. 271–92.

Richards, Spencer. Liner notes to *Live in Vienna.* By Cecil Taylor. Leo Records,
1988. LR 408/409 LP.

Smith, Christopher. "A Sense of the Possible: Miles Davis and the Semiotics of
Improvised Performance." *Drama Review* 39.3 (T147) (1995): 41–55.

Taylor, Cecil. *Chinampas.* London. Leo Records, 1988. LR 153 LP.

———. *Chinampas.* London. Leo Records. CD LR 153, 1991. LR 153 CD.

———. *In Florescence.* Hollywood, Calif. A & M Records, 1990. 5286 LP.

———. *Live in Vienna.* London. Leo Records, 1988. LR 408/409 LP.

———. Liner notes to *Unit Structures.* Blue Note Records, 1966.

Winn, James A. "Music and Poetry." *New Princeton Encyclopedia of Poetry and Poetics.*
3rd ed. Ed. Alex Preminger, T. V. F. Brogan, et al. Princeton: Princeton
University Press, 1993. 803–6.

PART THREE

Hearing Theories

SURROUNDINGS

MODERNISM'S SONIC WAIVER
Literary Writing and the Filmic Difference

GARRETT STEWART

> *Tongues* can *over-read* as well as *eyes*.
> **William Empson, *Seven Types of Ambiguity* (53)**

Unheard determinants quaver everywhere in "modernist" writing, waver there, crowding its textual surfaces, flooding its utterance with excess enunciation, drifting across its signifiers in the un-sounded racket of stray signification. And despite its estranging zing, this scud of lettered speech remains the very stuff of the everyday. We all have our Joycean accidents. In saving on computer disk a list of the film clips from *Apocalypse Now* that I planned to screen for a class recently, I resorted to my available eight-letter WordPerfect shorthand with the usual ad hoc decisions and elisions, coming up, I only noticed on later retrieval, with the all but letter-perfect overlapping portmanteau, "APOCLIPS." Abbreviation's lucky break? The fractal symmetry of a self-replicating scale model? In any case, the left hand often knows better than the right brain what the wrong spelling can get right. Literary modernism begins, is always beginning again, with such incursions of linguistic eccentricity into our habituation to lexical and syntactic code. Rather than thinking to listen in on such textual phenomena, as if writing somehow contained its sonic (or even phonetic) matter, one has only to listen up, to alert oneself: not giving voice so much as giving thought to voice. The waiver of orality in any text is what licenses its multiple overhearings.

However the silence of a page is intuitively felt to be sounded in the production of its full literary effect, the theoretical silence on the matter has grown deafening. The present essay would like to assist in breaking this silence by the odd route of including the silent—and mostly invisible—operations of the cinematic medium (before and apart from any dialogue on the soundtrack) as an unexpected parallel to the reeling-by of words held in syntactic focus. Across the stationary beam of the film projector, the frame-advance mechanism drops one photogram (the single celluloid image) after another, each re-framed by the aperture on its way—along another axis—toward the masked rectangle of the screen. The equivalent for writing in its production as text is the lateral racing of the eye from word to word as they are perceptually assimilated along an axis that is angled (again) at roughly ninety degrees to the flat page. The main point is this: just as the photograms that we register as continuous film images are in fact incremental textual imprints s/tripping over themselves from projected frame to frame, so too is the apparent ribbon of syntax a continual overlap of lexigrams and functional blanks spliced by conventions that exert no absolute control over the disruptive overrun of one word upon the next in the inevitable slippage of subvocal response. An obvious point follows: these latter verbal effects are in every sense marginal, rimming words, edging forward alternative junctures, hedging syntax, but mostly (if not always) ousted by sense.

One of the most obvious contrasts between film and writing in this regard is the very point of their intersection—as well as their immediate divergence. The filmstrip in hand, like the text on the page, manifests those seams between signifying units (edges in one case, blanks in the other) that the apparatus of cinematic projection deliberately masks and that, by contrast, the apparatus of reading insists on yet cannot help but let slide. The oddness of this comparison between the technical bases of these two differentially geared but otherwise strikingly different media is, therefore, meant to get at the fundamental oddness of the two processes separately, as well as at their joint inherence at times in a modernist program of disclosed textual materiality.

To be sure, when thinking of the raw material of the modernist text, sound is scarcely what comes to mind, let alone to ear. When not actually intoned by reading aloud; when not miked, broadcast on radio waves, tracked by analog recording, laid next to an image strip on celluloid, or digitalized either for video beam or laser imprint; and when not mystified as some aura of origin in such an otherwise dead metaphor as the "ironic voice" of poem or narrative, sound would seem to have as little to do with literary modernism as with the "protomodernist" telos (or mere leaning) in earlier eras of literary production. Even within variations on the dramatic monologue, doing the police in different voices (T. S. Eliot's ultimately suppressed homage to Dickens in his planned subtitle to *The Waste Land*) is never more than a manner of speaking about a manner of writing.

It is voice itself that has come increasingly to be policed. This essay has its work cut out for it if it wants, first, to recast the place of vocalization (sounded or not) in the generation of literary language, in high modernists and Victorians alike (not to mention in Shakespeare through Keats), and, second, to bring out the link between the structuring of enunciation in literary language and the work of cinema: cinema in its aspect not as an apparitional medium but as a material process(ion), cinema not so much as a modern(ist) aesthetic form but rather as a theoretical (precisely because technological) inroad into the textual poetics of modernism.

Reflecting on reading as one of the practices of everyday life — on reading not as it is conceptually defined but as it is actually practiced in the event — Michel de Certeau evokes its contingencies just about as well as it is possible to do while leaving unsaid a whole dimension of reading praxis: "From analyses that follow the activity of reading in its detours, drifts across the page, metamorphoses and anamorphoses of the text produced by the travelling eye, imaginative or meditative flights taking off from a few words, overlappings of spaces on the militarily organized surfaces of the text, it is at least clear, as a first result, that one cannot maintain the division separating the readable text (a book, image, etc.) from the act of reading" (170). This point catches the spirit of the reading energies I want to investigate here, but it is in turn captured too much by the letter of that reading: in literary instances, by the visible mark rather than the phonemic cue.

De Certeau's metaphors are spatial; their agency, the roving eye. Detours and leaps, skimmings and skewings, anamorphic warpings and morphological mutations: all of this is true of and true to the reading act as an encounter with the visual ground of textual legibility ("book, image, etc."). But that "etc." is by no means exhaustive if we take it to encompass merely any other such readable surface. Distinct from the opened and marked page of a book are the acoustic signals triggered by linguistic inscription: what I have elsewhere called the "phonotext" of subvocal enunciation running simultaneously across, and sometimes fractionally out of sync with, the scriptive phenotext. Such syncopation must be kept, so to say, in syntactic line. Similarly, within a broad acceptation of de Certeau's deciphered "image," there is also the visual skimming of the cinematic field. To remain legible as image system, cinema must actively resist any "reading" that submits itself to a correlative (and equally constitutive) syncopation within the meshed increments of its representation. As with its literary counterpart, this resistance cannot always be assured. High modernism is only one name for a more than ordinary letting down of the guard.

The Shape and W/Ring of Words

When the habit of reading becomes embroiled in the textual densities of such a modernist program, it is for the most part merely an aggravation of standard practice. Inadvertent phonemic hurdles are always being overcome in literary reading, as well as desired intensifications undergone. This is not often recognized by literary-historical schemata. According, for instance, to Fredric Jameson, Joseph Conrad's denaturing and anything but transparent style makes him in effect (at least among novelists) the first modernist *writer*, an early master of *écriture* (Jameson 206). This seems absolutely right as far as it goes. Pinning the assertion to instances, however, one senses how much of Conrad's textual experiment rings familiar, borrowing as it does from the trusted vein of Victorian rhetorical sonority and its more tactical phonetic emphases.

Conrad's preface to *The Nigger of the "Narcissus"* is, of course, one of the leading early manifestos for a new turn in prose fiction. Though his stress falls most famously on making the reader *see*, there is a little-noted and self-exampling passage on the aural contour of fictional writing, on prose as a timbre as well as a structure of prompted images. Here Conrad insists that "it is only through an unremitting, never-discouraged care for the shape and ring of sentences that an approach can be made to plasticity, to color, and that the light of magic suggestiveness may be brought to play for an evanescent instant over the commonplace surface of words" (Conrad 12). The notion of "plasticity" in this passage does not give way to that of "color" fast enough to rule out its transitional reference to the malleable acoustic matter of language. Nor is it just the internal slant rhymes of "scent" against "stant," "place" against "face," "evanescent" against "instant" that catch the resonance as well as the glint of which he speaks. Even in dismissing that slackness of language that must be forsworn, Conrad makes its very devaluation ring. For he glosses that "commonplace surface of words" as follows after a colon: "of the old, old words, worn thin, defaced by ages of careless usage." Capped by the further echo of "ages" against "usage," this implied economy in the use value of words is one in which the dead metaphor of "defaced" suggests by contrast the chink—or "ring"—of a newly minted narrative lexicon. So that finally what the modernist writer as craftsman must eschew, in rejecting (here via imitative redundancy) the "old, old words," is something exactly halfway between the poverty of "old, doled" and the numbness of "old, dulled" words. It is one (metaphoric) thing to have the rhetorical edge of language blunted by a cheapening wear and tear;

it is another (phonemic) thing to have the surfaces of words wear away at each other, productively, under the duress of sheer attention.

Shortly after finishing a book on more or less the latter subject, I chanced upon a Modern Language Association session about music and literature at which Marshall Brown was giving a paper in part on Keats's "Ode on a Grecian Urn." I myself had written about the relaxing slack in enunciation that turns "dost tease us out of thought" into the elided "dost ease us out of thought" (Stewart 160).[1] But Brown "heard" something earlier in the poem as well, when figures on the static, voiceless urn are called upon to "Pipe to the spirit ditties of no tone" (l. 14). He noted the "note" in no tone. Thinking of this phantom scriptive annotation as evoking the way in which all sound in literature exists only under erasure as text is a way of starting to think forward through the evidence I want here to examine. The question remains: Why are these textual "notations" so easy to hear and so hard to speak—that is, to speak about in critical discussion (Brown's happy discovery a decided exception at this or any other MLA)? There is at least one ready answer.

The Ear Inert: Conspiracy Theory

When Roman Jakobson writes of the "'figure of sound'" ("Linguistics" 312; his own quotation marks), the concept itself is figurative. So also when he writes of "the sound shapes of words," where he has in mind a decidedly *mixed* but not a dead metaphor, even when language takes the form of written text.[2] In its literary manifestations, Jakobson's object of study is of course the graphically fashioned but in large part phonemically realized formal infrastructure of textual representation. Literary writing is, in other words, shaped or configured by sound patterns even when they are not voiced. Recently, however, it is just this formal infrastructure of literature that has been questioned, flattened, vitiated by poststructuralist attacks from opposite directions, a prominent brand of deconstruction on one side, a leading mode of discourse analysis on the other. Each manner of attack summarily conflates the "sound figure" or "sound shape" with variously supposed manifestations of Voice, that shibboleth of the humanist literary tradition. Any such conflation, however, is premature and disabling for a full account of the reading dynamic. This is because it conspires theoretically against a differential tension fundamental to the linguistic structure of literary textuality.

From one direction, in service to a deconstruction of textual reference, the signifying system of literary representation is now widely understood not as a trace or index of the imagined world (or, more to the point here, speaker) it evokes, but instead as a series of differential *traces*. The term is of course Derrida's, along with its own often misleading metaphoric associations.[3] Though such a trace is for Derrida by no means simply the mark on the page, it has come to be thought of in these terms by many of his Anglo-American followers: more like a tracery of letters as phantom afterimage of presence than like a marked (but always invisible) difference within each letter from its pertinent opposite in word formation. And once trace is subsumed to script in this way, the phonematic dimensions of difference and deferral are consigned to silence.[4] From another direction, in the service of exposing and dismantling literature's constructed subjectivity as a strategically devised discourse of autonomous interiority, the literary system has been taken as the intentional fabrication of a unitary speaking voice. Thus, from each perspective by turns, a speech-based linguistics and an ideology of the subject are seen as literature's twin mystifications. The irony is that the phonemic texture of literary language is given almost opposite weight in these two frequent moves against the centering Voice, against text as voicing.

I speak mostly of tendencies adding up rather than of considered positions shored up. Yet the animus against phonological response is widely apparent. From the point of view of a narrowly conceived deconstruction, the phonocentric text is an illusion promoted by the figurative notion of "expressive utterance" where there is only writing. Alternately, the critique of the subject as a literary fiction finds in the poetic text a surplus of phonemic material, of enunciative options, that must be curtailed in order to sustain the myth of the univocal point of origin. Where deconstruction (in the hands of a practitioner such as Paul de Man) wholly subordinates phonological issues to the tropological indeterminacy of signification as mute inscription, a critic such as Antony Easthope in *Poetry as Discourse* attempts to historicize the enshrinement of a speaking subject as the necessary staving off of too much extraneous (rather than an altogether nonexistent) voicing. Though exiled by linguistic definition in certain deconstructive practices and so theorized out of existence, Voice is instead seen constrained only up to a certain point according to Easthope's discourse analysis, with the enunciating subject certified by classic texts precisely when its acknowledged phonemic multiplicity is held in check. Either way, the detectable phonophobia of these approaches—whether braced against the notion of sound's materialization through script or steeled against babble's invasion of simulated vocal discourse—sells short the linguistic tensility (and phonemic undertow) of literary writing in any period.

To force an uneasy wedding of the two positions is not, of course, impossible or unfamiliar. Phonemic along with graphic turmoil can become not an encumbrance to but, rather, the star-crossed destiny of literary writing in a certain version of the historical long view. Discourse eventually submits in this way to the maddening incestuous embrace of its own origin in a less regimented textuality. Something like this. So far, I have polarized the ruling claims only to expose the suppression of phonological textures that they each—and oppositely—entail. Their most obvious point of contact occurs in leading accounts of the "modernist" advent (loosely defined), with "modernity" understood either as an ahistorical condition of disclosed materiality in one approach or as a telos of literary history in the other—advent as an unscheduled adventure or a timed arrival. For deconstruction, especially and explicitly in Derrida, textual "modernity" is a dehistoricized term for the eruption into literary writing of what J. Hillis Miller would later call (in a book by that name) "the linguistic moment," a moment that disperses any vestige of naive mimesis (including of the speaking voice) to unfold the production of language itself under the sign of grammatology rather than phonology.[5] By contrast, literary history is for Easthope founded on and maintained by the vigilant "overcorrection" (106) of a certain signifying surcharge in text production. With coherent speaking subjects emerging from texts only via the protocols of containment by which phonemic excess is kept in place rather than at play, modernism is nevertheless the end in view. It is the breached limit that proves the rule.

On this showing, Renaissance poetic practice closes ranks around the speaking persona, where in Shakespeare's Sonnet 73, for example (the example is Easthope's, 106), the phrase "Death's second self" must be articulated to defeat a pointless elision of sibilants that no integrated persona could be conceived to intend, not to mention (as Easthope does not) the anarchic irruption of an entire clause from these three slurred words: "Death seconds self." Orchestrating the institution of the modern (though not the modernist) lyric, we are told, is a "coherent polysemy" that permits "very little sliding of the signifier over the signified" (99). Following on this Renaissance consolidation of integrated (however mystified) phonocentric origin, the Augustans, according to Easthope, only tightened the reins. The Romantics cut loose again in their own way, though still within the dispensation of a centered lyric utterance. Modernism then arrives as the point of no return for the foregrounded inscription (rather than transcribed utterance) of verse and prose fiction alike, where all aura of vocalization dissipates into a (strictly metaphoric) textual noise.

Before this ruptural turning point, however, as many such arguments would go, the constructed—and all too easily deconstructed—persona of a Shakespeare sonnet or a first-person Victorian bildungsroman (each expressive and introspective at once; each, in other words, the work of a speaking and of a subject) rules the practices of literary representation. All such literary personae betray an ideology of the subject so deeply implicated in the artificially buttressed myth of an uttering agency that a double imperative is found to hold sway: namely, that the sound shapes of literary language must not only veil their purely graphic origin but fence in their textual truancy in order to sustain the notion of a generative psychic center. So runs the prevailing assumption, but what happens when it runs up against disturbing (because all too prevalent) counterexamples?

We will be moving to some classic "readerly" instances (Barthes's sense) from the Victorian period after a brief further reflection on the tendency in criticism to hold such reading hostage to the labors of the deciphering eye alone. The tendency is still very much with us. In 1993's *Black Riders: The Visible Language of Modernism*, Jerome McGann consistently highlights the graphic physicality of the textual medium as its predominant modernist dimension, his commentary often tuning out entirely the aural register. As it happens, he tracks the high modernist emphasis on literary typography, on the biblio/graphic in this sense, back to the Victorian renaissance of printing in the work of William Morris. Against the maximized physical aspects of the protomodernist text as iconic rather than vehicular, inscriptive before signifying, McGann sets (almost nostalgically) "the material features (morphemic and phonemic) of poetic language as we have received them through a first-order set of (ballad) conventions" (46)—with (we might add) the implied derivation of such features, as in Easthope and others, from the bardic discourse of the speaking subject. Even when remarking in connection with the modernist Wallace Stevens that there "are graces available to writing when it gives its entire faith over to Language" (24), McGann's emphasis falls on the former, on the mechanical production of inscription and its print formats, rather than on the full ensemble of linguistic properties as produced in reading. In this respect it seems appropriate that McGann's title, alluding to a typesetter's inked rollers or "riders," should make no allusion to the potential play on such technical argot in the title of Wallace Stevens's famous essay, "The Noble Rider and the Sound of Words," a play that may perhaps be operable beneath the more obvious phonemic pun on "writer." What Stevens's title goes on to spell out—on the other side of the conjunction—is of course the aural authority for any and all such verbal free rides. This is to say that the "sound of words" evokes not simply (as is the main point of Stevens's essay) the differing force of writing's humanist reception from generation to generation, but also (as in Stevens's poetic practice, to which we will later be turning) the differential roll and rumble of words in their gallop across the page.

Another recent study, though concentrating on certain theoretical resistances to the rule of the visual in Western culture, has little to say of the reading ear as alternative. If one scans Martin Jay's *Downcast Eyes: The Denigration of Vision in Twentieth-Century French Thought* (1993) for any sustained emphasis on the relegation of print textuality to phonemic production, one searches in vain. This is mostly as it should be, historically speaking, since vision is "denigrated" from Jay's perspective largely in being *decried* by major French thinkers for its ideological hegemony, not in being intermittently *demoted* as the dominant textual register of literary practice. In such an overview, however, certain theories of writing do get short shrift. The granulated vocality of Barthes's "pleasure of the text," for instance, is decidedly marginalized in its force as a countering seduction to the visual monopoly explored elsewhere in Barthes's work on photographically based images (437–58). Only at the end of Jay's survey, arrived at the phonemic resistances of an antispecular *écriture feminine*, is a programmatically theorized modernist textuality given full hearing, a modernism *athwart* the letter that finds its peculiar version of "writerliness" distilled in an epigraph from Hélène Cixous: "I always privilege the ear over the eye. I am always trying to write with my eyes closed" (Jay 493). In this same spirit, we will soon be attempting to come at even some "transparent" nineteenth-century writing with our ears open.

On the way, a third recent point of departure. In *Anti-Mimesis from Plato to Hitchcock*, Tom Cohen accords no privilege in the undermining of explicit signification to high modernist over nineteenth-century texts, arguing for an antimimetic or "pre-figural" (prerepresentational) reading of Edgar Allan Poe and Herman Melville as much as of Conrad and Alfred Hitchcock. The trouble is, they all end up sounding, or at least looking, like minor Joycean imitators. Cohen's emphasis on "the facticity of the textual event itself . . . thematized on the level of inscription, sound, letters, signature, and other figures" (1) is a retroactive postmodernist inroad into the bastions of semantic coherence carried out both in the nonname of a no longer coherent (writing or reading) subject and in the institutional service of a "materialist" reading that might outlast and reroute the turn from textual to contextual studies. So far so good. The effort is, for him, a stand against "retro-humanism" (1), and it derives from his opening question: "What is the interventionist role of 'reading' (indeed of too close reading) after the era of cultural studies?" (1). That phrase "too close reading" might seem an invitation to demurral, but one ends up concurring. His readings tend to bring the verbal "material" up so close to the eye, rather than ear, that words break up into sheer letters, surrendering not only their mimetic function within the field of semantics but their phenomenality as read language. Cohen borrows from Poe to call such effects "runic rhyme." As such, they generate an echoism not of chimes but of runes, marked fragments, as for instance in "The Bells," where we are asked to think of "crystalline *de*light" as the "foreclosure of light" (112) or to free associate as follows: "If the letters E-A-R almost reproduce the initials E.A.P., Poe may be said to seek his runic signature in the ear, much as the 'mad ex*pos*tulation' of the third stanza involves an external positing of sense on the acoustic stuff of language in which Poe's own *name* is echoed" (113–14). As outré and indulgent as such claims may seem, Poe, read this way, operates for Cohen within an abiding American tradition: executing a truer pragmatism than neopragmatism imagines, carrying us back to the verbal *pragma*, the thing itself. In a like manner, Conrad's signature effect is supposedly heard to echo through various permutations of the letter *c*. Further, the infamous "The horror! The horror!" from *Heart of Darkness*, in association with Marlow's final lie to Kurtz's Intended, dissolves into various bilingual perversities, "including the double play on or-or, error, or the *hors-hors* that names her as the outside (of an outside)" (201).

When shifting his "too close" readings to film, the spirit of Cohen's approach recedes even farther from the medium-specific phenomenality of textual generation I am trying in this essay, against the more obvious tread of script or images, to hold in mind. The signifying materiality of Hitchcock depends for Cohen on rebuslike effects in *The Thirty-Nine Steps* such as "the question to Mr. Memory about the distance between *M*ontreal and *W*innepeg, in which the inversion of W and M reminds us that they are the same, and also without distance" (245). Thus does the material, prefigural thing, the letter, prompt a reading less "gentrified," in his view, than Slavoj Žižek's Lacanian decoding of Hitchcock, for it respects the necessary precedence of the thing, the *pragma*, even over the psychoanalytic Thing as a scandalous intrusion of the real. Cohen's "anti-mimetic" cryptography of the linguistic signifier on film bears certain affinities with the work of Marie-Claire Ropars-Wuilleumier (unmentioned by him but discussed below). In this respect, it must be distinguished from what I might call the *counter*mimetic stress of my own reading, which audits a text sequence not only working against the grain of manifest sense but cutting parallel grooves of sensualized representation in the (contrapuntal) process. By contrast with Cohen's avowedly "havoc-wreaking" (6) dispersions of the letter, the attention of this essay will be trained on the misfires and discharges of literary language as they get—if I may let pun come to the rescue of mixed metaphor—immediately rehired at overtime wages within an unstable but relentless economy of pertinent textual connotation. At one pole of the generic spectrum, traditional prose fiction as much as modernist verse participates in such an economy, oscillating always between the supply of signification and the demand for sense. A pair of classic nineteenth-century narratives should do the job of demonstrating this.

Lending an Inward Ear

The immediate appeal of my first Victorian example is to common sense, before we turn in any detail to the sensed commonalities of adjacent letters and syllables—either through multiplication or overlap—in an exemplary passage. Do we, could we ever, "overcorrect" the linguistic thickening and heightened phonic echoism of *Jane Eyre* (1847) in order to lend a more convinced ear to the novelistic document as Jane Eyre's transcribed voice? Are we not steadily asked to sense that *Jane Eyre*, read as written, is the model for Jane Eyre herself as text (rather than text maker), the psychological subject under the regime of the sliding signifier? I speak with a theoretical anachronism—or nondiachronism—that seems well enough advised, derived as it is from my commonsensical premise. If aesthetic modernism, on one prevailing account, is understood as a mode of art determined by the concerted revelation of its own medium, abstracted from the dutiful protocols of mimesis, then what literary modernism programmatically discloses about the materiality of language is a fact about such language that it is only reasonable to conceive being glimpsed, if not fully excavated, in the most intensive literary activity of any period. My topic is therefore a modernism less historically cataclysmic than often claimed, more continuous with the discontinuities of literary language itself. Brontë's prose gives teeth to this view.

I will be closing in on a passage as far from hermetic or autotelic modernism as the Victorian novel gets. It involves an overtly propagandistic set piece of ethical peroration that nonetheless erodes the lexical foundation of its own rhetorical platform. In it, aural dilapidation undermines the lapidary periods of a quasi-oratorical intrusion. This is the long paragraph ending with the insistence that it is "thoughtless to condemn [women], or laugh at them, if they seek to do more or learn more than custom has pronounced necessary for their sex" (12:96). By sudden juxtaposition, that thoughtlessness, that very irrationality, seems immediately embodied in the goading mockery of Bertha's laugh, at this point mistaken for a servant's:

"When thus alone I not unfrequently heard Grace Poole's laugh." In the mood Jane describes just before this intrusion, during her spells of elevated solitude at Thornfield, "my sole relief was to walk along the corridor of the third story . . . and, best of all, to open my *inward ear* to a tale that was never ended—a tale my imagination created, and narrated continuously" (12:96; emphasis added). Commanding a perch on one kind of "stor(e)y," the building's third, Jane yields to another—one perhaps known to her in her wish-fulfillment fantasies, as is the novel to us, by a name coincident with her own unfolding sense of self-consciousness. Jane Eyre tries listening as often as she can, in short, to Jane Eyre.

The narrator of one story becomes in this way the narratee of its redemptive counterplot. And when we open our *sense* of hearing to Brontë's novel, when we audit it with our own inward ear, we serve to enact this level of Jane's privately sustaining imagination. (The mind's ear is of course continually on alert in a novel where, in brief, plain Jane, airing her despair at the eyrie-like isolation that has been her life ere now, craves in her psychic errancy that heroism she is heir to.) Fleshing out the nature of the subjective narrative whose audition is in turn audited by the reader, Jane further characterizes her inward tale as "quickened with all of incident, life, fire, feeling, that I desired and had not in my actual existence" (12:96). If the typical interplay of assonance and alliteration in Brontë's prose—all too easy to discount as an overwrought lyric drag on narrative momentum—can better be read as part of a "cryptonymy" of repressed desire, then we have all the more reason to trust our subvocalization of the immediate lexical pressure points in this passage.[6] The metonymic skid within the temptingly metaphoric (hence appositional) interchangeability of "life, fire, feeling" disrupts sequence with secret equivalence, so that we come to hear in this passage the veritable insistence and slippage of the letter in the unconscious.

Words end up signifying only the spectral doubles of themselves as signifiers, with self-identity thus surrendered, structurally sundered, from the lexical level up. Bertha's cackling laughter, the eruptive flouting of all discourse, is not therefore the only appearance made by the Voice of the Other at this point in the novel. For within the phonemic buckling of Jane's own self-utterance, there is the chiastic switch at "life, fire" by which a large part of "life" is, as it were, swallowed up by "fire." This happens when an elision releases from within the juxtaposition of "life, fire" an otherwise bracketed and contained lexeme that obtrudes now as a further appositive. Out of the friction of letters, that is, the ignition of a further signifier: out of "life, fire"—either "Eyre" if pronounced as in "eyrie" (with the optional long *i* rather than long *a* sound) or, more to the point here, its homonym (and vocabular succubus) *ire*. At which point we hear named in advance, if by moments only—and only on the sly, or slide, of the signifying chain itself—the vocalized sarcastic rage of Jane's alter ego in Bertha. That this "ire," not the "fire" from which it has been smelted out in the heat of reading, yields not only a closer alliterative link with "I" but a closer morphemic common denominator with "desire" itself (quoting again: "that *I* des*ir*ed and had not") is a coincidence only in the mode of all those other accidents that manifest desire in language.

From Stevenson toward Stevens

This entrenching of identity's echoes along the phonemic groove of the long *i* sound is carried to almost garbled exaggeration in Robert Louis Stevenson's *The Strange Case of Dr. Jekyll and Mr. Hyde* (1886). Speaking of the double whose depravity is a vicarious extension of his own, Dr. Jekyll writes (of himself in third person) that this "insurgent horror was knit to *him* closer than a wife" (53; emphasis added). Discourse thus opens the cleft of self-surveillance at the very moment of erotic analogy. To this Jekyll adds, just as unexpectedly, and with an assonant echo of the long vowel in "wife," "closer than an eye." By this he would seem to mean, beyond the timeworn homophonic pun on an "I" hereby undergoing drastic redefinition, that Hyde is actually *inside* rather than adjacent to or embraced by him, "knit" up with his life by being "caged in his flesh" (53). Putting the *I* back in "w*i*fe" within the homeostatic eroticism of this vicarious soul-mating is not the only echoic thickening of this sort in which Jekyll is caught up. Twice before he has stumbled over an ejaculation as if it were the redundant designation of his own faltering—stuttering—identity. To Utterson, in explaining why he cannot say more, Jekyll multiplies the monosyllables of selfhood even as he is trying to keep his own multiplicity under wraps: "*I* would trust you before any man alive, *ay*, before myself, if *I* could" (44). Later, when explanation can no longer be postponed, Jekyll's reflexive grammar, turning back on itself, again snaps open more selves than it has intended, for "by the sleeplessness to which I now condemned myself, *ay*, even beyond what *I* thought possible to man, *I* became, in my own person, a creature eaten up" (95). Echoing in both passages across the long vowel of "my" and "myself," the homophonic "ays" have it. So, too, do they have Jekyll himself right where language wants him, with the "ay" stammered out only as the affirmation of negativity and self-division.

This is perhaps the least obtrusive streak of wordplay in a novel that rides on verbal duplicities of all sorts, dead metaphors sprung to sudden life, ambivalence thematized as psychotic doubling—everything from the distinguished Dr. Jekyll losing moral "stature" (44) when transformed into his dwarfish twin to the discovery by Dr. Lanyon of the "single word: double" (38) to indicate the dosage of the corrective drug meant to ward off the alter ego. Let me put it succinctly. The strangeness of *The Strange Case of Dr. Jekyll and Mr. Hyde*, its fable of self-estrangement, consists in its radical transformation of form into content, of literary anomaly into fantastic plot. The "profound duplicity" (42) of Stevenson's story is the story of one made two, a pun made flesh. It is saturated by a perversely pertinent wordplay that splits as many subjects as it can find. Even a negligible idiom of recognition at one early point—the dead metaphor of dissociated personality in Enfield's being "surprised out of myself" (34) by the unfolding story—can return burdened with the weight of the entire tale, as when Jekyll, coming to consciousness, "came to myself once more with the character . . . of Henry Jekyll" (85).

Comparison is invited with *Jane Eyre*. There, the logic of the unconscious as manifested in textual production appears in the homophonic undulation of Jane Eyre's discourse in describing that persistent, if continually interrupted, narrative audited by her inward ear. As banked fires are once again deformed to ire in the shearing off of Jekyll into Hyde, the inward clefts, defiles, and drifts of subjectivity are delivered from latency not merely as the syncopated phasing in and out of desire but as the reified—and so rent—faces of the self's contradictory impulses. Stevenson's mastertrope of ambivalence goes like this: A second or double meaning stands to a first—a read suggestion to a written sign—as Hyde stands to Jekyll. This does not exhaust the macabre physiology of the double, of course, but it goes far toward naturalizing it within the only range of experience that counts for its realization: the experience of the reading rather than the social subject. Where else but in language can the one be made two? In dream or nightmare, or its waking pharmacological equivalent, where the ego shivers into multiplicity like a rogue signifier. But, for most of us, only in literary language: that is, in language *recognized* for its layered and multivalent associations. In *Dr. Jekyll and Mr. Hyde*, the pun, as a paradoxically duplex singular, generates a kind of metalinguistic matrix (multiple signification) for this narrative of the multiplied self. The derivatives of this matrix are relentless, as we have begun to see, ranging from the homophonic through the syntactical.

Another minor and passing example from *Dr. Jekyll* comes to mind, one beginning to chafe at lexical borders as if in anticipation of the eroded envelope of self-identity. The foul alleyway into which Hyde is first seen to disappear—the unrecognized backside of Jekyll's house—is rather routinely personified when first described, especially the threshold of his den, with its "blind forehead" and the egregious neglect of "every feature" (30). But there is a further quirk of such metonymic personification in the image of loitering tramps striking matches on the "blistered and distained" panels of the door (30). Especially because that second participle is already archaic by Stevenson's time, the phrase's curious phonemic decontraction (and over-accentuation) of the semantically equivalent "blistered and *s*tained" implies that the locals have in fact "disdained" or despised the portal as if it were the obnoxious Hyde himself.

Metonymically revealed by his environs—but still unglimpsed in his own person by Utterson, the reader's surrogate—Hyde remains naggingly enigmatic in his absence, figured only by the cryptic knots of discourse: "And still the figure had no *face* by which he [Utterson] might know it; even in his dreams, it had no *face*" (8; emphasis added). Three more reiterations of the term "face" are added to this fixated repetition—all in phonemic reply to a curious anticipatory echo. For in the sentence just before this, as if in a homophonic matrix for the fivefold litany of "face" to come, we have a summary of the hyperactive "figure" of Hyde, now running down a girl in the street, now appearing at Jekyll's bedside to will the latter into doing his bidding: "The figure in these two faces haunted the lawyer all night."[7] So Stevenson had originally written, striking out "faces" at the last minute (effacing Hyde yet again) and inserting "phases" above the line: the normative constraint of a linear *distinction* (phases or stages) exerted on the intolerable *composite*.[8] As with the aurally materialized overlap of "disdained" upon the lexical boundary dispute and risked phonemic assimilation of "an*d* *di*stained" earlier, here too homophony speaks in tongues: those overreading Empsonian tongues from my epigraph. At this later crux of narrative sequence (the horizontally arrayed "phases" of degradation) reconfigured as a vertical imposition and pressure point, the internal force of language in subvocal production may once again be said to mime the alternatives it cannot graphically perform.

What I do not mean to be saying here is either of the things that might seem most obvious about this revision: either that Stevenson did not want the shadow self resulting from the degradation of Jekyll into Hyde to be confusingly two-faced in its own right, or that Stevenson's manuscript alteration has suppressed a virtual dead metaphor ("faces" for something like "aspects") in order to postpone any foreshadowings of the doppelgänger's countenance at this premature point in the arc of building anticipation. I would not put it this way precisely because the erasure is actually retained in the shadow of a pun. I want therefore to suggest instead that homophobic shock (Utterson's shudder at the thought of Hyde at Jekyll's bedside) is taken up rather than kept down by the shudder of homophonic recoil. In the imposed sequential logic of "phases" (temporal rather than corporeal), we have thus—and by a metamorphosis, or anamorphosis, internal to language—caught the alternative face of a phrasing that, like its referent, refuses self-identity. We have caught it, moreover, caught on to it, as if glimpsing it in superimposition: the prosopopoeia of the pun itself as a material inscription rather than an overtone, a kind of lexical mirage, a specter, a deformed scriptive double. This phantom manifestation operates on the model of a dreamlike parapraxis, as a working (out) of fleeting, amorphous apprehensions in and through language. Quite apart from the manuscript's apparent corroboration of wordplay (however unconscious), the published text as we have it has its divided way with us. Even while in a state of quickened, edgy alertness—a kind of textual paranoia—we may think it is we who are writing over, by reading in, the given by its equivocation, the stable substantive by the pun ("phases" by the "faces" that demarcate them). Instead, we are all the while being written with—conscripted at the level of phonemic demarcation itself.

The described anxieties of the passage rise to the surface as a warping doubleness of language itself. To think that this could operate credibly within the classic discourse of bourgeois realism only with a certain "overcorrection" of these fugitive folds of enunciation (Easthope's position above) would be woefully untrue to the workings (on us) of narrative textuality—even if the passage were not devoted in the first place, as of course it is, to transcribing the febrile half-consciousness of Utterson's fitful waking-dream state. To lean in this way on the constraints of overcorrection is to cut the text off from its affiliations with the modernist verbal instress of a Hopkins, a Conrad, a Woolf, a Joyce, an H. D., or a Stevens, all with their hospitality to the incorrigible in language.

Moreover, just as the stray letter insists (on itself) in Utterson's represented unconscious-structured-like-a-language (to paraphrase Lacan), so too is the general shape of Utterson's obsession a symptom of literature in embryo. Prosopopoeia—the quintessential literary activity of giving face to absence—is just what Utterson craves in his compulsion to look on Hyde's face. But whereas he is finally gratified, we are not, except by the feeble approximation of words—or except when we realize that in realizing Hyde in the space of his absence, we as readers are functioning rather like Jekyll himself. It is, in short, when we start hearing double that we end up seeing Jekyll-eyed.

In this passage from Stevenson, then, prosopopoeia is in the ear of the beholder. So too with a poem by Wallace Stevens about the sun whose face cannot be seen, a kind of cosmological catachresis, the name for whose every effect is always a figurative deflection from the source. In the modernist Stevens as well as in the Victorian Stevenson, the process of literary manifestation from the blank page entails the return of repressed absences within the linguistic economy of redistributed differential signification, whether the differential is between a word and its bordering blank (and [di]stained) or between a letter and its absentation by another (phases/faces). To Wallace Stevens's sequestering of the letter in the very image of imaging's invisible condition, the unsighted sun, we now turn.

"The Red Fern" Reread

Stevens's little-known and unreprinted poem tests the limits—or, to be more precise, the lexical lower limit—of a certain figural reading initiated by Paul de Man and promulgated further by J. Hillis Miller. "The Red Fern" (1947) is in fact a text on which Miller has written at the top of his bent. Stevens's verses develop across four stanzas as an elaborate exfoliation of their title, itself a metaphor for the unfurling light of day in the first stanza. This is the stanza to which we will mostly limit our concern here:

> The large-leaved day grows rapidly
> And opens in this familiar spot
> Its unfamiliar, difficult fern
> Pushing and pushing red after red.

Procreative and phallic at once, day dawns aggressively, its tendrils many and penetrant. This is where Miller too begins, but what we have now to register goes in a direction different from his emphasis on figural contradiction in the text.

In this poem about the very presupposition of the ocular in solar radiation, there is a sense, too, of revealed phonemic presupposition—as if to say that as the sun is to seeing, so are vocables as well as syllables to reading. A mediated internal rhyme from the second stanza, by which the "doubles of this *fern* in clouds" are "Less *firm* than the pate*rn*al flame," may indeed—via a further association of homophonic echoes across divergent orthography—augment one's suspicion that an unsaid half-pun may be operating as one avoided "matrix" of the entire poem: the day's blazing uprush figured as a "red furn/ace." This is, as it were, only half said, half written. I will be concentrating on the yet deeper-going lexical play in the first stanza, one that is entirely (if almost invisibly) manifested by script (pace Miller). According to his analysis (sounding in his local reading rather like Riffaterre as the global theorist of poetic signification), "the unspoken law of the poem is that though the poem has as its goal to name the sun the word *sun* may not be used" (217). Though this closely resembles that "expanded" and "converted" matrix pursued in Riffaterre's analysis of poetic semiosis, it must be remembered that for Riffaterre the "goal" is not a naming that is banned but precisely the sustained and elaborate deflection and forestalling of that name. Hence troping, "turning"—instanced here in a poem that we may come to think reads like a pervasively evaded autotelic pun: the fern as helio*tropic* image of its very source in the literary circumlocution for sun.

Veiling like cloud-cover the always invisible, because otherwise blinding, origin of all sight, a figure like the "fern" becomes (in the other sense) figure to the always unrepresentable ground of perception. "Day is a name for everything under the sun but the sun" (220), quips Miller. Within this understanding, though, one of the things that is for Miller "anomalous" in the poem, a figurative detail deliberately staged so that it "does not make sense," is the tropological conversion by which the first quatrain moves from the metaphoric equation between day and "large-leaved plant" to "the day as the locus, milieu, or 'spot' within which the invisible and unnamable sun grows as a red fern" (220). Yet looking at the lines more closely, in their lineation as well as figuration, we may find that they resolve their own apparent contradiction.

"The large-leaved day grows rapidly / And opens in this familiar spot." So far one potential grammar is complete. As specified by the title, the red fern has by line 2 opened (itself). The unexpected transition—which for Miller fails to "make sense"—comes when "opens" slips from intransitive to transitive verb form around the turn of the enjambment, releasing "Its unfamiliar, difficult fern." What Miller seems to rule out here is a genitive sense of "its" other than the expected possessive, a sense that would prevent the fern from seeming like some illogical component of the larger plant—even though everything so far would have led us to assume that the whole dawning day and "its" spreading fern were represented as equivalents. Another rhetorical option presents itself, however. Is this not in fact a case of the "genitive metaphor" so closely related to catachresis (as in, so it happens, such a prototypical example "eye of the sun," where the sun *is* rather than *has* an eye)?[9] On this understanding, then, the sun opening its eye would be like the day opening its fern, in other words unfolding itself to view. If this metaphoric subcategory—marshaling what Jakobson might characterize as "the poetry of grammar, and its literary product, the grammar of poetry" (Jakobson 319)—were brought to bear in helping solve Miller's problem at this turn, it would only support his sense that all of this figuration is floated on the structuring absence of the seen sun: the fern made available by metonymy for a daylight that, in illuminating the proximate causes (atmospheric conditions) of the fern's figurative effects, always remains hidden behind it.

But what about the fact, emphasized by the heavy beat of lexical invariance within antithesis, that in a "familiar" spot the fern is, and presumably always, "unfamiliar"? This may be just—and must be at least—a perfectly apt description of a day's always unique dawning in the inevitable East. Yet what else, if I may put it this way, does difference within familiarity here permit? Miller insists on "the impossibility or at least the impropriety of naming the sun in so many words, looking it in the eye, so to speak" (317). We never do quite look its inscription in the eye, but this does not mean— especially in a poem titled to permit its own aural transliteration to "The Read Fern"—that we are not in a position to *read* "sun." My claim is that we cannot help but do so, and yet never more than under erasure, at precisely that enjambment from second to third line. Across the at least momentarily ambiguous "its" (genitive versus equative), the text yields (by liaison rather than elision this time) the sibilant whisper—the aural penumbra—necessary to say the unseeable "sun" on the underside of "it*s un*familiar, difficult fern." It would seem that the "noble riders" of inked inscription are here blurred by their phonemic materialization as the "sound of words." If so, then the repressed matrix has been instantiated after all, if only on the slope between the falling off of one word and the uptake of the next. With "The Red Fern" read this way, its never more than covert assertion of the backing "sun" replays any text's resistance to complete and literalizing *dis*figuration. The effects of such resistance are indeed "difficult"—defacilitating, that is, defamiliarizing—if only in order to be registered in the first place, registered as the figures that wrest themselves from blank literality.

In this sense I would carry Miller's de Manian argument about the priority of figure to ground one step farther—farther back—to the material basis of language itself within (if not before) the mark, language as a structure of double articulation (phonemes/morphemes). The annihilating brightness of unfigured light is the always present but masked cause of its epiphenomena, then, just as the blank obliterating space glimpsed between lexically bunched letters is the very ground of enunciation repressed in process. The cross-lexical effects I am examining enjoy, it should be clear, a privileged if not strictly legible relation to this textual ground. They institute in fact the morphophonemic (the scriptive, subvocal) rather than pictorial version of those gestalt drawings in which the figure/ground relationship oscillates beyond easy containment: the duck looking one way that almost simultaneously becomes a rabbit looking the other, or the vase that flip-flops to two faces staring at each other in profile. That last fabled example carries with it a happy lexical coincidence in English that allows one to produce a veritable gestalt phrasing dependent on a slip of the ear rather than the eye: "How does shifting perception sometimes recei*ve faces*?" The answers lies immanent along the very phonemes that phrase the question. It is what I have taken to calling the duck/grab-it-while-you-can syndrome.

This is the same effect, not in Stevens but in Stevenson, that we saw in that phasing-out of "faces" by the "phases" that alone gave form to the perversity at play in the protagonist as living pun. It is also the effect that I would like now to imagine in its relation to film, as a way of imagining film's relation not just to the international modernism it accompanied and informed, but to a history of the modernist moment in the literature of earlier periods. If the sun's invisibility in relation to the traces of the day it generates is like the page's functional disappearance beneath the marks that manifest a given text as signification, then the cinematic equivalent of this might seem, pretty much as with a slide projector, to be the bright and effectively invisible light behind the image as projected. But in the kinetic medium of film, as analogously in the workings of textuality, there is another level of the material base, requiring not just projection but also the serializing of difference. This is the spatiotemporal materiality that develops a closer parallel, after all, between the filmstrip passing in front of the projector lamp and the eye's assimilation of a scriptive text than between movies and sun-drenched mornings. As we will see, this (so far hypothetical) parallel may be linked ultimately to an unexpected teleology of text-based representation on the way toward silent film's automatism of difference in the first decades of this century. Indeed, on the issue of modernism's general turn toward the minimal increment of textual generation across various aesthetic forms, there is a suggestive remark from the linguistic vantage of Roman Jakobson: "The autonomization of minimal formal units, a characteristic procedure of the arts and sciences around World War I, was saliently manifested in the growing inquiry into the sound shapes of language" (Jakobson and Waugh 181).

Phonemic Montage: The Word D/Riven by Syntax

In entertaining the cinematic process itself as something like a photo-mechanical equivalent for the interlinked phonological and graphic basis of textual generation, I will be offering finally an epitomizing—if by no means typical—moment of sheer homophonic wordplay. This is an imbricated phrasal pun that may be found to rehearse the most eccentric visual operations of the film that passes under its name(s). I take it that this is no harder to do because the wordplay I have in mind appears only in the film's title and is nowhere mobilized within the functional syntax of the voice-over narrative. The avant-garde text in question is the late-modernist photographic montage ("photoroman" or "ciné-roman") by Chris Marker, *La Jetée* (1962), whose most famous (or only?) "scene" (the narrative is comprised otherwise of still photographs in overlapping succession) is a few seconds of teased-out moving-image footage. What this experimental narrative serves to distill of the medium's own standard operations is, we will find, a composite textuality that the impacted title has already acted out in advance.

Then, too, for the lexical splaying of Marker's title there may indeed be a notable high modernist prototype in cinema's own avant-garde canon. In his silent, anagrammatically titled *Anemic cinema* (1927), Marcel Duchamp inscribes a series of homophonic puns—"esquimaux au mots esquise" and the like—on a set of spiraling disks. Simulating the spooling of the cinematic reel in its own silent visual slippage from one celluloid frame to another, frames that blur like Duchamp's high-speed wordplay into various signifying permutations, these spirals bespeak a moment of alliance between the linguistics of literature and the mechanics of a recently arrived and rival medium. From here to the punning title of another nondialogue film half a century later, *La Jetée*, is a shorter step than it may seem in the history of modernist experiment in verbal and visual succession.

Moreover, this step is effectively halved by a direct link recently demonstrated between another of Duchamp's kinetic investigations, this time on canvas (*Nude Descending a Staircase* [1912]), and the late nineteenth-century protocinematic studies of the biomotor "trace" conducted via the chronophotography of Etienne-Jules Marey (Dagognet 140–51). These last are experiments that went so far in the direction of my present thesis (if I may put it this way) as to include—but always without full success in the cinemalike resynthesizing of its analytic breakdowns—a "phonoscope" designed to reinscribe the precise facial and lip movements necessary for the execution of speech patterns (Dagognet 160–62). At the center of its narrative almost a full century later, *La Jetée* embeds an exercise in such analysis-cum-synthesis that may be found to replay the technological origins of both pictorial and literary modernism, each in their own way cubist and polysemous, diffracted and multivalent.

Photogrammatology

Given the psychoanalytic topic (and subject) of Marker's film—a self vanished into his own artificially induced and self-displacing memory traces as visual fixations—the thematizing of the medium as the carrier of consciousness seems inevitable. For Lacan, the *aphanisis* of self-consciousness, its phased fading in and out, constitutes the subject only as "flickering in eclipses" within the metonymic slide of its own enunciation (Jacques-Alain Miller 34). Comparably, in Marker's "photoroman"—composed all but exclusively of still photographs edited together—we are made uniquely aware of kinetic representation in cinema as the flickering-in-eclipses of the single photogram on the image track. This fact is brought out most forcefully by that cinematically "realized" moment when the flow of discrete images of the hero's dream woman asleep is sped up to the point where it begins to resemble, and then actually becomes, a moving-image shot of her waking face in close-up. Just before the photographic encroaches in this way on the cinematic, the separate images have grown so nearly coincident with each other that they narrow to that differential spread necessary to the process of animation. Even before the filmic achieves itself momentarily in a brief stretch of "moving pictures," then, its mechanisms have been rehearsed and asserted in what we might call a *pressure toward* cinema.

Brought forward here is the so-called phi effect at the basis of filmic projection, dependent on that "persistence of vision" that bridges the dis/juncture between separate photograms in order to produce the illusion of continuous motion across the succession of single frames.[10] In the sequence where an all but animated montage of hairbreadth deflections builds toward a fugitive engagement with the full cinematic process, Marker's ontological point is perhaps best captured by precisely the impossibility of capturing this moment through illustrative frame enlargements in an essay like this. Once they were blocked out in sequence, one could not "read" the difference between those stills that, on one hand, remain within the thematic logic of perpetually fading fixations and those that, on the other hand, accelerate toward the enhanced cognitive (and emotional) dimension of the moving image. My own point is that the mechanical rudiments of the apparatus may well evoke at such a moment, as if standing in for all filmic projection, that flickering signification that film shares, while literalizing, with the file of the signifier in writing. Within the filmic flow, that is, the automatized serial displacement of images offers the new medium's loose but illuminating equivalent to the continuously decentered activation of script in subvocal text production, with its recurrent jostling of lexigraphic material by phonemic encroachments. This connection is all the more tempting in the case of Marker's film because, again, it is a connection staged—if only in lexical pantomime—by the ambiguities of its very name. To these I will return after bringing out some further points about the mechanics of cinema that should help to gloss such wavering valences even in their related linguistic register.

Let me first advert to a cinematic happenstance as a way of coming round—via the relation of the phases/faces (rather than faces/vase) syndrome of *Dr. Jekyll and Mr. Hyde*—to the flickering-in-eclipses of the cinematic chain. I refer to the manner of producing the transformations of Jekyll into Hyde in the 1941 film version with Spencer Tracy (as well as in previous cinematic adaptations going back to 1912).[11] By the device of superimposition, one avatar of self fades away as the other materializes behind or upon it, the successor self getting stabilized only at the completion of the overlapping dissolve. Any number of other scenic evocations or editing tricks *might* have been used. So that at the level of directorial decision, this device is only a probability, not a structural inevitability. Yet at the level of film history, and the very evolution of its syntax, such a laboratory effect encapsulates a longer view of such technical devices.

This is the view, outlined and exemplified by Christian Metz, whereby the history of editing codes in the cinema is in part the record of the gradual naturalizing of special or trick effects (*trucage*). Superimposition (to choose one of Metz's examples, 666) was once perceived as all magic, all trick— and inevitably foregrounded as such, part of the available spectacle of early cinema. This remained the case until, over time, the device became normalized (in Metz's terms, de-diegeticized)—transferred from message to code—as the operable grammar of temporal and spatial transition in film narrative. To borrow from Stevenson, it was as if the lap dissolve comes eventually to be read not to mark a fantastic simultaneity of "faces" but to generate the "phases" of a narrative as dovetailed episodes. In order for the werewolf-style special effect of *Dr. Jekyll and Mr. Hyde* to operate again as the monstrous, as the preternatural rather than the merely grammatical, it must negotiate in this way a certain return of the media-historical repressed: a reactivation of the unnerving artifice of imposed overlaps. In so doing, it becomes the exception that proves the rule of this general outmoding of original narrative topos by sheer editing technique. The resurgence of such a device as figure rather than grammar, in short, manifests a return of form as content.

Linguistic evolution may occasionally operate in much the same way, with a tension between syntax and lexicon that, over etymological time, turns a too easily mispronounced phrase such as "a napple" into "an apple" (Jesperson 133). If "at ease" had once been "a tease," then a moment such as that mentioned above in Keats's "Ode on a Grecian Urn" would be the reanimation of a linguistic fossil. One does not need a specific etymological contingency of this sort, however, to apprehend a general tendency. It is a tendency never far from impinging on—even while readily overridden by—the local histrionics (rather than history) of language at play and at risk in a given literary text. The tendency is that of lexical border crisis under shifting syntactic duress. The point I now wish to clarify is the way in which this crisis finds an unexpected parallel in the constitutive suppression of differential advance in the photogrammar of the filmstrip: a temporal specificity apart from all special effects.

Cinégation as *Écriture*

In "The Ideological Effects of the Basic Cinematographic Apparatus," Jean-Louis Baudry speaks of the cinematic phenomenon in explicitly psychoanalytic terms. Cinematic images seize attention by means of denial, repression, and negation. In regard to the minimal differentia of images on film, Baudry seeks to demonstrate that cinema as process operates by "the denial of difference: difference is necessary for [cinema] to live, but it lives on its negation" (Baudry 290). This process depends on an enforced cognitive succession—rather than disjunctive series—of photograms clamping down on the unconscious "as it is found in dreams, slips of the tongue, or hysterical symptoms." In this way does the unconscious, if released, find manifestation "as continuity destroyed, broken, and as the unexpected surging forth of a marked difference" (290).

With film and consciousness both understood as networks of containment, of suppressed disruption, the unspoken third term for Baudry is writing. But it is not unspoken for long: "Couldn't we thus say that cinema reconstructs and forms the mechanical model (with the simplifications that this can entail) of a system of writing [*écriture*] constituted by a material base and a countersystem (ideology, idealism) which uses the system while also concealing it?" (291). We can. But only, once more, with the provisos that (1) in certain discursive situations the concealment incident to such writing is not so extreme as the discourse analysis of an Antony Easthope would suppose, and that (2) in those same situations—call them literary moments as such—the unruly deviations of marked *différance* do not get conceptually degraded to inscribed marks per se. Film is, in short, so perfect an illustration of Derrida's "trace" that it reminds us of the term's inevitably metaphoric status in the not purely visual (graphological) medium of literature, with its system of double articulation rather than (as in cinema) a mechanized indexical relation to an action once before the camera.

Baudry's own claims are indirectly renewed (without explicit comparison) by the work of Marie-Claire Ropars-Wuilleumier. In an "antidisciplinary" survey not unrelated to the cross-disciplinary links attempted by this essay, John Mowitt's *Text* gives considerable space to Ropars's work. For Mowitt, its interest rests with the way Ropars theorizes the film image "by first showing how its effacement of the spacing (the enunciative ordering) that conditions the image (as a recognizable visual phenomenon) makes film complicit with phonecentrism [phonocentrism], that is, the ideological system that, among other things, reduces writing to a seamless representation of speech" (Mowitt 170). Instead, Ropars unravels the seams. She sets out (and we turn here to her own translated essays) to deconstruct speech precisely as it founders on "the space of intervals" ("Film Reader" 26). She is concerned, therefore, with its "overlapping of multiple circuits, both heterogeneous and simultaneous" (26). In a parallel reading of a novel by Maurice Blanchot and a film by Alain Resnais, Ropars claims to have "pushed the deconstruction of the sign by the overlapping of letters to its most vertiginous point" (26). She does so, for instance, through the byplay latent in Blanchot's *L'Arrêt du mort* on the proper noun "Louise" (with its hidden "oui") and the pronoun smuggled into the enunciation "ote elle" (26). When Ropars takes up a similar impaction of syllabic matter in "Nevers," a town in the remembered past of the heroine in *Hiroshima mon amour*, the place-name is found overlain in context with, among other monosyllabic infratexts, *verre* (glass), *vers* (toward), and *vert* (green).

This "process of unbinding" directed on "the intertangling and reciprocal disintegration of the elements where meaning is undone" (30) is extended in another of her essays (as it will soon be in my own) to the homophonically loaded title of a single film, in her case Godard's *Breathless*. On Ropars's hearing, the "cinéscripture" ("The Graphic" 147, 158) of the film's French title, *À bout de souffle*, reveals how a "single graphic tracing ('*souffle*') . . . generates elements ('*sous*') which are figurable or phonetically combinable into 'souvenirs brises' (broken memories)" (151). As in the case of Cohen's "anti-mimetic" disturbances earlier, there often appears something forced rather than found in her examples, anything but immanent, yet the general claim may hold. The analytic rather than just synthetic power of cinema, conceived as writing, is such that "editing" (she means the internal exertions of the whole montage system) has the "ability to make the alphabet err into protean anagrams," materialized on "multiple channels" (158).

This is, in short, the "hieroglyph hypothesis" (158), and it comes nearest to my own formulation about the recurrence of a transegmental drift at lexical borders when Ropars asserts that this alphabetic errancy is engaged only "if the voice frees from the hold of the written word the text whose mark it will continue to bear" (159). To cast this in the explicit grammatological terms that she repeatedly courts: The "multiple channels" of signification interfere with each other in a shaking off of the letter that involves, at the same time, a further shackling to the trace.

Words S/Crawling By, Text T/Racing On: Toward a Dialectics of Succession

Ropars's "hieroglyph hypothesis" of course calls to mind the more famous "ideogram hypothesis" of half a century before. It is indeed Sergei Eisenstein who may lead us to a closer tie between the phi effect of the filmic apparatus and the ripple effect of cinematic *écriture*. For it was Eisenstein who defiantly minimized the element of succession itself in the filmstrip, subsuming sequence instead to a perceptual dialectic. Despite the rolling-past of images, film does not *read* as a textual scrolling but rather as a reciprocal displacement and mutual exclusion of image flashes. This is the base level of Eisenstein's claims for the destabilizing essence of the montage principle apart from—and before—an actual montage sequence. Eisenstein drives his ideogrammatic thesis (signification through visual collision) past even the contrasts within a single shot down to the vanishing borders between single photograms in the process of projection. Though on the strip we have the successive and sequential displacement of one image by its adjacent other, in the phenomenality of screen viewing, Eisenstein insists, there is no patient sequence of frames. There is only the instantaneous superimposition of one upon the other in that mix of sameness and difference—of perpetually deferred self-identity, if you will—that transforms the race of photograms into the fact of film: a continuously unsettled palimpsest. "For, in fact, each sequential element is perceived not *next* to the other, but on *top* of the other" (105)—in a perceptual "conflict" (105) that generates not so much the moving image (images are already speeding by) but the held image of another and *represented* motion, one autonomous rather than automated. Cinema is, in short, a conflictual tension that looks like action. It is, in a word, dialectical.[12] And to retrieve Eisenstein's dead metaphor for my literary model, some of the intervals involved in the conflicted lexicality of literary momentum do become all but "audible" in their graphonic syncopation. They do so through a process that grammatology itself would recognize as a "'dialectic' of protention and retention" (Derrida, *Of Grammatology* 117): the continuous alter(n)ation of phonemes and constitutive *blancs*.[13]

We are therefore ready to consider how the dialectical tension of the photogrammatic sequence takes what might be sensed as its homologous lexical toll on the narrative as well as the title of Chris Marker's *La Jetée*. In ways almost uncannily matched to the ironies of the film's tacit psychoanalytic plotting, its self-mutating title is a gestalt all its own, now alternative noun phrases, now wavering full clauses. Framing the story's post-Proustian allegory of psychic time travel, in a narrative pitched between science-fiction thriller and existential reverie, the uninvolving phrase *La Jetée* refers most obviously (and trivially) to the jetty (or outdoor passenger platform) at Orly airport, the walkway—and psychological transit zone—that locates the story's primal scene of eroticism and death. It was there, as a young boy, that the hero, smitten with a woman's face, saw what he realized only later must have been a man murdered. World War III follows precipitously, and in the aftermath the hero is made the subject of psychological experiments designed to send him back into his own fixated past as a way of training him for projection into the future, where he can gain access to the power supply necessary to keep the present remains of civilization moving along on its way into just that future. When the hero seeks finally to escape the underground laboratory of these experiments, he finds, back again on the jetty, that it was his own death that he had once (fore)seen—finds, in other words, that in the very moment and the very fact of going back again he has obliterated his own future, has killed off his own succession from boy to man.

It is according to something like this double pattern of anticipation and retrospection—or in an extrapolation from Derridean trace to the track of plot, of protention versus retention as a narrative double-cross—that the title begins to unravel its layers of imbricated syntactic pertinence. At issue here is of course not the instance but the principle. It does not matter for my argument that any given film text (whether by Marker or Godard) indulges in lexically erosive wordplay, but that all films perform something like the cinematic counterpart of this frictional byplay in the confounding (as well as foundational) overlap of simultaneity upon succession. For Joan Copjec's psychoanalytic reading of Marker's film, in which the plot turns on the hero's psychotic incapacity to disengage from the libidinal cathexis of an obsessional childhood image, the title ironically evokes that throwing-off, that "ejection," which has failed to release him (Copjec 36). In my reading, however, the lexical dynamic of the phrasing sustains a multiple self-ejection that removes all priority and therefore all possible exile. What it sustains is exactly that paradox of simultaneous alternatives that, in terms of the plot's time-loop narrative, presents for its spatiotemporal agent an impossible double bind.

Ventrilogos

A related example may justify a brief further delay. Postponing the analytic breakdown of Marker's (two-, three-, or four-word) title along its shifting internal fault lines, a comparison may be drawn from the actual soundtrack of another film. Though equally concerned with the parapraxis of the unconscious, the destabilizing overlays incident to dream life, this cinematic narrative does not intervene quite so irruptively in its own medium, as *La Jetée* does, to theorize the photogram's place in the metonymic slide of desire. The film I am thinking of, also a time-loop narrative in the genre of the uncanny, is the 1945 British thriller *Dead of Night*. It narrates, and hence comes to inhabit, a weird recurrent dream in which, by a dizzying regress, the participants tell the dreamer stories of their own uncanny past. The last of these, from a psychiatrist who happens to be on hand, concerns a ventriloquist's dummy who gradually siphons off the life of his master. This last inset story is launched in the retrospective telling by a marked narrative framework laying bare nothing less than sound cinema's own constitutive ventriloquism (human images wedded to voices issuing from a separate source): a close-up on a legal affidavit timed to the detached voice-over of the psychiatrist who is silently reading the narrative deposition to himself.

Inside the subsidiary plot evolved in this way, the first scene with the ventriloquist introduces us at once to the facile punning that characterizes his stage act. Hugo, the aggressive dummy, mishears his master's phrase, "Why, Hugo, that's clairvoyance" (in response to the dummy's offer to read a pretty customer's thoughts), and instead introduces himself to the woman with a vaguely lascivious "Good evening, Clair." From here out, the dummy's patter, onstage and off, is laced with just such puns, right down to the moment when he threatens to desert his master for a rival ventriloquist. The master seeks reassurance that Hugo would never leave, and the latter's ominously repeated "Wouldn't I?"—with its fleeting homophonic ambivalences—returns for threefold iteration in the violent finale of the frame narrative's encompassing nightmare. There, the hero, the original recurrent dreamer, has openly taken up the position of the ventriloquist (all dream avatars being merely the "throwing" of one's own voiced—or otherwise manifested—desires into the figure of the other) and finds himself being strangled to death by the dummy.

Now all articulation is the latter's alone. Where before there was a trisyllabic noun operating as phonemic rebus for a proper name (clairvoyance = Clair Voyance), at this point the homicidal enunciation of "Wouldn't I" installs a more lexically splintering torsion. From its obvious status as contracted rhetorical question, the wrenched because overinflected phrasing vacillates—as if sounded once for each of three possible decodings—between the slurred "wooden I" of the dummy's asserted identity (carved as well as constructed) and the too crisply enunciated "wouldn't die" of his homicidal self-preservation.[14] That last valence of this ambivalent phrasing is thereby rotated in rapid, emphatic repetition to "I wouldn't die." This stands—or, better, slips out from under itself—as a low modernist example of the same phonemic torque that springs that mystic transfiguration in Forster's *A Passage to India* (1922) by which the name Mrs. Moore, via the syllabic laxity of "Miss/es Moore," gets r/evolved into the Hindu goddess "Esmiss Esmoor" (225), its own bilingual version of what Forster calls in a different context "a religious pun, not a religious truth" (276).[15]

In that climactic repetition from *Dead of Night*, like the broken record of a denatured voice, we cannot, certainly on first viewing, be sure exactly what we have heard. What limits the interest of this example for my present argument is simply that we *have* heard it, however we decide to take it—that the relation of language to dreamplay, to the condensations and displacements of the unconscious, is in this case sounded out (and so *potentially* disambiguated) rather than merely, as in literary writing, inscribed for a ventriloqual if silent enunciation of our own. The latter case of hovering halftones in the reading experience, of course, involves a variety of phantasmal manifestation at least as close as is the audiovisual materiality of film to the undecidable fluxions—though not of course the specularity—of the unconscious. More than with the reception of continuous motion on film, however, such reading defers with a nervous resistance to those instantaneous deferrals of signifying elements that make for cognitive engagement with film and literary text alike. Encountered on page rather than screen, and maximized as *écriture*, is a signifying energy that can at any moment seem spun from the marginal doubling, duping, or punning—the overlapping "slant rhyme"—of a verbal shape (as in Stevenson's homophonic gothic) fractionally out of phase with the passing alterity for which it rushes to substitute itself.

Here I depart from Ropars, if only by taking her own logic a step farther. On her view, "vertical montage," the layering for instance of aural upon visual effects, opens that undecidable space of *différance* that is exactly what turns audiovisual automatism into "cinéscripture." I wish, though, to follow this lead into the plane of "horizontal montage" as well, and its cellular constituents. There, by analogy with the "fracture internal to every graphic trace" ("Film Reader" 28), film is found to operate only by performing in eclipses its own version of an incremental default in continuity. Yet this jagged differential operates both to engineer and define a technological motion that simulates another sort of movement, and that does so by a vertical superimposition after all: Eisenstein's dialectic of frame advance as a tensed perceptual laminate rather than graded progression.[16]

Sans son: The Self-Jettisoned Signifier

The lexical and syntactic lamination of Marker's title, we are now primed to recognize—its dialectic conflation, I am now ready to argue—says it all, if only because its mode of saying is replayed within his film's most famous scene of liminal cinematic signification, its photograms coming awake as cinema. I have been delaying discussion of this title, this titular common noun phrase, until what I want to call its climactic *gratuitousness* for my argument should be obvious. Even when activated so that it "undercorrects"—and so undermines—the normative work of utterance, this phrasing as such remains one more "literary" example. At the same time, its relation to the analytic breakdown of filmic flow within this one film lends it an exemplary (if not explanatory) frisson. In its own frictional anamorphonics, it offers an isomorph of filmic articulation. More specifically, it evokes that cinemachination whose constitutive effects were necessarily more obvious in the "primitive" (and so in its own way modernist) phase of the medium's history. For what *La Jetée* recovers for strategic deployment, the new mimesis of the early cinema could not help but disclose, at least until developments in "flicker fusion" smoothed over the very traces of photogrammatic origin. It is in this sense that cinema as a modern representational system sheds a kind of stroboscopic light on the graph/phonic (graphonic) segues of letteral as well as visual signification.

How, then, is this line of thought entitled, finally, by the unprepossessing designation of Marker's film? The first break with lexical borders begins with the elision that would permit *Là j'étais* (the imperfect mode of a continuous past: "There I was") to emerge by close echo with the inscribed *La Jetée*, offering on the sly the hero's locative testimony of original and abiding presence on the jetty of his memory. No sooner has narrative displaced the naming of its in/augural (because ominous) dramatic site—by verbalizing at the same time the avowed presence to that place of the protagonist—than this elegiac clause begins stripping its linguistic gears. It slips or drifts, in other words, toward a more precisely demarcated temporality in its slide from imperfect to perfect mode: the homophonic (and further elided) over-tone of *Là j'ai été* ("There I have been").[17] This is a phrasing shadowed in turn by the faint adverbial expectancy of something like "once" or "often" or "until just now"—but no longer. For in the *there* of that having been, no here and now sustains its foothold. Even the past itself melts away toward the conjectural in yet a third modal overlay of the composite verb form: this time the past subjunctive ("[que] là j'aie été"), as in "I believed (hypo-thetically) that *I had been there*," with adverbial predication suspended in the ontological as well as grammatical limbo of all things "contrary to fact." Such is the last gesture of presence for a life lived wholly in the mood—as well as mode—of conjectural retrospect. If any verbal alternative of this sort occurs to or accurses our ears, bedeviling the linearity of this particular mimesis, then we are all the more likely to allow Marker's overcrowded title a last sem/antic latitude. The slippage would insinuate, this time, a less than strictly grammatical figure for the ironized season of an at once unrecover-able and inescapable past: *l'âge été*, that phantasmatic summer before the fall.

In all this we are registering a more site-specific and grammatically con-cretized (however fractured) version of the errant cinéscripture theorized and spottily audited by Ropars, whose suitably involuted formulation I take space to repeat: the sliding signifier of deconstruction does its work only "if the voice frees from the hold of the written word the text whose mark it will continue to bear." It is in this sense, and within a literary-historical framework, that I have hoped to elaborate on what Ropars has set herself more locally to demonstrate, namely, the "capacity of montage to con-stitute an operator of reading" ("Film Reader" 30). This is a montage, in Marker's case, only at its reductive lower limit. It is a montage that struc-tures the almost visible *succession*, not just the self-succeeding visibility—the almost visible *différance*—of the cinematographic series. This is a series built upon the enchained photogram that differs from, but only by way of de-ferring, the phantasmal (and fractionally discrepant) double that is always overtaking it in order to take it over—or in Eisenstein's sense of dialecti-cal superimposition, in order to put one over on it, one of the same-but-different.

To return, then, to our final example: That all of this greased significa-tory slippage along the gathering creases of adverb, pronoun, and verb in their various contractions and decontractions (enunciatable on the run as *l'/là/âge/je/j'/é/ai/aie/été/ais*) should transpire to entitle a film so strikingly keyed, in its one moment of cinematic activation, to the skid of photograms underlying the flow of motion seems to me one culmination of an impor-tant "modernist" strain (both senses) of textual procedure. By analogy with

Marker's unprecedented bringing to light of "persistence of vision" as a founding phenomenon of the moving image, we may therefore speak in connection with the literary text of a certain "persistence of (subvocal) audition." This is the lexical (per)severing or syntactic s(p)licing that makes for meaning even while generating a sense of wording in excess of words. In both literary and cinematic cases, as they happen to collaborate in *La Jetée* at textual as well as thematic levels, evanescence and loss do not rob meaning but constitute it. Cinema proceeds on the serial trace of a vanishing, a forgetting-in-progress that is dialectically infused into each new intrusion within the frame. Persistence of vision explains the retention of the ephemeral as the dialectical other of the suddenly arrived. So, too, with the passage of word after word into the cognitive frame of sequential syntactic positioning, with a rapidity that keeps lexical integrity at risk. The superimposition (Eisenstein's model transposed to script) of one word upon another may surrender a letter or two, and hence reshuffle the phonemic sequence—but only as a subvocal drift cresting over the inscribed blank with a force sufficient to draw off the trace of the predecessor for the materialization of the subsequent lexeme. It all happens in the flick of an inscription, the blink of an eye, the flash of an inner ear. To the extent that such a phenomenon thwarts (or at least multiplies and so postpones) mimesis, it does so not as its antithesis but as its analysis, degrammatizing the fluent in service to the constituent, while in the process "turning structure into event."[18]

Such is the enunciated (even when unspoken) fluxion, both form and overflow at once, that sustains the filaments of ambiguity across the gaping integument of script. This is an oscillation beyond all operable signifying, one that the rival medium of cinema works at once to mechanize and to mask. Within the context of an international modernism newly detached from traditional mimetic obligations in verbal as well as pictorial media, film's alternative visuality marks its distance from experimental writing not only, as image system, by the seen world it simulates but also, as text, and here the distance narrows, by the different means of difference required to sustain that illusion. Within a common microdialectic of form, film suppresses what modernist writing releases. Movies elide the gap, the splice, that all reading must honor and at the same time surmount—an intermittent eclipse of script that intensive literary reading further unsettles, vexing the interval in the self-regrouping drive of lettered sense. But this is not to deny, precisely not, that a filmstrip becomes a movie in much the same way that writing becomes text. For all the divergences between arbitrary and analogous signification, it might in this sense be observed—according to a different teleological destiny than is usually sketched for either medium—

that cinema makes good on everything in literature that it fails to outmode as mimetic system, even as literature is divesting many of its own representational mandates. In so doing, filmic process renders almost tangible, albeit invisible, something very close to the underlying textual dynamism of a literary writing with which cinema's manifest kinetic picturation would never, at least before Marker's extremity, expect comparison.

The filmstrip, too, like the sentence, is an articulated sequence of signs. Montage on screen is to the incremental collage on the strip what the read page is to lexical structure and its bordering blanks. Photogram as much as phoneme, therefore, must disappear into the processed unit of signification as its inner lining and its negative imprint, at one and the same time the rudiment and the undoing of its linear effect. In this way cinema lends itself to the ethos of modernism in part to make palpable not the strict binarism of the linguistic system so much as the more mobile and fluid counterplays on which the flicker effect — and flicker fusion — of literary writing is also, and always, mounted. Or, to bring the metaphor closer to home in this essay, try figuring these signifying vibrations within the aural register of silent text production: as evidence, once again, of that sonic waiver in reading that imposes no ban on subvocalization. In reading between words, we no sooner produce than we process the extraneous phonic enunciation. Still within the orbit of an emergent cinematic paradigm, here modernist writing gets its new lease on subliminal vocalization. Without the insulation against background interference ordinarily provided by discourse (a normative discourse that protects its lexical flanks), the flicker effect of literary writing is accompanied at intervals — exactly at lexical intervals — by sensed tremors that penetrate the sound barrier of standard inscription. Here is the sprocket noise of textual machination as the very engine of reading's second sense: a whir that is every so often urged toward wording by the listening eye.

NOTES

1. Since my argument for the "transegmental drift" as the lexical limit case of the literary "phonotext," two recent publications tend (I like to think) to confirm as well as extend my line of inquiry. Kittler, without mentioning Kristeva, historicizes the importance of maternal orality in the inculcation of phonetic principles in childhood reading (25–69) in a way that anticipates the "maternal" core (*chora*) of semiotic pulsion in Kristeva's work (Stewart 125, 270–71). So that "when later in life children picked up a book, they would not see letters but hear, with irrepressible longing, a voice between the lines" (Kittler 32). Part of this tendency toward the "oralization" of reading Kittler draws from Foucault's history of the linguistic episteme in *The Order of Things* (32). It is an earlier aspect of Foucault's work, on

the modernist literary experimentation of Raymond Roussel (Stewart 118–26), that has been taken up more recently by Douglas Kahn in "Death in the Light of the Phonograph: Raymond Roussel's *Locus Solus*" (Kahn and Whitehead 69–104): "Despite what has been noted as Foucault's antivisualism, he does not demonstrate any heightened sense of aurality; for him Roussel is text, that is mute" (70). So "Why listen to a Roussel novel?" asks Kahn (70), stressing the "homophonics" (72) of Roussel's post-phonographic inscription in a way that can be readily assimilated, as Foucault's own best examples go to show, to a notion of "text" that, however "mute," is not narrowly graphological.

2. See especially his and Linda R. Waugh's last chapter, punningly titled "The Spell of Speech Sounds" (181–234), for the application of certain phonological principles to literary structure.

3. For which Derrida himself is scarcely to be held accountable, having gone out of his way in both commentary and example to honor the phonematic stratum of language. Indeed, in "+ R (Into the Bargain)," he unites instance and exegesis when closing in on an explicitly cross-lexical wordplay in the opening line of a poem he published at age seventeen: "*Glas* emerges twice in it, in pieces, cut from itself, . . . once in a single word, once inapparent or inaudible, detached from itself by the chasm between two words: it is read, seen written or drawn, held to silence (etang *lait* [pond milk], entity [*étant*] become milk [*lait*] again" (161). It is just this "chasm between words" whose aleatory bridging I have called the "transegmental drift," and whose further workings this essay has set out to explore.

4. For a fuller discussion of the Derridean position and the confusion it has sometimes sown in its application by other critics, see Stewart 104–7.

5. Against the *epos* of the speaking voice Derrida stresses up to a point "the purely graphic stratum within the structure of the literary text within the history of the becoming-literary of literality, notably in its 'modernity' " (*Of Grammatology* 117).

6. For a testing on *Jane Eyre* of the theories of Nicholas Abraham and Maria Torok, I am indebted to Herman Rapaport's tentative integration of their version of psychoanalytic reading ("cryptonymy") with that of Lacan. Rapaport's claims about a "poetic of hauntedness" (1093) center on the mourninglike effects of those encrypted signifiers in Brontë that circle the unsaid bilingual *mère* both of Jane's patriarchal "nightmare" (1101) and of the orphaned Jane's own paternal name: the Law of the Father thus manifested and evaded at once in the "psychotic voices" (1103) of a signifying maternal Other. In the context of echoing phonic chains such as "ère, air, aware, beware, nightmare, glare, terror, but also eye, ire, Ireland, I, Vampyre, wild" (1098), Rapaport finds a subterranean "verbarium" strung together in Brontë's novel out of what Abraham and Torok call lexical "allosemes." These are ghostly, self-haunted echoes of one another slipping into signification along "paths of avoidance" (1107) that one might call repression were it not for their perpetual return, a return both within and upon themselves. As for the passage presently under discussion from *Jane Eyre*, my own sense of "ire" and "I" in relation to the "Eyre" of both "Ireland" and "Eyrie" finds such lexical dissemination taking a different "path of avoidance" — via the frictional erosion of what might instead be called overlapping "allophonic" variants.

7. In this specialized use of the term "matrix" (here and with the Stevens pas-

sage below), I allude to Riffaterre's *Semiotics of Poetry*, despite his own disinclination to operate at this phonemic level.

8. See William Veeder, "Collated Fractions of the Manuscript Drafts of *Strange Case of Dr. Jekyll and Mr. Hyde*" (Veeder and Hirsch 20).

9. See the treatment of such "appositive genitives" in Brooke-Rose 154–60, where perhaps the most immediately apparent example is "the fire of love" (154).

10. This continuity is also made possible by the projector's shutter interrupting the beam often enough (two or three times per frame at twenty-four frames per second) to mute or smooth the oscillating recurrence of nearly identical frames, thus inducing "critical flicker fusion" (Bordwell and Thompson 6).

11. See Veeder and Hirsch for an illustration of the 1912 instance (212), as well as for an earlier publicity shot, also involving superimposed images of the title characters, used to advertise an 1887–88 stage adaptation.

12. Metz has a similar point in mind when he declares that "montage itself, at the base of all cinema, is already a perpetual *trucage*, without being reduced to the *false* in usual cases" (Metz 672).

13. Without reference to Eisenstein's dialectic of succession as superimposition, Mowitt's account of Ropars's attempt to get past "the complicity between phonecentrism [*sic*] and iconic fetishism" (Mowitt 17) in the alignment of film with a grammatological model highlights her recourse to Eisenstein's concept of the ideogram, the composite signifier, or in other words, "the hieroglyph's graphic embodiment of a cohabitation of figurative, symbolic, abstract and phonetic elements" (Mowitt 171). Though Mowitt follows Ropars in a sense of spacing that extends far beyond my concern here with the Derridean *blanc* between words, still Mowitt's next formulation, and not least in its relation to Eisenstein's thought, coincides with my own emphasis on a "modernist" sense of the cinematic image in its constitutive failure (as in the case of the literary lexeme) entirely to coincide with itself: "From this perspective, filmic writing qualifies as 'writing,' not because it generates aesthetic effects (like literary writing), but because it is, in many ways, a consummately 'modern' articulation of the heterogeneous spacing that comprises writing *in general*" (Mowitt 171).

14. It is in the nature of these dialectical auditions that they often emerge from the dialogics of interpretative discussion. I am grateful to Jeff Netto for pointing out to me the second of these punning overtones, via the dental liaison that assimilates *t* to *l* in a context where, as it were, the *die* is immediately cast.

15. The locus classicus, whether before or after the fact, of any such rotational phrasing, all such spun punning, is of course Joyce. The famous section of the *Wake* that begins "O / tell me all about / Anna Livia" (196) quickly reiterates the command with "Tell me all. Tell me now" (196), only to close twenty pages later, after the speaker's identification with the insentient environs ("I feel as old as yonder elm" [215]), with "Tell me, tell me, tell me, elm!" (216), where the vocative syllable is transegmentally released from the belling repetition of the imperative form.

16. It should be clarified that Ropars uses the term "horizontal" (as in "Graphic" 148) in something of the way I am applying it above to the sequential unfolding of plot "phases" in *The Strange Case of Dr. Jekyll and Mr. Hyde*. This is not to be confused with the actual passage of the strip through the projector, which is in turn not the

sense of "vertical" when it is applied to the editorial (rather than projective) work of montage. Where "vertical montage" (Ropars-Wuilleumier, "Film Reader" 22) designates the layered elements that make up the projected ensemble of image and sound, "horizontal montage" captures the sense that this material elapses in time, moving from here to there (often *as if* laterally, and quite possibly by analogy with the left-to-right movement of the reading rather than viewing eye in Western culture) while the image track races (from top to bottom) through the projector.

17. My thanks to Nataša Ďurovičová for first calling to mind's ear this instance of the French perfect tense.

18. This was a phrase used by Michael Holquist to characterize my investigation when part of this essay was read as a conference paper at the University of Aarhus, Denmark, in 1994.

WORKS CITED

Barthes, Roland. *S/Z*. Trans. Richard Miller. New York: Hill & Wang, 1974.

Baudry, Jean-Louis. "Ideological Effects of the Basic Cinematographic Apparatus." *Narrative, Apparatus, Ideology: A Film Theory Reader*. Ed. Philip Rosen. New York: Columbia University Press, 1986. 286–97.

Bordwell, David, and Kristin Thompson. *Film Art: An Introduction*. New York: McGraw, 1990.

Brontë, Charlotte. *Jane Eyre*. Ed. Richard J. Dunn. New York: Norton, 1971.

Brooke-Rose, Christine. *A Grammar of Metaphor*. London: Secker and Warburg, 1958.

Certeau, Michel de. *The Practice of Everyday Life*. Trans. Steven F. Rendall. Berkeley: University of California Press, 1984.

Cohen, Tom. *Anti-Mimesis from Plato to Hitchcock*. Cambridge: Cambridge University Press, 1994.

Conrad, Joseph. Preface to *The Nigger of the "Narcissus," Typhoon, and Other Stories*. Baltimore: Penguin, 1963. 11–14.

Copjec, Joan. "Vampires, Breast-Feeding, and Anxiety." *October* 58 (Fall 1991): 24–43.

Dagognet, François. *Etienne-Jules Marey: A Passion for the Trace*. Trans. Robert Galeta with Jeanine Herman. New York: Zone, 1992.

Derrida, Jacques. *Of Grammatology*. Trans. Gayatri Chakravorty Spivak. Baltimore: Johns Hopkins University Press, 1976.

——. "+ R (Into the Bargain)." *The Truth in Painting*. Trans. Geoff Bennington and Ian McLeod. Chicago: University of Chicago Press, 1987: 155–81.

Easthope, Antony. *Poetry as Discourse*. London: Methuen, 1983.

Eisenstein, Sergei. "A Dialectic Approach to Film Form." *Film Theory and Criticism: Introductory Readings*. 2nd ed. Ed. Gerald Mast and Marshall Cohen. New York: Oxford University Press, 1979. 101–22.

Empson, William. *Seven Types of Ambiguity*. New York: New Directions, 1947.

Forster, E. M. *A Passage to India*. New York: Harcourt, 1924.

Foucault, Michel. *The Order of Things: An Archaeology of the Human Sciences*. New York: Random House, 1970.

Jakobson, Roman. "Linguistics and Poetics." *Essays on the Language of Literature*.
    Ed. Seymour Chatman and Samuel R. Levin. Boston: Houghton Mifflin, 1967.
    296–322.
Jakobson, Roman, and Linda R. Waugh. *The Sound Shape of Language*. 2nd ed.
    Berlin: Mouton de Gruyter, 1987.
Jameson, Fredric. *The Political Unconscious: Narrative as a Socially Symbolic Act*. Ithaca:
    Cornell University Press, 1981.
Jay, Martin. *Downcast Eyes: The Denigration of Vision in Twentieth-Century French
    Thought*. Berkeley: University of California Press, 1993.
Jesperson, Otto. *Language: Its Nature, Development, and Origin*. New York:
    Macmillan, 1922.
Joyce, James. *Finnegans Wake*. Harmondsworth: Penguin, 1976.
Kahn, Douglas, and Gregory Whitehead, eds. *Wireless Imagination: Sound, Radio, and
    the Avant-Garde*. Cambridge, Mass.: MIT Press, 1992.
Kittler, Friedrich A. *Discourse Networks, 1800/1900*. Trans. Michael Metteer, with
    Chris Cullens. Stanford: Stanford University Press, 1990.
McGann, Jerome. *Black Riders: The Visible Language of Modernism*. Princeton:
    Princeton University Press, 1993.
Marker, Chris. *La Jetée: Ciné-roman*. New York: Zone, 1992.
Metz, Christian. "*Trucage* and the Film." Trans. Françoise Meltzer. *Critical Inquiry* 3
    (1977): 657–75.
Miller, J. Hillis. "Impossible Metaphor: (Stevens' 'The Red Fern' as example)."
    Tropes, Parables, Performatives: Essays on Twentieth Century Literature. Durham:
    Duke University Press, 1990. 213–26.
Miller, Jacques-Alain. "Suture (Elements of the Logic of the Signifier)." Trans.
    Colin MacCabe. *Screen* 18.4 (1977–78): 24–34.
Mowitt, John. *Text: The Genealogy of an Antidisciplinary Object*. Durham: Duke
    University Press, 1992.
Rapaport, Herman. "*Jane Eyre* and the *Mot Tabou*." *MLN* 94 (1979): 1093–1104.
Riffaterre, Michael. *Semiotics of Poetry*. Bloomington: Indiana University
    Press, 1978.
Ropars-Wuilleumier, Marie-Claire. "Film Reader of the Text." Trans. Kimball
    Lockhart. *diacritics* 15.1 (1985): 18–30.
———. "The Graphic in Filmic Writing: *À bout de souffle*, or the Erratic
    Alphabet." *enclitic* special issue (1982): 147–61.
Stevens, Wallace. "The Noble Rider and the Sound of Words." *The Necessary Angel:
    Essays on Reality and the Imagination*. London: Faber & Faber, 1951. 3–36.
Stevenson, Robert Louis. *The Strange Case of Dr. Jekyll and Mr. Hyde and Other
    Stories*. Baltimore: Penguin, 1979.
Stewart, Garrett. *Reading Voices: Literature and the Phonotext*. Berkeley: University of
    California Press, 1990.
Veeder, William, and Gordon Hirsch, eds. *Dr. Jekyll and Mr. Hyde: After One
    Hundred Years*. Chicago: University of Chicago Press, 1988.

POETRY'S VOICE-OVER

A prevalent shorthand today associates the poem with "the voice of the poet," anchoring the language of poetry in the language of subjectivity. This is obviously the case for believers in self-expression, but it is equally the case in any discussion of the vatic role of poetry and the rhetoric of the high sublime. No matter how depersonalized the poetic voice may appear, the voice remains a calculus of the speaking subject. In fact, inasmuch as we talk about poetry, we assume poetry to be talking about us. I suggest that poetry begins to lose touch with its voice-over—its inspiring double and alien prompter—when it appropriates voice for the purposes of subjectivity. This is not a recent development, however, and I propose it in the spirit of Wittgenstein's remark that philosophy is a struggle against the fascination of words. Poetry may be a struggle *in* words against the allures of subjectivization. Poetry since the eighteenth century has been an exercise of the Kantian faculties. Poems are engines for affirming space, time, causality, and the unity of consciousness, registering Understanding as cognition, pleasure and pain as Judgment, will and desire as Reason: the Faculties, those blind mice (*Anschauung, Einbildungskraft, Verstand, Vernunft*) who persevere in their orthodontic regulation (straightening and ordering, sometimes involving extractions) of raw sensory experience— experience of the sort that constitutes subjectivity, which is the electromagnetic energy required for animating Cartesian puppetry (subjectivity does not include batteries). I bring up the Cartesian cogito, encased in the Enlightenment technology of Kant's "faculties," in order to emphasize the wizardry of the construct and to situate it *as* a construct (poems continue to be voice loops prerecorded by the Kantian faculties). The hypothesis of rational self-interest that underwrites the Cartesian as well as the Kantian projects is obviously askew, but poetry is still inspected for evidence of rational self-interest. This compulsion persists because poetry has a traditional association with subjectivity. I have in mind something far more archaic than the Romantic sublime, which is in fact concurrent with and thus responsive to Enlightenment claims for rationality as anchorage of identity. To address the subordination of poetry to the development of subjectivity, I recount some mythopoetic scenarios of poetic origins, inaugural episodes in the history of voice-over, for it is in precisely such scenes that we can detect a subjectivity inseparable from prosthetic augmentation.

This essay reiterates a simple point in a variety of ways, so it is best to state it bluntly at the outset. I would unsettle the customary association of poetry with subjectivity, for two reasons. First, I adhere to Foucault's familiar view of subjectivity as a social technique for producing and legislating—what else?—subjects ("Subject" 420). There is thus no innate subjectivizing impulse, no pure cry of the human, that is not socially stipulated or fabricated. By "voice-over" I mean the mode of production that authorizes these sounds of autonomous subjectivity—a point that will require further clarification and refinement since my concept of voice-over is intended in neither a wholly negative nor positive sense. Rather, voice-over doubles the voice, splitting its allegiance in ways that can be traumatizing as well as humanizing. It is, in Levinas's terms, exposure and risk: prayer, mantra (149). But more fundamentally, "the poet disappears behind his own voice," says Octavio Paz, "a voice which is his because it is the voice of language, the voice of no one and of all. Whatever name we give this voice—inspiration, the unconscious, chance, accident, revelation—it is always the voice of *otherness*" (160).

While poetry is one of the archaic acts of the species, it is not a primitive or unsophisticated one. Poets are "technicians of the sacred," in Jerome Rothenberg's sense, and I would emphasize the technological incentive. If poetry has on occasion been subject to attack, most famously by Plato, it is not because of the infractions of inspired simpletons but because poetry by definition utilizes the most sophisticated and volatile of our technologies—language. Furthermore, poetic traditions make a great display of *technē*, of the precise means by which the honeyed voice is skillfully engineered, even while masquerading at being engendered. Poetry is often likely to be an affront to the ideologues of the Republic, then, because it mounts a display, an extravagant show, of ways the "natural" is culturally styled.

Technē not only precedes but pre*codes* the subject, anchoring it in subjectivity by its appeal to natural force and primacy. The noun comes from the Latin verb "to throw [down]": *sub-jacere*. Heidegger's concept of *Geworfenheit* (thrownness) and Freud's hydraulic model of the unconscious are influential accounts of subjectivity as abasement. The enabling scenarios of poetry, however, do not imply a corresponding unilateral plunge—at least not without a corollary ascent. The culturally specific requirements of fidelity versus innovation admit, in either case, a vision of poetry as liminality, threshold, or twilight experience. The extremities are handsomely evoked in the Ostyak image of the tomcat: "There is a mill which grinds by itself, swings of itself, and scatters the dust a hundred versts away. And there is a golden pole with a golden cage on top which is also the Nail of the North. And there is a very wise tomcat which climbs up and down this pole. When he climbs down, he sings songs; and when he climbs up, he tells tales" (qtd. in Santillana and Dechend 96).

The tableaux discussed here reanimate certain primal episodes that illustrate the mythic protocols of the poetic voice enabled by its technical voice-over to converse with the dead, reassemble a crumbled cosmos, awaken and inhabit the phantasms of love and spiritual ascesis, enumerate theogonies, and even "do the police in different voices" (as in Eliot's first—Dickensian—title for *The Waste Land*). My topic is ostensibly poetic inspiration, but I have sought to estrange the familiar preconception that haunts the topic—the premise of an autonomous speaking subject—by substituting a different term: the voice-over. The substitution is suggested by certain traditionally authorizing primal scenes of poetic empowerment.

It is in the spirit of the primal scene, in Freud's sense, to regard the troublesome wish as traumatically manifested in masquerade. Pleasure, always compromised by reality, moves in detours, meanders, and entanglements. The act of creation, in whatever medium—whether in the flesh or by aesthetic extension into other materials—deposits a residue distinct from the literal outcome. This is a palpitation, a rhythmic cue that needs to be absorbed into a contextual sonority, an ensemble of polyrhythms. I have in mind a choice formulation of Freud's, when he contends that "palpitations that occur in hysteria and anxiety-neurosis are only detached fragments of the act of copulation" (96–97). In Freud's view of (in this instance) the Dora case, parental coition overheard by the child is preserved acoustically. Since the original acoustic cues were only fragmentarily available in the first place—and since sexual innocence turns out to be the perfect preservative, because it does not permit the child to assemble the fragments into a coherent representation—the sensory traces of the primal scene prompt a provisional embodiment. Perhaps because Freud was preoccupied with elucidating unconscious thoughts as evidence of an integral (if submerged) system, he overlooked a key implication: namely, that the mnemonic traces of the primal scene are preserved in the body. Freud identifies his patient's troubled breathing with her father's asthmatic huffing during coitus but fails to notice in this primal scene a primal symmetry: the life-bestowing heavy breathing is sheltered and continued in the life bestowed, which carries forward the breath principle of the (sexually) animated body. Dora breathes in gasps, replicating the paternal stammer of procreation. The fact of respiration is the unconditional precedent for sex; and sex, the unconditional proponent of life, germination. Freud regards breathing as a latent memory of sex but does not see that sex is itself *the primal scene of breathing*.

Freud was still caught up in the metaphysics of anamnesis or recollection, in which the present moment always refers back to a prior occasion. Yet his thought was inspired by biology, which at the phylogenetic level works as a system of productive overflow and expenditure, not retention as implicit in his topography of the primal scene. The primal scene labors on behalf of production, not recollection; projection, not commemoration. The full pressure of coital abandon blurs rather than reinforces boundaries of the self. To procreate is literally to forget or lose oneself, a point reinforced by the radical proximity of sex with death (not only linguistically, but biologically in the case of certain animal species). Freud curiously "remembers"—to use the term in a sense antithetical to his—the function of the primal scene in the reiterative primal scenario of analysis, in which the analyst is self-effacing, saying little or nothing, and by this instructive abstinence lending all the breath, the *inspiration* as it were, to the patient. It is a mutual if imbalanced pact, since the moment the "talking cure" is terminated, the activated voice is perpetuated by the analyst in the surrogate medium of *writing*. Dora leaves, but Freud painstakingly revisits *her* words, generating in the process his own. Freudian theory is literally a rewriting of linguistic pathogenesis. The patient's disclosures presuppose concealment, as Freud surmised, yet what is hidden is not withdrawn from circulation but preserved on behalf of it. *Concealment preserved*: this is the very definition of a hermetic tradition, and Hermes, after all, is patron of boundaries, thresholds, and interpretation.

Writing and "inspiration" are thoroughly implicated in this epicycle of primal scenes. "The primal scene is always the primal scene of words," writes Ned Lukacher, in which "voice has always been a mode of distortion and concealment, for along with its promise of presence, voice has also proclaimed, by virtue of its 'fading,' a haunting message of distance and absolute separation" (68, 80).[1] It is not surprising that Lukacher's subtly polyphonic interweaving of Freud, Heidegger, Nietzsche, Derrida, Lacan, and Barthes should impinge so on the question of writing. Not only are these authors themselves preoccupied with language and with both acoustic and grammatological signs, but they are all mesmerized by the *inconsolability of transmission*, by the thought that every act is compromised by the medium of its enactment. The radical interdependence of inspiration and breathing, spirit and act, reveals an act helplessly repetitive and dependent. By choosing to call the mythopoetic scenarios of poetic inception "primal scenes," I adhere to the paradoxes of an *enabling disablement* and a *superior subordination*. The episodes I have focused on retain a sense of incommensurability between voice and voice-over; but that is as it should be, given the fact that I regard voice-over as *empowerment* with an attendant sense of *ambiguous gratification*.

The poet's individual voice is too frail to attain prominence by itself. This is not simply to conflate voice-over with inspiration. Instead, I follow the lead of Lacan and Althusser, identifying a certain power of the free-floating voice to affix itself with uncanny exactitude on the seemingly innocent bystander—the "hey you" that they call *interpellation*. The voice of the poet, then, is a calling, and in turn hails us in the mode of an ideologically prefabricated voice-over. I do not mean to suggest by this anything in the way of the formulaic (whether positively, as in oral recitation, or negatively, in the poetaster's flailing). The voice-over as it coalesces around poetic voice is not purely ideological. Like the witches' cauldron in *Macbeth* it brews to a fine broth the unpalatably dense residue of plots that need leavening and watering down to be properly heard. For that reason the myths suggest a divine source for the voice-over, as is the case with Hesiod's Muses, who select a specific poet as medium precisely because the *concentrate* of their utterance has no purchase on human ears otherwise. From a different perspective, that of ideology critique (which may be nothing other than the anamorphic shape of mythopoeisis), the notion of an individual voice serves as subpoena for an entire cultural habitus, a way of disposing as personal and inviolable something that has been dictated, by ventriloquism, well in advance of the poem itself.

The contemporary media environment is saturated with stagings of voice-over, to the extent that we are hard pressed to imagine a naive one-on-one encounter with a poem. Film subtitles, prerecorded sales pitches, audience sampling calls at dinnertime, canned laughter, public address systems, intercoms, musical overdubs, background music, lip-sync, karaoki, catastrophe footage with broadcast voice-over, and sportscasters reviewing instant replay all converge in a congestion of voice-over scenarios. It is not surprising that one of the most popular recent television shows is "Murphy Brown," about television's talking heads whose drone accompanies a world on view, starring the daughter of a ventriloquist who spent his career doing voice-over for his lap dummy. Murphy herself is a cue card for a generation; her angst and trials of identity serve to reconnect the demographically pinpointed audience with its hippie youth, its yuppie success, and its politically correct maturity. The driving force behind Murphy's character is music, specifically Motown, an icon that provides yet another complex cultural interface. Murphy Brown is energized as well as guided by the sonorous voices of the music, and the tacit message of Murphy's attachment to Motown is that subjectivity requires an aesthetic (poetic) support: self-consciousness is a voice-activated technology.

Contemporary monitors and transmitters of heritage—including textbooks, prefaces and introductions to anthologies, and reviews in *The New York Times Book Review* and elsewhere—participate in the voice-over function. The voice-over lays out guidelines, coordinates the reader's attention, and delineates the territory native to what is called "the poet's voice." The poet's voice has long been our cultural paradigm for a voice that compels assent by imputing to all who hear it an agreement about its priority. The poet's honeyed voice is a benchmark of the irresistible, the voice one cannot help but attend to. The poet's voice, complicit with a cultural voice-over, is intimately bonded to ecstatic inertia. Stunned with gratitude, we gape openmouthed at the sound of a voice, a voice ringing in our ears in the museum headset: the voice of the other implanted directly in our heads, a technical effect, a consoling voice-over.

Primal Scenes: *Technē* 1

Hesiod, a shepherd tending his lambs on the flank of Mount Helikon, is rudely addressed (in the plural) by the Muses: "'Shepherds [*Poimenes*] of the wilderness, wretched things of shame, mere bellies, we know how to speak many false things as though they were true; but we know, when we want to, how to tell the truth.' So said the ready-voiced daughters of great Zeus, and they plucked and gave me a rod, a shoot of sturdy laurel, a marvellous thing, and breathed into me a divine voice to celebrate things that shall be and things that have been; and they bade me sing of the race of the blessed gods that are eternally, but ever to sing of themselves both first and last" (*Theogeny* 1.26–35). To be inspired by the Muses is to be filled with their spirit, their breath or *pneuma*, which may or may not coincide with truth. (For this reason Plato expelled poets from his Republic, since in their trances they were out of their minds, unreliable citizens, blithely vocalizing words not their own, and worse, words that the Muses concede might be untrue but the veracity of which cannot be confirmed.) There is ventriloquism at work here, in this confidential insinuation of another's voice into one's own mouth and words. And the truth of words is henceforth bound up with the problem of "voice" as a security deposit for any subsequent claim of authenticity.

The lesson of Hesiod and the potential duplicity of the Muses is a lesson about language and about voice. For Hesiod, taking dictation, the voice precedes the words. That is, the voice compels transcription as immediate obligation. The semantic content of the words received in such a state is beyond mediation. Hesiod willingly becomes a radio transmitter or a solid-state amplifier for the Muses, and this is not rational. He succumbs to the glamour of the voices that croon the words, inaugurating a condition that has plagued poetry ever since: for to cede authority to the Muses, with their acknowledged power of duplicity, is to concede the unsuitability of the logos as a means of distinguishing true from false. The logos, with its "vicarious, rhetorical, supplementary nature," precipitates ambiguity and duplicity, and it is implicit that those who throw in their lot with the Muses may be intent on dissimulation (Pucci 19).

Poetry emerges, under Hesiod's proxy authorship (first among ancients to attach his personal name to his poem), as a way of pondering a bifurcation in language itself. Insofar as writing is thought to succeed orality, writing assumes control of an echo. Writing is, in effect, the ventriloquial means of transposing an acoustic event onto an optic event, thereby pacifying the sensory incertitude of hearing by substituting another sense as legislator. The proprioceptive and exteroceptive ambiguities of sound are suspended, as the voice is fixed by graphic interception. Such a paradox makes poetry the phantom double of language. By means of its metrics (measure) poetry displays a stylistic control that is not supported by semantic control, for the truth or falsity of what is said is referred to the inscrutable Muses; and the measures of the poem can support the parasitic violence of falsehood.

A rift is thus introduced between the mind and the tongue, thought and word. A mythopoetic prototype is the nymph Echo, who suffers perpetual grief at the dislocation of her voice, its unchecked proliferation in a state of nature.[2] The mocking multiplication of Echo's voice by the streams, cliffs, and forest glens dispels the aura of speakerly control in ways that parallel Hesiod's mimicry of the Muses. But surely all words are echoes in an unending babble — this is the *turf* of that subterranean darkbook *Finnegans Wake* — an echolalia of prolific sentience that stirs tongues as well as leaves on trees. For the Tukanos of the Columbian rain forest, the word for "measure" is also the word for "echo," *keori*. An echo, in other words, is "the measure of sound." It is instructive to compare the synaesthetic connotations of rain forest echo-measures with those measures or *metrics* of a poetry that develops in concordance with the measuring *ratios* of Western rationality.[3] On the shore of Walden Pond Henry Thoreau came to a different estimation of Echo: "The echo is, to some extent, an original sound, and therein is the magic and charm of it. It is not merely a repetition of what was worth repeating in the bell, but partly the voice of the wood; the same trivial words and notes sung by a wood-nymph" ("Sounds"). The words may be trivial, but the sound is original, casting a spell or charm; and spells and charms return us to the archaic mantic provocations of poetry before it is fully distinguished from prophecy.

It is the echo that certifies the strangeness of identity, the peculiarity of repetition and self-sameness. Robert Frost's poem "The Most of It" is a revolt against the intolerable monomania of the repetition compulsion, registered in a fear of echoes:

> He thought he kept the universe alone;
> For all the voice in answer he could wake
> Was but the mocking echo of his own
> From some tree-hidden cliff across the lake.
> Some morning from the boulder-broken beach
> He would cry out on life, that what it wants
> Is not its own love back in copy speech,
> But counter-love, original response. (451)

Frost goes on to envision originality as a wilderness creature, an "embodiment that crashed / In the cliff's talus on the other side" that turns out to be a buck, as if to confirm in advance Deleuze and Guattari's notion of "becoming-animal": "Singing or composing, painting, writing have no other aim," they write, but "to unleash these becomings" (272). "Becoming-animal" is for them complicitous with rhizomatic proliferation, "following alogical consistencies or compatibilities" (250). It is not surprising, they insist, to find that "becoming and multiplicity are the same thing," or to discover that "the self is only a threshold, a door, a becoming between two multiplicities" (249). The stability of the self is threatened, for Hesiod, by a fear of contagious falsehoods, yet poetic inspiration necessitates exposing the self to this risk of infection. It is a justifiable concern if we recall instances of monstrous alliance such as the Minotaur or, more recently, Ahab's becoming-whale. But what is exposed here in this concern about truth and falsity is a deeper issue, which is that the true and the false are merely veils deflecting attention from the disturbing hybridity implied by inspiration. The voice of an other, penetrating the poet's consciousness, threatens to turn him into another species altogether, usurping his biological ground and leaving him scattered, trapped like the nymph Echo in alienating matter. In Frost's terms, at issue is not true and false but copy-speech and counter-love—both of which harbor a kind of madness.

The notion of poetry as madness or furor—the poet's eye "in a fine frenzy rolling"—is a late supplement to mythopoetic scenes of instruction. As the Chadwicks exhaustively elucidated in their three-volume survey of the world's oral literatures (1932–40), and as N. K. Chadwick summarized in *Poetry and Prophecy* (1942), mantic inspiration requires elaborate procedural controls. More recently, Penelope Murray has concluded that "the idea of poetic inspiration in early Greece differs in a number of important ways from subsequent conceptions. It was particularly associated with knowledge, with memory and with performance; it did not involve ecstasy or possession, and it was balanced by a belief in the importance of craft" (100). Hesiod's initiatory encounter is interpreted by Gregory Nagy as a conciliatory threshold in the creation of a "pan-Hellenic theogony" in which "the Muses have to come down from Helikon and go up to Olympus, through the intermediacy of Hesiod" ("Ancient Greek Poetry" 60). Nagy arrives at this conclusion by noting the parallel between the Muses' disconcerting ability to utter both truths and falsities and the Bee Maidens of Parnassos in the Homeric "Hymn to Hermes," who tell the truth when fed honey but lie when deprived of it. There is also a significant alliance being forged between poetry and prophecy. The "Hymn to Hermes" has to do with the rivalry between Hermes and Apollo, concluding with a significant exchange of implements that signals accord: Hermes gives Apollo his lyre, receiving the bees in return. Susan Scheinberg notes that "the imagery in which the bee maidens are clad, with its traditional evocation of both poets and seers, enables them to bring to a fitting close a hymn whose chief concern is the rivalry, and then the harmony, between the poetic and mantic spheres" (28).[4] Insofar as mantic divination provoked, for the Greeks, anxieties about accuracy (both of report and interpretation), these same anxieties will apply to poetry as long as it has prophetic connotations.

The archaic ambiguity about truth and falsity becomes, in late antiquity and the Middle Ages, a matter of concern in faculty psychology. As the medieval Jewish commentator Abraham Ibn Daud puts it, in a formulation close to those regarding the Muses and the Bee Maidens, the danger of imagination is that "sometimes it creates a false form . . . and sometimes it brings forth a true form" (qtd. in Cooper 39). The history of the transformation of the Greek concepts *phantasia* and *eikasia* into their Latin correlates, *fantasia* and *imaginatio*, is too involved to rehearse here.[5] But the underlying concerns derive from the role of the imagination and whether images are divinely inspired or a merely human production. The varied expositions of the matter, from Plato to the Neoplatonists and Aristotle to the Stoics, through Augustine and Maimonides, Aquinas and Dante, do not move out of the orbit traced here involving inspiration in poetry and prophecy, and mimetic repetition in the myth of Echo. Whether *phantasia* is an afterimage of sense experience, or an imprint in the soul from a divine source, it is subject to a dynamic of repetition or duplication. The Muses' acknowledged duplicity becomes, by the Middle Ages, a trauma of the incarnate rational soul, for whom fantasy can lead downward to carnal image or upward to divine vision: the way of regress and dissolute materiality versus the path of purification and ascesis.

The axis of ascent and descent is retained as a model of temporality in modern psychoanalysis, in part because of Freud's preoccupation with archaeology. The logic of the primal scene stipulates that phylogenesis is recapitulated in ontogeny, that extrapersonal (or species) trauma intervenes in the deepest reservoirs of individual psychosis. Deep time is retained, monstrously, in deep psychic space. Hesiod's, of course, was not a voyage into interiority, despite the Muses' eruption into the proprioceptive balance center of his ears. But, significantly, the Muses *do* bring him knowledge of the past, so Hesiod's concerns about the Muses, in this light, reflect the anxieties of historians and psychoanalysts alike in their concern with techniques for verifying the past. The soft spot in rationalism is not the present, which is under administrative control, or even the future, which is susceptible to forecasting and planning, but the past, which is at once delimited and thus tantalizingly inviting to review, yet maddeningly out of reach. The mantic resources of poetry propose themselves as "inspired" to the degree that they apprehend the past. Homer invokes the Muses' aid to enumerate the names of the ships and their captains headed for Troy:

Tell me now, Muses, dwelling on Olympos,
as you are heavenly, and are everywhere,
and everything is known to you—while we
can only hear the tales and never know—
who were the Danáän lords and officers? (II.254)

Despite this ancient urge to consult the Muses in order to get the facts straight, the skeptical tone that prevails in scholarship today suggests that even the most devoted readers of poetry favor form over content. Admittedly, we do not go so far as to regard poetry as an outright pack of lies. But documentary works like Doughty's *Dawn in Britain*, Pound's exhaustive rehearsal of the Adams administration, Olson's chronicle of Gloucester, or Susan Howe's captivity narratives tend to be characterized as idiosyncratic and unreliable. The poet's task may be capacious, but it is not seen as having any responsibility for information—a situation Ed Sanders sought to correct in his manifesto *Investigative Poetry*. Sanders's belief that "poetry should again assume responsibility for history" (3) might seem out of step with the times, but these "times" have prevailed since Aristotle elevated poetry above history, contending that "poetry is something more philosophic and of graver import than history, since its statements are of the nature rather of universals, whereas those of history are singulars" (9:6–7). Aristotle goes on to associate this universality with probability, implying that the law of averages favors poetic truth, which is replicable, whereas historic fact, being contingent, is unique. The Aristotelian distinction that prioritizes poetry as the vehicle of universality inaugurates voice-over as the prevailing concept, the legislative installation of an autonomous function (which comes to be known as the speaking subject), regulated as a probabalistic ratio. This formulation rushes the account, however, for I do not mean to suggest that Aristotle stipulates a robotic voice-over as the ideal average of the aggregate of speaking voices. But what Aristotle does establish is the tradition based on Hesiod's experience of the Muses' duplicity, in which the falsity of a voice may be converted, through the medium itself, into a simulated "truth," and that which is most common and replicable is misconstrued as the unique sign of individuation.

Aristotle's is thus an inaugural moment in the capture of poetry for information technologies, probabilistic thinking, and serial access memory. Poetry is not definitively linked to this endeavor until the Cartesian endowment of mathematics and poetry as formal languages, one commensurate with material extension, the other with the ego-logical requirements of intension and intensity that Milton convenes as the "paradise within." If mathematics constitutes the objective coordinates of modern Cartesian idealism, the subjective coordinates are engineered in poetry. The poem becomes implicated—particularly in the high sublime—in this uninhabitable but unforgettable dimension. The Cartesian cogito, transfigured into the Romantic ego, becomes a finitude resonating in the echo chamber of the infinite, the cogito replicating exponentially in the reflexive domain of self-reference. The residues of a haunting anxiety—the tension precipitated by the Cartesian split between mirroring idealisms of subject and object, each endowed with a private infinity—begin to accumulate a cultural legacy; so now we have a nostalgia for this trauma, a sentimentality aspiring to reclaim the authenticity of the original affront, a compulsion to repossess a primal rather than a merely derivative hurt. In its pursuit of this phantasm the poem — swollen with its Cartesian-Kantian-Hegelian-Freudian helium of the sublime — develops a squeaky novelty voice. Susceptible to hermeneutic delirium, its interpretations follow the path of hypermaterialization insofar as the poem itself is regarded as an ideal object, an object which is somehow distinct from the words on the page, an object that participates in that reverberatory hyperspace called "the tradition," which (thinking of Eliot's version) settles for an infinite regress as the proper image of its magnitude, or the magnitude (suggested by the concept of the sublime) to which it aspires.

Hesiod's legacy suggests that poetic interiority is mesmerizing because of its alterity. The poet's voice both is and is not that of the person, just as words are and are not true, and the force of an event retained in the mind is distinct from — and so develops differently from — the original stimulus. So if "The mouth of lyric is an ear" (Zwicky 336), then "the tongue is an eye" (Stevens, *Opus* 167). Poetry is a manifestation of such thresholds, conveyer of a delicious duplicity, as well as a doubling of resources. Language, transmitted by the Muses, is enriched but also disabled inasmuch as its semantic nature is ambiguated. Paradox is native to poetry as well as to philosophy, in the sense indicated by Louis Zukofsky's concise definition of poetry as "an order of words that as movement and tone (rhythm and pitch) approaches in varying degrees the wordless art of music as a kind of mathematical limit" (27). Poetry's words aspire to wordlessness in their musicality, and in their physicality poetry claims words as resources of embodiment, reconnecting poetry with music on another plane. In poetry, music is approached at two extremes, abstraction and concreteness, and the oscillation between them can make of poetry a "hyperanimacy" comparable to that which Ellen Basso attributes to the "powerful beings" of the rainforest Kalapo people, whose "multiplicity of essence or 'hyperanimacy' is coupled on the one hand with a multiplicity of feeling and consequent unpredictability and on the other with a monstrous intensity of some feeling or trait; hence powerful beings are dangerous beings" (69). These powerful beings turn out to incarnate the essence of music, and for the Kalapo, humans can only copy music, not originate it (a function reserved for language) (70).

When Zukofsky outlines the ways poetic musicality may be perceived, he cites the prospect of someone listening to Homer without knowing Greek, enabled thereby "to 'tune in' to the human tradition, to its voice which has developed among the sounds of natural things" (28). The voice reclaims for itself an alignment with natural sounds. Poetic voice is not strictly human, and this complicates the assumption that would place subjectivity at the center of poetic ambition. Poetry may not be humanizing, but dehumanizing. Sound, as Charles Olson said, is a dimension mankind has extended.

The reciprocity implied in Zukofsky's formulation, between natural sound and human voice, facilitates a suggestive reversal of Olson: the human is a dimension that has been extended by sound, and voice is the signature of this extension. Speech may be felt as reversible, as what is spoken invariably inducts its referents into that somatic interiority in cranium and solar plexus where the "things" of the world reverberate and are shaken apart seismically into an intangible *materia prima*, not unlike the way ultrasound pulverizes gallstones. We change ourselves by the sounds we make and practice these changes on the world evoked in utterance—that realm of the "infinite rehearsal" in Wilson Harris's telling phrase. In the Vedic heritage the word (*vâc*) is a pulsation that is integrated into a cosmological vibration (*spanda*) that generates and destroys worlds (Padoux 427).

Poetry is not a "language art" but a *play on words*—in several senses. It seeks to activate words in the dimension of sound. Words are an instrumental plectrum of beseeching sonorities. Poetry also plays in the sense of trading on semantic instabilities. Such play may seem too specific unless we recall that tropes themselves are a species of semantic multiplication, guided less by a spirit of replacement than proliferation, generation. The gift of the Muses compounds the sense that dread and wariness are indistinguishable from mastery and ecstasy. Poetic accomplishment is a threat, specifically the threat implied by an *accomplice*, a sacred share. Possession and dispossession are intertwined in the Muses's bestowal of voice-over to the poet's personal voice. To cite the legacy of the Muses in this way is to place poetic inspiration in the realm of prosthetic technologies, or elaborations of human propensities in alien material, ultimately adaptable to corporeal agency and recuperable to physiognomic identity. Inspiration is alienation, or at least *alieniloquiam*, "speaking otherwise." Hesiod's initiation into poetry is at once an affirmation of voice and a disturbance of identity.

The gift of the Muses becomes an insurgency in speech itself; speech as an originary inspiration is revealed to be a secondary mimicry, and the poet's authority is at once exalted by divine support and undermined by the Muses' acknowledgment that they tell lies as well as truth. This is of course much the same scenario concocted in what Derrida calls "Plato's Pharmacy," which adds yet another necessary source of anxiety to poetry's voice-over: writing. Poetic voice plays itself out, expends itself, grammatologically. According to Derrida, the empowering tropology of poetic language is also its downfall: "Metaphoricity is the logic of contamination and the contamination of logic" (149). The supplementarity with which writing contaminates speech is what Derrida means by dissemination: vocal force and mnemonic inspiration is expended (this is Plato's fear) in writing, but what is worse, these degrading expenditures have the capacity to proliferate on their own, sow stray seeds, and reap their own vagabond crops. Insofar as poetry negotiates the transition from oral to written culture, then, it begins to accommodate ever more diverse and intolerable aspects of play—play as performance, play as juvenile, play as unalleviated expenditure, play as the labile exhaustion of purpose—until it arrives utterly spent on Kant's doorstep, exemplifying to him "zwecklichkeit ohne Zweck," purposiveness without purpose.

Memory invested in the Muses—those daughters of Mnemosyne and Zeus—is memory abandoned to celestial seizure, in which the agent or medium may be divine, but the human is dispossessed, becoming subordinate to what seemed initially a prosthetic tool. The effective poet, as in Pindar's sixth Olympian ode, becomes a graphic implement (a sharp whetstone on the tongue [ll. 83–84]), a cipher-stick of the Muses (l. 92), and a vacant container (a mixing-bowl of thunderous songs [l. 93]). There is a reversal of function, then, as the poet turns out to be *accessed* from above and beyond, by Muses, or by Apollo: a human megaphone, a prosthetic stylus. Before the metal stylus of the pen, there is the quill, a diminutive switch or rod, by which the deepest resources of Indo-European linguistics and mythology refer writing to wood (from the Ygdrassil tree to bark/book). Writing is woodlore, magic skill. The Muses give Hesiod a laurel staff, and laurel ("daphne" in Greek) is also associated with Apollo. The scepter of the king and the wand of the magus derive from similar associations. The Indo-European roots *uat* (inspire) and *ueid* (behold) knot together a resounding complex of associations, from which we derive wisdom, prophecy, fury, sight, idea, and *wood*. To further investigate primal scenes, then, we should bear in mind the technological dimension as implicit in even the most "primitive" poetics. It is best to reiterate, following Jerome Rothenberg, that any poetics is "a question of technology as well as inspiration; & we may as well take it as axiomatic . . . that where poetry is concerned, 'primitive' means complex" (Rothenberg xxvi). Such a directive stipulates mythology as a medium in which the primitive apparition camouflages complex technological specifications. The pastoral myth of Hesiod's Muses represents, then, *the state of the art.*

In its primeval inception, poetry cohabits a landscape of premonitions along with oracle, prophecy, testimony, oath, proclamation, and glossolalia. These may all be regarded as technical systems, media networks, even if they appear to be natural omens. The hiss of wind in a rock channel, scrutinized for vocable semiosis, converts the topographic space into a cultural implement. A cleft in rock is a primitive computer terminal. The oral roots of Hellenic poetry are well known. But Jean-Pierre Vernant, in "Speech and Mute Signs," has made the enlightening suggestion that the Greeks favored oracles because vocal utterance kept the priests at bay, with all the sacerdotal custodianship that attends written scripture. The voice of conviction, compulsion, and possession—whether in trance or in conscious exhortation—is an early invitation to prioritize poetic voice by affirming it as the most progressive technology available. But what was formerly symptomatic of divine inspiration, poetic furor, or even madness has subsequently constituted another kind of *terminal* altogether, in the coordinates of our latest communications heraldry, the threat of which is its manifest externalization of everything formerly ascribed to the interiority of the subject: language, logic, and computational power as the virtual index of the rational soul. The Muses, having been born of Mnemosyne, now begin, here and there, to pass by the names Database, Hypertext, and World Wide Web. Metrical regulation is no longer necessary for poems once poetry has ceased to be the encyclopedic register of the culture; so instead of metrics we have programming languages, and the sonnet has been bypassed by COBOL and ASCII. In the process, the instructive gendering of the Muses has been abandoned, or reconverted to the masculinist dream of pure thought, calculation without expenditure, language unpolluted, a regained paradise of unity without strife or division. Inspiration as computation.

Primal Scenes: *Bios*

Poetry is simultaneously celebration and loss, commemoration and grievance: this is the slippage introduced by the Muses. The supplementary character of language ("words add to the senses," said Wallace Stevens ["Variations" 172]) troubles the body by blurring its boundaries. In contrast to the seriality of languages, Apollo (god of the bow and the lyre, patron of poetry and the Muses) is "all seeing," taking in all at a glance. Hence the incommensurability of divine vision with human witness; the revelation is dissipated, scattered. Giovanni Manetti attributes the semiotics of Greek divination to a lack of fit between god and human: "Divinatory logic . . . allows for the reintroduction at the human level of the 'obscurity' of Fate (reduced, if not entirely eliminated, by the very nature of divine omniscience) by means of the ambiguity of the sign" (19). The sign, then, is a token of what cannot be read or comprehended. Prophetic utterances like those given by the oracles resemble an index ripped out of a book (in Sybilline prophecy the book itself is torn apart). Whatever can be gleaned from ciphers will have to suffice when the text is nowhere at hand. Inasmuch as the world is full of signs, unlimited semiosis is a consequence of perception. To bear something in mind is to pluck a thing from its mooring in the quotidian and dispose of it in the twilight realm of interiority, where muses and madness intermingle.[6]

In the primal semiosis of poetic origins, however, a different belief arises—one that finds solace in a homology of linguistic seriality with the proliferation of forms in nature. A mutual and simultaneous declaration makes words and the world congruent. The principle, it is important to note, is not a doctrine of *correspondences* but a code, a ratio of integrations and integrities—a decorative or *cosmic* concord, not a *universal* compulsory consent.[7] The specter of harmony haunts the cosmic code because it is in fact Pythagorean. The Hellenic model of a speaking, or at least euphonious, universe derives from Pythagoras. Aristotle belittled the Pythagorean doctrine of universal harmony by suggesting we do not actually hear the music of the spheres: "It appears unaccountable that we should not hear this music, [but the Pythagoreans] explain this by saying that the sound is in our ears from the very moment of birth and is thus indistinguishable from its contrary silence" (*De Caelo* II.9 24–6). Aristotle's skepticism gives way to a curious equation: if silence is all we "hear" of the cosmic symphony, the act of hearing is synonymous with deafness. It is, however, possible to hear the equation otherwise. Pythagorean cosmology posits a harmony that exceeds the perceptual range of human ears, to which we may nonetheless be attuned. Hearing is therefore a domain that the ears sample but cannot master. Just as we recognize visionary experience that is by no means contingent on eyesight, the Pythagorean worldview stipulates a "visionary" experience in the auditory mode, in which we have proprioceptive assurance of harmonies we cannot hear.

For the Pythagoreans the universal harmony did not take the form of a voice. If we hanker after a measurable acoustic perception of cosmic harmony or wish to hear a deific voice in lexical utterances, we need an aid, a prosthetic means of extending our hearing. To consider the nature of voice-over any further, we therefore need to look at a different primal scene, one that acknowledges prosthetic augmentation of an initially "natural" if deaf (or unresponsive) state. The prosthesis rearticulates the boundaries of body and self, so that the voice of the other may appear out of the deepest resources of interiority, and interiority, reckoned as the fount of subjective nature, can then be retrofitted with the symptoms of primacy that are culturally endowed as *natural*.

The prophetic sensibility attunes itself to the vaporous moaning of chasms, the groan of trees in wind, and the bubbling of springs, extending vocalization throughout a sacred landscape. The world speaks, and this is Orphic. Orpheus allows us to hear the world speak, while at the same time obliging *us* to be the ventriloquists if we would hear nature's voice in our own language. Nature "speaks" on the condition that we do the talking. As with the silent harmony of the Pythagoreans, humans have to supplement a primal language with prosthetic amplification. The speaker (or singer, *aiodos*) must become a speaker (*technē*, broadcaster). The figure of Orpheus signifies the emergence of a *human* language from a world of expressive sentience, but this emergence is always partial and conditional. "The myth [of Orpheus] oscillates between the power of form to master intense passion and the power of intense passion to engulf form" (Segal 8).[8] Besides inaugurating poetry as a specifically human enterprise, Orpheus is the first talking head, his sumptuous singing persisting long after his decapitation by the Maenads. The Orphic perspective signifies a reversal, not only of sound to silence but of life to death, and vice versa. In the Orphic cosmogony, Orpheus was a prophet, a magus empowered by his access to the secrets of the dead. These shamanistic abilities are technical skills, which are somewhat muted in the familiar rendition of his underworld descent to fetch Eurydice.[9] Under Orpheus's tutelage we discover voice as *technē*. He is a primary figure, then, among technicians of the sacred, proposing an interface between ancient and contemporary resources of poetry. To turn to this legacy is not primitivism; as Elizabeth Sewell insists, concluding *The Orphic Voice*, "We have to return to it, not as a vague ornament of life but as one of the great living disciplines of the mind" (405).

As Sewell elaborates, the Orphic "disciplines of the mind" are enabled by techniques of the body. This is in fact the root of Orphism in poetry, which thrives on the rediscovery of mind as embodied, and body *minded*: "The only choice for the mind lies not between mythology and logic but between an exclusive mythology which chooses to overlook the body's participation and an inclusive mythology which is prepared in varying degrees to admit the body, the notion of the organism as a whole, as a partner in that very odd operation known as thought" (38). The "voice" Sewell speaks of is a somatic insistence that manifests itself in the form of language. Language, in the Orphic view, is a biological epiphenomenon.[10] Poetry is that linguistic occasion in which the body orchestrates thought, moved by a prelinguistic density, a corporeal engagement that has its affiliations with the Hesiodic voice-over. Orpheus's mother was a Muse (Calliope is usually cited), and the Muses impinge on the speech act from inside the cranium. Orphic embodiment is thus an attunement to the estrangement of proprioceptive awareness, the sense that the bodily habitus itself is saying something that the mind generally ignores; it is in fact perilous *not* to ignore this cenesthetic amplitude. That we literally *inhere* in our bodies is to find ourselves inhabiting a paradoxical condition, for the body as *ground* of awareness recedes from attention to the degree that the *figures* of perception are in focus, thereby rendering ground (and body) invisible. The most adept realization of the body's articulation, then, is unconscious.

To call on the Muses for aid in memory is not the whole story. The proprioceptive occasion of Orphic corporeality demands another sort of retrieval, a descent into the body. Orpheus's descent signals an expedition into somatic topography to retrieve lost images, configured as vital persons of the soul. At one level this is figured as Orpheus's descent into the underworld. To conceive descent in terms of a memory that has somatic overtones is to associate self-knowledge not with the past but with the present. Orpheus's resourcefulness, in this light, is a kind of yoga, involving integral postures of expansion and contraction, to which end breath control is primary. To the inspiration or breathing-in with which the Muses endow Hesiod, there is also the *expiration* of Orpheus, the completion of respiration. So Orpheus's legends are necessarily as much about depletion as about animation.

It is in this spirit that one of the great nineteenth-century Orphic reveries is Whitman's "Crossing Brooklyn Ferry," a poem that rekindles a memento mori out of the turbulent froth worked up from the ferry's prow. "Flood tide below me, I see you face to face," he begins, as though seeing himself at once prefigured in and dissolved in the river as a kind of amniotic seething. "I too knitted the old knot of contrariety," he writes in section 6. Embodiment is the knot: "I too had been struck from the float forever held in solution, / I too had receiv'd identity by my body, / That I was I knew was of my body, and what I should be I knew I should be of my body" (#5). The "solution" here is simultaneously preservative and key and indicates the terms of a colossal reciprocity of meaning and being, life and death. (It also reiterates Emerson's opening declaration in *Nature*: "Every man's condition is a *solution* in hieroglyphic to those inquiries he would put" (7; my emphasis). As a poem of the body, it is a poem of Orphic release and *sparagmos*— "The simple, compact, well-join'd scheme, myself disintegrated, every one disintegrated yet part of the scheme" (#2)—in which Whitman beholds his head reflected in the water as he gazes down from the ferry railing:

> I too many and many a time cross'd the river of old . . .
> Saw the reflection of the summer sky in the water,
> Had my eyes dazzled by the shimmering track of beams,

> Look'd at the fine centrifugal spokes of light round the shape of my
> head in the sunlit water . . . . (#3)

The head, transfigured by its spokes into a rind emitting light, is transcendentally iconic. Interpreters have frequently commented on the Christlike image, and we have only to recall that in the Middle Ages Orpheus was regarded as a precursor of Christ to see what sort of figure Whitman is discovering in himself as bard.[11] Orpheus took on Christlike attributes as a guide of souls after death—his relation to Eurydice expanded to include humankind in general—and as Whitman rhetorically affirms, "What gods can exceed these that clasp me by the hand, and with voices I love call me promptly and loudly by my nighest name as I approach? / What is more subtle than this which ties me to the woman or man that looks in my face? / Which fuses me into you now, and pours my meaning into you?" (#8). As these lines suggest, Orpheus represents a recovery of the body in the act of speech. But this is too simple a formulation. As patron of poetry, Orpheus favors an act of speech that is *not* a "speech act," but a *song*, and even a *text*. Woven as integument, speech is disclosed as nonverbal; vocalized as song, words are charmed into music, extralinguistic.

Beginning as a mute signal in the head, then a coordinated feeling (of Pythagorean cosmic harmony) in the body, emerging finally as vatic utterance, it turns out that the resources of the speech act are confoundingly multiple, polymorphously perverse. One speaks, but "one" is two, or many. The poet "sings," but the song is an act of writing. In the Dionysian *sparagmos* or dismemberment, Orpheus's head goes on singing by itself. Whitman's scenario suggests a merger of the Orphic and Pythagorean traditions, as the head recollects remote impulses of the body to which it is no longer attached, vocalizing them as if the body were instantaneously proximate to the whole universe: as in the case of Orpheus, the singing head is a mediumistic phantom that gathers up the entire cosmic order on its way to song.

An Orphic proponent not mentioned by Sewell is the French aphorist Alain, whose treatise *The Gods* affirms that "the reality of the imagination is always in some impulse of the body." Alain sees in the Orpheus myth a schema for phantom sensations:

Orpheus bringing Eurydice back, is the essential text of the imagination. For it is true that emotions like fear, anxiety, surprise, create a kind of presence in our bodies, one that is even sensitive to touch, which is, as we see, the most deceptive of the senses; and it is also true that our senses are quickened by our own blood and disposition so as to produce the beginnings of phantoms—a humming in the ears, spots of color, butter-flies in the stomach, pricklings, salivation, nausea, and other effects of heightened expectation; but these disturbing forms, if we should pay attention to them, would present us with nothing more than the structure of our own body, though in a state of flux. (37)

Eurydice, in Alain's account, is an anthropomorphized model of neuronal firings, synaptic leaps, electrochemical impulses of the central nervous system, most of which are invariably lost when we attempt to retrieve them from the somatic underworld. So the poetic sensibility is an attunement to what is below attention, ungraspable except in those heightened states of distraction otherwise known as *inspiration*, and even then realized only as expenditure, as jubilation and lament.

In "The Gaze of Orpheus" Maurice Blanchot reads descent as erasure, memory as inseparable from forgetfulness. "Orpheus' gaze links inspiration to desire. Desire is linked to *carelessness* by *impatience*. He who is not impatient will never achieve that carelessness which merges care with its own limpidity." This rehearsal of the outlines of Orpheus's descent is instructive for Blanchot about writing as such, the inauguration of which he attributes to Orpheus's gaze: "We can only write when we have reached that point which we can only reach in the space to which writing gives access. To write we must already be writing" (181). Poetic inspiration is a tautology that challenges the foundations of poetry. That is, the mantic or divinatory energy that provides the literal force of inspiration leads mind down into body, submerging it in an extralinguistic somatic environment where it no longer recognizes what it has to say. Orpheus's descent suggests something about the dangers of language. His turning to verify that Eurydice is still behind him is an instance of the conduit theory of words. In this view, the mind, being sensually and prelinguistically attached to its objects, has no use for words but as cognitive glue. The other facet of the myth, having to do with Orpheus's enchanting songs as a prodigal élan vital, links the resources of poetic expression with expenditure: nature's creatures are animated by the gratuitous promptings of his charmed voice. These two faces of Orpheus are instructions about linguistic nominalism versus realism, testifying to the dual pathos of losing the beloved object or being smothered in the disjecta of our own fertility.

Not surprisingly, then, Blanchot sees in Orpheus a necessary resistance to accomplishment and completion: Orpheus "links poetry with an outrageous urge to vanish" (173). Expression is expenditure. To return to the surface is to efface the trail leading down to the underworld and the subconscious. Blanchot's attribution of "carelessness" to poetry is echoed by Stephen Owen in *Mi-Lou: Poetry and the Labyrinth of Desire*. "Poetry may call to that part of us that hungers for straying," he says. "Poetry is . . . a precise art of negligence" (5, 74). The sense of vagrancy and deviation solicited here can be compared with Thoreau's determined assertion, at the end of *Walden*, on behalf of extravagance ("I fear chiefly lest my expression may not be *extra-vagant* enough"). "The volatile truth of our words should continually betray the inadequacy of the residual statement," Thoreau insisted (580). Mallarmé held that the mind is "volatile dispersal," developing his own field composition strategies of spacing and scattering, about which Blanchot observes, "For Mallarmé, language is not made of words, even unadulterated words: it is that into which words have always already disappeared." The poet's efforts, in *Un Coup de dés*, are guided in this encounter with pure space (which Rilke, in the 8th Elegy, would call "das Offene," the Open) not by words but by "a rhythmic scansion of life" (Blanchot 247). "Space does not accommodate things; instead," says Levinas in a Mallarméan perception, "through their erasures, things delineate space" (146).

These formulations are all Orphic, which means they adhere to an image of creation as latency and squandering, in which accomplishment is abandoned to *bios*, the order of physical dispersal. In contrast to Hesiod — for whom inspiration is marked as a technical augmentation, a conceptual supplement establishing a secure and distinct space for a "song" uttered in writing — Orpheus represents that poetic longing for unmediated expression embodied in *phonē* or voice. The enigmas that emerge from Mallarmé and Blanchot have to do with their attempts to transpose Orphic song to the space of a text by intuiting significant resemblances between the blank page and the profound vacancy of cenesthesic (or somatic) perception. This interior sense of balance, intactness, and postural readiness was not fully addressed in terms of poetics until Charles Olson's ruminations on proprioception. In his view, "Neither the Unconscious nor Projection (here used to remove the false opposition of 'Conscious'; consciousness is self) have a home unless the DEPTH implicit in physical being . . . is asserted, or found-out as such. Thus the advantage of the value 'proprioception'" (*Additional Prose* 18). Proprioception, for Olson, provided the model for enacting the ancient hermetic dictum *Quod inferius, sicut superius est* (as above, so below). Because the internal "sense" of well-being is not of the same order as the exterior senses, we know ourselves in this interior extension only as a blank depth, an inner cosmos that excites analogies with the starry sky, both being equally ungraspable yet oddly intimate. A star chart is a recovery of the body in a stellar vocabulary, a gazing at seams that bind not only by analogy but which reconstitute the sundered *corpus* that the figure of Orpheus signifies:

> I looked up and saw
> its form
> through everything
> —it is sewn
> in all parts, under
> and over. (*Maximus Poems* 343)

Orpheus was linked by Blanchot to vanishing, but in light of Olson's poetics—based on Whitehead's sense of the cosmic imbricating the moment, the perpetual penetrating the transitory—Orpheus naturally results in an "Orphic cosmology" because his vanishing is a motivating reminder of space and distance. Orpheus never vanishes; rather, he is simply diminished amidst our ever increasing awareness of the immensity of his context. Astray in the cosmos, Orpheus becomes that accidental apparition that reminds us how far we have to go to have a chance at ever retracing our own steps. As a warning against the craving for duplication, corroboration, and repetition, Orpheus is at the same time the figure of rhythmic recurrence.

Every trace of passage consists of disseminated contours of an ongoing passing, the most elegant version of which is not Orphic at all, but an Ashante tale of the trickster Ananse. A rival comes to his house and asks to see him, but Ananse, having foreseen this, has instructed his children in what to say: that their father's penis broke in seven places, and he has gone to the smith for repairs. The rival asks for the mother, and the children reply that she went to the river to fetch water, dropped her pot but luckily caught it just in time. So why is she not here now? She did not quite finish catching it and has gone back to the river to do so.

Primal Scenes (Modern): *Technē* 2

For the Dogon people of West Africa, language is pragmatically akin to weaving. To speak and to weave both involve fabrication. In the Dogon creation myth a spirit ancestor combines the functions: "By opening and shutting his jaws the Spirit caused the threads of the warp to make the movements required in weaving. His whole face took part in the work, his nose studs serving as the block, while the stud in his lower lip was the shuttle" (Griaule 28). This labor is made richly complex by additional elements, including a sexual anthill that is essential to the propagation of words (the loom is grounded just over the mouth of the anthill, so that the weaving is congruent with the disclosure of words by an ant).[12] "Thus there was recreated by human lips the concept of life in motion, of the transposition of forces, of the efficacy of the breath of the Spirit . . . and thus the interlacing of warp and weft enclosed the same words, the new instruction which became the heritage of mankind and was handed on from generation to generation of weavers to the accompaniment of the clapping of the shuttle and the creaking of the block, which they call the 'creaking of the Word' " (Griaule 29). Nathaniel Mackey has taken up the Dogon myth as a more generalized insight into the ambiguous nature of language as possession/dispossession. For him, the creaking of the Word "is the noise upon which the word is based, the discrepant foundation of all coherence and articulation, of the purchase upon the world fabrication affords" (19). Mackey then clarifies the derivation of the title of his book, *Discrepant Engagement*, from these considerations: "Discrepant engagement, rather than suppressing or seeking to silence that noise, acknowledges it. In its antifoundational acknowledgment of founding noise, discrepant engagement sings 'base,' voicing reminders of the axiomatic exclusions upon which positings of identity and meaning depend" (19). The pun on singing "bass" as *base* discloses foundation as abasement. Undertones stabilize but also remind of traumatic breakage and ancestral violations. For Mackey, "Poetic language is language owning up to being an orphan, to its tenuous kinship with the thing it ostensibly refers to" (234). The orphan peregrination of language renders poetry itinerant. Poetry enacts the exile of language, which is not so much banishment as it is the constant displacement of the power of the word into other media, signified by the shuttle in the Dogon myth.

Walter Benjamin's formula for the storyteller is an "old co-ordination of the soul, the eye, and the hand" (108). Benjamin's insistence on the hand is traceable to orality, in that the storyteller, working out of traditions of recital, assimilates versions and variants in the mode of *weaving*, a handiwork. In addition, Benjamin wants us to respect storytelling literally as *manual* labor (an "artisan form of communication" [91]). Storytelling has been replaced by the cult of information, in Benjamin's view. Story arises from the security of companionship, a solidarity formed by mutual presence of reciter and auditor and above all by the assimilative lassitude of mental relaxation and boredom. Nothing now supports this unique archaic web, according to Benjamin, whereas the rustle of daily life proliferates in its place a surface static of data. Had he written his essay "The Storyteller" now rather than in 1936, he might make his point by suggesting that stories arise from humans; information, from technical systems.

The *graphē* that supplemented voice with writing, in one traditional version of cultural succession, persists in another medium equally intent on capturing voice: the phonograph. Michael Taussig describes the role of the phonograph as a cross-cultural instrument of intimidation:

> To take the talking machine to the jungle is to emphasize and embellish the genuine mystery and accomplishment of mechanical reproduction in an age when technology itself, after the flurry of excitement at a new breakthrough, is seen not as mystique or poetry but as routine. Taking the talking machine to the jungle is to do more than impress the natives and therefore oneself with Western technology's power. . . . It is to reinstall the mimetic faculty as mystery in the art of mechanical reproduction, reinvigorating the primitivism implicit in technology's wildest dreams, therewith creating a surfeit of mimetic power. (208)

Mimesis, under the aegis of such technology, becomes a lure or bait to snare others, subjecting them to the repetition-compulsion of "developmental" masquerade—progress as mimesis. But Taussig's account is not altogether about the obviously imperialist dimension in that he recognizes as an anthropologist what Benjamin, as flâneur, did not: namely, "the primitivism implicit in technology's wildest dreams," the foremost conviction of which is in "the power of the copy to influence what it is a copy of" (250). To the soul-eye-hand nexus of the storyteller, then, Taussig adds the phonographic complex of copy-contact-contagion. The phonographic copy, unlike writing, registers a bodily index like the fingerprint, and this point of contact suggests a corresponding possibility of contagion—the sound of a cough emanating from either a recording or a telephone receiver had people worrying about germs. This is what Taussig means by a surfeit of mimetic power. Mimesis and alterity reciprocate so vigorously in the enhanced zone of reproductive (cultural) technologies that the distinction of self from other is no longer tenable.

The concept of mimetic surplus inclines to an Aristotelian rather than a Platonic version of mimesis, biological reproduction versus devolution of an archetype, adherence to a pulsion, not replication of a form. "The process is not mimetic, imitation of a prior imitation, but ontomimetic, imitation of 'being' itself" (Lawler 20). Mimesis does something quite different from hastening after the real with a copy; it reanimates somatic purpose with its excess. The power vested in Hesiod or Homer by the Muses is the power not only to know but to *feel* and *see*, to *taste* the manifold of difference that in Sanskrit poetics is known as *rasa*. To reread is to burn with ardor for being contaminated once again; immersion, not termination, is the goal. The trajectory of narrative has a paradigmatic storyteller in Scheherezade, a figure of unbounded fertility, but whose lifespan is strictly contingent on her narrative persistence. For her, death is proximate to narration.[13] The performative intensity incorporated into the tales of Orpheus, of Narcissus, and of the Sirens, draws on the anxiety of destruction. I am not concerned here with the funereal lament, elegy, or thanatopsis as such. Rather, it is the *technical* injunction of the apparatus, the voice-over, that stages fantasies of loss, dismemberment, or discorporation.

In "The Phonograph's Horned Mouth," Charles Grivel characterizes the Muses as a "repeating machine inside poetry" (33), a machine externalized in modernism as the phonograph. "The phonograph emphasizes the self in the lack of subject," Grivel writes, which introduces a paradoxical split: "It identifies a voice, fixes the deceased (or mortal) person, registers the dead and thus perpetuates his living testimony, but also achieves his automatic reproduction *in absentia*" (35). The phonograph resurrects the deceased in an uncanny simulation, uncannily responsive to Lyotard's question, "Can thought go on without a body?" But the phonograph also affirms that the speaking voice may subsist without a body—a paradox like trying to think of bodiless *running* or *sleeping*. Grivel sees in this not a technological misadventure but a poetic longing: "At just about the same time [as the invention of the phonograph in 1877], Rimbaud was writing that '*je est un autre*' (I is someone else), Mallarmé that a blank volume is his expression, Lautréamont that poetry is made up of everything and by everyone, and Nietzsche, of course, that since God is dead, the voice, without reservation, dissolves. A machine arrives in the nick of time to capture all this and give it an appearance" (33). Reviewing Hesiod in this light, the Greek shepherd turns out to have participated in an initial dispossession, an initial retooling for prosthetic interface, entering the Muses' listserve with all the enthused wariness of Case "jacking in" to the matrix in William Gibson's *Neuromancer*. "I am buried in its entrails (or it is in me): I am the equal of this imitating device. When it speaks to me, it also represents to me, outside of me and without me, the absence of subject: it repeats me without my being there." Predictably, then, "the first consequence of the mechanical reproduction of the voice was to break the bond unifying sign and person, the self and its support or medium" (Grivel 52). Thereafter, the body subsists as biologically unfit for new technologies, with a remedial relation to the social skills that institutionalize these technologies.

Modern poetry openly embraces the normative functions of a speaker in order to attest to the savor of individual experience. But poetry can lose touch with its voice-over when it appropriates voice for subjective instrumentality, particularly when subjectivity becomes a socialized medium of technical affiliations. As Foucault tirelessly elaborates, the modern modes of subjectivization are not modes of subjugation and repression; power is less likely to circulate now (at least in democratic societies) as repressive constraint. "What makes power hold good, what makes it accepted, is simply the fact that it doesn't only weigh on us as a force that says no, but that it traverses and produces things, it induces pleasure, forms knowledge, produces discourse" (*Power/Knowledge* 119). The incitement of productivity is none other than an injunction to become cathected to prosthetic junctures, in which subjectivity itself becomes a matter of negotiating consoles and interfaces, and communication is discharged on the model of dataflows and serial processing. Subjectivity is that process of *subjection* or insertion into what Scott Bukatman calls "terminal identity," in which transcendence of the human takes on the dystopic character of assimilation to telematic paraphernalia, and we begin to endure the wonder of our creations by enlarging them to a scale that requires our (in)habitation of them, and ultimately our own *rehabilitation* to them.[14]

The episode on Mount Helikon prepares us for a poetic legacy that will court subjectivity as an alternative to the epistemological discrimination of true from false, recuperated by Kant as a transcendental idealism. In modern regimes of enticed/enforced subjectivization, language becomes an ideological medium of adjustment and self-maintenance. Poetry becomes complicitous with the regulative endeavors of selfhood. But before the self could emerge as an irresistible intoxicant, the world of the senses had to fade away under the punitive glamour of the voice-over. The paralytic freeze-frame of ecstasy is encoded in this hallucino-literary medium: "Poetry as a 'possession of the inner mind' arises in erotic and alcoholic intoxication; authorship arises in rereading what had been unconsciously written in the delirium; poetic works, finally, are media for the hallucinatory substitution of realms of the senses" (Kittler, *Discourse* 109). Poetry is proximate to engineering, not humanities: "In the discourse network of 1800, the Book of Poetry became the first medium in the modern sense. Following McLuhan's law, according to which the content of a medium is always another medium, poetry supplemented the data of the senses in a way that was reproducible and multiplicatory" (Kittler, *Discourse* 115). Poetry, in Friedrich Kittler's hypothesis, forecasts our current fantasies about virtual reality. The poem becomes a technical support in a random-access memory device—a *hard drive*, as it were, for activating the serial components of an identity that can no longer identify itself in the reflective screen of a monitor.[15] It is as if self-awareness had been subcontracted to a prosthetic memory, an outside agency. Poetry is the terminal that accesses the database; the subcontractor is the discourse network that writes (and patents) the software.

Hesiod preserved the trauma of voices inside his own head, perpetuating the anxiety of introjected alterity as a legacy of poetry. Poetry from its beginnings has prepared us for the allure of a disembodied voice—and a beheaded body—software mysteriously tracing its commands on a resistant medium. This specter is memorably documented in the 1919 essay "Ur-Geräusch" (Primal noise), in which Rilke recalls his boyhood encounter with the phonograph. What most impressed Rilke was not the magical appearance of sound from the technical device, but "the markings traced on the cylinder," which he later came to identify with the coronal suture of the human skull. The thought of applying the phonographic needle to the suture led him to reveries of returning the entire world to Orphic audibility: "What variety of lines then, occurring anywhere, could one not put under the needle and try out?" ("Was für irgendwo vorkommende Linien möchte man da nicht unterschieben und auf die Probe stellen?") (53–54). The verb *unterschieben* also carries implications of substitution, which is altogether accurate to Rilke's intuition that the compelling element of the phonograph is not the recording but the needle, which might well be applied to surrogates.

Just as the Dogon figure of the weaver gives us an insight into the handicraft of textuality, Kafka's writing machine/torture device in "In the Penal Colony" provides an unsettling image of writing as haptic *sentence*. This helps us feel the dimension Rilke adds to the auditory aspect of the phonograph, in which the needle on the stylus makes explicit its tactile claim. A similar tactility occasions Michel Leiris's celebrated reverie "Persephone" (in *La Règle du jeu I: Biffures* 84). Leiris's childhood experience of the "slightly fatty quality" of static produced by the sound of the needle in the grooves of a record fractures the otherwise "tranquil flow of time," leading him ultimately to a speculative traversal of subterranean openings associated with gnomes in mines, the penetration of the body by foreign (metallic) substances, and much more. These associations return us to "der Seelen wunderliches Bergwerk" of Rilke's poem "Orpheus. Eurydike. Hermes"—the marvelous mine of souls through which the figures travel to the underworld as if through veins of ore.

The lines followed by the stylus of the phonograph bear an uncanny conceptual kinship with lines of poetry, and poetry in its Orphic dimension can become audible or legible anywhere, as in Whitman's encounter with "the trail of drift and debris" on Paumanok's shore, "seiz'd by the spirit that trails in the lines underfoot." Rilke, like Whitman, pursues voice as a para-doxical integration of jubilation and lament, significantly rendered as erotic adhesiveness. The stylus, in this light, is a source of sexual friction arousing a voice. In Whitman's other great seashore poem, "Out of the Cradle End-lessly Rocking," the scene of poetic calling is one of interspecies vocalism, animal vampirism, as the young boy hears the mockingbird calling his lost mate and is poetically *infected* by the lamentation. "O you singer solitary," the grown Whitman responds across the years, "singing by yourself, pro-jecting me . . . never more shall I cease perpetuating you." This *Liebestod* aria culminates in the answering sea that "Lisp'd to me the low and deli-cious word death . . . / Creeping thence steadily up to my ears and laving me softly all over, / Death, death, death, death, death. // Which I do not forget, / But fuse the song of my dusky demon and brother." This is a poem not so simply about death and inspiration, but about the death involved in expiring from one state and assuming another, shedding the human in order to be empowered as a poet.

Osip Mandelstam notes a similar becoming-bird on the part of Paster-nak, whose poetry he sees as "a direct mating call" and "the direct conse-quence of a special physiological structure in the throat." "To read Paster-nak's verses is to clear one's throat, reinforce one's breathing, renovate the lungs" (83). Reading Dante, he discovers a "peculiar labial music" distend-ing the lips into a proboscis (34). The entirety of the *Commedia* becomes, for Mandelstam, a challenge to "imagine how it would be if bees had worked at the creation of this thirteen-thousand-faceted shape, bees endowed with instinctive stereometric genius, who attracted more and still more bees as they were needed" (15). The discovery of the world as animate and elo-quent is euphorically enabling, but it can result in a paralytic arrest as well. The phonographic needle, resembling bee stinger, pen, and hypodermic, equates writing with inoculation, or subdermal descent.[16]

The voluble world can share the burden of voice with the poet; it can also usurp the poet's role. Rilke's boyhood fascination with the phonograph portends a chattering environment that strikes the poet dumb with amaze-ment. Eye and voice — attraction and distraction — converge in that peculiar animation that is poetic reverie, in which the voices of others vibrate in-side the head, inducing that "vision" that the poet is said to compose. The voice-over turns the body into a vanishing point. All of this is dramatized in the Eurydice myth, in which Orpheus suffers an uncharacteristic lapse of confidence in auditory cues and turns to look at his wife before surfacing from the underworld. His distraction is manifested as a scopic compulsion, and this becomes the first of a series of losses that culminate in the ritual *sparagmos*, his dismemberment by the Maenads. In any event, there is either too much to look at (or look for), or too much to listen to; there is a sensory overload, resulting in an imbalance that fatally usurps one sense by the demands of another sense.

We have seen how Hesiod's voice is occupied by — filled up with — the Muses. He is the Muses' medium. We can hear this in several ways. The poet is the medium, the raw material instrument through which the poem is transmitted. He is also a "control," in the mediumistic sense (at a seance the control is the person transmitting spirit voices), a proxy for phantoms. There is a final, more contemporary sense of control, which Norbert Wiener derived from the Greek word for steersman: cybernetics. Hesiod — putting his voice at the mediumistic disposal of the Muses — converts poetry into cybernetics. As a theory of control in systems behavior, cybernetics has always been poised at the prosthetic interface, that juncture at which the tool may become an extension of the person, or the person an extension of the tool. The swarm of voices clinging like bees to the media web arouses connotations of language for us that are different from those of Hesiod. Instead of oracles we now have artificial intelligence. Cognitive science has modeled language on neurology, and language in turn has become a paradigm of codes and systems. Poetry, meanwhile, seems like raw industrial sewage from the immense transformations required here. Language macroprocessors flit about weightlessly in the superconductive environs of cognitive science and the hyperspace of critical theory, while the diesel-driven bigrigs of poetry still chug along the interstates, belching smoke. Poetry is dirty language. Poetry emerges from the technological menu as a vestigial residue of the primitive, as the very elements that initially made poetry appear dangerously progressive and autonomous — the Muses's headgear — have migrated into other media. The voice-over function is now more likely to emanate positively from the charged tensions of video, film, or photography.[17] Poetry for the most part remains bound up with Enlightenment fantasies of humanism. But of course the fantasy of the human projected by Enlightenment ideals has become today's cyborg, or recombinant person.[18] So even the Enlightenment has left poetry behind, discarding it as unfit for its long-range instrumentality like a booster-rocket ejected on liftoff.

In the atmosphere of the voice-over, most of the voices we hear no longer remember or display their paths to and from (adult) bodies. Instead they are equations of infantile laminar flow, free-floating tourniquets marking the interface between anxiety and authority. We hanker after the reassuring sound of a voice, no longer attending to what it says and untroubled by its disembodiment. We are frightened less by dark than by quiet. After World

War II the Swiss philosopher Max Picard wrote, "By taking it away from silence we have made language an orphan. The tongue we speak today is no longer a mother-tongue but rather an orphaned tongue" (41). An orphanage is the institution of surrogate parenthood. Norman Bates, although adult, is still an orphan, desperately intent on speaking the (m)other('s) tongue, much as it makes him stutter, gagging on the words as they protrude through his mouth, a mouth as vaginal envelope preserving in its mummy embryo the hieroglyphic papyrus of a ventriloquialized ~~muse~~ voice.

From the Pythagorean prospect, confronting the exasperating incommensurability of our senses with the sensory waveband of the cosmos, we infer a language exceeding the scope of words. The Orphic perspective awakens a sense that language is at once a glorious and an awkward augmentation of the world, and Orpheus's decapitation is a grisly reminder that somewhere along the continuum of words there is a human disjunction. The Orphic breach is sewn up in the (somewhat monstrous) form of Hesiod, who bears traces of a prosthetic rearticulation of the shape and boundaries of the human. Before Hesiod, poetry in its Orphic demeanor rambunctiously adds to, and awakens echoes throughout, the world at large. With Hesiod the world itself is condensed to a single compelling (yet alien) voice inside the head—and it is only a matter of time until Descartes condenses even the figure of the human to a glistening mote of ego, in which a voice persists, if only as a technical simulation. Poetry henceforth develops an alliance with subjectivity, requiring compulsory speech from a world (of "muses") that had hitherto resounded freely, but which now begins to endure its lengthy subjugation to the human subject, and in its subjugation develops that sullen, unspeaking demeanor that its masters read as evidence of a brute, unresponsive nature (Caliban to Prospero). Cartesian subjectivity demands of the voice-over that it offer compelling evidence of its resources and its identity—that it testify on its own behalf. Voice-over is to be the authentic, inspired version of the voice as such. Any experience of voice that resists such alignment is evidence of demonic intervention, psychological neurosis, or technical malfunction, and gender has been the generic fate of these technical malfunctions. Gender *is* the primal scene, the site of ambiguous transit between nature and culture, biology and tool. Bearing in mind that gender is construed as prediscursive or mute facticity, Hesiod's relation to the Muses illustrates the process by which the male voice of poetic authority is underwritten by a female voice-over. His poem is not so much "inspired" (in the convention to which we are accustomed) as it is prearticulated inside him, in a voice that is differently gendered.[19] To experience voice as inner—that is, as *unvoiced*—is to be initiated in the emergence of gender, particularly gender understood in affiliation with genius, speech with fertility.

In the primal scene of poetic inspiration, the volatility of the medium itself is indistinguishable from that cauldron of subjectivity that can only be tamed or quenched by the special linguistic and cultural technique of gender. The issue of the gendered voice is not simply a matter of authority, then. The archaic resources of language trouble authority even before it establishes itself. The *Odyssey* is an epic of erotic *vocations* that disturb the man who would be king. The narrative that engenders his triumph must submit to an itinerary of other voices, a polyphony that is sampled and synthesized, as it were, into an access code. The voice of heroic epic is masculine, reverberating in compassionate timbre with the voice of the hero, since the hero is merely a figure for the engineering miracle that has generated the tale and at the same time gendered it. Narrative is a foundry, in which narratological (and I should stress the logical) techniques filter out and set aside the female *prima materia*, without which there is no engendering heat, but the presence of which requires purification ("rites" in antiquity, "procedures" in modernity). What is at issue is never so simply the right to speak, but the timbre of the voice that finally does speak, especially when the "universal" is at stake.

Cybernation

Poetry is a receptacle of the most archaic associations of the linguistic function, which makes it seem inept if not simply irrelevant today. But poetry lingers on as a low-tech material base for high theory. The "linguistic turn" in the human sciences has ironically accentuated and valorized the very contingencies that made poetry appear fallible. Poetry now has to struggle with the multiple legacies it shares with the epistemological status of a debased medium, classical rhetoric, while at the same time signifying the dignity and impunity of the more exalted functions of "literature." The parameters of poetry's voice-over are now beyond reckoning, since every definition of poetry necessarily excludes something that returns, in the mobility of our communications environment, like the unforeseen siren call of an unacknowledged Muse, depositing a new litter of poems in its wake. The voice returns in an environment of disconnections, amputations, in a prodigal prosthetic congress, in which the "power" and "authority" of the voice can no longer be traced to a plausible speaker.

The pathos of signification at the present time is a mourning for the sign, a mourning for the innocent, natural, uncoerced sign that precedes what Herbert Schiller has called the "corporate takeover of public expression." "The corporate 'voice' now constitutes the national symbolic environment," he writes, noting the ominous significance that inheres not so much in the specific claims expressed by any given corporation, but "the organic process by which the corporate 'voice' is generalized across the entire range of cultural expression" (44).[20] After the corporate voice-over becomes generically indistinguishable from public discourse, any act of communication is a tacit form of bereavement, insofar as it is an active reminder of how we perpetuate our own captivity. To speak is to perform a duet with the corporate voice-over, and any attempt to struggle or resist simply strengthens the bonds that constrain us, since the bonds are nothing less than "our own" words.

Captured and enraptured by mediaspeak, we settle into the dismayed inertia of the mammal mesmerized by fatal headlights. So we mourn the signs that would protest the kidnapping of our means of expression, *as if* there were in fact "means of expression" not already overtaken (and underwritten) by pre-expressive voice-over and reinforced scopically by the continuum of an image track. In scholarly discourse this lament has been ingeniously displaced by synecdoche, so instead of protesting an erosion of the right to language as such, we have developed a pathological awareness of the "arbitrariness of the sign." The systematicity with which the sign has been revoked—privatized for corporate purposes—is rendered as an arbitrariness of the sign itself. In other words, a historical determinant of late capitalism as it impinges on language is misdiagnosed as a congenital defect of language as such.

In our media environment (an environment, to be precise, inseparable from its media), the frantic mobility of voices amounts to a vast spectacle of dissociative turbulence. The voice-over now functions to attach some remnant of the body to the spin cycle of information and control, which can variously masquerade as entertainment, news, politics, or even education. The voice-over itself acts as a gentle summons, an intimate command. The voice-over is what calls out to us from the other room to return to the monitor, to stay tuned to a specific transmitting channel.[21] The confidentiality of the voice-over itself, however, is effaced by the universality of the voice-over function. We are cocooned in a surrogate multiplicity; the voices we are accustomed to are utopian, belonging nowhere, regionless, without accent, rendering neutrality enticing, even exemplary.

If the oral rhetoric of print culture aspired to do the police in different voices (from Dickens to Eliot), the compulsion today is to homogenize the proliferation of voices—and internalize the police. We have yet to reckon with the punitive role of the voice-over. Excessive preoccupation with the reign of the visual—the centrality of the panopticon as brute enforcer—has, if anything, played along with the power brokers of the scopic regime. The duet of the ruler's eyes has swollen into the grotesque choral aggregate of the panopticon. There is something hypnotic about the lure of the carceral voice. From silent film through radio days and into the postwar supplementation of voice with its televisual component, the voice-over has been consistently pitched in the mode of command.

The concept of voice-over hails from film, of course, where the primary distraction of the visual element easily absorbs and effaces the subordinate labor of the off-screen voice. In the earliest film exhibitions, a century ago, lecturers addressed the audience as a sequence of short films was screened. These living vocal accompanists were replaced by subtitles (or intertitles between scenes), the graphic foreground of voice-over. In its presound era film was busy knitting a shroud of compensations for the missing voice. In silent movies, Mary Ann Doane suggests, "The absent voice reemerges in gestures and the contortions of the face—it is spread over the body of the actor" (335). When the talkies came, voice-over migrated decisively to documentation and newsreels, bonding the (inevitably male baritone) voice to a transcendent authority. The important thing to note is that voice-over initially developed as compensation for a lack. (It is fitting that Hollywood's most consistent use of voice-over for fictional narration is in film noir, a genre obsessed with lack, disorientation, and loss.) For some time now we have been citizens of a cybernation, occupying a mental homeless shelter that harbors Dan Rather, Roseanne Barr, and Bullwinkle. If Loony Tunes return (in John Ashbery's "Daffy Duck in Hollywood") as tour de force of the American sublime, it is altogether relevant to compare Pound's "news that stays news" with network news and the way the voice of the "anchor" underwrites the braille of the daily Real.

The voice-over of the concept stipulated by Aristotle and reaffirmed by Kant continues in the compulsion to hear individual voices as components of a larger and more "universal" voice,[22] the "voice that is great within us," in Wallace Stevens's phrase. The unity of consciousness, initially conceived as a matter of ethical dignity, then as superiority of intellect, eventually appears in the cyborg as unlimited circuitry in a technohuman system. Such a biotechnical mind is no longer congruent with a voice, so the specificity of the speaking subject gives way to the ventriloquial mimicry prevalent today. Poetic "license" is deflated when voice is licensed for commercial applications, carrying language along with it as an effluvia accompanying the image protocols that anatomize populations and bodies into spectacles of need, whose deficit can be compensated in service centers and distribution warehouses. In such scenes an assembly of autonomous consumers is promoted, but at the cost of dissipating the carnal sociality of congregation in the agora.

The great irony of the situation is that poets, patiently laboring under a cultural misconception, imagine that authenticity can be conflated with subjectivity, not realizing that subjectivity is simply the most acutely engineered of all our technologies—voice activated, setting in motion a replay of cultural "memories" that are generic, belonging to everyone and no one. Such simulated memories are more effective for being customized, like those provided for the "replicants" in Ridley Scott's film *Blade Runner*, or injected as a neocortex "vacation" for Arnold Schwarzenegger in *Total Recall*—for whom the one-size-fits-all snapshot supports a reverie of intimacy that cannot be contradicted by experience because there is no distinction between the subject and the semiotic cue. The replicants savor their simulated past just as, now, poets are compelled to nurture a simulated present, convulsively tuning in to the solace of "immediacy." But I recommend heeding Friedrich Kittler's reminder that aesthetics are always preceded by media. That is surely the import of Hesiod's Muses. The *aisthesis* preparatory to performance is subject to the broadcasting capabilities of the medium: "The pictures in the cinema can be fuzzy, or a beloved voice on the telephone can be filtered. The dependent variable of this compromise is what we take for our sense perception" ("Gramophone" 103). In the primacy now accorded the mass electronic media, our own physical natures acquire a supplementary, exotic aura—"dependent variables" that are to be ascertained in the final equation at our own initiative. The senses have become "theoreticians," as Marx put it, which is to say, witnesses to their own nomadic dispersal as industrial by-products. In these circumstances the senses fail to "add up" to a composite identity, because that sort of arithmetic is already proposed as the model for gratifying simulations of self—and I have in mind here the agenda of virtual reality, promoted as the exhilarating freedom to sample and reassemble the "meat" in more subjectively alluring and "site specific" ways.[23]

The ego, defining itself in the logic of market equivalence, is autistic, substituting the seriality of consumption for the laborious recursive structures of autopoiesis. Inasmuch as voice is designated as the colophon of the subject, it increasingly appears in prosthetic subordination to mind or computational power. Because the voice is always shadowed by a voice-over, a split not *in* but *prior* to the subject, marking the spot where the subject is indubitably embodied, the subject is hounded and ridiculed by the trickster impertinence of voice as phantom double. Voice is not a clothing of the naked body of language (though that is always a claim of voice-over); language does not recall itself as bodied forth in speech, adding voice to itself as a supplementary coloration. Quite the contrary: voice primordially calls the body to its acoustic materiality, its hollows and ducts and tubes, its respiration. The implication of voice with language is thus much more complex than anything that can be generated out of Saussure's binary, *langue/parole*. Voice includes, and is included in, laughing and crying, grunting and gurgling and moaning, none of which can be thought of as prearticulations, much as articulation seems to harken back to these bodily pulsions as roots. But even the term "root" is misleading inasmuch as it suggests a central stability. Philosophical anthropology (in the German school) sees a vital dissymmetry in the biological template of homo sapiens. Adolf Portmann's concept of an extra-uterine prematurity (also elaborated as "neoteny"), Max Scheler's "world-open" precondition of human instinct, Arnold Gehlen's insistence on our unspecialized nature—these all point to an ontogenic opportunism, a congenital indeterminacy, in which development is experimental, not teleological. The entirety of human development is regulated by something like Vaihinger's philosophy of the *as if*. Helmuth Plessner's work in philosophy of biology has made it clear that human existence is ambiguously grounded, occupying an "eccentric positionality." "As an eccentrically organized being, the human must *make itself* into what it *already is*" (309; my translation). In Plessner's view, "culture" is that collective mode of self-recuperation, a reservoir absorbing and stabilizing the seething decentering energy implicit in eccentric positionality. "Man would overcome the unmanageable eccentricity of his being, and would compensate for his divided existence, yet can only achieve this by way of things that are weighty enough to serve as counterweights for this existence" (311). Language is foremost among our counterweights. It is a detached bodily function orbiting as a paradoxical individuating/collectivizing impulse outside the body. Language, as biocultural artifact, is a pooling of the resources of what Whitman called "vocalism," which is a condition shared by humans with many other creatures. Where vocal emissions of other creatures are unmediated (and evaporate instantly), human vocalism derives from an *eccentric* positionality in which vocal expression is never complete. Voice is a biological countenance seeking semiotic discharge, continuously shunted into those relays and junctions, those semantic reservoirs that we call *language*. For humans there is no end of utterance; speech is teleologically indeterminate.

Heidegger's title *Unterwegs zur Sprache* captures the import. We do not possess or subsume language but are always "on the way to language." The sound-poetry ejaculations of Raoul Hausmann, Hugo Ball, Antonin

Artaud, and others are neither pre- nor postlinguistic but vocalizations at a tempo different from that generally permitted by the semantic assignments of "voice." Kurt Schwitters's grand *Ur-Sonate* is not preparatory to linguistic function, but a kind of counter-love, a reciprocal comportment of voice *on the way* to language but without any particular incentive to arrive. Heidegger regarded language as a power, a force in which we awaken, not a tool. This is the thrust of his inversion of the customary formula that poetry is a language art, when he says that "poetry never takes language as a raw material ready to hand, rather it is poetry which first makes language possible" (283). This is also the Viconian perspective of language as a residue of primal matter, *Urstoff* of creation, coevolving with humans.[24] Voice-over is thereby predicated on a biological unrest—whether or not we call it, with Plessner, eccentric positionality—a turbulence that animates voice and sets it on its path toward language, which is also where it overlaps with the human, not as substrate but as palimpsest. Language is a residual capacity, and poetry is that specific *residue* that alerts us to the leakage, the "creaking of the word," the "discrepant engagement," the improbable attraction of the fact that "like a piece of ice on a hot stove the poem must ride on its own melting" (Frost viii).

Voice "precedes the subject, which means, of course, that it is intimately linked with the subject. . . . Voice frays a path for the subject. But it is not the subject's voice" (Nancy 240).[25] Because so much contemporary verse practice presumes the equivalence of subjectivity and authenticity, we have become estranged from what Viktor Shklovsky referred to as "defamiliarization," forwarding or baring the aesthetic/technical device. The primal scenes of poetic inspiration suggest the unnerving realization that *voice is alien*. Poetry thus becomes the "practice of outside" in Robin Blaser's phrase, the *art of othering*. "It is within language that the world speaks to us with a voice that is not our own," Blaser writes (279). Along the same lines Shklovsky holds that "art removes objects from the automatism of perception," dis-habituating us from the sensory anesthetizing of the objects of awareness, something especially consequent upon the use of language (13). Shklovsky's views are frequently cited, but few retain his additional observation that "I personally feel that defamiliarization is found almost everywhere form is found" (18). Form is most useful as deformation, or violation of pattern recognition. "The language of poetry is, then, a difficult, roughened, impeded language. . . . We can define poetry as *attenuated*, *tortuous* speech" (22–23). Poetry is language pulverized. Poets have been traumatized by any intimation that "the voice that is great within us" has gotten into us by forces outside our control. The *device* that is great within us, then, is the swollen sum of our erasures. So the compulsion is to retrieve the present in a medium (in this case print) that facilitates fantasies of the unmediated. Voice has been nominated as the icon of this fantasy, but the wish-fulfilling association of voice with the speaking subject's authenticity (also known as phonocentrism) has exacted a price. Poets have lost touch with the archaic parables of voice-over, which instruct us in the ways in which inspiration always divests us of that security we so desperately crave as the sign of an empowerment we forever wish was ours alone, and not a sport of the gods or a bewitchment of the Muses.

NOTES

For their responses to drafts and their encouragement, I would like to thank Adalaide Morris, Chris Keep, Clayton Eshleman, David Cuthbert, and Kevin McGuirk.

    1. Lukacher is using "fading" with reference to Roland Barthes: "For Barthes, Being gives itself not through the presence of the voice but through the rhythm of its 'fading' " (77).

    2. Echo is of course the nymph in love with Narcissus who, in Ovid's account, is punished by Juno for concealing Jupiter's trysts. The punishment deprives her of originary speech, so her attempts at professing her love for Narcissus result in the senseless repetition of everything *he* says. My synoptic reference above neglects the more nuanced implications that Lawrence derives from Echo's plight as necessarily related to Narcissus, whose self-absorption she sees predicated on the elimination of dialogic exchange: "And so Echo fades away, unable to contact Narcissus once he ceases to speak, sound's absence established as a precondition for the image's irresistible allure." Lawrence takes the tale as an instructive parable about gender hierarchy: "The man's tragic obsession with the image is more important than the woman's problems of expression, her death simply preparation for the grand climax of his death. Woman and sound are allied on the 'weak side' of the story" (2).

    3. Levin brings considerable sagacity to his recommendation that we redirect our attention to *hearing* as the ground of Being. On the Tukano's *keori*, see 236–37.

    4. Bees also figure in Vergil's *Georgics*, in his augmentation of the Orphic descent to Hades, narrated within the frame of apiculture patron Aristaeus, who loses his bees after lustfully pursuing Eurydice to her inadvertent death. On prophecy and the underworld, see Clark.

    5. An excellent resource is Bundy.

    6. Gregory Nagy's etymological speculations are pertinent: "The very form *Mousa* may well be derived from the same root **men-* as in *mania*. If this etymology is correct, then the very word for Muse reflects an earlier stage when not only the one who is inspired and the one who speaks the words of inspiration are the same, but even the type of mental state marked by *mania* is not yet differentiated from the type of mental state marked by formations with **men-t-* and **men-h—*, 'remember,' 'have the mind connected with' " ("Ancient Greek Poetry" 61). Nagy's speculations are foreshadowed by Plato's in *Phaedrus* (244a–c), in which an etymological back-

ground is sketched linking *mantike* (divination) with *manike* (craziness). As Socrates said, the simple addition of a letter is sufficient to render *manic* as *mantic*.

7. In Kant this is a prearticulate murmur of consent, since in his view "in the judgment of taste nothing is postulated but . . . a *universal voice*."

8. Segal goes on: "Whereas the success of Orpheus reflects the power of language, raised to its furthest limits, to cross the boundaries between opposing realms of existence, matter and consciousness, and finally life and death, his failure reflects the inability of the language of art to empty itself of the subjectivity of the artist, to reach beyond emotion and obey the laws of an objective reality outside, in this case the conditions that the gods of the underworld impose for Eurydice's return" (8). Segal succumbs, in this account, to the recent tendency to emphasize Orpheus as a figure of the poet, to endow him with character traits, and constitute him as a patron of subjectivity.

9. See Warden ix–x for a summary of the Orphic cosmology.

10. Sewell proposes an Orphic lineage of inquiry into two related questions: "*What power and place has poetry in the living universe?*" and "*What is the biological function of poetry in the natural history of the human organism?*" (4) The "main people" of this tradition of inquiry, according to Sewell, are Bacon, Shakespeare, Milton, Hooke, Vico, Linnaeus, Swedenborg, Erasmus Darwin, Goethe, Novalis, Coleridge, Wordsworth, Shelley, Emerson, Renan, Hugo, Mallarmé, and Rilke (5).

11. On Orpheus-Christus, see Friedman chap. 2.

12. The Dogon myth works in concert with the Greek myth of Psyche's tasks, a necessarily dark subordination in Robert Duncan's "Poem Beginning with a Line by Pindar." The ants, those paradigms of minute detail, come to the aid of those, like Psyche, who "must follow to the letter / freakish instructions" (Duncan 65). Duncan also evokes in his poem the image of Pound at Pisa, for whom the ant was a figure of survival in a time of desperation ("an ant's forefoot shall save you").

13. "Death is the sanction of everything that the storyteller can tell," writes Benjamin. "He has borrowed his authority from death" (94).

14. Virilio has recently warned of a conversion of paradigms of social mobility to those of handicapped access. The fate of the individual, then, is that of a "*terminal citizen*" who will soon be equipped with interactive prostheses whose pathological model is that of the 'motorized handicapped'" (11). The original science fiction vision of such a prosthetic world is Bernard Wolfe's novel *Limbo* (1950).

15. Monitor: Minotaur. The near homonym invites reflection on the sorts of transgression involved in migratory lusts and Daedalian transpositions. The Minotaur was offspring of an unholy union between Pasiphaë and a bull, a copulation arranged by Daedalus by prosthetic means (Pasiphaë occupying the hollow interior of a bovine mannequin of sufficient attraction to the bull). The ghost in such a machine, being a flesh and blood woman, gives birth to a monster who ends up being imprisoned in a labyrinth—which is exactly what a microchip looks like.

16. Mandelstam also notes that Dante wrote with a quill and would have been mindful of the winged materiality of such an implement. "A pen is a small piece of bird's flesh. Of course Dante, who never forgets the origin of things, remembers this. His technique of writing in broad strokes and curves grows into the figured flights of flocks of birds" (40).

17. Jorie Graham, for instance, has attempted to integrate the cinematic techniques of lap dissolve and slow motion into her poems. See especially *Materialism*.

18. The figure of the poet as cyborg I want to evoke here is from Chris Marker's documentary meditation *Sans Soleil*, in which we see a mannequin in a men's clothing department of a Tokyo department store. The mannequin is fabricated to resemble John F. Kennedy and is outfitted with a tape loop of his voice from the famous inauguration speech: "Ask not what your country can do for you, ask what you can do for your country." (The Muses appear here as a female choral accompaniment, a supra-voice-over, seconding the emotion in a Tokyo Motown motif.)

19. For an expanded version of the following, see Rasula, "Gendering the Muse."

20. Colloquial expressions claimed as corporate slogans—such as "Just do it!" and "You deserve a break today"—become a form of private property that is not off limits to the public at large. Quite the reverse: the public is enticed to adopt the corporate slogan by recognizing it as already idiomatic, as if it were "part of nature, part of us," in Wallace Stevens's line. The "language of the tribe" is thus broadcast by sound and image back to the population, but having been run through a corporate vocoder.

21. Altman has made the penetrating observation that approximately half of the time television sets are on in the United States, they are not being watched but are heard or, rather, *overheard* from other rooms. Such use of the medium potentially converts all television voices into voice-over, since the voice hails from an unseen speaker and applies to a (temporarily) unseen image or situation.

22. "We may now see that in the judgment of taste nothing is postulated but such a *universal voice*, in respect of the satisfaction without the intervention of concepts, and thus the *possibility* of an aesthetical judgment that can, at the same time, be regarded as valid for everyone (for that can only be done by a logically universal judgment because it can adduce reasons); it only *imputes* this agreement to everyone, as a case of the rule in respect of which it expects, not confirmation by concepts, but assent from others" (Kant 50–51).

23. For two precautionary views on the ascetic overtones of the rush into cyberspace, I recommend "The Erotic Ontology of Cyberspace," by Michael Heim, and "Will the Real Body Please Stand Up?: Boundary Stories about Virtual Cultures," by Allucquere Stone, both in Benedikt.

24. For a much more extensive presentation of these thoughts, see Rasula and McCaffery.

25. Nancy is summarizing Hegel in this passage. See also Žižek's expositions of Lacan, via classic Hollywood cinema, regarding ways "the voice functions as a foreign body, as a kind of parasite introducing a radical split" (*Enjoy* 2). Žižek draws on Michel Chion's concept of the uncannily displaced voice, *la voix acousmatique*, as the auditory form of what is more famously referred to as the *gaze*: "the superegoic voice, for example, addressing me without being attached to any particular bearer . . . functions again as a stain, whose inert presence interferes like a strange body and prevents me from achieving my self-identity" (*Looking* 126).

WORKS CITED

Alain. *The Gods*. Trans. Richard Pevear. New York: New Directions, 1974.

Altman, Rick. "Television/Sound." *Studies in Entertainment*. Ed. Tania Modleski. Bloomington: Indiana University Press, 1986. 39–54.

Aristotle. *Poetics. The Complete Works of Aristotle: The Revised Oxford Translation*. Ed. Jonathan Barnes. Princeton: Princeton University Press, 1984.

Basso, Ellen. *A Musical View of the Universe: Kalapalo Myth and Ritual Performances*. Philadelphia: University of Pennsylvania Press, 1985.

Benedikt, Michael, ed. *Cyberspace: First Steps*. Cambridge, Mass.: MIT Press, 1991.

Benjamin, Walter. "The Storyteller." *Illuminations: Essays and Reflections*. Ed. Hannah Arendt. Trans. Harry Zohn. New York: Schocken, 1968. 83–109.

Blanchot, Maurice. *The Siren's Song: Selected Essays*. Ed. Gabriel Josipovici. Trans. Sacha Rabinovitch. Bloomington: Indiana University Press, 1982.

Blaser, Robin. "The Practice of Outside." *The Collected Books of Jack Spicer*. Ed. Robin Blaser. Los Angeles: Black Sparrow, 1975. 271–329.

Bukatman, Scott. *Terminal Identity: The Virtual Subject in Postmodern Science Fiction*. Durham: Duke University Press, 1993.

Bundy, Murray Wright. *The Theory of the Imagination in Classical and Mediaeval Thought*. Vol. 12, nos. 2–3. University of Illinois Studies in Language and Literature. Urbana: University of Illinois Press, 1927.

Clark, Raymond J. *Catabasis: Vergil and the Wisdom-Tradition*. Amsterdam: B. R. Gruner, 1979.

Cooper, Alan. "Imagining Prophecy." *Poetry and Prophecy: The Beginnings of a Literary Tradition*. Ed. James L. Kugel. Ithaca: Cornell University Press, 1990. 26–44.

Deleuze, Gilles, and Felix Guattari. *A Thousand Plateaus: Capitalism and Schizophrenia*. Trans. Brian Massumi. Minneapolis: University of Minnesota Press, 1987.

Derrida, Jacques. *Dissemination*. Trans. Barbara Johnson. Chicago: University of Chicago Press, 1981.

Doane, Mary Ann. "The Voice in the Cinema: The Articulation of Body and Space." *Narrative, Apparatus, Ideology: A Film Theory Reader*. Ed. Philip Rosen. New York: Columbia University Press, 1986. 335–48.

Duncan, Robert. *The Opening of the Field*. New York: Grove, 1960.

Emerson, Ralph Waldo. *Essays and Lectures*. New York: Literary Classics, 1983.

Foucault, Michel. *Power/Knowledge: Selected Interviews and Other Writings, 1972–1977*. Ed. Colin Gordon. Trans. Colin Gordon et al. New York: Pantheon, 1980.

———. "The Subject and Power." *Art after Modernism: Rethinking Representation*. Ed. Brian Wallis. Boston: Godine, 1984. 417–34.

Freud, Sigmund. "Analysis of a Case of Hysteria." *Collected Papers*. Vol. 3. *Case Histories*. Trans. A. and J. Strachey. London: Hogarth, 1925. 13–146.

Friedman, John B. *Orpheus in the Middle Ages*. Cambridge, Mass.: Harvard University Press, 1970.

Frost, Robert. *Complete Poems of Robert Frost*. New York: Holt, 1949.

Graham, Jorie. *Materialism*. Hopewell, N.J.: Ecco, 1993.

Griaule, Marcel. *Conversations with Ogotemmêli: An Introduction to Dogon Religious Ideas.* London: Oxford University Press for the International African Institute, 1965.

Grivel, Charles. "The Phonograph's Horned Mouth." Trans. Stephen Sartarelli. *Wireless Imagination: Sound, Radio, and the Avant-Garde.* Ed. Douglas Kahn and Gregory Whitehead. Cambridge, Mass.: MIT Press, 1992. 31–61.

Heidegger, Martin. "Hölderlin and the Essence of Poetry." *Existence and Being.* Chicago: Regnery, 1949. 270–91.

Hesiod. *The Homeric Hymns and Homerica.* Trans. Hugh G. Evelyn-White. Cambridge, Mass.: Harvard University Press, 1936.

Homer. *The Iliad.* Trans. Robert Fitzgerald. Garden City, N.Y.: Anchor, 1975.

Kahn, Douglas. "Death in Light of the Phonograph: Raymond Roussel's *Locus Solus.*" *Wireless Imagination: Sound, Radio, and the Avant-Garde.* Ed. Douglas Kahn and Gregory Whitehead. Cambridge, Mass.: MIT Press, 1992. 69–103.

Kant, Immanuel. *Critique of Judgment.* Trans. J. H. Bernard. New York: Hafner, 1951.

Kittler, Friedrich A. *Discourse Networks, 1800/1900.* Trans. Michael Metteer, with Chris Cullens. Stanford: Stanford University Press, 1990.

———. "Gramophone, Film, Typewriter." Trans. Dorothea von Mücke and Philippe Similon. *October* 41 (Summer 1987): 101–18.

Lawler, Justus. *Celestial Pantomime: Poetic Structures of Transcendence.* New Haven: Yale University Press, 1979.

Lawrence, Amy. *Echo and Narcissus: Women's Voices in Classical Hollywood Cinema.* Berkeley: University of California Press, 1991.

Leiris, Michel. *Rules of the Game I: Scratches.* Trans. Lydia Davis. New York: Paragon, 1991.

Levin, David Michael. *The Listening Self: Personal Growth, Social Change, and the Closure of Metaphysics.* New York: Routledge, 1989.

Levinas, Emmanuel. *The Levinas Reader.* Ed. and trans. Séan Hand. Oxford: Blackwell, 1989.

Lukacher, Ned. *Primal Scenes: Literature, Philosophy, Psychoanalysis.* Ithaca: Cornell University Press, 1986.

Mackey, Nathaniel. *Discrepant Engagement: Dissonance, Cross-Culturality, and Experimental Writing.* Cambridge: Cambridge University Press, 1993.

Mandelstam, Osip. *Selected Essays.* Trans. Sidney Monas. Austin: University of Texas Press, 1977.

Manetti, Giovanni. *Theories of the Sign in Classical Antiquity.* Trans. Christine Richardson. Bloomington: Indiana University Press, 1993.

Murray, Penelope. "Poetic Inspiration in Early Greece." *Journal of Hellenic Studies* 101 (1981): 87–100.

Nagy, Gregory. "Ancient Greek Poetry, Prophecy, and Concepts of Theory." *Poetry and Prophecy.* Ed. James L. Kugel. Ithaca: Cornell University Press, 1990. 56–64.

———. *Greek Mythology and Poetics.* Ithaca: Cornell University Press, 1990.

Nancy, Jean-Luc. *The Birth to Presence.* Trans. Brian Holmes et al. Stanford: Stanford University Press, 1993.

Olson, Charles. *Additional Prose: A Bibliography on America, Proprioception, and Other*

Notes and Essays. Ed. George F. Butterick. Bolinas, Calif.: Four Seasons Foundation, 1974.

————. *The Maximus Poems*. Ed. George F. Butterick. Berkeley: University of California Press, 1983.

Owen, Stephen. *Mi-Lou: Poetry and the Labyrinth of Desire*. Cambridge, Mass.: Harvard University Press, 1989.

Padoux, André. *Vāc: The Concept of the Word in Selected Hindu Tantras*. Trans. Jacques Gontier. Albany: State University of New York Press, 1990.

Paz, Octavio. *Children of the Mire: Modern Poetry from Romanticism to the Avant-Garde*. Trans. Rachel Phillips. Cambridge, Mass.: Harvard University Press, 1974.

Perloff, Marjorie. *Radical Artifice: Writing Poetry in the Age of Media*. Chicago: University of Chicago Press, 1991.

Picard, Max. *The World of Silence*. Washington, D.C.: Regnery Gateway, 1988.

Plessner, Helmuth. *Die Stufen des Organischen und der Mensch: Einleitung in die philosophische Anthropologie*. 2nd ed. Berlin: Walter de Gruyter, 1965.

Pucci, Pietro. *Hesiod and the Language of Poetry*. Baltimore: Johns Hopkins University Press, 1977.

Rasula, Jed. "Gendering the Muse." *Sulfur* 35 (Fall 1994): 59–76.

Rasula, Jed, and Steve McCaffery, eds. *Imagining Language*. Cambridge, Mass.: MIT Press, 1997.

Rilke, Rainer Maria. *Selected Works*. Trans. G. Craig Houston. Vol. 1. New York: New Directions, 1960.

Rothenberg, Jerome. "Pre-Face (1967)." *Technicians of the Sacred: A Range of Poetics from Africa, America, Asia, Europe, and Oceania*. Berkeley: University of California Press, 1968. xxv–xxxiii.

Sanders, Ed. *Investigative Poetry*. San Francisco: City Lights, 1976.

Santillana, Giorgio de, and Hertha von Dechend. *Hamlet's Mill: An Essay on Myth and the Frame of Time*. Boston: Gambit, 1969.

Scheinberg, Susan. "The Bee Maidens of the Homeric *Hymn to Hermes*." *Harvard Studies in Classical Philology*. Vol. 83. Cambridge, Mass.: Harvard University Press, 1979. 1–28.

Schiller, Herbert I. *Culture, Inc.: The Corporate Takeover of Public Expression*. New York: Oxford University Press, 1989.

Segal, Charles. *Orpheus: The Myth of the Poet*. Baltimore: Johns Hopkins University Press, 1989.

Sewell, Elizabeth. *The Orphic Voice: Poetry and Natural History*. New Haven: Yale University Press, 1960.

Shklovsky, Viktor. "Art as Technique." *Russian Formalist Criticism*. Ed. and trans. Lee Lemon and Marion Reis. Lincoln: University of Nebraska Press, 1965. 3–24.

Stevens, Wallace. *Opus Posthumous*. Ed. Samuel French Morse. London: Faber, 1957.

————. "Variations on a Summer Day." *The Palm at the End of the Mind*. Ed. Holly Stevens. New York: Knopf, 1971. 170–73.

Taussig, Michael. *Mimesis and Alterity: A Particular History of the Senses*. New York: Routledge, 1993.

Thoreau, Henry. "Sounds." *Walden*. Ed. Robert Sayre. New York: Library of America, 1985.

Vernant, Jean-Pierre. *Mortals and Immortals: Collected Essays*. Ed. Froma Zeitlin. Princeton: Princeton University Press, 1991.

Virilio, Paul. "The Third Interval: A Critical Transition." *Rethinking Technologies*. Ed. Verena Andermatt Conley. Minneapolis: University of Minnesota Press, 1993. 3–12.

Warden, John, ed. *Orpheus: The Metamorphoses of a Myth*. Toronto: University of Toronto Press, 1982.

Whitman, Walt. *The Complete Poetry and Prose*. New York: Library of America, 1982.

Žižek, Slavoj. *Enjoy Your Symptom! Jacques Lacan in Hollywood and Out*. New York: Routledge, 1992.

———. *Looking Awry: An Introduction to Jacques Lacan through Popular Culture*. Cambridge, Mass.: MIT Press, 1991.

Zukofsky, Louis. *Prepositions: The Collected Critical Essays of Louis Zukofsky*. New York: Horizon, 1968.

Zwicky, Jan. *Lyric Philosophy*. Toronto: University of Toronto Press, 1992.

BIBLIOGRAPHY

ARCHIVES AND PRINTED SOURCES

Adorno, T. W., and M. Horkheimer. "The Culture Industry: Enlightenment as Mass Deception." *Mass Communication and Society.* Ed. James Curran, Michael Gurevitch, and Janet Woollacott. London: Edward Arnold, 1977. 349–83.

Ahl, Frederick. *Metaformations: Soundplay and Wordplay in Ovid and Other Classical Poets.* Ithaca: Cornell University Press, 1985.

Alain. *The Gods.* Trans. Richard Pevear. New York: New Directions, 1974.

Algarín, Miguel, and Bob Holman. *Aloud: Voices from the Nuyorican Poets Cafe.* New York: Holt, 1994.

Allen, Donald M., ed. *The New American Poetry, 1945–1960.* New York: Grove, 1960.

Allen, Donald M., and Warren Tallman, eds. *The Poetics of the New American Poetry.* New York: Grove, 1973.

Altieri, Charles. *Enlarging the Temple: New Directions in American Poetry during the 1960's.* Lewisburg, Pa.: Bucknell University Press, 1979.

———. "The Postmodernism of David Antin's *Tuning.*" *College English* 48 (1986): 9–26.

Altman, Rick. "Television/Sound." *Studies in Entertainment.* Ed. Tania Modleski. Bloomington: Indiana University Press, 1986. 39–54.

Anderson, Laurie. *Collected Videos.* Los Angeles: Warner Reprise, 1990.

———. *United States.* New York: Harper, 1984.

Anderson, Perry. *A Zone of Engagement.* London: Verso, 1992.

Angus, Robert. "History of Magnetic Recording: Part I." *Audio* 68.8 (1984): 27–33, 96–97.

———. "History of Magnetic Recording: Part II." *Audio* 68.9 (1984): 33–39.

Antin, David. "tuning." *tuning.* New York: New Directions, 1984. 105–42.

———. "whos listening out there." *tuning.* New York: New Directions, 1984. 269–96.

Arcand, Pierre-André. "Traffic Somewhere between Media." *Performance au Canada, 1970–1990.* Ed. Alain-Martin Richard and Clive Robertson. Quebec: Editions Intervention, 1991. 209.

Archer, Gleason L. *History of Radio to 1926.* New York: American Historical Society, 1938.

Aristotle. *Poetics* 9:6–7. *The Complete Works of Aristotle: The Revised Oxford Translation.* Ed. Jonathan Barnes. Princeton: Princeton University Press, 1984.

Arnheim, Rudolf. *Radio.* Trans. Margaret Ludwig and Herbert Read. London: Faber & Faber, 1936.

Arnold, Matthew. *Culture and Anarchy.* Ed. J. Dover Wilson. Cambridge: Cambridge University Press, 1932.

Austin, J. L. *How to Do Things with Words.* Cambridge, Mass.: Harvard University Press, 1975.

Bakhtin, M. M. *The Dialogic Imagination.* Ed. Michael Holquist. Trans. Caryl Emerson and Michael Holquist. Austin: University of Texas Press, 1981.

Baker, Houston A., Jr. *Modernism and the Harlem Renaissance*. Chicago: University of Chicago Press, 1987.

Ball, Hugo. *Flight out of Time: A Dada Diary*. Ed. John Elderfield. Trans. Ann Raimes. New York: Viking, 1974.

Baraka, Amiri. "Four for Trane." *Black Music*. New York: Morrow, 1967. 156–61.

———. "History as Process." *Black Magic: Sabotage, Target Study, Black Art: Poetry, 1961–1967*. Indianapolis: Bobbs-Merrill, 1969. 38.

———. "Lines to García Lorca." *New Negro Poets USA*. Ed. Langston Hughes. Bloomington: Indiana University Press, 1964. 55.

———. "Words." *Tales*. New York: Grove, 1967. 89–91.

Barrett, Leonard E., Sr. *The Rastafarians: Sounds of Cultural Dissonance*. Boston: Beacon, 1988.

Barthes, Roland. "Listening." *The Responsibility of Forms: Critical Essays on Music, Art, and Representation*. Trans. Richard Howard. New York: Hill & Wang, 1985. 245–60.

———. *S/Z*. Trans. Richard Miller. New York: Hill & Wang, 1974.

Barzun, Jacques. "Voix, Rythmes, et Chants Simultanés — Esthétique de la Poésie Dramatique." *Poème et Drame* 4 (May 1913): 6–13.

Basso, Ellen. *A Musical View of the Universe: Kalapalo Myth and Ritual Performances*. Philadelphia: University of Pennsylvania Press, 1985.

Bataille, Georges. *The Accursed Share: An Essay on General Economy*. Trans. Robert Hurley. 3 vols. New York: Zone Books, 1988–91.

———. *The Impossible*. Trans. Robert Hurley. San Francisco: City Lights, 1991.

Baudry, Jean-Louis. "Ideological Effects of the Basic Cinematographic Apparatus." *Narrative, Apparatus, Ideology: A Film Theory Reader*. Ed. Philip Rosen. New York: Columbia University Press, 1986. 286–97.

Bauman, Zygmunt. "Modernity, Postmodernity, and Ethics: An Interview with Zygmunt Bauman." *Telos* 93 (Fall 1992): 133–44.

Beckett, Samuel. *Krapp's Last Tape*. Ed. James Knowlson. Vol. 3. *The Theatrical Notebooks of Samuel Beckett*. New York: Grove, 1982.

Begnal, Michael H., and Grace Eckley. *Narrator and Character in "Finnegans Wake."* Lewisburg, Pa.: Bucknell University Press, 1975.

Benedikt, Michael, ed. *Cyberspace: First Steps*. Cambridge, Mass.: MIT Press, 1991.

Benjamin, Walter. "The Storyteller." *Illuminations: Essays and Reflections*. Ed. Hannah Arendt. Trans. Harry Zohn. New York: Schocken, 1968. 83–109.

———. "The Work of Art in the Age of Mechanical Reproduction." *Illuminations: Essays and Reflections*. Ed. Hannah Arendt. Trans. Harry Zohn. New York: Schocken, 1968. 217–51.

Bennett, Tony. "Useful Culture." *Cultural Studies* 6 (1992): 395–408.

Benson, Steve. *Blindspots*. Cambridge, Mass.: Whale Cloth Press, 1981.

Bergman, Par. *"Modernolatria" et "simultaneita": Recherches sur deux tendances dans l'avant-garde litteraire en Italie et en France à la veille de la première guerre mondiale*. Doctoral thesis. Uppsala University, 1962. Uppsala: Svenska bokforlaget/Bonniers, 1962.

Bernstein, Charles. *Content's Dream: Essays, 1975–1984*. Los Angeles: Sun & Moon, 1986.

————, ed. *Close Listening: Poetry and the Performed Word*. New York: Oxford University Press, forthcoming.

Bernstein, Michael André. *The Tale of the Tribe: Ezra Pound and the Modern Verse Epic*. Princeton: Princeton University Press, 1980.

Berry, James, ed. *News for Babylon: The Chatto Book of West Indian-British Poetry*. London: Chatto & Windus, 1984.

Bhabha, Homi K. "DissemiNation: Time, Narrative, and Margins of the Modern Nation." *Nation and Narration*. Ed. Homi K. Bhabha. New York: Routledge, 1990. 291–322.

————. "Interrogating Identity: The Postcolonial Prerogative." *Anatomy of Racism*. Ed. David Theo Goldberg. Minneapolis: University of Minnesota Press, 1990. 183–209.

Biocca, Frank A. "The Pursuit of Sound: Radio, Perception, and Utopia in the Early Twentieth Century." *Media, Culture, and Society* 10 (1988): 61–79.

Blanchot, Maurice. *The Siren's Song: Selected Essays*. Ed. Gabriel Josipovici. Trans. Sacha Rabinovitch. Bloomington: Indiana University Press, 1982.

Blaser, Robin. "The Practice of Outside." *The Collected Books of Jack Spicer*. Ed. Robin Blaser. Los Angeles: Black Sparrow, 1975. 271–329.

Boone, Elizabeth Hill. "Introduction: Writing and Recording Knowledge." *Writing without Words: Alternative Literacies in Mesoamerica and the Andes*. Ed. Elizabeth Hill Boone and Walter D. Mignolo. Durham: Duke University Press, 1994. 3–26.

Bordwell, David, and Kristin Thompson. *Film Art: An Introduction*. New York: McGraw, 1990.

Bornstein, George. "What Is the Text of a Poem by Yeats?" *Palimpsest: Editorial Theory in the Humanities*. Ed. George Bornstein and Ralph G. Williams. Ann Arbor: University of Michigan Press, 1993. 167–94.

Bourdieu, Pierre. *Homo Academicus*. Trans. Peter Collier. Stanford: Stanford University Press, 1988.

Brathwaite, Edward Kamau. "Contradictory Omens: Cultural Diversity and Integration in the Caribbean." Monograph no. 1. Mona, Jamaica: Savacou Publications, 1974.

————. *History of the Voice: The Development of Nation Language in Anglophone Caribbean Poetry*. London: New Beacon, 1984.

Brenton, Myron. *The Privacy Invaders*. New York: Coward-McCann, 1964.

Breslin, James E. B. *From Modern to Contemporary: American Poetry, 1945–1965*. Chicago: University of Chicago Press, 1984.

Brontë, Charlotte. *Jane Eyre*. Ed. Richard J. Dunn. New York: Norton, 1971.

Brooke-Rose, Christine. *A Grammar of Metaphor*. London: Secker and Warburg, 1958.

Brown, Bob. *The Readies*. Bad-Ems: Roving Eye Press, 1930.

————. *1450–1950*. Paris: Black Sun, 1929. New York: Jargon, 1959.

Brown, Lloyd W. *West Indian Poetry*. London: Heinemann, 1984.

Bukatman, Scott. *Terminal Identity: The Virtual Subject in Postmodern Science Fiction*. Durham: Duke University Press, 1993.

Bundy, Murray Wright. *The Theory of the Imagination in Classical and Mediaeval Thought*.

Vol. 12, nos. 2–3. *University of Illinois Studies in Language and Literature.*
Urbana: University of Illinois Press, 1927.

Burroughs, William S. "The Art of Fiction." *Paris Review* 9.35 (1965): 12–49.

———. "The Cut-up Method of Brion Gysin." *Re/Search* 4–5 (1982): 35–38.

———. *The Ticket That Exploded.* New York: Grove, 1967.

Cage, John. "Art Is Either a Complaint or Do Something Else." *Aerial* 6/7.
Washington: Edge, 1991. 1–35. Repr. in revised form in Retallack, *Musicage:
Cage Muses on Words, Art, Music.* Hanover, N.H.: Wesleyan University Press,
1996. 3–42.

———. "Diary: How To Improve the World (You Will Only Make Matters
Worse) Continued, 1971–72." *M: Writings '67–'72.* Middletown, Conn.: Wesleyan
University Press, 1973. 195–217.

———. *Empty Words: Writings '73–'78.* Middletown, Conn.: Wesleyan University
Press, 1979.

———. *For the Birds: John Cage in Conversation with Daniel Charles.* Salem, N.H.:
Marion Boyars, 1981.

———. *I–VI.* Cambridge, Mass.: Harvard University Press, 1990.

———. "James Joyce, Marcel Duchamp, Erik Satie: An Alphabet." *X: Writings
'79–'82.* Middletown, Conn.: Wesleyan University Press, 1983. 53–101.

———. *M: Writings '67–'72.* Middletown, Conn.: Wesleyan University Press, 1973.

———. "Notes on Compositions III, 1967–78." *John Cage, Writer: Previously
Uncollected Pieces.* Selected and introduced by Richard Kostelanetz. New York:
Limelight, 1993. 93–108.

———. Preface to *"Lecture on the Weather." Empty Words: Writings '73–'78.*
Middletown, Conn.: Wesleyan University Press, 1979. 3–5.

———. *Roaratorio: An Irish Circus on Finnegans Wake.* Ed. Klaus Schoning.
Munich: Atheneum, 1985.

———. "Second Conversation with Joan Retallack." *Aerial* 6/7. Washington:
Edge, 1991. 97–130. Repr. in revised form as "Cage's Loft, New York City:
September 6–7, 1990," in Retallack, *Musicage: Cage Muses on Words, Art, Music.*
Hanover, N.H.: Wesleyan University Press, 1996. 43–79.

———. *Silence: Lectures and Writings.* Middletown, Conn.: Wesleyan University
Press, 1961.

———. "Time (Three Autokus) (1986)." *John Cage II.* Ed. Heinz-Klaus Metzger
and Rainer Riehn. *Musik-Konzepte* II (Munich 1990). 264–304.

———. "Toyko Lecture and Three Mesostics." *John Cage: Writer: Previously
Uncollected Pieces.* Selected and introduced by Richard Kostelanetz. New York:
Limelight, 1993. 177–82.

———. "What You Say . . . ." *Formations* 4.1 (Spring–Summer 1987): 52–67. Repr.
in *John Cage II.* Ed. Heinz-Klaus Metzger and Rainer Riehn. *Musik-Konzepte* II
(Munich 1990). 267–77.

———. "Writing for the Second Time through *Finnegans Wake*." *Empty Words:
Writings '73–'78.* Middletown, Conn.: Wesleyan University Press, 1979. 133–76.

Camras, Marvin, ed. *Magnetic Tape Recording.* New York: Van Nostrand
Reinhold, 1985.

Carpenter, Humphrey. *A Serious Character: The Life of Ezra Pound.* New York: Delta, 1988.

Carpentier, Alejo. *The Lost Steps.* Trans. Harriet de Onís. New York: Noonday, 1989.

Certeau, Michel de. *The Practice of Everyday Life.* Trans. Steven F. Rendall. Berkeley: University of California Press, 1984.

Chabert, Pierre. "Samuel Beckett as Director." Trans. M. A. Bonney and J. Knowlson. *Krapp's Last Tape: A Theatre Notebook.* Ed. James Knowlson. London: Brutus, 1980. 85–107.

Chambers, Iain. *Migrancy, Culture, Identity.* New York: Routledge, 1994.

Chevannes, Barry. "The Literature of Rastafari." *Social and Economic Studies* 26 (1977): 239–62.

Clark, Raymond J. *Catabasis: Vergil and the Wisdom-Tradition.* Amsterdam: B. R. Gruner, 1979.

Cliff, Michelle. *No Telephone to Heaven.* New York: Dutton, 1987.

Clough, Rosa Trillo. *Futurism: The Story of a Modern Art Movement, a New Appraisal.* New York: Philosophical Library, 1961.

Clover, Joshua. "The Avant-Garde Art of Noise." Review of *Wireless Imagination: Sound, Radio, and the Avant-Garde.* Ed. Douglas Kahn and Gregory Whitehead. *San Francisco Review of Books* 18.2 (1993): 30–31.

Cohen, Tom. *Anti-Mimesis from Plato to Hitchcock.* Cambridge: Cambridge University Press, 1994.

Collins, Hugh. "Political Ideology in Australia." *Australia: The Daedalus Symposium.* Ed. Stephen R. Graubard. North Ryde, N.S.W., Australia: Angus and Robertson, 1985. 147–69.

Compact Edition of the Oxford English Dictionary. Oxford: Oxford University Press, 1971, 1988.

Connor, James A. "RADIO free JOYCE: *Wake* Language and the Experience of Radio." In this volume.

Conrad, Joseph. Preface to *The Nigger of the "Narcissus," Typhoon, and Other Stories.* Baltimore: Penguin, 1963. 11–14.

Cook, Deborah. "Umbrellas, Laundry Bills, and Resistance: The Place of Foucault's Interviews in His Corpus." *CLIO* 21 (1992): 145–55.

Cooper, Alan. "Imagining Prophecy." *Poetry and Prophecy: The Beginnings of a Literary Tradition.* Ed. James L. Kugel. Ithaca: Cornell University Press, 1990. 26–44.

Cooper, Carolyn. *Noises in the Blood: Orality, Gender, and the "Vulgar" Body of Jamaican Popular Culture.* Durham: Duke University Press, 1995.

Copjec, Joan. "Vampires, Breast-Feeding, and Anxiety." *October* 58 (Fall 1991): 24–43.

Cory, Mark E. "Soundplay: The Polyphonous Tradition of German Radio Art." *Wireless Imagination: Sound, Radio, and the Avant-Garde.* Ed. Douglas Kahn and Gregory Whitehead. Cambridge, Mass.: MIT Press, 1992. 331–71.

Creeley, Robert. "The Language." *The Collected Poems of Robert Creeley, 1945–1975.* Berkeley: University of California Press, 1982. 283.

Crisell, Andrew J. *Understanding Radio*. London: Methuen, 1986.

Culler, Jonathan. "The Call of the Phoneme." *On Puns: The Foundation of Letters*. Ed. Jonathan Culler. New York: Blackwell, 1988. 1–16.

———, ed. *On Puns: The Foundation of Letters*. New York: Blackwell, 1988.

Czitrom, Daniel J. *Media and the American Mind: From Morse to McLuhan*. Chapel Hill: University of North Carolina Press, 1982.

Dagognet, François. *Etienne-Jules Marey: A Passion for the Trace*. Trans. Robert Galeta with Jeanine Herman. New York: Zone, 1992.

Damon, Maria. *The Dark End of the Street: Margins in American Vanguard Poetry*. Minneapolis: University of Minnesota Press, 1993.

"Dance Beaters." Kingston, Jamaica, *Abeng* 19 July 1969.

Davidson, Michael. " 'By ear, he sd': Audio-Tapes and Contemporary Criticism." *Credences* n.s. 1.1 [1981]: 105–20.

———. *The San Francisco Renaissance: Poetics and Community at Mid-century*. Cambridge: Cambridge University Press, 1989.

———. "Writing at the Boundaries." *New York Times Book Review* 24 February 1985: 1, 28–29.

Davies, Hugh. "A History of Recorded Sound." *Poésie Sonore Internationale*. Ed. Henri Chopin. Paris: J. M. Place, 1979. 13–40.

Davis, Stephen. *Bob Marley*. Garden City, N.Y.: Doubleday, 1985.

Debord, Guy. "Détournement as Negation and Prelude." *Situationist International Anthology*. Ed. and trans. Ken Knabb. Berkeley: Bureau of Public Secrets, 1981. 55–56.

Debray, Régis. *Teachers, Writers, Celebrities: The Intellectuals of Modern France*. Trans. David Macey. London: Verso, 1981.

Deleuze, Gilles, and Felix Guattari. *A Thousand Plateaus: Capitalism and Schizophrenia*. Trans. Brian Massumi. Minneapolis: University of Minnesota Press, 1987.

Derrida, Jacques. *Cinders*. Ed. and trans. Ned Lukacher. Lincoln: University of Nebraska Press, 1991.

———. *Dissemination*. Trans. Barbara Johnson. Chicago: University of Chicago Press, 1981.

———. *Of Grammatology*. Trans. Gayatri Chakravorty Spivak. Baltimore: Johns Hopkins University Press, 1976.

———. "Onto-Theology of National-Humanism (Prolegomena to a Hypothesis)." *Oxford Literary Review* 14 (1992): 3–23.

———. *Writing and Difference*. Trans. Alan Bass. Chicago: University of Chicago Press, 1978.

———. "+ R (Into the Bargain)." *The Truth in Painting*. Trans. Geoff Bennington and Ian McLeod. Chicago: University of Chicago Press, 1987: 155–81.

Dery, Mark. "Signposts on the Road to Nowhere: Laurie Anderson's Crisis of Meaning." *South Atlantic Quarterly* 90 (1991): 785–801.

Dirlik, Arif. "The Postcolonial Aura: Third World Criticism in the Age of Global Capitalism." *Critical Inquiry* 20 (1994): 328–56.

Doane, Mary Ann. "The Voice in the Cinema: The Articulation of Body and

Space." *Narrative, Apparatus, Ideology: A Film Theory Reader*. Ed. Philip Rosen. New York: Columbia University Press, 1986. 335–48.

Donner, Frank J. *The Age of Surveillance: The Aims and Methods of America's Political Intelligence System*. New York: Knopf, 1980.

Drucker, Johanna. *The Visible Word: Experimental Typography and Modern Art, 1909–1923*. Chicago: University of Chicago Press, 1994.

Dukore, Bernard J. "Krapp's Last Tape as Tragicomedy." *Krapp's Last Tape: A Theatre Notebook*. Ed. James Knowlson. London: Brutus, 1980. 146–50.

Duncan, Robert. *Caesar's Gate: Poems, 1949–50*. Berkeley: Sand Dollar, 1972.

———. *The Opening of the Field*. New York: Grove, 1960.

Dutoit, Thomas. "Translating the Name?" *On the Name*. By Jacques Derrida. Ed. Thomas Dutoit. Trans. David Wood, John P. Leavey Jr., and Ian McLeod. Stanford: Stanford University Press, 1995. lx–lxvi.

Dygert, Warren G. *Radio as an Advertising Medium*. New York: McGraw-Hill, 1939.

Eagleton, Terry. "The Crisis of Contemporary Culture." *New Left Review* 196 (1992): 29–41.

Easthope, Antony. *Poetry as Discourse*. London: Methuen, 1983.

Eco, Umberto. *Travels in Hyper Reality: Essays*. Trans. William Weaver. San Diego: Harcourt, 1986.

Edgerton, Samuel Y., Jr. "From Mental Matrix to *Mappamundi* to Christian Empire: The Heritage of Ptolemaic Cartography in the Renaissance." *Art and Cartography: Six Historical Essays*. Ed. David Woodward. Chicago: University of Chicago Press, 1987. 10–50.

Edmunds, Susan. *Out of Line: History, Psychoanalysis, and Montage in H.D.'s Long Poems*. Stanford: Stanford University Press, 1994.

Eisenstein, Elizabeth. *The Printing Press as an Agent of Change: Communications and Cultural Transformations in Early-Modern Europe*. 2 vols. New York: Cambridge University Press, 1979.

Eisenstein, Sergei. "A Dialectic Approach to Film Form." *Film Theory and Criticism: Introductory Readings*. 2nd ed. Ed. Gerald Mast and Marshall Cohen. New York: Oxford University Press, 1979. 101–22.

Eliot, T. S. *The Waste Land and Other Poems*. New York: Harcourt, 1934.

Emerson, Ralph Waldo. *Essays and Lectures*. New York: Literary Classics, 1983.

Empson, William. *Seven Types of Ambiguity*. New York: New Directions, 1947.

Engel, Friedrich Karl. "Magnetic Tape: From the Early Days to the Present." *AES: Journal of the Audio Engineering Society* 36 (1988): 606–16.

Eribon, Didier. *Michel Foucault*. Trans. Betsy Wing. London: Faber & Faber, 1991.

Esslin, Martin. "Samuel Beckett and the Art of Broadcasting." *Encounter* 45.3 (1975): 38–46.

Etzioni-Halevy, Eva. *The Knowledge Elite and the Failure of Prophecy*. London: Allen & Unwin, 1985.

Forrest, Leon. *Two Wings to Veil My Face*. Chicago: Another Chicago Press, 1988.

Forster, E. M. *A Passage to India*. New York: Harcourt, 1924.

Foucault, Michel. *The Archaeology of Knowledge*. Trans. A. M. Sheridan Smith. London: Tavistock, 1972.

———. "The Concern for Truth." Trans. John Johnston. *Foucault Live: (Interviews, 1966–84)*. Ed. Sylvère Lotringer. Foreign Agents Ser. New York: Semiotext(e), 1989. 293–308.

———. "The End of the Monarchy of Sex." Trans. Dudley M. Marchi. *Foucault Live: (Interviews, 1966–84)*. Ed. Sylvère Lotringer. Foreign Agents Ser. New York: Semiotext(e), 1989. 137–55.

———. *The History of Sexuality*. Trans. Robert Hurley. Vol. 1. *An Introduction*. New York: Vintage, 1980.

———. *The History of Sexuality*. Trans. Robert Hurley. Vol. 2. *The Use of Pleasure*. London: Penguin Books, 1986.

———. "How Much Does It Cost for Reason to Tell the Truth?" Trans. Mia Foret and Marion Martius. *Foucault Live: (Interviews, 1966–84)*. Ed. Sylvère Lotringer. Foreign Agents Ser. New York: Semiotext(e), 1989. 233–56.

———. "The Masked Philosopher." Trans. John Johnston. *Foucault Live: (Interviews, 1966–84)*. Ed. Sylvère Lotringer. Foreign Agents Ser. New York: Semiotext(e), 1989. 193–202.

———. *The Order of Things: An Archaeology of the Human Sciences*. New York: Random House, 1970.

———. "Politics and the Study of Discourse." Trans. Anthony M. Nazzaro. Rev. Colin Gordon. *Ideology and Consciousness* 3 (Spring 1978): 7–26.

———. "Power and Form: Notes." Trans. W. Suchting. *Michel Foucault: Power, Truth, Strategy*. Ed. Meaghan Morris and Paul Patton. Sydney: Feral Publications, 1979. 59–66.

———. *Power/Knowledge: Selected Interviews and Other Writings, 1972–1977*. Ed. Colin Gordon. Trans. Colin Gordon et al. New York: Pantheon, 1980.

———. "Questions of Method." *The Foucault Effect: Studies in Governmentality*. Ed. Graham Burchill et al. London: Harvester Wheatsheaf, 1991. 73–86.

———. "The Subject and Power." *Art after Modernism: Rethinking Representation*. Ed. Brian Wallis. Boston: Godine, 1984. 417–34.

———. "Truth and Power." Trans. Paul Patton and Meaghan Morris. *Michel Foucault: Power, Truth, Strategy*. Ed. Meaghan Morris and Paul Patton. Sydney: Feral Publications, 1979. 29–48.

———. "What Calls for Punishment?" Trans. John Johnston. *Foucault Live: (Interviews, 1966–84)*. Ed. Sylvère Lotringer. New York: Foreign Agents Ser. Semiotext(e), 1989. 279–92.

Frank, Joseph. *The Widening Gyre: Crisis and Mastery in Modern Literature*. New Brunswick, N.J.: Rutgers University Press, 1963.

Freud, Sigmund. "Analysis of a Case of Hysteria." *Collected Papers*. Vol. 3. *Case Histories*. Trans. A. and J. Strachey. London: Hogarth, 1925. 13–146.

———. "On Beginning the Treatment (Further Recommendations on the Technique of Psycho-analysis I)" (1913). *Complete Works of Sigmund Freud* (1911–1913). Ed. and trans. James Strachey. Vol. 12. London: Hogarth, 1958. 123–44.

———. "Recommendations to Physicians Practicing Psycho-analysis." *Complete Works of Sigmund Freud* (1911–1913). Ed. and trans. James Strachey. Vol. 12. London: Hogarth, 1958. 109–20.

Fried, Debra. "Rhyme Puns." *On Puns: The Foundation of Letters*. Ed. Jonathan Culler. New York: Blackwell, 1988. 83–99.

Friedberg, Anne. "Cut-Ups: A Synema of the Text." *William S. Burroughs at the Front: Critical Reception, 1959–1989*. Ed. Jennie Skerl and Robin Lydenberg. Carbondale: Southern Illinois University Press, 1991. 169–73.

Friedman, John B. *Orpheus in the Middle Ages*. Cambridge, Mass.: Harvard University Press, 1970.

Friedman, Susan Stanford. *Psyche Reborn: The Emergence of H.D.* Bloomington: Indiana University Press, 1981.

Frith, Simon. "Contemporary Culture and the Academy: Notes towards a Research Strategy." *Critical Quarterly* 35.1 (1993): 1–7.

Frith, Simon, and Jon Savage. "Pearls and Swine: Intellectuals and the Mass Media." *New Left Review* 198 (1993): 107–16.

Frizzell, Rev. Dwight, and Jay Mandeville. "Early Radio Bigwigs." *Semiotext(e)* 6.1, no. 16 (1993). Ed. Neil Strauss. 39–46. *Semiotext(e)* no. 16 is also titled "Radiotext(e)."

Frost, Robert. *Complete Poems of Robert Frost*. New York: Holt, 1949.

Garfinkel, Harold, and Harvey Sacks. "On Formal Structures of Practical Actions." *Theoretical Sociology: Perspectives and Developments*. Ed. John C. McKinney and Edward A. Tiryakian. New York: Appleton-Century-Crofts-Meredith, 1970. 337–66.

Gefin, Laszlo K. "Collage Theory, Reception, and the Cutups of William Burroughs." *Perspectives on Contemporary Literature: Literature and the Other Arts* 13 (1987): 91–100.

Gilroy, Paul. *The Black Atlantic: Modernity and Double Consciousness*. Cambridge, Mass.: Harvard University Press, 1993.

Ginsberg, Allen. *Collected Poems, 1947–1980*. New York: Harper, 1984.

Glück, Louise. "Death and Absence." *Proofs and Theories: Essays on Poetry*. Hopewell, N.J.: Ecco, 1994. 125–28.

Goody, Jack. *The Interface between the Written and the Oral*. Cambridge: Cambridge University Press, 1987.

Gordon, John. *"Finnegans Wake": A Plot Summary*. Syracuse: Syracuse University Press, 1986.

Gorham, Maurice. *Forty Years of Irish Broadcasting*. Dublin: Talbot, 1967.

Gouldner, Alvin W. *The Future of Intellectuals and the Rise of the New Class: A Frame of Reference, Theses, Conjectures, Arguments, and an Historical Perspective on the Role of Intellectuals and Intelligentsia in the International Class Contest of the Modern Era*. New York: Continuum, 1979.

Graham, Jorie. *Materialism*. Hopewell, N.J.: Ecco, 1993.

Gray, Obika. *Radicalism and Social Change in Jamaica, 1960–1972*. Knoxville: University of Tennessee Press, 1991.

Griaule, Marcel. *Conversations with Ogotemmêli: An Introduction to Dogon Religious Ideas*. London: Oxford University Press for the International African Institute, 1965.

Grivel, Charles. "The Phonograph's Horned Mouth." Trans. Stephen Sartarelli. *Wireless Imagination: Sound, Radio, and the Avant-Garde*. Ed. Douglas Kahn and Gregory Whitehead. Cambridge, Mass.: MIT Press, 1992. 31–61.

Gunst, Laurie. *Born Fi' Dead: A Journey through the Jamaican Posse Underworld*. New York: Holt, 1995.

H.D. *The Gift*. Abr. ed. New York: New Directions, 1982.

——. *H.D.: Collected Poems, 1912–1944*. Ed. Louis L. Martz. New York: New Directions, 1983.

——. *Helen in Egypt*. New York: New Directions, 1961.

——. *HERmione*. New York: New Directions, 1981.

——. Letters to Norman Holmes Pearson. Beinecke Rare Book and Manuscript Library. Yale University.

——. "The Mask and the Movietone: The Cinema and the Classics III." *Close-Up* 5 (November 1927): 18–31.

——. *Notes on Thought and Vision and the Wise Sappho*. San Francisco: City Lights, 1982.

——. *Trilogy*. New York: New Directions, 1973.

Habekost, Christian. *Verbal Riddim: The Politics and Aesthetics of African-Caribbean Dub Poetry*. Amsterdam: Rodopi, 1993.

Haraway, Donna J. "A Cyborg Manifesto: Science, Technology, and Socialist-Feminism in the Late Twentieth Century." *Simians, Cyborgs, and Women: The Reinvention of Nature*. New York: Routledge, 1991. 149–81.

Hardison, O. B., Jr. *Disappearing through the Skylight: Culture and Technology in the Twentieth Century*. New York: Penguin, 1989.

Harris, Wilson. "History, Fable, and Myth in the Caribbean and Guianas." *Explorations*. Ed. Hena Maes-Jelinek. Mändelsträp, Denmark: Dangaroo, 1981. 20–42.

Havelock, Eric A. *The Literate Revolution in Greece and Its Cultural Consequences*. Princeton: Princeton University Press, 1982.

——. *The Muse Learns to Write: Reflections on Orality and Literacy from Antiquity to the Present*. New Haven: Yale University Press, 1986.

——. *Preface to Plato*. Cambridge, Mass.: Harvard University Press, 1963.

Head, Brian. "Introduction: Intellectuals in Australian Society." *Intellectual Movements and Australian Society*. Ed. Brian Head and James Walter. Melbourne: Oxford University Press, 1988. 1–44.

Hebdige, Dick. *Cut-'n-Mix: Culture, Identity, and Caribbean Music*. New York: Methuen, 1987.

——. *Subculture: The Meaning of Style*. London: Methuen, 1979.

Heidegger, Martin. "Hölderlin and the Essence of Poetry." *Existence and Being*. Chicago: Regnery, 1949. 270–91.

Hentoff, Nat. Liner notes to *Nefertiti, the Beautiful One Has Come*. By Cecil Taylor. New York: Arista/Freedom Records, 1975. FLP 40106 LP. First published in *Down Beat* 25 February 1965, 16–18.

Herr, Cheryl. *Joyce's Anatomy of Culture*. Urbana: University of Illinois Press, 1986.

Hesiod. *The Homeric Hymns and Homerica*. Trans. Hugh G. Evelyn-White. Cambridge, Mass.: Harvard University Press, 1936.

Higgins, Dick. *Some Poetry Intermedia*. Barrytown, N.Y.: Unpublished Editions, 1976.

Hill, Jonathan. *The Cat's Whisker: Fifty Years of Wireless Design*. London: Oresko, 1978.

Hoffmeister, Adolph. "Portrait of Joyce." Trans. Norma Rudinsky. *Portraits of the Artist in Exile: Recollections of James Joyce by Europeans*. Ed. Willard Potts. Seattle: University of Washington Press, 1979. 127–36.

Homer. *The Iliad*. Trans. Robert Fitzgerald. Garden City, N.Y.: Anchor, 1975.

Horkheimer, Max, and Theodor Adorno. "The Culture Industry: Enlightenment as Mass Deception." *Dialectic of Enlightenment*. Trans. John Cumming. New York: Seabury, 1972. 120–67.

Hošek, Chaviva, and Patricia Parker, eds. *Lyric Poetry: Beyond New Criticism*. Ithaca: Cornell University Press, 1985.

Howe, Susan. *Articulation of Sound Forms in Time*. Windsor, Vt.: Awede, 1987.

Ingalls, Jeremy. "The Epic Tradition: A Commentary." *East-West Review* 1 (1964): 42–69.

———. "The Epic Tradition: A Commentary II." *East-West Review* 1 (1964): 173–211.

Jaffé, Hans L. C. *De Stijl*. Trans. R. R. Symonds and Mary Whitall. New York: Abrams, 1967.

Jakobson, Roman. "Linguistics and Poetics." *Essays on the Language of Literature*. Ed. Seymour Chatman and Samuel R. Levin. Boston: Houghton Mifflin, 1967. 296–322.

Jakobson, Roman, and Linda R. Waugh. *The Sound Shape of Language*. 2nd ed. Berlin: Mouton de Gruyter, 1987.

Jameson, Fredric. "The Cultural Logic of Late Capitalism." *Postmodernism: Or, the Cultural Logic of Late Capitalism*. Durham: Duke University Press, 1991. 1–54.

———. "On 'Cultural Studies.'" *Social Text* 34 (1993): 17–52.

———. *The Political Unconscious: Narrative as a Socially Symbolic Act*. Ithaca: Cornell University Press, 1981.

Jay, Martin. *Downcast Eyes: The Denigration of Vision in Twentieth-Century French Thought*. Berkeley: University of California Press, 1993.

Jerry, Bongo. "Mabrak." *Savacou* 3/4 (December 1970–March 1971): 13–15.

Jesperson, Otto. *Language: Its Nature, Development, and Origin*. New York: Macmillan, 1922.

Johns, Jasper. "Interview with Jasper Johns." *Writings, Sketchbook Notes, Interviews*. New York: Museum of Modern Art, 1996. 188–97.

Johnson-Hill, Jack A. *I-Sight, the World of Rastafari: An Interpretive Sociological Account of Rastafarian Ethics*. Metuchen, N.J.: American Theological Library Association and Scarecrow Press, 1995.

Jolas, Eugene, ed. *Vertical: A Yearbook for Romantic-Mystic Ascensions*. New York: Gotham Bookmart, 1941.

Joyce, James. *Finnegans Wake*. New York: Penguin, 1967.

———. *Ulysses*. New York: Vintage, 1961.

Kahn, Douglas. "Death in Light of the Phonograph: Raymond Roussel's *Locus Solus*." *Wireless Imagination: Sound, Radio, and the Avant-Garde*. Ed. Douglas Kahn and Gregory Whitehead. Cambridge, Mass.: MIT Press, 1992. 69–103.

————. "Introduction: Histories of Sound Once Removed." *Wireless Imagination: Sound, Radio, and the Avant-Garde*. Ed. Douglas Kahn and Gregory Whitehead. Cambridge, Mass.: MIT Press, 1992. 1–29.

Kahn, Douglas, and Gregory Whitehead, eds. *Wireless Imagination: Sound, Radio, and the Avant-Garde*. Cambridge, Mass.: MIT Press, 1992.

Kant, Immanuel. *Critique of Judgment*. Trans. J. H. Bernard. New York: Hafner, 1951.

Kaplan, Alice Yaeger. *Reproductions of Banality: Fascism, Literature, and French Intellectual Life*. Minneapolis: University of Minnesota Press, 1986.

Kaufman, Bob. *The Ancient Rain: Poems, 1956–1978*. New York: New Directions, 1981.

Kaufman, Michael. *Jamaica under Manley: Dilemmas of Socialism and Democracy*. Westport, Conn.: Lawrence Hill, 1985.

Kelly, Robert. "Song XVII." *Songs I–XXX*. Cambridge, Mass.: Pym-Randall, 1968. 52–53.

Kenner, Hugh. *The Mechanic Muse*. New York: Oxford University Press, 1987.

————. *The Pound Era*. Berkeley: University of California Press, 1971.

Kittler, Friedrich A. *Discourse Networks, 1800/1900*. Trans. Michael Metteer, with Chris Cullens. Stanford: Stanford University Press, 1990.

————. "Gramophone, Film, Typewriter." Trans. Dorothea von Mücke and Philippe Similon. *October* 41 (Summer 1987): 101–18.

Kloepfer, Deborah Kelly. *The Unspeakable Mother: Forbidden Discourse in Jean Rhys and H.D.* Ithaca: Cornell University Press, 1989.

Knabb, Ken, ed. and trans. *Situationist International Anthology*. Berkeley: Bureau of Public Secrets, 1981.

Knowlson, James. "The Beginnings of Krapp's Last Tape." *Krapp's Last Tape: A Theatre Notebook*. Ed. James Knowlson. London: Brutus, 1980. 45–48.

Kostelanetz, Richard. *Conversing with Cage*. New York: Limelight, 1987.

————, ed. *The Avant-Garde Tradition in Literature*. Buffalo: Prometheus, 1982.

Kostelanetz, Richard, and John Cage. "A Conversation about Radio in Twelve Parts." *John Cage at Seventy-Five*. Ed. Richard Fleming and William Duckworth. Lewisburg, Pa.: Bucknell University Press, 1989. 270–302.

Kristeva, Julia. *Revolution in Poetic Language*. Trans. Margaret Waller. New York: Columbia University Press, 1984.

Lange, Art, and Nathaniel Mackey, eds. *Moment's Notice: Jazz in Poetry and Prose*. Minneapolis: Coffee House, 1993.

Lanham, Richard A. *The Electronic Word: Democracy, Technology, and the Arts*. Chicago: University of Chicago Press, 1993.

————. "The Implications of Electronic Information for the Sociology of Knowledge." Printed in summary form and available through the Internet at http://www.cni.org/docs/tsh/www/TOC.html.

Lapidus, Edith J. *Eavesdropping on Trial*. Rochelle Park, N.J.: Hayden Book, 1974.

Lauretis, Teresa de. *Technologies of Gender: Essays on Theory, Film, and Fiction*. Bloomington: Indiana University Press, 1987.

Lawler, Justus. *Celestial Pantomime: Poetic Structures of Transcendence*. New Haven: Yale University Press, 1979.

Lawrence, Amy. *Echo and Narcissus: Women's Voices in Classical Hollywood Cinema.* Berkeley: University of California Press, 1991.

Leiris, Michel. *Rules of the Game I: Scratches.* Trans. Lydia Davis. New York: Paragon, 1991.

Levin, David Michael. *The Listening Self: Personal Growth, Social Change, and the Closure of Metaphysics.* New York: Routledge, 1989.

Levinas, Emmanuel. *The Levinas Reader.* Ed. and trans. Séan Hand. Oxford: Blackwell, 1989.

Levinson, Stephen. *Pragmatics.* Cambridge: Cambridge University Press, 1985.

Lévi-Strauss, Claude. *The Raw and the Cooked.* Trans. John Wightman and Doreen Wightman. New York: Harper & Row, 1969.

———. *Structural Anthropology.* Vol. 2. London: Allen Lane, 1977.

Lilly, John Cunningham. *The Center of the Cyclone: An Autobiography of Inner Space.* New York: Julian, 1972.

Lippard, Lucy, ed. *Dadas on Art.* Englewood Cliffs, N.J.: Prentice-Hall, 1971.

Lipsitz, George. "Cruising around the Historical Bloc: Postmodernism and Popular Music in East Los Angeles." *Cultural Critique* 5 (Winter 1986–87): 157–77.

Long, Edward V. *The Intruders: The Invasion of Privacy by Government and Industry.* New York: Praeger, 1967.

Lorca, Federico García. *Deep Song and Other Prose.* Ed. and trans. Christopher Maurer. New York: New Directions, 1980.

———. *Poet in New York.* Ed. Christopher Maurer. Trans. Greg Simon and Steven F. White. New York: Noonday, 1988.

Lord, Albert B. *The Singer of Tales.* Cambridge, Mass.: Harvard University Press, 1960.

Lubeck, Heinz. "Magnetic Sound Recording with Films and Ring Heads." *Magnetic Tape Recording.* Ed. Marvin Camras. New York: Van Nostrand Reinhold, 1985. 79–111.

Lukacher, Ned. *Primal Scenes: Literature, Philosophy, Psychoanalysis.* Ithaca: Cornell University Press, 1986.

Lydenberg, Robin. "Sound Identity Fading Out: William Burroughs' Tape Experiments." *Wireless Imagination: Sound, Radio, and the Avant-Garde.* Ed. Douglas Kahn and Gregory Whitehead. Cambridge, Mass: MIT Press, 1992. 409–33.

———. *Word Cultures: Radical Theory and Practice in William S. Burroughs' Fiction.* Urbana: University of Illinois Press, 1987.

Lyotard, Jean-Francois. *Peregrinations: Law, Form, Event.* New York: Columbia University Press, 1988.

McCaffery, Steve. "Insufficiencies of Theory to Poetical Economies." *The Ends of Theory.* Ed. Jerry Herron et al. Detroit: Wayne State University Press, 1996. 257–71.

McCaffery, Steve, and bp Nichol, eds. *Sound Poetry: A Catalogue.* Toronto: Underwhich Editions, 1978.

McCullough, David. *Truman.* New York: Simon, 1992.

Macey, David. *The Lives of Michel Foucault.* London: Hutchinson, 1993.

McGann, Jerome. *Black Riders: The Visible Language of Modernism*. Princeton: Princeton University Press, 1993.
———. "What Is Critical Editing?" *Text* 5 (1991): 15–29.
McHoul, Alec. "Con/versation." *Pretending to Communicate*. Ed. Herman Parret. Berlin: Walter de Gruyter, 1993. 196–211.
Mackey, Nathaniel. *Bedouin Hornbook*. Callaloo fiction ser. 2. Lexington: University Press of Kentucky, 1986.
———. "Cante Moro." In this volume.
———. *Discrepant Engagement: Dissonance, Cross-Culturality, and Experimental Writing*. Cambridge: Cambridge University Press, 1993.
———. "Ohnedaruth's Day Begun." *Eroding Witness*. Urbana: University of Illinois Press, 1985. 70–74.
———. "Sound and Sentiment, Sound and Symbol." *Callaloo* 10 (1987): 29–54. Repr. in *Discrepant Engagement: Dissonance, Cross-Culturality, and Experimental Writing*. Cambridge: Cambridge University Press, 1993. 231–59.
Mac Low, Jackson. "Selected Poems from *Stanzas for Iris Lezak* in Roughly Chronological Order (May–October 1960)." *Representative Works, 1938–1985*. New York: Roof, 1986. 71–105.
McLuhan, Marshall. *The Gutenberg Galaxy: The Making of Typographic Man*. Toronto: University of Toronto Press, 1962.
———. *Understanding Media: The Extensions of Man*. New York: McGraw-Hill, 1964.
McNeill, Anthony. *Reel from "The Life Movie."* Savacou 6. Mona, Jamaica: Savacou Publications, 1972.
Mandelstam, Osip. *Selected Essays*. Trans. Sidney Monas. Austin: University of Texas Press, 1977.
Manetti, Giovanni. *Theories of the Sign in Classical Antiquity*. Trans. Christine Richardson. Bloomington: Indiana University Press, 1993.
Manley, Michael. *A Voice at the Workplace: Reflections on Colonialism and the Jamaican Worker*. Rev. ed. Washington, D.C.: Howard University Press, 1991.
Marinetti, Filippo Tommaso. "Destruction of Syntax—Wireless Imagination—Words in Freedom." *Lacerba* 11 May, 15 June 1913. Translated in Richard J. Pioli, *Stung by Salt and War: Creative Texts of the Italian Avant-Gardist F. T. Marinetti*. New York: Lang, 1987. 45–53.
———. *Marinetti: Selected Writings*. Ed. R. W. Flint. Trans. R. W. Flint and Arthur A. Coppotelli. New York: Farrar, Straus and Giroux, 1972.
Marker, Chris. *La Jetée: Ciné-roman*. New York: Zone, 1992.
Markov, Vladimir. *Russian Futurism: A History*. London: MacGibbon & Kee, 1969.
Marvin, Carolyn. *When Old Technologies Were New: Thinking about Electric Communication in the Late Nineteenth Century*. New York: Oxford University Press, 1988.
Melhem, D. H. *Heroism in the New Black Poetry*. Lexington: University Press of Kentucky, 1990.
Metz, Christian. "*Trucage* and the Film." Trans. Françoise Meltzer. *Critical Inquiry* 3 (1977): 657–75.

Millard, Andre. *America on Record: A History of Recorded Sound*. Cambridge: Cambridge University Press, 1995.

Miller, Arthur R. *The Assault on Privacy: Computers, Data Banks, and Dossiers*. Ann Arbor: University of Michigan Press, 1971.

Miller, J. Hillis. "Impossible Metaphor: (Stevens' 'The Red Fern' as example)." *Tropes, Parables, Performatives: Essays on Twentieth Century Literature*. Durham: Duke University Press, 1990. 213–26.

Miller, Jacques-Alain. "Suture (Elements of the Logic of the Signifier)." Trans. Colin MacCabe. *Screen* 18.4 (1977–78): 24–34.

Miller, James. *The Passion of Michel Foucault*. New York: Simon, 1993.

Miller, Toby. *The Well-Tempered Self: Citizenship, Culture, and the Postmodern Subject*. Baltimore: Johns Hopkins University Press, 1993.

———, ed. "Radio-Sound." *Continuum* 6.1 (1992).

Mink, Louis O. *A "Finnegans Wake" Gazetteer*. Bloomington: Indiana University Press, 1978.

Molesworth, Charles. *The Fierce Embrace: A Study of Contemporary American Poetry*. Columbia: University of Missouri Press, 1979.

Moran, Albert. "Media Intellectuals." *Intellectual Movements and Australian Society*. Ed. Brian Head and James Walter. Melbourne: Oxford University Press, 1988. 109–26.

Morris, Meaghan, and Paul Patton, eds. Preface to *Michel Foucault: Power, Truth, Strategy*. Sydney: Feral Publications, 1979. 7–10.

Moten, Fred. "Tragedy, Elegy, Improvisation: Voices of Baraka II." *Semiotics 94*. Proceedings of the Semiotic Society of America. Nineteenth Annual Meeting. New York: Peter Long, 1995. 431–49.

Mowitt, John. *Text: The Genealogy of an Antidisciplinary Object*. Durham: Duke University Press, 1992.

Murray, Penelope. "Poetic Inspiration in Early Greece." *Journal of Hellenic Studies* 101 (1981): 87–100.

Nagy, Gregory. "Ancient Greek Poetry, Prophecy, and Concepts of Theory." *Poetry and Prophecy*. Ed. James L. Kugel. Ithaca: Cornell University Press, 1990. 56–64.

———. *Greek Mythology and Poetics*. Ithaca: Cornell University Press, 1990.

Nancy, Jean-Luc. *The Birth to Presence*. Trans. Brian Holmes et al. Stanford: Stanford University Press, 1993.

Nänny, Max. *Ezra Pound: Poetics for an Electric Age*. Bern: Franke, 1973.

Nelson, Cary. "The End of the Body: Radical Space in Burroughs." *William S. Burroughs at the Front: Critical Reception, 1959–1989*. Ed. Jennie Skerl and Robin Lydenberg. Carbondale: Southern Illinois University Press, 1991. 119–32.

———. *Repression and Recovery: Modern American Poetry and the Politics of Cultural Memory, 1910–1945*. Madison: University of Wisconsin Press, 1989.

New Princeton Encyclopedia of Poetry and Poetics. Ed. Alex Preminger, T. V. F. Brogan, et al. Princeton: Princeton University Press, 1993.

Odier, Daniel. *The Job: Interviews with William S. Burroughs*. New York: Grove, 1969.

Olson, Charles. *Additional Prose: A Bibliography on America, Proprioception, and Other*

Notes and Essays. Ed. George F. Butterick. Bolinas, Calif.: Four Seasons Foundation, 1974.

———. *The Maximus Poems*. Ed. George F. Butterick. Berkeley: University of California Press, 1983.

———. "Projective Verse." *Selected Writings of Charles Olson*. Ed. Robert Creeley. New York: New Directions, 1966. 15–26.

O'Neill, Ynez Violé. *Speech and Speech Disorders in Western Thought before 1600*. Westport, Conn.: Greenwood, 1980.

Ong, Walter J. *Orality and Literacy: The Technologizing of the Word*. London: Methuen, 1982.

———. *The Presence of the Word: Some Prolegomena for Cultural and Religious History*. New Haven: Yale University Press, 1967.

Owen, Stephen. *Mi-Lou: Poetry and the Labyrinth of Desire*. Cambridge, Mass.: Harvard University Press, 1989.

Owens, Craig. "Amplifications: Laurie Anderson." *Art in America* 69 (1981): 120–23.

Owens, J. V. "Literature on the Rastafari: 1955–1974." *Savacou* 11–12 (1975): 86–105.

Packard, Vance. *The Naked Society*. New York: McKay, 1964.

Padoux, André. *Vāc: The Concept of the Word in Selected Hindu Tantras*. Trans. Jacques Gontier. Albany: State University of New York Press, 1990.

Parkin, David. "Ritual as Spatial Direction and Bodily Division." *Understanding Rituals*. Ed. Daniel de Coppet. London: Routledge, 1992. 11–25.

Paterson, Elmer. *Tristan Tzara: Dada and Surrational Theorist*. New Brunswick, N.J.: Rutgers University Press, 1971.

Payne, Anthony J. *Politics in Jamaica*. New York: St. Martins, 1988.

Paz, Octavio. *Children of the Mire: Modern Poetry from Romanticism to the Avant-Garde*. Trans. Rachel Phillips. Cambridge, Mass.: Harvard University Press, 1974.

Pei, Mario. *A Glossary of Linguistic Terminology*. New York: Columbia University Press, 1966.

Perloff, Marjorie. "Can(n)on to the Right of Us, Can(n)on to the Left of Us: A Plea for Difference." *Poetic License: Essays on Modernist and Postmodernist Lyric*. Evanston: Northwestern University Press, 1990. 7–29.

———. *The Dance of the Intellect: Studies in the Poetry of the Pound Tradition*. Cambridge: Cambridge University Press, 1985.

———. "'A duchamp unto my self': 'Writing through' Marcel." *John Cage: Composed in America*. Ed. Marjorie Perloff and Charles Junkerman. Chicago: University of Chicago Press, 1994. 100–124.

———. "A Lion in Our Living Room: Reading Allen Ginsberg in the Eighties." *Poetic License: Essays in Modernist and Postmodernist Lyric*. Evanston: Northwestern University Press, 1990. 199–230.

———. "'No More Margins': John Cage, David Antin, and the Poetry of Performance." *The Poetics of Indeterminacy: Rimbaud to Cage*. Princeton: Princeton University Press, 1981. 288–339.

———. *Radical Artifice: Writing Poetry in the Age of Media*. Chicago: University of Chicago Press, 1991.

Picard, Max. *The World of Silence*. Washington, D.C.: Regnery Gateway, 1988.

Plessner, Helmuth. *Die Stufen des Organischen und der Mensch: Einleitung in die philosophische Anthropologie*. 2nd ed. Berlin: Walter de Gruyter, 1965.

Potter, Russell A. *Spectacular Vernaculars: Hip-Hop and the Politics of Postmodernism*. New York: State University of New York Press, 1995.

Pound, Ezra. *ABC of Reading*. New York: New Directions, 1934.

———. *The Cantos of Ezra Pound*. New York: New Directions, 1970.

———. "I Gather the Limbs of Osiris, II. A Rather Dull Introduction." *New Age* 10.6 (7 December 1911): 130.

———. "I Gather the Limbs of Osiris, IV. A Beginning." *New Age* 10.8 (21 December 1911): 179.

———. *Literary Essays*. Edited with an introduction by T. S. Eliot. New York: New Directions, 1935.

———. "Three Cantos." *Poetry* 10.3 (June 1917): 113–21. Unrevised version of Canto 1.

Pucci, Pietro. *Hesiod and the Language of Poetry*. Baltimore: Johns Hopkins University Press, 1977.

Radhakrishnan, R. "Postcoloniality and the Boundaries of Identity." *Callaloo* 16 (1993): 750–71.

Rapaport, Herman. "*Jane Eyre* and the *Mot Tabou*." *MLN* 94 (1979): 1093–1104.

Rappaport, Joanne. "Object and Alphabet: Andean Indians and Documents in the Colonial Period." *Writing without Words: Alternate Literacies in Mesoamerica and the Andes*. Ed. Elizabeth Hill Boone and Walter D. Mignolo. Durham: Duke University Press, 1994. 271–92.

Rasula, Jed. "Gendering the Muse." *Sulfur* 35 (Fall 1994): 59–76.

Reed, Ishmael. *Mumbo Jumbo*. Garden City, N.Y.: Doubleday, 1972.

Reiman, Donald H. *Romantic Texts and Contexts*. Columbia: University of Missouri Press, 1987.

Revill, David. *The Roaring Silence: John Cage, a Life*. New York: Arcade, 1992.

Richards, Spencer. Liner notes to *Live in Vienna*. By Cecil Taylor. Leo Records, 1988. LR 408/409 LP.

Richman, Michele H. *Reading Georges Bataille: Beyond the Gift*. Baltimore: Johns Hopkins University Press, 1982.

Richter, Hans. *Dada: Art and Anti-Art*. Trans. David Britt. New York: Abrams, 1965.

Riffaterre, Michael. *Semiotics of Poetry*. Bloomington: Indiana University Press, 1978.

Rilke, Rainer Maria. *Selected Works*. Trans. G. Craig Houston. Vol. 1. New York: New Directions, 1960.

Rohlehr, F. Gordon. "Afterthoughts." *BIM* 14.56 (January–June 1973): 227–32.

———. *Pathfinder: Black Awakening in the Arrivants of Edward Kamau Brathwaite*. Tunapuna, Trinidad: College Press, 1981.

———. "West Indian Poetry: Some Problems of Assessment." *BIM* 14.54 (January–June 1972): 80–88 and 14.55 (July–December 1972): 134–44.

Ronell, Avital. *The Telephone Book: Technology, Schizophrenia, Electric Speech*. Lincoln: University of Nebraska Press, 1989.

Ropars-Wuilleumier, Marie-Claire. "Film Reader of the Text." Trans. Kimball Lockhart. *diacritics* 15.1 (1985): 18–30.

———. "The Graphic in Filmic Writing: *À bout de souffle*, or the Erratic Alphabet." *enclitic* special issue (1982): 147–61.

Rose, Tricia. *Black Noise: Rap Music and Black Culture in Contemporary America*. Hanover, N.H.: Wesleyan University Press, 1994.

Rose, Tricia, and Andrew Ross, eds. *Microphone Fiends: Youth Music and Youth Culture*. New York: Routledge, 1994.

Rosenthal, Mark. *Jasper Johns: Work since 1974*. London: Thames and Hudson, in association with the Philadelphia Museum of Art, 1988.

Rothenberg, Jerome. "Pre-Face (1967)." *Technicians of the Sacred: A Range of Poetics from Africa, America, Asia, Europe, and Oceania*. Berkeley: University of California Press, 1968. xxv–xxxiii.

Rumi, Jalaluddin. *Teachings of Rumi: The Masnavi*. Trans. E. H. Whinfield. London: Octagon Press, 1979.

Saakana, Amon Saba. *Jah Music*. London: Heinemann, 1980.

Salkey, Andrew. *Jamaica: An Epic Poem Exploring the Historical Foundations of Jamaican Society*. London: Bogle-L'Ouverture, 1973.

Sanders, Ed. *Investigative Poetry*. San Francisco: City Lights, 1976.

Santillana, Giorgio de, and Hertha von Dechend. *Hamlet's Mill: An Essay on Myth and the Frame of Time*. Boston: Gambit, 1969.

Sayre, Henry. *The Object of Performance: The American Avant-Garde since 1970*. Chicago: University of Chicago Press, 1989.

Schegloff, Emanuel, and Harvey Sacks. "Opening up Closings." *Semiotica* 8 (1973): 289–327.

Scheinberg, Susan. "The Bee Maidens of the Homeric *Hymn to Hermes*." *Harvard Studies in Classical Philology*. Vol. 83. Cambridge, Mass.: Harvard University Press, 1979. 1–28.

Schiller, Herbert I. *Culture, Inc.: The Corporate Takeover of Public Expression*. New York: Oxford University Press, 1989.

Schillingsburg, Peter L. "Text as Matter, Concept, and Action." *Studies in Bibliography*. Vol. 44. Charlottesville: University Press of Virginia, 1991. 31–82.

Schlegel, Friedrich von. *The Philosophy of Life and Philosophy of Language in a Course of Lectures*. Trans. A. J. W. Morrison. London: Henry G. Bohn, 1847.

Scott, Dennis. "And it's true." *Dreadwalk: Poems, 1970–78*. London: New Beacon, 1982. 36.

———. "Apocalypse dub." *Dreadwalk: Poems, 1970–78*. London: New Beacon, 1982. 37.

———. "No Sufferer." *Uncle Time*. Pittsburgh: University of Pittsburgh Press, 1973. 53.

———. "Squatter's Rites." *Uncle Time*. Pittsburgh: University of Pittsburgh Press, 1973. 42–43.

Segal, Charles. *Orpheus: The Myth of the Poet*. Baltimore: Johns Hopkins University Press, 1989.

Sewell, Elizabeth. *The Orphic Voice: Poetry and Natural History*. New Haven: Yale University Press, 1960.

Sexton, Adam, ed. *Rap on Rap: Straight-Up Talk on Hip-Hop Culture*. New York: Delta Trade, 1995.

Shannon, Claude E. "A Mathematical Theory of Communication." *Bell System Technical Journal* 27 (July, October 1948): 379–423, 623–56. Repr. in *Claude Elwood Shannon: Collected Papers*. Ed. N. J. A. Sloane and Aaron D. Wyner. Piscataway, N.J.: IEEE Press, 1993. 5–83.

Shklovsky, Viktor. "Art as Technique." *Russian Formalist Criticism*. Ed. and trans. Lee Lemon and Marion Reis. Lincoln: University of Nebraska Press, 1965. 3–24.

Silverman, Kaja. *The Acoustic Mirror: The Female Voice in Psychoanalysis and Cinema*. Bloomington: Indiana University Press, 1988.

Smith, Anthony. *The Shadow in the Cave: The Broadcaster, His Audience, and the State*. Urbana: University of Illinois Press, 1973.

Smith, Christopher. "A Sense of the Possible: Miles Davis and the Semiotics of Improvised Performance." *Drama Review* 39.3 (T147) (1995): 41–55.

"Sound." *Encyclopedia Britannica: Macropoedia*. 1992.

Soupault, Philippe. "James Joyce." Trans. Carleton W. Carroll. *Portraits of the Artist in Exile: Recollections of James Joyce by Europeans*. Ed. Willard Potts. Seattle: University of Washington Press, 1979. 108–18.

Spicer, Jack. *The Collected Books of Jack Spicer*. Ed. Robin Blaser. Los Angeles: Black Sparrow, 1975.

Stephens, Evelyne Huber, and John D. Stephens. "The Transition to Mass Parties and Ideological Politics: The Jamaican Experience since 1972." *Comparative Political Studies* 19 (1987): 443–83.

Stevens, Wallace. "The Noble Rider and the Sound of Words." *The Necessary Angel: Essays on Reality and the Imagination*. London: Faber & Faber, 1951. 3–36.

———. *Opus Posthumous*. Ed. Samuel French Morse. London: Faber, 1957.

———. "Variations on a Summer Day." *The Palm at the End of the Mind*. Ed. Holly Stevens. New York: Knopf, 1971. 170–73.

Stevenson, Robert Louis. *The Strange Case of Dr. Jekyll and Mr. Hyde and Other Stories*. Baltimore: Penguin, 1979.

Stewart, Garrett. *Reading Voices: Literature and the Phonotext*. Berkeley: University of California Press, 1990.

Stone, Carl. *Class, Race, and Political Behaviour in Urban Jamaica*. Mona, Jamaica: Institute of Social and Economic Research, University of West Indies, 1973.

———. "Ideology, Public Opinion, and the Media in Jamaica." *Perspectives on Jamaica in the Seventies*. Ed. Carl Stone and Aggrey Brown. Kingston, Jamaica: Jamaica Publishing, 1981. 308–29.

Strauss, Neil. "Talk Radio." Rev. of *Wireless Imagination: Sound, Radio, and the Avant-Garde*. Ed. Douglas Kahn and Gregory Whitehead. *Village Voice* 2 February 1993: 62.

Sussman, Elisabeth, ed. *On the Passage of a Few People through a Rather Brief Moment in Time: The Situationist International, 1957–1972*. Cambridge, Mass.: MIT Press, 1989.

Talarico, Ross. *Spreading the Word: Poetry and the Survival of Community in America*. Durham: Duke University Press, 1995.

Tan, Margaret Leng. " 'Taking a Nap, I Pound the Rice': Eastern Influences on John Cage." *John Cage at Seventy-Five.* Ed. Richard Fleming and William Duckworth. Lewisburg, Pa.: Bucknell University Press, 1989. 34–58.

Tarde, Gabriel. *Les Lois de l'Imitation.* Paris: Etude psychologique, 1895.

Taussig, Michael. *Mimesis and Alterity: A Particular History of the Senses.* New York: Routledge, 1993.

Taylor, Cecil. Liner notes to *Unit Structures.* Blue Note Records, 1966.

Tedlock, Dennis. "Learning to Listen: Oral History as Poetry." *Boundary 2* 3 (1975): 707–26.

————. "The Speaker of Tales Has More Than One String to Play On." *Vox Intexta: Orality and Textuality in the Middle Ages.* Ed. A. N. Doane and Carol Braun Pasternack. Madison: University of Wisconsin Press, 1991. 5–33.

Terrell, Carroll F. *A Companion to the Cantos of Ezra Pound.* Vol. 1 (Cantos 1–71). Berkeley: University of California Press, 1980.

Thiele, Heinz H. K. "Magnetic Sound Recording in Europe up to 1945." *AES: Journal of the Audio Engineering Society* 36 (1988): 396–408.

Thoreau, Henry. "Sounds." *Walden.* Ed. Robert Sayre. New York: Library of America, 1985.

Tichi, Cecelia. *High Lonesome: The American Culture of Country Music.* Chapel Hill: University of North Carolina Press, 1995.

Tindall, William York. *A Reader's Guide to "Finnegans Wake."* New York: Farrar, Straus and Giroux, 1969.

Titon, Jeff Todd. *Early Downhome Blues: A Musical and Cultural Analysis.* 2nd ed. Chapel Hill: University of North Carolina Press, 1994.

Tzara, Tristan. "Note 6 sur l'art nègre." *Sic* 21–22 (1917): unpaginated. Repr. in "Note sur l'art nègre." *Lampisteries; Precedees des sept manifestes dada.* [Paris]: Pauvert, 1963. 87–88.

Veaux, Micheline. "Réflexions Vocales dans un miroir et voix mythiques." *Bulletin d'Audiophonologie* 16.4 [1983]: 435–47.

Veeder, William, and Gordon Hirsch, eds. *Dr. Jekyll and Mr. Hyde: After One Hundred Years.* Chicago: University of Chicago Press, 1988.

Vernant, Jean-Pierre. *Mortals and Immortals: Collected Essays.* Ed. Froma Zeitlin. Princeton: Princeton University Press, 1991.

Virilio, Paul. "The Third Interval: A Critical Transition." *Rethinking Technologies.* Ed. Verena Andermatt Conley. Minneapolis: University of Minnesota Press, 1993. 3–12.

Walker, Roy. "Love, Chess, and Death." *Krapp's Last Tape: A Theatre Notebook.* Ed. James Knowlson. London: Brutus, 1980. 48–51.

Wallis, Roger, and Krister Malm. *Big Sounds from Small Peoples: The Music Industry in Small Countries.* New York: Pendragon, 1984.

Walmsley, Anne. *Caribbean Artists Movement, 1966–1972: A Literary and Cultural History.* London: New Beacon, 1992.

Warden, John, ed. *Orpheus: The Metamorphoses of a Myth.* Toronto: University of Toronto Press, 1982.

Waters, Anita M. *Race, Class, and Political Symbols: Rastafari and Reggae in Jamaican Politics.* New Brunswick, N.J.: Transaction, 1985.

Watten, Barrett. "Total Syntax: The Work in the World." *Total Syntax*. Carbondale: Southern Illinois University Press, 1985. 65–114.

Weaver, Mike. "Concrete Poetry." *Lugano Review* 5–6 (1966): 100–125.

Wendt, Larry. "Henri Chopin and Sound Poetry." *Furnitures* 10 (1993): 2.

———. *Sound Poems for an Era of Reduced Expectations*. Toronto: Underwhich Editions, 1981.

White, Timothy. *Catch a Fire: The Life of Bob Marley*. New York: Holt, 1989.

Whitehead, Gregory. "Out of the Dark: Notes on the Nobodies of Radio Art." *Wireless Imagination: Sound, Radio, and the Avant-Garde*. Ed. Douglas Kahn and Gregory Whitehead. Cambridge, Mass.: MIT Press, 1992. 253–63.

Whitman, Walt. *The Complete Poetry and Prose*. New York: Library of America, 1982.

Whitney, Malika Lee, and Dermott Hussey. *Bob Marley: Reggae King of the World*. New York: Dutton, 1984.

Wicke, Jennifer. *Advertising Fictions: Literature, Advertisement, and Social Reading*. New York: Columbia University Press, 1988.

Wiener, Norbert. *The Human Use of Human Beings: Cybernetics and Society*. New York: Da Capo, 1954.

Williams, William Carlos. *Paterson*. New York: New Directions, 1958.

Winn, James A. "Music and Poetry." *New Princeton Encyclopedia of Poetry and Poetics*. 3rd ed. Ed. Alex Preminger, T. V. F. Brogan, et al. Princeton: Princeton University Press, 1993. 803–6.

Yeats, William Butler. "Byzantium." *Poems*. New York: Macmillan, 1960. 243–44.

Žižek, Slavoj. *Enjoy Your Symptom! Jacques Lacan in Hollywood and Out*. New York: Routledge, 1992.

———. *Looking Awry: An Introduction to Jacques Lacan through Popular Culture*. Cambridge, Mass.: MIT Press, 1991.

Zukofsky, Louis. *Prepositions: The Collected Critical Essays of Louis Zukofsky*. New York: Horizon, 1968.

Zurbrugg, Nicholas, and Marlene Hall, eds. *Henri Chopin*. Morningside: Queensland College of Art Gallery, Griffith University, 1992.

Zwicky, Jan. *Lyric Philosophy*. Toronto: University of Toronto Press, 1992.

TAPES, RECORDS, AND CDS

Benson, Steve. Reading at 80 Langton Street. Audiotape. University of California, San Diego. Archive for New Poetry L-714, 1981.

Brathwaite, Edward Kamau. *Atumpan*. Introduction by Carolivia Herron. Audiocassette. Watershed Tapes, 1989.

Comic, Sir Lord. "Jack of My Trade." *Keep on Coming through the Door: Jamaican Deejay Music, 1969–1973*. Trojan Records, 1991, 1988. Originally recorded 1970.

Davis, Miles. "Saeta." *Sketches of Spain*. Columbia CS 1480.

Davis, Miles, and John Coltrane. "All Blues." *Miles Davis and John Coltrane Live in Stockholm, 1960*. Dragon DRLP 90191.

H.D. *Helen in Egypt*. Audiocassette. Watershed Tapes, 1981.

I-Roy. "Heart Don't Leap." *Keep on Coming through the Door: Jamaican Deejay Music, 1969–1973*. Trojan Records, 1991, 1988. Originally recorded 1971.

Kirk, Rahsaan Roland. "The Business Ain't Nothin' but the Blues." *I Talk with the Spirits*. Limelight LS82008.

Last Poets. "Jazzoetry." *Chastisment*. Celluloid, 1992.

"Love Song." *Folk Music of Iran*. Lyrichord LLST 7261.

McDowell, Mississippi Fred. "Everybody's Down on Me" and "Jesus Is on the Mainline." *I Do Not Play No Rock 'n Roll*. Capitol ST-409.

Mutabaruka. "The People's Court." *Blakk Wi Blak . . . k . . . k . . . .* Shanachie 43083, 1991.

Pavón, Pastora. "Ay Pilato." *La Niña de los Peines*. Le Chant du Monde LDX 274859.

Rollins, Sonny. "East Broadway Rundown." *East Broadway Rundown*. Impulse! A-9121.

Taylor, Cecil. *Chinampas*. London. Leo Records CD LR 153, 1991.

―――. *In Florescence*. Hollywood, Calif. A & M Records, 1990. [5286 LP].

―――. *Live in Vienna*. London. Leo Records, 1988. [LR 408/409 LP].

ADDITIONAL DISCOGRAPHY

Camarón. *Calle Real*. Phillips 814–466–1.

―――. *La Leyenda del Tiempo*. Phillips 63–28–255.

Ketama. *Ketama*. Hannibal HNBL-1336.

―――. *Songhai*. Hannibal HNBL-1323.

―――. *Y Es Ke Me Han Kambiao los Tiempos*. Mango 539.879–1.

Lebrijano, Juan Peña, and the Andalusian Orchestra of Tangier. *Encuentros*. Ariola 1–207240.

Lole and Manuel. *Casta*. CBS S-26027.

―――. *Lole y Manuel*. CBS S-82276.

―――. *Nuevo Día*. Movieplay 15.2320/3.

Manitas de Plata. *Manitas de Plata: Flamenco Guitar*. Vol. 2. Connoisseur Society CS-965.

Manzanita. *Poco Ruido y Mucho Duende*. CBS S-83188.

Maya, José Heredia, and the Andalusian Orchestra of Tetuan. *Macama Jonda*. Ariola I-295400.

Pata Negra. *Blues de la Frontera*. Hannibal HNBL-1309.

Pepe de la Matrona. *Pepe de la Matrona*. Vol. 2. Hispavox 150–055.

Singing Preachers. Blues Classics BC-19.

Louis Armstrong's "Gone Fishin' " (track 1) licensed by the Harry Fox Agency.

H.D.'s readings from *Helen in Egypt* (tracks 2–4) reproduced by permission of Alan Austin, Executive Producer, Watershed Tapes. *Helen in Egypt*, number C-158, Watershed Tapes Archive Series, is available from Watershed Tapes, P.O. Box 50145, 6925 Willow Street NW, Washington, D.C. 20091. All sections on the tape come from *Helen in Egypt* by H.D.; copyright © 1961 by Norman Holmes Pearson. Reproduced by permission of New Directions Publishing Corporation.

Excerpt from John Cage's performance of "What You Say . . ." (track 5) reproduced by permission of Laura Kuhn, Executive Director, John Cage Trust, courtesy of the John Cage Trust.

Bengt af Klintberg's "Calls" (track 6) reproduced by permission of the artist. Available from Fylkingen Records, Box 17044, S-104 62, Stockholm, Sweden.

F. T. Marinetti's "Bombardamento di Adrianopoli" (track 7) reproduced from *Futurism & Dada Reviewed*, CD SUBCD 012–19, Sub Rosa.

Sound poems by Hugo Ball, Christian Morgenstern, Paul Scheerbart, Raoul Hausmann, Isadore Isou, and Aleksei Kruchenykh (tracks 8–13) from a boxed collection titled *Futura poesia sonora: A Critical-Historical Anthology of Sound Poetry*, edited by Arigo Lora-Totino, Cramps Records. The cuts were taken from different discs as follows: Kruchenykh from 5202 302; Morgenstern, Ball, Scheerbart, and Hausmann from 5202 303; and Isou from 5202 306.

François Dufrêne's "Cri-rhythme 67" (track 14) and Henri Chopin's "Le Ventre de Bertini" (track 15) reproduced by permission of Henri Chopin.

Lee "Scratch" Perry's "Well Dread" (track 16) reproduced by permission of Trojan Records. Available on *The Upsetter Compact Set*, by Lee "Scratch" Perry, the Upsetters & Friends, TRLS 195, Trojan Recordings Ltd., Iwyman House, 34–39 Camden Road, London NW1 91E, UK.

King Tubby's "A Rougher Version" (track 17) reproduced by permission of Trojan Records. Available on *King Tubby's Special, 1973–1976*, by King Tubby, the Observer and the Aggrovators, CDTRD 409, Trojan Recordings Ltd., Iwyman House, 34–39 Camden Road, London NW1 91E, UK.

Anthony McNeill's "Ode to Brother Joe" (track 18) reproduced by permission of Caedmon Audio, Harper Collins. Available on *Poets of the West Indies Reading Their Own Works*, CDL 51379.

Edward Kamau Brathwaite's "Wings of a Dove" (track 19) reproduced by permission of Alan Austin, Executive Producer, Watershed Tapes, from *Atumpan*, number 229, Watershed Tapes Archive Series. Available from Watershed Tapes, P.O. Box 50145, 6925 Willow Street NW, Washington, D.C. 20091.

Mutabaruka's "The People's Court" (track 20) reproduced by permission of Shanachie Entertainment Corporation. Available on *Blakk Wi Blak . . . k . . . k . . .*, CD 43083, from Shanachie Records Corp., 37 East Clinton Street, Newton, NJ 07860.

Pastora Pavón's "Ay Pilato" (track 21) reproduced by permission of Le Chant du Monde. Available on *La Niña de los Peines*, Le Chant du Monde LDX 274859.

Miles Davis's "Saeta" (track 22) reproduced by permission of SONY Records. Available on *Sketches of Spain*, Columbia CS 1480.

Miles Davis's and John Coltrane's "All Blues" (track 23) reproduced by permission of Dragon Records. Available on *Miles Davis & John Coltrane Live in Stockholm 1960*, Dragon DRLP 90/91.

Mississippi Fred McDowell's "Everybody's Down on Me" (track 24) and "Jesus Is on the Mainline" (track 25) reproduced by permission of Capitol Records Inc. Available on *I Do Not Play No Rock 'n Roll*, Capitol ST-409.

Rahsaan Roland Kirk's "The Business Ain't Nothin' but the Blues" (track 26) reproduced by permission of Polygram Records. Available on *I Talk with the Spirits*, Limelight LS82008. Under license from PolyMedia, a division of PolyGram Group Distribution, Inc.

"Love Song" (track 27) reproduced by permission of Lyrichord Discs Inc. Available on *Folk Music of Iran*, Lyrichord LLST7261.

Sonny Rollins's "East Broadway Rundown" (track 28) reproduced by permission of Sonny Rollins and MCA Records, Inc. Available on *East Broadway Rundown*, Impulse! A-9121. Courtesy of GRP Records under license from Universal Music Special Markets.

Cecil Taylor's "Chinampas" (track 29) reproduced by permission of Leo Records. Available on *Chinampas*, Leo Records LR153 1988.

Loretta Collins received her M.F.A. in poetry from the Writer's Workshop at the University of Iowa, where she is now completing a Ph.D. in twentieth-century American and Caribbean literature. Her writing has appeared in journals and anthologies such as *TriQuarterly New Writers* and the 1996 Pushcart Prize anthology. She has received research grants to Britain and a Fulbright Graduate Fellowship to Jamaica to conduct research for "Trouble It: Rebel Soundspace in the Caribbean Diaspora," a study of Caribbean sound politics, oral traditions, performance literature, and carnival arts in Trinidad, Jamaica, Britain, and Canada.

James A. Connor teaches communications at St. Louis University, where he specializes in technology and culture studies. In addition to "RADIO free JOYCE," he has published essays in *Science Fiction Studies* and *The Critic*. His collection of short stories is titled *God's Breath and Other Tales* (1989).

Michael Davidson teaches at the University of California, San Diego. He is the author of six books of poetry. His book *The San Francisco Renaissance: Poetics and Community at Mid-century* was published by Cambridge University Press in 1989. His new book, *Ghostlier Demarcations: Modern Poetry and the Material Word*, is published by the University of California Press.

N. Katherine Hayles, Professor of English at the University of California at Los Angeles, teaches and writes on literature and science in the twentieth century. She is the author of *The Cosmic Web: Scientific Field Models and Literary Strategies in the Twentieth Century* (1984) and *Chaos Bound: Orderly Disorder in Contemporary Literature and Science* (1990) and editor of *Chaos and Order: Complex Dynamics in Literature and Science* (1991). She is currently completing a book project titled "Virtual Bodies: Evolving Materialities in Cybernetics, Literature, and Informatics."

Steve McCaffery, currently John Logan Fellow at the State University of New York, Buffalo, is an internationally known poet, interdisciplinarian, and critic. He has taught at the University of California, San Diego; Queen's University, Canada; and the California Institute of Arts. He is the author of more than twenty books, the latest of which is *The Cheat of Words*. His anthology, *Imagining Language*, coedited with Jed Rasula and forthcoming in 1997, is an annotated gathering of three millennia of linguistic conjectures.

Alec McHoul teaches communication studies at Murdoch University, Western Australia. He has written books on Pynchon, Foucault, and Wittgenstein. His most recent book is *Semiotic Investigations* (1996).

Nathaniel Mackey teaches literature at the University of California, Santa Cruz. He is the author of four chapbooks of poetry, *Four for Trane* (1978), *Septet for the End of Time* (1983), *Outlantish* (1992), and *Song of the Andoumboulou: 18–20* (1994), and two books of poetry, *Eroding Witness* (1985) and *School of Udhra* (1993). *Strick: Song of the Andoumboulou: 16–25*, a CD recording of poems with Royal Hartigan and Hafez Modirzadeh, was released in 1995 by Spoken Engine Company. Two volumes of his ongoing prose composition *From a Broken Bottle Traces of Perfume Still Emanate* have been published: *Bedouin Hornbook* (1986) and *Djbot Baghostus's*

Run (1993). He is editor of the literary magazine *Hambone*, coeditor (with Art Lange) of the anthology *Moment's Notice: Jazz in Poetry and Prose* (1993), and author of a book of critical essays, *Discrepant Engagement: Dissonance, Cross-Culturality, and Experimental Writing* (1993).

Toby Miller teaches cinema studies at New York University. He is the author of *The Well-Tempered Self: Citizenship, Culture, and the Postmodern Subject* (1993), *Contemporary Australian Television* (with Stuart Cunningham, 1994), *The Avengers* (British Film Institute, forthcoming), and *Technologies of Truth: Cultural Citizenship and the Pursuit of the Popular* (forthcoming). He is editor of the *Journal of Sport and Social Issues* and a member of the Social Text collective.

Adalaide Morris teaches and writes on modern and contemporary poetry and poetics at the University of Iowa. In addition to editing two collections of contemporary poetry, she has published a book on Wallace Stevens and essays on Emily Dickinson, H.D., Adrienne Rich, the contemporary American canon, and the state of the profession.

Fred Moten was born in Las Vegas, currently lives in Los Angeles, and teaches at the University of California, Santa Barbara. He has published articles on Amiri Baraka, Nathaniel Mackey, and other figures in the African American aesthetic traditions. He is completing a book tentatively titled "Graphaphone Resistance: The Transference of Music in Afro-American Literature."

Marjorie Perloff is Sadie Dernham Patek Professor of Humanities at Stanford University. Her books include *The Poetics of Indeterminacy: Rimbaud to Cage* (1981), *The Futurist Moment* (1986), *Radical Artifice: Writing Poetry in the Age of Media* (1992), and most recently, *John Cage: Composed in America* (edited with Charles Junkerman, 1994), and *Wittgenstein's Ladder: Poetic Language and the Strangeness of the Ordinary* (1996).

Jed Rasula teaches English at Queen's University in Kingston, Ontario. He holds a Ph.D. in the history of consciousness from the University of California, Santa Cruz. He is coeditor of *Imagining Language, an Anthology* (forthcoming) and co-author, with Don Byrd, of *Tactics of Attention*, a collection of essays on the poetry scene in America from 1975 to 1995 (forthcoming). His most recent critical book is *The American Poetry Wax Museum: Reality Effects, 1940–1990* (1996).

Garrett Stewart, James O. Freedman Professor of Letters at the University of Iowa, is the author of *Dickens and the Trials of the Imagination*, *Death Sentences: Styles of Dying in British Fiction*, *Reading Voices: Literature and the Phonotext*, and *Dear Reader: The Conscripted Audience in Nineteenth-Century British Fiction*, as well as numerous articles on film.

INDEX

238, 276; influence on Caribbean poets, 185

Ellington, Duke, 215, 226

Emerson, Ralph Waldo, 291

Empson, William, 237, 251

Esslin, Martin, 80

Ethnopoetics, 98

Etzioni-Halevy, Eva, 65

Faulkner, William, 17

Forrest, Leon, 196

Forster, E. M., 265

Foucault, Michel, 56–60, 62–63, 68–69, 71 (n. 3), 87, 99, 269–70 (n. 1), 275, 299

Frank, Joseph, 34

Freud, Sigmund, 46–47, 275–78, 283, 285

Fried, Debra, 2

Frith, Simon, 66–67, 71

Frost, Robert, 281–82, 309; "The Most of It," 281–82

Garrison, Jimmy, 210

Gaudier-Brzeska, Henri, 42

Gehlen, Arnold, 308

Gibson, William, 298

Gillespie, John Birks "Dizzy", 231 (n. 3)

Ginsberg, Allen, 98, 103–6, 107, 117, 121; "Howl," 100, 117, 146–47 (n. 5); *Fall of America*, 104; "Wichita Vortex Sutra," 104–6

Gligo, Niksa, 134

Glück, Louise, 6–7

Godard, Jean-Luc, 261, 263

Gomringer, Eugen, 171

Goody, Jack, 2, 3, 43

Gordon, John, 21, 22

Graham, Jorie, 312 (n. 17)

Gray, Obika, 179

Grivel, Charles, 298

Guattari, Felix, 281

H.D., 8, 36, 38, 44, 51 (n. 16), 252; *Helen in Egypt*, 32, 34, 36, 43, 44–50, 52 (n. 22); *Trilogy*, 32, 49, 51 (n. 11); *HERmione*, 34–35, 52 (n. 23); and telephone, 34–35; and radio, 35–36, 42; and tape,

36, 45, 47; *Notes on Thought and Vision*, 50

Haraway, Donna, 113

Harlem Renaissance, 195. *See also* Hughes, Langston

Harris, Wilson, 286

Hausmann, Raoul, 149, 153, 164 (n. 7), 308–9

Havelock, Eric A., 1, 2, 3, 11, 33–34, 43–44, 47, 49, 74, 99–100

Hebdige, Dick, 173

Hegel, G. W. F., 285

Heidegger, Martin, 275–76, 277–78, 308–9

Henderson, David, 98

Hendrix, Jimi, 211

Herr, Cheryl, 24

Hesiod, 10, 278, 279–88, 290, 291, 294, 297, 298, 300, 302, 303, 307

Higgins, Dick, 163 (n. 5)

Hitchcock, Alfred, 245, 246

Hitler, Adolf, 44, 49, 52 (n. 24)

Homer, 36, 283, 285, 297; *Odyssey*, 304

Hopkins, Gerard Manley, 252

Horkheimer, Max, 52 (n. 24), 122–23 (n. 16)

Howe, Susan, 7, 284

Huelsenbeck, Richard, 152, 163 (n. 1)

Hughes, Langston, 6, 195, 218

Ibn Daud, Abraham, 282

Isou, Isadore, 154, 157, 158

Italian Futurism. *See* Marinetti, F. T.

Jakobson, Roman, 164 (n. 8), 241, 254–55, 256

Jameson, Fredric, 61, 121, 240

Janco, Marcel, 152

Jane Eyre, 10, 247–49, 250, 270 (n. 6)

Jay, Martin, 245

Jazz, 4, 98, 185, 224, 233 (n. 23)

"Jazzoetry," 8, 11

Johns, Jasper, 135, 139, 140, 145, 146; *Fizzles*, 135

Johnson, Linton Kwesi, 169, 179–80

Johnson, Lyndon, 105–6

Jolas, Eugene, 152, 163 (n. 2)

Marker, Chris, 10; *La Jetée*, 10, 257–59, 263–64, 265–69; *Sans Soleil*, 312 (n. 18)

Marley, Bob, 175, 177, 180

Martin, Jean, 81

Marx, Karl, 307

Melville, Herman, 105, 245

Metz, Christian, 259

Miller, J. Hillis, 243, 253–55

Miller, Robyn and Rand, 8

Miller, Toby, 8, 11

Milton, John, 36, 284

Moholy-Nagy, László, 153–54, 164 (n. 7)

Monk, Thelonius, 231 (n. 3)

Moran, Albert, 62

Morgenstern, Christian, 149, 152

Morris, Mervyn, 182

Morris, William, 6, 244

Motte, Warren F., 171

Movietone cinema, 46

Mowitt, John, 261, 271 (n. 13)

"Murphy Brown," 278–79

Murray, Penelope, 282

Mutabaruka, 179, 188–89

Myer, Ernst, 43

Myst, 8

Nagy, Gregory, 282, 310 (n. 6)

Nelson, Cary, 6

New American Poetry, 1945–1960, 197, 199, 201, 202

New Criticism, 2, 7, 43, 98

Newton, James, 208

Nichol, bp, 165–66 (n. 20)

Nietzsche, Friedrich, 277–78, 298

Niña de Los Peines. *See* Pavón, Pastora

Nixon, Richard, 103, 122 (n. 12)

Noigandres poets, 132

Nuyorican Cafe, 8

O'Connell, Daniel, 23

O'Hara, Frank, 98, 117

Olson, Charles, 97, 100, 107, 117, 161, 162, 165 (n. 18), 166 (n. 21), 285–86, 294; *The Maximus Poems*, 97, 100, 283–84, 294–95; "Projective Verse," 97–98, 99, 162, 166 (n. 22)

Ong, Walter J., 1, 2, 3, 11, 20, 33–34, 47–48, 74, 99, 165 (n. 17). *See also* Orality

Onuora, Oku, 179–80

Orality, 296; secondary, 3, 20, 34, 37, 51 (n. 13), 74, 99, 157, 160; primary, 36, 42, 47–49, 280, 287–88

Orpheus, 10, 290–95, 298, 301–3, 311 (n. 8)

Orwell, George, 102, 115

Oulipo, 171

Owen, Stephen, 294

Owens, Craig, 113

Parker, Charlie "Yardbird," 231 (n. 3)

Parkin, David, 218–20, 221

Parmenides, 226

Pasternak, Boris, 301

Pavón, Pastora, 196, 204, 207

Paz, Octavio, 275

Pearson, Norman Holmes, 36, 46, 47

Perloff, Marjorie, 9, 11, 11 (n. 6), 34, 37, 121–22 (n. 1)

Perry, Lee "Scratch," 174

Perry, Milman, 99–100

Phonocentrism, 6, 99, 107, 242, 261, 310; and contemporary poetics, 97, 100

Phonograph, 4, 76, 160, 296–97, 298–301

Phonophobia, 6, 242

Phonotext, 2, 3, 4, 6, 33–34, 42–43, 47–49, 239, 269 (n. 1). *See also* Stewart, Garrett

Picard, Max, 303

Pindar, 287

Plato, 49, 86, 111, 199, 223, 275, 279, 283, 286, 297, 310–11 (n. 6), *Symposium*, 86; *Phaedrus*, 310 (n. 6)

Plessner, Helmuth, 308, 309

Poe, Edgar Allan, 245, 246

Poetics of the New American Poetry, 194–95

Portmann, Adolf, 308

Poulsen, Valdemar, 76, 100

Pound, Ezra, 6, 8, 36, 38, 44, 49, 97, 98, 106, 306, 311 (n. 12); *Cantos*, 32, 34, 36, 42, 283–84; and telephones, 34–35; and radio, 35; *Cantos* and John Cage, 133, 138, 146 (n. 5)

Telephones, 34–35, 42, 50 (n. 2), 76, 160, 297, 307; and Freud, 46; and Laurie Anderson, 115–17
Thoreau, Henry David, 4, 281, 294
Torre, Manuel, 195–96, 197
Typewriters, 98
Tzara, Tristan, 149, 152, 163 (n. 4)

Veaux, Micheline, 5
Veloso, Caetano, 171
Vergil, 33, 36, 310 (n. 4)
Vernant, Jean-Pierre, 288

Walker, Roy, 80–81
Walmsley, Anne, 180–81
Waters, Anita M., 178
Waters, Muddy, 211
Watt, Ian, 43
Watten, Barrett, 117
Weber, Max, 66
Weiner, Norbert, 17, 302

Wendt, Larry, 158, 161, 166 (n. 22)
Whitehead, Gregory, 5, 6, 10, 11, 42, 121 (n. 3)
Whitman, Walt, 33, 104, 105, 106, 164 (n. 10), 300–301, 308; "Crossing Brooklyn Ferry," 291–92; "Out of the Cradle," 301
Wicke, Jennifer, 27
Williams, William Carlos, 6, 36, 44, 49, 98; *Paterson*, 32, 34
Wittgenstein, Ludwig, 142, 274
Woolf, Virginia, 252
Wynter, Sylvia, 172

Yeats, William Butler, 6, 8, 18, 42; "The Tower," 8; "Byzantium," 37–38

Zaum poetry, 149, 154–55, 164 (nn. 9–10), 171
Žižek, Slavoj, 246
Zukofsky, Louis, 203, 285–8